"God has created us for relationship and work for his honor—to bring hope and justice to the nations and our neighbors, and joy and purpose to our own hearts. In *Work Matters*, Tom Nelson examines how God uses our work, even the ordinary and routine, to transform us and to reveal our gifts and calling. I have known Tom for several years, and his life and work exemplify these profound and practical truths. His book will inspire and encourage you to reexamine not only your understanding of work but of yourself as well."

Ravi Zacharias, Founder and President, Ravi Zacharias International Ministries; author, *Jesus Among Other Gods* and *From East to West*

"Tom Nelson does a marvelous job of walking his readers through a robust theology of work, and he does so in a very provocative way. We are all Jesus's apprentices and our work lives are filled with opportunities for spiritual growth and discipleship. *Work Matters* will compel you to approach work differently."

Moe Girkins, author, *Mother Leads Best* and *50 Women Who are Transforming Leadership*

"Nelson's conclusions, insights, and examples will help many people get a better grip on serving God and finding purpose in the work place. This book is thoughtful, practical, entertaining, and true to Scripture. The lights are going to suddenly come on in many readers' minds, and that's not just great fun but a good thing as well."

John Yates, Rector, The Falls Church, Falls Church, Virginia

"By definition, every Christian is in full-time ministry. Unfortunately, many of us see a great divide between the secular and spiritual, ministry and work. In *Work Matters*, Tom Nelson helps to bridge the artificial and unbiblical gap that keeps us from fully realizing our calling and full potential in Christ. Read it. It will change the way you think about Monday to Friday."

Larry Osborne, Pastor, North Coast Church, Vista, California; author, *Sticky Church*

"More than just a book, *Work Matters* is a kaleidoscopic testimony to the power of calling in the lives of a vibrant local church, inspired to engage their community and city. If every pastor taught like this and every church lived like this, America would be a very different country."

Os Guinness, author, *The Dust of Death* and *The Last Christian on Earth*

"Not many pastors are adept at encouraging the Christians they serve to think deeply about the work they undertake during the six days when they are not gathering for corporate worship. So many of our applications and exhortations, as important and as faithful as they are, deal with prayer, Bible reading, family relationships, and evangelism, and not with the work that takes up much of our time and that we are called to offer up to God. I first heard Tom Nelson bring some clarity to these matters in some addresses at Trinity Evangelical Divinity School, and I am delighted to see his reflections expanded and put into print. This book is greatly needed."

D. A. Carson, Research Professor of New Testament,
Trinity Evangelical Divinity School

"Each week people gather to experience a time of worship. The idea that this moment on Sunday can actually be a time for both celebrating the Savior *and* for strategically shaping what happens when we leave those four walls is rarely considered. *Work Matters* takes a look into the Christian's life, offering strategic insight into the workplace as a key part of God's kingdom agenda and explaining how Sunday's worship experience can spill over into Monday through Saturday. A great work indeed."

Stan Archie, Vice President, Missouri State Board of Education; Senior
Pastor, Christian Fellowship Church, Kansas City, Missouri

"This is a very important book written by a pastor whom I respect immensely. *Work Matters* will change how you view your vocation and in the process it may just change your life."

Adam Hamilton, Senior Pastor, The United Methodist Church
of the Resurrection, Leawood, Kansas; author, *The Journey:
Walking the Road to Bethlehem*

"Tom Nelson offers the world a profoundly rich vision of vocation as integral to the mission of God in history—by a pastor who has spent the years of his life helping his people understand what they do and why they do what they do in light of the truest truths of the universe. Theologically serious and pastorally aware, no one has tried to do what he has done and has done so well. For pastors and for their people, indeed for everyone who wants to connect the vocation of the ministry with vocations in the marketplace, it will change the conversation about calling because it will change the way we understand worship and work."

Steve Garber, Director, The Washington Institute for Faith,
Vocation, and Culture; author, *The Fabric of Faithfulness*

WORK MATTERS

CONNECTING SUNDAY WORSHIP TO MONDAY WORK

Tom Nelson

 CROSSWAY

WHEATON, ILLINOIS

Published by Crossway
               1300 Crescent Street
               Wheaton, Illinois 60187

Cover design: Tobias' Outerwear for Books

Cover photo: iStock

Page design and typesetting: Dawn Premako

Notebook page: © iStockphoto.com/CGinspiration

First printing 2011

Printed in the United States of America

Trade paperback ISBN:	978-1-4335-2667-1
PDF ISBN:	978-1-4335-2668-8
Mobipocket ISBN:	978-1-4335-2669-5
ePub ISBN:	978-1-4335-2670-1

Library of Congress Cataloging-in-Publication Data
Nelson, Tom, 1956-
  Work matters : connecting Sunday worship to Monday work /
Tom Nelson.
    p. cm.
  Includes bibliographical references and index.
  ISBN 978-1-4335-2667-1 (tp)
  1. Employees—Religious life. 2. Work—Religious aspects—
Christianity. I. Title.
  BV4593.N45 2011
  248.8'8—dc23   2011020712

Crossway is a publishing ministry of Good News Publishers.

VP	20	19	18	17	16	15	14	13	12	11
11	10	9	8	7	6	5	4	3	2	1

To my wonderful bride, Liz,
whose contagious faith inspires me,
and to my dear friends Dave and Demi
whose seamless lives of work and worship
are a constant encouragement

CONTENTS

ACKNOWLEDGMENTS

The rich texture of thoughtful and collaborative friendships is one of our greatest gifts of grace. I am grateful to God for the many individuals who have encouraged my faith journey and helped shape the contours of my thought. I would like to especially acknowledge Don Carson, Stephen Garber, Os Guinness, James Hunter, David Miller, Dallas Willard, and Ravi Zacharias. Their collective imprint is evident throughout the book.

I want to express my most heartfelt gratitude for my precious family. Liz, Schaeffer, and Sarah offered much encouragement and provided many insights along the way. I also want to thank Justin Taylor, Mattie Wolf, and the entire Crossway staff for their commitment and enthusiastic support. A special thanks to Kristen Brown, who was of indispensible help in preparing the manuscript for submission.

Let me also express my deepest appreciation to the staff and members of Christ Community Church. Thank you for allowing me the amazing privilege of sharing life with you. Thanks, Dave, Mike, Jay, Peggy, Debbie, Kevin, Matt, Gayln, David, and Kori for telling your stories of a gospel-centered faith that connects Sunday to Monday. Most of all I am grateful for the gospel and the gracious calling to be an apprentice of Jesus.

Tom Nelson
Soli Deo Gloria

INTRODUCTION
CONNECTING SUNDAY TO MONDAY

It was on a curvy stretch of California's picturesque Pacific Coast Highway that in our rental car we made a quick stop. Our family vacation guidebook had piqued our interest about the rugged shoreline of the Point Arguello area. The day was bright and sunny. A light ocean breeze greeted us as we stepped out of the car. The view of the Pacific Ocean was simply stunning.

As we breathed in the beauty of the moment, my mind drifted to a tragic event that had occurred on these treacherous, rugged shores. The day was September 8, 1923. A squadron of US destroyers steamed southward down the California coast. Led by the USS *Delphy*, the squadron was on a twenty-four–hour training mission from San Francisco to San Diego. Just north of Point Arguello, a thick blanket of fog rolled in. Unaware of the danger that lurked in the fog dead ahead of them, the navigator on the USS *Delphy* directed the column of ships to swing a few degrees east. Relying on the skill of his navigator, Captain R. A. Dawes confidently cruised through the fog, maintaining a fast speed of twenty knots. Suddenly, the *USS Delphy* smashed broadside into the rocky Point Arguello shoreline. The sheer force of the massive collision of welded steel and jagged rock split the hull of the *USS Delphy* in half. Before Captain Dawes could notify the rest of the squadron, six other destroyers had run aground on the rocky shoreline, their once-impressive hulls lying bruised and battered, listing in the pounding waves. On that fateful, foggy day off California's rocky coast the United States not only lost some very fine sailors, the Navy also lost more combat ships than they would during the entire course of World War I.

As I stood overlooking the Pacific Ocean, reflecting on the naval tragedy that had occurred there, I was reminded of how perilous a heavy blanket of fog can prove to be in our lives. It is all too easy to find ourselves fogged in when it comes to those things that matter most in life. Of course we have good intentions of not running aground on the rocky shorelines we inevitably encounter, yet we often cruise through life in a fog, at breakneck speed, without gaining the necessary navigational wisdom we need.

When it comes to your work, perhaps you are feeling a bit fogged in at the moment. It could be that your work has you simply living for the weekend. Maybe you are looking for some clearer direction about your work, and you need some timely wisdom to guide you. Whether you really like your present work or you are stoically enduring your job, I am hopeful that a small investment of your time will be well worth your effort. In our technologically driven, complex, and ever-changing modern world, navigating our work and the workplaces we inhabit requires thoughtful reflection.

Thanks to our laptop computers, cell phones, and other technological advances, our work can take place almost anywhere. We can do our work at home, on a factory floor, in a cubicle of a corporate office, at a desk in a classroom, on an athletic field, or in a small business setting. Sometimes we are paid for our work, and sometimes financial remuneration is not part of the picture. But regardless of the setting, the often unsettling truth is that while we shape our work, our work shapes us and the world around us. As we look around our fragmented world, we feel a sense of responsibility to positively contribute to the common good, yet we wonder if our work is really making any difference.

I believe how we view our work and how we do our work matters a great deal more than we might imagine. Yet when it comes to this important area of my life, particularly how my work connects to my Christian faith, I must confess I have often found myself in a thick fog. Sad to say, as both a follower of Jesus and as one whose work is to assist others in their spiritual growth, I have repeatedly run aground on some pretty rocky theological shorelines. With the best of intentions and the sincerest of heart, I have led others aground on some faulty ideas about faith and work. I have wrongly viewed some kinds of work as being more important than others. On several occasions in my life, I have drifted to the perilous edge of workaholism, conveniently making an idol out of my work. For way too long, I did not see work as an essential component of a broader, robust theology of Christian calling, nor did I see how the gospel transforms work. I failed to grasp that a primary stewardship of my pastoral work was to assist and equip others to better connect the professions of their Sunday faith with the practices of their Monday work. As a pastor, I regret that I have often given minority attention to what most of us do the majority of our time. I am most grateful for the extra measure of grace extended to me by so many as I have wrestled to more integrally incorporate a biblical theology of vocation into my own life and ministry.

Out of my own inadequacies and shortcomings, an increasing passion has been birthed in my heart. Even in a small way, I long to help clear the fog that has settled in the minds of many followers of Jesus who deeply desire to faithfully integrate their Christian faith into their work. David Miller, who is one of the foremost thinkers on faith and work, speaks of the growing number of us who live increasingly bifurcated lives in which faith and work seldom seem to connect. David observes, "Many who are Christians complain of a 'Sunday-Monday gap,' where their Sunday worship hour bears little to no relevance to the issues they face in their Monday workplace hours."[1] If you feel fogged in when it comes to your faith and your work, if you sense a sizable

Sunday-to-Monday gap, let me assure you that in God's sovereign grace there is a transforming and rewarding way forward.

But before we begin our exploration of work, it is important for us to clarify a few things about Christian vocation in general. The theology of Christian vocation is wide and sweeping in its breadth and significance. The word *vocation* simply means "calling." Properly understood, Christian vocation is centered in a sovereign God who calls us to embrace the gospel of Jesus Christ and to follow him in the power of the Holy Spirit as his disciples. The good news of the gospel is that a transforming relationship with God is not based on anything we have done or could ever do, but on what Christ has already done for us by shedding his atoning blood on the cross. In Christ we experience a new birth and we live brand-new lives in his kingdom here and now. We are and continue to be transformed in and through the power of the gospel. Our work, too, is transformed. When we come to the foot of the cross, we bring with us what we do as well as who we are. The gospel, properly understood, leads us to a seamless faith.

Os Guinness has given considerable thought to a robust theology of vocation. Keeping the gospel central, Os makes a helpful distinction between our primary calling and our secondary callings. He rightly points out that Scripture first and foremost emphasizes our primary calling to Christ. Os writes, "Our primary calling as followers of Christ is by him, to him and for him. First and foremost we are called to Someone, not to something or to somewhere."[2] But Os also insightfully points out that each one of us has also been given a secondary calling, and an essential aspect of this particular calling is to do a specific work. Yet because we refer to work as a secondary calling, we must not in any way minimize work's importance in living lives of Christian faithfulness. A large portion of our time on earth is given to our work, and we would be wise to take this stewardship seriously.

On the pages that follow we will focus our attention on our secondary calling to work. In the first section of the book, we will look at our work through a biblical lens. What does Scripture say about our work? What does God intend for our work? The second section will focus on how God shapes our lives in and through our work. What would it really look like if our Sunday faith connected seamlessly to our Monday work? What are the important implications and opportunities that our work provides for us and for our world as we seek to live out a gospel witness and be a faithful presence in our workplace? We are going to discover that what we do each and every day during the majority of our waking hours really matters not only now, but also for all eternity. We all find ourselves at different places in our faith journeys, but as we explore together the rich truths of Scripture, my prayerful hope is that some of the fog in your mind may clear, and you will experience a more integral, seamless faith. I pray that your calling to a specific work may bring with it a new dynamism of heartfelt joy and purpose.

Questions for Reflection and Discussion:

- Do you see your work as a calling?

- How might thinking of work as a calling transform the way you do your work and the kind of work you do?

- What are some ways you currently connect your Sunday faith and your Monday work?

- How might connecting Sunday faith to Monday work change the way you view work?

1

CREATED TO WORK

*All vocations are intended by God to
manifest His love in the world.*[1]
THOMAS MERTON

The animated movie *WALL-E* is a cute story of a curious robot whose job is to clean up a trashed earth. While humans once inhabited the earth, we soon discover that they have been evacuated from earth with the hopes of returning one day after robots clean up the mess. Though a hardworking robot, WALL-E has a rather lonely existence. But that changes when WALL-E meets another robot by the name of Eve. WALL-E quickly gains a fondness for his newfound friend whose name evokes a biblical image of creation.

WALL-E enthusiastically pursues EVE to the point of making an unplanned journey, via spaceship, to a high-tech space station where humans who have made a real mess of planet Earth are now living a "utopian," carefree, work-free existence. As residents of the space station, humans are waited on hand

and foot by robots attending to their every whim and desire. As a result, the pampered humans have become self-indulgent, bored couch potatoes. With the passage of time, adult humans now resemble giant babies with soft faces, rounded torsos, and stubby, weak limbs—the tragic deforming and atrophying result of human beings doing nothing but cruising around on cushy, padded, reclining chairs, their eyes fixed on video screens, taking in large amounts of calories, and sipping from straws sticking out of giant cups.

As a movie watcher, the high-tech space station filled with human couch potatoes is anything but appealing. The creators of *WALL-E* explore many important themes, but possibly none more compelling than what it means to be human. *WALL-E* reminds us that a do-nothing couch potato existence is actually repulsive and dehumanizing. But why is this? As human beings we were not created to be do-nothings; we were created with work in mind.

CREATED WITH WORK IN MIND

As human beings, we have been designed not only to rest and to play but also to work. From the very beginning of Scripture we see that the one true God is not a couch potato God, nor did he create a couch potato world. As the Genesis storyline opens, we read, "In the beginning, God created the heavens and the earth." Here we are immediately introduced to God as a thoughtful and creative worker. At first glance we observe the triune God as an active deity. The Spirit of God is hovering over the waters. God's infinite creativity, omnipotence, and omniscience are unleashed, and he is intimately engaged in his good creation.

As God's work of creation unfolds, humankind—the crown of creation—emerges on the literary landscape. God the Creator places a distinguishing stamp of uniqueness on human beings, one that sets humanity apart from the rest of creation. Then God said,

"Let us make man in our image, after our likeness. And let them have dominion over the fish of the sea and over the birds of the heavens and over the livestock and over every creeping thing that creeps on the earth." So God created man in his own image, in the image of God he created him; male and female he created them. And God blessed them. And God said to them, "Be fruitful and multiply and fill the earth and subdue it, and have dominion over the fish of the sea and over the birds of the heavens and over every living thing that moves on the earth." (Gen. 1:26–28)

The Genesis writer wants us to grasp the unique place of human beings in creation. We observe this uniqueness in two foundational ways. First, humans are designed by God to exercise proper dominion over creation, which is a divinely delegated stewardship role. Second, humans are designed by God to be his image-bearers, to uniquely reflect who God is to his good world. The repeated use of the word *image* by the Genesis writer tells us of the importance of this concept for our understanding of what it means to be human.

IMAGE-BEARERS OF GOD

As God's image-bearers, we were created to mirror the glory and excellence of the triune God. An image-bearer is designed to reflect the image of another. I was reminded of this truth as my wife, Liz, and I were cheering on our Kansas City Royals baseball team. While enjoying a beautiful summer evening at Kauffman Stadium, we had a delightful conversation with the wife of a professional baseball player whose present work and vocational calling is being a mom and raising her children. Sitting in the row right in front of us were two of her beautiful children whom we had not seen for a couple of years. The last time we had seen them they were still infants, and now at three and five years old, their budding personalities and appearances were emerging. As I looked at their five-year-old son, I was simply stunned at how much he was like his dad. The closer I looked, the more amazed I

21

became. His physical appearance remarkably resembled his dad, though on a smaller scale. The boy's voice sounded the same. Even as a five-year-old he had similar mannerisms, and like his dad he was already into baseball. I couldn't help but comment to my wife, Liz, "Look at him; he is the spitting image of his dad!"

I am not in any way suggesting that we are somehow little gods or that we will ever be God, but as human beings we were created to reflect our heavenly Father. In a sense we were created to be his spitting image. We were created to worship God and to display a glimpse of God's glory to a vast and expanding universe. This glimpse of God's glory reveals many things about the character and magnificence of the one true God, and at a very foundational level, we must recognize our image-bearing reveals that God is a creator, a worker. God is not some cosmic do-nothing deity.

WHY DO WE WORK?

While commuting to my office, on more than one occasion I have seen a bumper sticker that provides one answer to this question of why we work: "I owe, I owe, it's off to work I go." Paying the many bills that come to us each month is no small matter. We can all give testimony to the high cost of modern-day living, but is economic transaction the foundational reason why we work?

Scripture tells us that the most bedrock answer to the question of why we work is that we were created with work in mind. Being made in God's image, we have been designed to work, to be fellow workers with God. To be an image-bearer is to be a worker. In our work we are to show off God's excellence, creativity, and glory to the world. We work because we bear the image of One who works. This is why the apostle Paul writes to a group of first-century followers of Jesus who have embraced the gospel, "If anyone is not willing to work, let him not eat" (2 Thess. 3:10). At first blush, Paul's rather blunt words seem cold and lacking

Christian compassion, but upon further theological reflection, Paul's words convey to us some needed insight. Paul does not rebuke those who, for various legitimate reasons, cannot work, but he does say that an unwillingness to work is no trivial thing. For anyone to refuse to work is a fundamental violation of God's creation design for humankind.

When we grasp what God intended for his image-bearers, it is not surprising that throughout the book of Proverbs the wise are praised for their diligence and the foolish are rebuked for their laziness. When we hear the word *fool*, we often think of someone who is mentally deficient. However, a foolish person in Scripture is not necessarily one who lacks intelligence but rather one who lives as if God does not exist. The psalmist puts it this way: "The fool says in his heart, 'There is no God'" (Ps. 14:1). A fool is one who rejects not only the Creator but also creation design, including the design to work. Throughout Scripture slothfulness is rightly viewed in a negative light. A slothful Christian is a contradiction in terms. We should not be shocked to see that the Christian church throughout history has reflected negative sentiments about slothfulness. Sloth finds a prominent place in Pope Gregory the Great's listing of the seven deadly sins. The Protestant Reformers spoke of the poverty of slothfulness and laziness. Consistently they made the connection that those who spend their time in idleness and ease should rightly doubt the sincerity of their Christian commitment.

God could have placed Adam and Eve in the garden of Eden and made it much like the world of humans in *WALL-E*, where they could sit around with food coming to them, sipping their life-giving nutrients out of giant cups. This was not God's desire or his design for his good world. Because God himself is a worker, and because we are his image-bearers, we were designed to reflect who God is in, through, and by our work. The work we are called to do every day is an important part of our image-bearing nature and stewardship. As human beings we were created to do things.

In this sense we are not only human beings, we are also human doings. We have been created to contribute to God's good world.

CREATED TO CONTRIBUTE

First and foremost, work is not about economic exchange, financial remuneration, or a pathway to the American Dream, but about God-honoring human creativity and contribution. Our work, whatever it is, whether we are paid for it, is our specific human contribution to God's ongoing creation and to the common good. Work is an integral aspect of being human, an essential aspect of loving God and his created world, and a vital part of loving our neighbor as ourselves. Gilbert Meilaender presses into the rich implications of the truths presented to us in the Genesis account. He writes, "To regard work as a calling is to suggest that we live to work, that our work is of central significance for our person. Still more, the calling gives to work a religious significance which it is not likely to acquire in any other way."[2] For us to view work outside a theological framework is to inevitably devalue both work and the worker.

The creation account recorded for us in Genesis 2 emphasizes God's design for humanity and the significant contribution the crown of creation is to make in his good world. Prior to God forming man from the dust of the earth and breathing life into him, before sin entered the world, the Genesis writer raises a tension regarding the incompleteness of God's creation. In Genesis chapter 2:5 we read that "there was no man to work the ground." In other words, God created humans not only to worship him and to delight in him, but to make an important ongoing contribution to his creation. From Genesis 2 we see that the earth itself was created in order to be cultivated and shaped by humankind. Unspoiled pristine nature is not necessarily a preferred state. God desired that there would be harmonious human cooperation within the creation order. Not only would the crown of creation have joyful intimacy with their Creator, but they would also be given the joyful privilege of contributing to the work of God in his good world.

As Genesis chapter 2 continues, we get a further picture of a human being as a worker. We observe work as it was originally designed to be, before sin and death entered the world. In Genesis 2:15 we read these words, "The LORD God took the man and put him in the garden of Eden to work it and keep it." The Lord God takes the initiative and places humankind in the garden of Eden with a particular task in mind. The emphasis here is not about personal human choice but rather divine initiative and divine calling. Already in Genesis we see that vocation is not something we ultimately choose for ourselves; it is something to which God calls us. Contrary to much of our present cultural emphasis that deifies personal choice, a biblical worldview begins not with human choice, but with a good and sovereign God who is not only the Creator but also the Caller. Here in the Genesis narrative, before humanity's fall into sin and resulting corruption of the world and our work, we are given two bedrock truths regarding human work and vocation: we were created with an important stewardship in mind, to cultivate creation and to keep it; and we are commissioned by God to nurture, care for, and protect his creation.

A STEWARDSHIP POSTURE

Humankind, the crown of creation, was created for the glory of God and entrusted with a remarkable stewardship exercising dominion over the earth. A vital aspect of this stewardship is the essential work not only of tending things and making things but also of cultivating and creating culture. Andy Crouch convincingly undermines the rationale for both Christian withdrawal from the common culture and for Christian hubris that projects a kind of utopian triumphalism of changing the world. Crouch suggests Christians adopt a stewardship posture anchored in cultivation and creation, what he often refers to as culture making.

25

The stewardship of culture making involves both cultivators and creators. Crouch describes cultivators as "people who tend and nourish what is best in human culture, who do the hard and painstaking work to preserve the best of what people before us have done." Creators, he says, are "people who dare to think and do something that has never been thought or done before, something that makes the world more welcoming and thrilling and beautiful."[3] Andy Crouch makes an important point. Humanity's creative work is varied, broad and far reaching. We not only make things or fix things, but also we are actively involved in creating and cultivating human culture itself.

AVODAH

The language of work as cultivation and creation in Genesis 2:15 is embedded in the Hebrew word *avodah,* which is behind the English translation "to cultivate." The Hebrew word *avodah* is translated in various ways in the Old Testament. It is rendered as "work," "service," or "craftsmanship" in many instances, yet other times it is translated as "worship." *Avodah* is used to describe the back-breaking hard work of God's covenant people making bricks as slaves in Egypt (Ex. 1:14), the artisans building the tabernacle (Ex. 35:24), and the fine craftsmanship of linen workers (1 Chron. 4:21). *Avodah* also appears in the context of Solomon dedicating the temple. Solomon employs this word as he instructs the priests and Levites regarding their service in leading corporate worship and praise of the one true God (2 Chron. 8:14). Whether it is making bricks, crafting fine linen, or leading others in corporate praise and worship, the Old Testament writers present a seamless understanding of work and worship. Though there are distinct nuances to *avodah,* a common thread of meaning emerges where work, worship, and service are inextricably linked and intricately connected. The various usages of this Hebrew word found first in Genesis 2:15 tell us that God's original design and desire is that our work and our worship would be a seamless way of living. Properly understood, our work is to be thoughtfully woven into the integral fabric of Christian vocation, for God designed and intended our work, our vocational calling, to be an act of God-honoring worship.

WORK AS AN ACT OF WORSHIP

So often we think of worship as something we do on Sunday and work as something we do on Monday. However, this dichotomy is not what God designed nor what he desires for our lives. God designed work to have both a vertical and horizontal dimension. We work to the glory of God and for the furtherance of the common good. On Sunday we say we go to worship and on Monday we say we go to work, but our language reveals our foggy theological thinking. That our work has been designed by God to be an act of worship is often missed in the frenzied pace of a compartmentalized modern life.

One of our favorite family vacations was visiting England. Touring beautiful Westminster Abbey and Christopher Wren's truly breathtaking St. Paul's Cathedral was one of my personal highlights. As I walked through these beautiful and inspiring architectural works of art, I was reminded of the apocryphal story of the three stone masons who were engaged in conversation by a visitor. "What are you doing?" the visitor asked the first mason. "I am cutting stone," the mason replied. A second mason chimed in, "I'm making a living." "And how about you?" the visitor asked the third mason. "Me, I'm building a cathedral for God and his people." What a difference our perspective on work makes!

AN AUDIENCE OF ONE

When our children were young, my wife, Liz, and I tried to impress on them that we live and work before an Audience of One.[4] Our line of thought went something like this: If God is aware and cares for every sparrow that falls, then we know that our loving heavenly Father watches over us wherever we are and whatever we are doing. Nothing we think, say, or do ever escapes God's loving, caring, and watchful eye. Living before an Audience of One also means that all we do and say is to be an act of God-honoring worship. Of course we all fell short many times in keeping this perspective in mind, but, as a gymnast, our daughter, Sarah, latched on to this transforming truth.

Over the many years of her devotion to the sport of gymnastics, Sarah encountered the daily hard work of preparation, the exhilaration of victory, and the agony of defeat. Through the good and the bad times, Sarah remained remarkably focused and resilient. Sadly, Sarah's gymnastics career was cut short due to a severe ankle injury. Years later we were reminiscing about her years of being a competitive gymnast. I asked Sarah how it was that she stayed so buoyant during those years. She looked at me and said, "Dad, remember you and mom taught me to live before an Audience of One."

Doing our work before an Audience of One changes what we do and how we do it. Living with this mind-set helps us connect our faith with our work, for we live before the same Audience on Monday at work as we do on Sunday at worship. Dorothy Sayers, a contemporary of C. S. Lewis, gave a lot of thought to how followers of Christ who have embraced the gospel ought to see their work. She also spoke in a compelling way about how the church has so often dropped the ball when it comes to connecting our Sunday faith with Monday work. In a thoughtful essay simply titled "Why Work?" Sayers writes, "The Church's approach to an intelligent carpenter is usually confined to [moral instruction and church attendance]. What the Church should be telling him is this: that the very first demand that his religion makes upon him is that he should make good tables. . . ."[5] Dorothy Sayers is not saying that offering moral instruction and inspiring worship services is unimportant. Clearly this is an important stewardship of any gospel preaching and Christ-honoring local church. But what we must not miss in her insightful words is the importance of the church in teaching each one of us that our work, whatever it is, is to be an act of worship. With remarkable insight Sayers continues, "Let the church remember this: that every maker and worker is called to serve God in his profession or trade—not outside it. . . . The only Christian work is good work well done."[6]

So often we use the language of Christian work to refer exclusively to ecclesiastical, missionary, or parachurch callings, but this distorted understanding exposes our inadequate grasp of the transforming truths of Christian vocation. It is hard to imagine how our understanding of work and the quality of our work would change if we would truly live before an Audience of One and fully embrace the truth that *the only Christian work is good work well done.* Dorothy Sayers is not being novel; she is simply saying what the apostle Paul penned to the first century local church at Colossae: "Whatever you do, work heartily, as for the Lord and not for men, knowing that from the Lord you will receive the inheritance as your reward. You are serving the Lord Christ" (Col. 3:23–24).

RETHINKING WORK

Though our work may be difficult and at times exasperating, we do not have to hate our work or merely live for the weekends. We need to rethink how we think about our work. When we begin to embrace how work ought to be, then we begin to see what we do each and every day as an integral part of our worship of God. If you understand that God designed you to contribute to his creation, you will take seriously how and where you are called to make your important contribution in the world.

When we thoughtfully reflect on God's original design for our work, we are inspired with its beauty and grandeur, but we also realize that work and the workplaces we inhabit in our present world are not as God designed them to be. You may be thinking, *Tom, this reflection on God's design for our work all sounds well and good, but you don't know the difficulty of my work or the pressures of my workplace or what a difficult boss I work for!* And you are right in the sense that I don't know all that you are facing in this competitive, fast-paced world. I may not know the particularities of your work, but over the years I have interacted with many people about their work, and I do know that for each one of us who desires to connect our Sunday faith with our Monday work, the ongoing challenges are ever present and significant.

THE OFFICE

I must confess I am an enthusiastic fan of the television show *The Office*. Each week the Dunder Mifflin gang makes their way into our living room. The Scranton division of a fictitious paper company by the name of Dunder Mifflin and the cast of characters have become a lasting fixture in our imaginations. *The Office*, at first glance, gives a humorous depiction of work and workplace antics, but the more you enter into the lives of these characters and the workplace they inhabit, the more painfully broken it seems. On display every week for the entire world to see is the ongoing drama of very broken individuals who daily bump into each other in the workplace. Though the writers of *The Office* sometimes go over the edge for my tastes, each week they remind a watching world that work is an important part of what it means to be human. *The Office* says to us that we were created to work, yet unresolved tensions fill the air of every episode, and we are left to ponder that work now is not what it really ought to be.

Daily we are confronted by a sobering reality that our work, the workers we work with, and the workplaces in which we work are not as God originally designed them. In a myriad of ways we are painfully reminded each and every day that we live and work in a fallen and corrupted world. Like many other things in life, work in this less-than-perfect world is a mixed bag. This is the inescapable reality to which we will turn our attention next.

A Prayer for Our Work

Let your work be shown to your servants, and your glorious power to their children. Let the favor of the Lord our God be upon us, and establish the work of our hands upon us; yes, establish the work of our hands! (Ps. 90:16–17)

Questions for Reflection and Discussion:

- How does knowing that you are created in the image of a God who works change the way you view work?

- In what ways does your work serve to create and cultivate culture?

- What would change in your work if you maintained the mindset that you live and work before an Audience of One?

- How might you do your work as a God-honoring act of worship?

DAVE > CHIEF EXECUTIVE OFFICER

My wife, Demi, and I started our company in 1991, and I think, like many people, we had good intentions. We wanted to create a decent company, make a decent living, and perhaps do some good. At that point, we thought the "good" would come mostly at the end of the year when we figured out what our profits for the year had been and, therefore, what we should tithe. In the midnineties we started to study the fullness of the Christian story more, including the biblical narrative on vocation. I remember it seemed like water to a dry soul when we began to realize that we were made in the image of a God who worked and who created us to work. I remember for the first time understanding that I could feel God's pleasure in and through my work every day, not just when the accounting books were closed at the end of the year. And this idea that my Monday through Friday could be a sweet aroma to him, that the essence of my work could be pleasing to him, helped me make the transition from a job to a vocation. And it colored my world, literally.

Demi and I no longer have a sense that there are other more significant or "spiritual" vocations. God made us the way we are, and therefore, as entrepreneurs, we are doing that which he alone determines is our most sacred response to him. And so we try to create a place where every decision matters, where the way we negotiate contracts matters, where the beauty of the buildings we build matters, where the freedom or lack thereof that we create for our colleagues matters. We understand that each and every gift item we create has a story, and that we are implicated in the story it tells. We know that how we and our colleagues treat our partner factories, our UPS or FedEx drivers, the artisans we work with, and the kind of team that cleans our facility every night matters; it's a reflection of our beliefs and view of work. Each and every day, in the sacred of the mundane, we understand that our vocations matter to God, as he is the one who created and ordained us for those specific roles in life. None are more "spiritual" than others. Rather, we determine daily, through our thoughts and words and actions, whether we choose to honor him through our work. And what a joy it is to sense his pleasure when we do.

2

IS WORK A FOUR-LETTER WORD?

*God's curse after the Fall expresses the fact that alien-
ation is inherent to the human experience of work.*[1]
MIROSLAV VOLF

Whether you like your work, don't like your work, or simply put up with your work, I think you will agree with me that work can be a big pain. I am not a big-time yard guy, but I've always liked lawn work. That is, until something took the wind out of my sails. Frankly, it happened so very quickly I couldn't stop it. The momentum of my revved-up lawnmower devoured the extended sprinkler head hidden in the tall grass. Black pieces of my sprinkler flew all over my back yard. At that agonizing moment, words suddenly snuck out of my mouth that need not be repeated. I was not a very happy camper when my sprinkler head disintegrated before my eyes and my tongue revealed to anyone within hearing distance that I, the "right" reverend, was neither right nor reverent at the moment. Work. Sometimes it makes me want to curse.

It doesn't matter if our workplace is at home, in a classroom, on a factory floor, or in an office cubicle, work can be a source of great frustration in our lives. Facing an urgent deadline and having a computer crash is a big pain. Dealing with difficult customers or serving a demanding boss is a big pain. Having to let an employee go or downsize a labor force is a big pain. Facing a family's mountain of dirty laundry is a big pain. Lingering unemployment or underemployment is a big pain. Work can make us want to curse. But why is this? Why is work so often such a pain?

Though Scripture does not give us all the detailed answers to this question that we might desire, the Bible does provide a helpful framework that paves the way for understanding why work is a mixed bag of the good, the bad, and the ugly. Scripture doesn't hide the contrasting before and after pictures of the world of work as it is, but unlike all the television commercials and magazine ads, the before picture is dramatically better than the after. In the first three chapters of the book of Genesis we are given a contrasting before and after pictures of work.

In the last chapter we looked at the before picture highlighted in Genesis 1 and 2. Here we were presented with a delightful picture of work as God originally designed it to be. Adam and Eve are working in a pristine garden context, finding fulfillment in a joyful and intimate relationship with God and each other. What we see in the before picture is that God designed human work to be an exhilarating pleasure, not a frustrating pain. So what happened to God's good and perfect design for our work?

When we arrive in Genesis chapter 3, we discover the tragic answer. Here we encounter the after picture of work in a sin-ravaged world. Lured by Satan's lies, Adam and Eve commit an unthinkable and unconscionable act of folly. In eating the fruit of the tree of the knowledge of good and evil, Adam and Eve rebel against God. Sin and death enter God's good world. Adam and Eve are expelled from the garden of Eden. Paradise is lost and sin wreaks a devastating effect on human work.

WORK IN A SIN-RAVAGED WORLD

The Bible clearly tells us that while work is not a result of the fall, work itself was profoundly impacted. If we grasp what the biblical writers say, we realize that our work, whatever it may be, is now not at all what it ought to be. In this broken world, God's original design for our work has been badly corrupted, and we feel it in the depths of our being every day. To truly understand how work came to be what it is, we need to take a closer look at the narrative of Genesis 3.

After Adam and Eve's act of disobedience, God comes to them as they are hiding from him in the garden. In God's address to Adam and Eve in responding to this rebellion, we find these words about our work:

> And to Adam he said, "Because you have listened to the voice of your wife and have eaten of the tree of which I commanded you, 'You shall not eat of it,' cursed is the ground because of you; in pain you shall eat of it all the days of your life; thorns and thistles it shall bring forth for you; and you shall eat the plants of the field. By the sweat of your face you shall eat bread, till you return to the ground, for out of it you were taken; for you are dust, and to dust you shall return." (Gen. 3:17–19)

In this text we see the Genesis writer employ the word *curse* to describe a new reality and its massive and devastating effect on work. In our cultural context, the word *curse* often brings to mind images of a kind of mystical hocus-pocus. We envision a kind of occultist witch doctor voodoo sort of thing we might see in some movie. Perhaps we have images of someone casting spells on others like the Wicked Witch of the West in the classic film *The Wizard of Oz*. Though I don't want to minimize the very real presence and power of Satan, evil, demons, and occult practices in our world, the word *curse* here in this text is not primarily portraying a kind of voodoo spell. Rather, a careful look at the context reveals far-reaching and long-lasting changes regarding work. This curse means that the very nature and context of human work has fundamentally changed. The topography of human work has been altered.

The Genesis writer emphasizes that under the curse, work has a new dimension to it. Work is now toilsome and difficult. Thorns and thistles will bring the sweat of exertion to the human brow. I often think of Genesis chapter 3 when I am pulling weeds in my garden or removing wallpaper during a home project. Yet much more is going on here besides work's thorny challenges. As we read the account in Genesis 3, we can almost feel the intensity of hurricane-force winds rearranging the entire landscape of human existence and sense the intense groaning of creation and the weariness that is now a part of our work. Work has become a heavy yoke that humans were not originally designed to bear. The vivid biblical imagery of the curse paints the dire picture of the far-reaching and devastating consequences of rebellion against a good, just, and holy God.

C. S. Lewis captures well this curse language in his classic *The Lion, the Witch and the Wardrobe*. Lewis tells us that mythical Narnia once displayed the vibrant and flourishing warmth of summer, but now it faces the chilling cold of winter. One of Lewis's main characters is a young girl named Lucy. Lucy questions Mr. Tumnus about the White Witch whose curse has so dreadfully altered the land of Narnia. Mr. Tumnus responds, "Why, it is she that has got all Narnia under her thumb. It's she that makes it always winter. Always winter and never Christmas, think of that!"[2] An incredulous Lucy then blurts out, "How awful!" Lucy's response is quite appropriate to such a dreadful thing. Evil, sin, and death entering the world have a ravaging effect on all of creation. Lewis insightfully reminds us that we live and work in a fallen world where it is always winter and never Christmas. In this cursed world, there is alienation from God, alienation from other human beings, and yes, alienation from the good work we were created for. Genesis chapter 3 tells us in very riveting language that we are broken people who live and work in a broken world. Something has gone badly awry. Our work is not what it ought to be.

GROANING

When it comes to pain, I would rather not be there when it happens, but usually I am. I will never forget the time when, in a hurry to get to an appointment, I slammed my car door shut before my right hand had made it out of the car. My crushed fingers sent a pain through my body that was so intense I almost blacked out on the spot. After retrieving my crushed and quite bruised fingers from the door and wrapping my whole hand in ice, my swollen fingers still throbbed for hours.

When we experience excruciating pain from a physical injury or the despairing emotional pain of a deep loss, our visceral reaction is often a groan. This, too, is true of all of creation in this fallen world. In his letter to a group of first-century followers of Jesus in Rome, Paul makes the point that we, along with the cursed and fallen creation, feel the pain of alienation from our Creator and we groan deeply. With a sense of hope flowing through his inspired pen, Paul looks to the transforming power of the gospel and the glorious future of redemption, but he also describes an inherent groaning, one that presently permeates every aspect of our lives, our work, and our world. Paul writes, "For we know that the whole creation has been groaning together in the pains of childbirth until now. And not only the creation, but we ourselves, who have the firstfruits of the Spirit, groan inwardly as we wait eagerly for adoption as sons, the redemption of our bodies" (Rom. 8:22–23). Paul strikes many rich theological themes in these verses, but for our purposes his metaphor of childbirth is particularly instructive. Childbirth is a joyful thing, but it is also a painful thing. At this point in redemptive history, the work we do and the workplaces we inhabit are filled with difficulty and pain. Someday this will not be the case, but for now we must not expect otherwise. Our work has been deeply affected by the devastating consequences of sin.

PAINFULLY DIFFICULT WORK

Sin entering the world and corrupting God's design has made the very nature of work itself harder. Our work is often painfully difficult. The systems, technologies, economics, and structures we deal with every day reflect a fallen, broken world. We face difficult people in the workplace. We face intense dog-eat-dog competition on a global scale. Government regulation and the constant threat of possible litigation bring new complexities and greater demands to our work. Layoffs and reduction of workforces place greater burdens on those who still have a job. We encounter backstabbing and political maneuvering in the workplace. We observe the people in the cubicles next to us playing the power game to their career advantage.

I received an e-mail from a friend of mine describing the difficulty of his work in the highly competitive global corporate world. Facing the pressures of staff reductions and ever-increasing sales targets in a global economic downturn, he wrote, "It's like a daily Private Ryan hit-the-beach environment. . . . The goals are extraordinarily difficult to complete. Morale suffers under the carnage." The work environment many of us inhabit every day can only be described as painful and messy. There is a lot of groaning in our work.

Work is also painfully difficult when we have to do jobs that are less than desirable. One of my first work experiences was working long hours serving the public in a fast-food restaurant. Being given the task of cleaning the bathrooms in a fast-food restaurant was not my idea of fun, but I knew someone had to do it. I think that's why I like the show *Dirty Jobs*. Mike Rowe, the host, has become a stunning success by getting his hands dirty. Mike Rowe takes on the dirty jobs no one wants, from rattlesnake catching to septic tank cleaning. On his popular website, Mike invites all who are stuck in a dead-end job, combing through the classifieds, to consider a new calling. For example, Mike describes the job of road-kill collector in this job listing: "Must be able to work long hours braving oncoming traffic while picking up creatures of various size and breed and in various states of decay. Benefits include working outdoors. Strong stomach a plus!" I am not sure Mike has a lot of takers on this one, but in a fallen world, the job of collecting road-kill has to be done by someone. Though when approached rightly, this too can be seen as God-honoring work, it is still difficult and downright stinky and dirty. The curse of the fall means our work is often painfully difficult.

DISILLUSIONING WORK

Not only is our work painfully difficult, but the work we do can also seem empty and meaningless. In many cases the work we do is far removed from the beneficiaries of our efforts. Because of this distance, we do not receive the inherent satisfaction of seeing the direct benefit of our work. It all too often feels like we are one big meaningless cog in a giant global wheel. When I have a conversation with people about their work, I often hear this plea: "Tom, please tell me that what I do every day really matters." Behind these words lurks a haunting sense that our work really does not have much significance at all. The Old Testament book of Ecclesiastes transparently addresses the disillusionment that is part of this fallen world and our daily experience in it. The author's mad pursuit of power, pleasure, and material comforts leads him to the disillusioning conclusion that it is all for naught. Satisfaction and fulfillment elude him in his pursuits, particularly his work. It is as if he had before him the lyrics of the Rolling Stones' classic song, "I can't get no satisfaction; 'Cause I try and I try and I try."[3]

The writer of Ecclesiastes describes his disillusionment with work in a fallen world as futile and striving after wind:

> So I hated life, because what is done under the sun was griev-ous to me, for all is vanity and a striving after wind. I hated all my toil in which I toil under the sun, seeing that I must leave it to the man who will come after me.... What has a man from

41

all the toil and striving of heart with which he toils beneath the sun? For all his days are full of sorrow, and his work is a vexation. Even in the night his heart does not rest. This also is vanity. (Eccles. 2:17–18, 22–23)

Clearly the biblical writer is deeply disillusioned with his life and work, but he also offers a ray of hope seeing his work as a gift from God. Later on in Ecclesiastes we encounter these words, "I perceived that there is nothing better for them than to be joyful and to do good as long as they live; also that everyone should eat and drink and take pleasure in all his toil—this is God's gift to man (3:12–13).

The writer of Ecclesiastes reminds us that work in this fallen world is a mixed bag. Work is both a curse and a gift. Work greets us with both frustration and exhilaration. Our work gives evidence of our glorious creation as well as our great estrangement from God and our need for a Savior who will redeem us from sin's devastating curse.

DISTORTED WORK

The difficulty of our work and the disillusionment with work that we face distorts how we see our work. Rather than worship God through our work, we can easily and subtly begin to worship our work. Work can become an idol in our lives. The most destructive and dangerous idols we worship are seldom those figures made of wood or stone, but rather the idols that lurk in human hearts. But Scripture is clear. God will not share his glory with anyone or anything. God does not stutter when he declares, "You shall have no other gods before me" (Ex. 20:3). God will not allow any rivals. Our ultimate allegiance, the greatest love of our hearts, is to be God and God only.

THE DISTORTION OF WORKAHOLISM

One of the ways we make work an idol is workaholism. Workaholism is rampant in our day and often points to a deeper issue of idolatry in our lives. In this common form of idolatry, our entire lives center around what we do, and our identity becomes centered in it. Work idolatry can be driven by our pursuit of the American dream, of material comforts, of financial security, or by our attempts to prop up a certain image of success about ourselves. Work idolatry is often concealed in the language of organizational loyalty and commitment and is regularly legitimized in a competitive work environment as the required pathway to promotion and advancement. Workaholism can also be driven by overextended living, materialistic greed, and rebellion against God. Regardless of the form it takes, like a black hole from which light cannot escape, excessive devotion to work inevitably crowds out our relationship with God and others and sets work up as the ultimate reality in our lives. Work becomes an idol.

In Jesus's parable of the rich fool found in Luke 12, we are warned about the peril of a life lived without God, one that worships self, work, and personal comfort. Jesus gives a damning indictment of a man who lived as if God did not exist, who thought he had it all, but at the end of the day who truly had nothing. In death, the rich fool left his work and all he had accumulated behind, and God said to him, "Fool! This night your soul is required of you, and the things you have prepared, whose will they be?" (Luke 12:20).

Workaholism is destructive distortion of work that wreaks havoc on our physical health and our relationships. The sin of a hurried, harried, and preoccupied life is rampant in our fast-paced, competitive world. Much of this frantic pace is driven by our distorted view of work. When our work is out of whack, we can be assured our life will be out of whack, too.

THE DISTORTION OF SLOTHFULNESS

Instead of making work an idol, we can erroneously view our work as really no big deal. When work is distorted, we easily make leisure an idol and become a slothful person. When taking a slothful approach to our work, we may find creative excuses not to do our work, or do just enough of our work to keep our job and get a regular paycheck. We need to realize the seriousness of a slothful life, for slothfulness violates the very essence of our image-bearing nature. Slothfulness leads us to rely on the hard work and industry of others and to develop an entitlement mentality. It is all too easy for college students whose parents are footing the hefty tuition bill to party away their college years, taking for granted their parents' hard work that has made it possible. But it is not only younger adults who can live sloth-ful lives; older retired adults can do this as well. The common notion of a long, leisurely, and self-indulgent retirement is not something Scripture endorses, and in many ways it reflects the distortion of slothfulness.

The Bible repeatedly warns of this peril. The writer of Prov-erbs declares, "The sluggard does not plow in the autumn; he will seek at harvest and have nothing" (20:4). The apostle Paul, who modeled diligence in his work as a tentmaker, encourages the first-century followers of Jesus in Thessalonica to live lives of diligence in their everyday work. Paul writes, "Aspire to live quietly, and to mind your own affairs, and to work with your hands, as we instructed you" (1 Thess. 4:11). Slothfulness is a reflection of the corruption of God's design for our lives and his good world.

THE DISTORTION OF WORK DUALISM

Dualism, put simply, is wrongly dividing something that should not be divided. This all too often takes place in our work. When we wrongly distinguish one type of work from another, placing value on some types of work at the expense of others, we fall into the distortion of work dualism. Work dualism sees through a bifurcated lens in the form of a two–story world. The upper story is seen as a higher vocational calling, one devoted to the church or religious or sacred work. The lower story is viewed as a lower vocational calling, one devoted to secular work. This work dualism distortion is often perpetuated with subtle and very spiritual-sounding words. In the fourth century, Augustine spoke of the contemplative life and the active life. The contemplative life was given to sacred things and deemed a higher calling, while the active life was given to secular things and regarded as a lower calling. This kind of thinking helped spawn a distorted view of work that continues even to our modern time.

Work dualism can be seen in various Christian traditions. For example, the language of "full-time Christian work" is commonly used to describe those whose vocational calling is to be a pastor, missionary, or parachurch worker. However, a proper and biblical understanding is that all Christians are called to "full-time Christian work," doing good work well for the glory of God, regardless of their specific vocation.

It wasn't long after I began my pastoral ministry that a dear elderly lady approached me after a Sunday worship service to affirm the meaningfulness of the morning sermon. I was grateful for her warm and affirming words, but then she asked me a question, "Pastor, when did you receive your call?" I replied to her in a polite manner, but her carefully nuanced words reflected this common distortion about work. Somehow in her mind she believed that my calling to pastoral work was different than the work she had been doing for years. I wanted to ask her a question back, "Tell me, when did you receive your call?"

Many followers of Jesus live their entire lives in the workplace under the soul-suffocating distortion that their work is not as important and God honoring as the work of a pastor or missionary. But this is not the only place this work dualism is seen. Work dualism often prompts well-meaning and sincere people to leave the work to which they are uniquely called to pursue a "higher calling." The monastic impulse calling followers of Jesus to withdraw from the normal, day-to-day world in order to pursue a highly spiritual and highly mystical contemplative life in sacred spaces shows this distortion of work. In reality, there is no more sacred space than the

45

workplace where God has called you to serve him as you serve the common good.

Perpetuating this work dualism distortion reinforces the false two-story work world in which certain vocations are elevated over others, and bolsters the unbiblical idea of withdrawing from the world rather than engaging it and being faithfully present in it. Work dualism can raise its ugly head when some work we may be called to do is perceived as beneath us or not a good utilization of our gifts. As I interact with people who are in the middle years of life, I hear a subtle work dualism claw its way out from the shadows of well-meaning hearts as they pursue work they believe will somehow be more pleasing to God or more eternally impactful. Often this means a move to the nonprofit sector with the hope it will move them from a life of success to a life of significance. Because of sin's devastating and far-reaching effect on our world, we all find ourselves at times fogged in with blinding distortions about work. But we don't have to live in the fog. There is good news about our work that gives us hope in the midst of the painful difficulty.

THE STOCKDALE PARADOX

In his bestselling book, *Good to Great*, Jim Collins recounts the story of his interaction with Admiral James Stockdale who, as a young man, spent several years as a prisoner of war in what was dubbed the Hanoi Hilton. When asked by Collins what the difference was between those prisoners of war who lost hope and gave up, and those who endured such a torturous existence, Admiral Stockdale was quick to reply. The difference, he pointed out, was a kind of hopeful realism. The idealistic prisoners who convinced themselves they would be home by Christmas, simply caved in when Christmas after Christmas came and went. But those prisoners who prepared themselves for the likelihood of a long and difficult captivity, yet believed they would eventually triumph and make it back home, were the ones who survived.[4]

CULTIVATING A HOPEFUL REALISM

Though few of us will ever have to endure the torturous existence of a prisoner of war, when it comes to a lifetime of work, I believe we need to cultivate a hopeful realism if we are going to thrive in our work. Your mind may be filled with idealistic phantoms of the perfect dream job. You may be encountering great difficulties in your work. You may be feeling deeply disillusioned about your work. You may be sensing a growing lack of contentment in your work. You may be going from job to job because the grass seems greener on the other side of the work fence. But how are you approaching your work? Are you viewing your work through an idealistic or a realistic lens? A perfect job or career is not only unrealistic, it is theologically untenable. Even if you are blessed to have your dream job, I can assure you it will be hard and it will not be all you long for it to be. Whatever work we have been called to do will be a mixture of both the good and the not so good. We must recognize that at this point in redemptive history, our work will not be all we want it to be.

The after-picture the Bible paints for us about the toilsome nature of our work as a result of the devastating effects of sin is anything but encouraging. Our work is not how it was designed to be, and we feel it deeply. However, the good news of the gospel is that the tragedy of humankind's fall into sin is not the end of the story. There is good news for you and your work. Though your work may be difficult and demanding, you can approach your work with a sense of hope and excitement that God can and will do remarkable things in and through the work he has called you to do. Though sin entered the world, the good news is, so did the Savior, our Lord Jesus Christ. Through his death and resurrection, we see Jesus as the redeemer not only of human

47

souls but also of the whole fallen world. It is to this good news we turn our attention next.

A Prayer for Our Work

Almighty God, by whose will we were created, and by whose providence we have been sustained, grant to us your blessing this day. You have given to each of us our work in life; Lord, enable us to diligently perform our respective duties. May we not waste our time in unprofitableness and idleness, nor be unfaithful to any trust committed to us. By Your grace strengthen each of us for the performance of duties before us. (Henry Thornton)[5]

Questions for Reflection and Discussion:

- How have you experienced the brokenness of work in a fallen world?

- How does recognizing the brokenness of work change the way you view your work/workplace?

- Which distortion of work is most apparent in your workplace?

- Which distortion of work do you most easily fall into?

MIKE > EDUCATIONAL ADMINISTRATOR

After I came to faith as a teenager, my understanding of what it meant to "be called" was limited by the belief that just those in full-time Christian ministry were truly "called." Missionaries, pastors, youth ministers—those were the ones who were called by God, I reasoned, because a person couldn't ever be effective for God by holding anything but one of those esteemed positions. That belief led me to seek my calling at a Bible college and culminated with me trying to manufacture my calling by taking various roles in church settings. One of those roles was as a pastor at a small church in rural Nebraska for nearly three years. I focused on finding my calling in the way I understood calling—that is, to be effective for God, you had to be doing God's work, which meant full-time ministry. I had a deep desire to be the person I thought God wanted me to be. For so many years I missed understanding the person God created me to be, and how that person fits into God's kingdom work.

Over the past several years as I have deepened my understanding of calling, I have come to recognize that my true calling is found in understanding my interests, abilities, and gifts, and in the realization of responsibility that I, as a Christian, have to use those gifts for God's glory. It's an understanding of the person God made me to be and how that person fits into his kingdom work.

So what does that look like? What does it mean to provide educational leadership for a large suburban school district? As I have known to be true, God wants me to influence those with whom I have contact toward a faith in Jesus Christ. What I have learned recently is how this can be done, and needs to be done, within my calling as a school administrator. So many times throughout my career God has used me to help make his truths evident in my daily work, not just in daily interactions around the proverbial water cooler, but within my daily work activities. I have seen conversations with groups about such things as the nature of education, what constitutes good literature, the definition and implementation of tolerance, the proper role of student rights, and a host of other topics turn into springboards for other discussions about deeper spiritual matters. In my old way of thinking, I saw my work as a school administrator to be disconnected from calling and certainly not something that God was excited about. In my new way of thinking, I see everything I do as a school administrator as an opportunity to engage and influence those around me in discussions and thinking that ultimately points to God's truth about matters I deal with on a daily basis.

When I wake up in the mornings, not only do I get to go to a vocation that I love, I go there knowing God does not want me to be anywhere else. And in that I take great comfort.

3

THE GOOD NEWS OF WORK

The first Adam was cursed with labor and suffering; the redemption of labor and suffering is the triumph of the second Adam—the Carpenter nailed to the cross.[1]
DOROTHY SAYERS

His name meant "useful," but he proved himself to be anything but useful to his boss. As an enslaved household servant in the first century, the work Onesimus did every day was not all that appealing. The long hours and endless domestic duties that occupied his life must have seemed mundane and meaningless. Perhaps Onesimus had thought about running away for a long time, or maybe a particularly dehumanizing or painful incident in the workplace was the proverbial straw that broke the camel's back. What prompted Onesimus to make his escape remains a mystery, but one eventful day he left his boss and work behind and bolted to the big city of Rome.

While in Rome, something unexpected happened to Onesimus that changed his life forever. An imprisoned apostle Paul shared with Onesimus the good news of the gospel. Hearing the gospel proclaimed, Onesimus encountered the crucified and resurrected Christ and experienced transforming grace. Though a household slave, the chains of sin that had bound Onesimus were now gone. For the first time in his life, Onesimus was now truly free. He had been redeemed from slavery to sin, yet he still had a job to do. We know this from an inspired letter that makes its way into the New Testament. Named for its recipient, this letter written by the apostle Paul is simply called Philemon.

The apostle Paul sent Onesimus, with letter in hand, back to his boss Philemon and appealed to him to receive his household servant and put him back to work. Paul wrote, "I appeal to you for my child, Onesimus, whose father I became in my imprisonment. (Formerly he was useless to you, but now he is indeed useful to you and to me.)" (Philem. 10–11). Paul's heartfelt appeal to Philemon was not based on giving his household servant a humanitarian or altruistic second chance, however noble that might have been. Rather, Paul's persuasive appeal was based on the power of the gospel to bring true transformation to a human life. Paul's letter informs us that Philemon himself had experienced the power of the gospel. Philemon's life, too, had been changed. With this in mind, Paul urged Philemon to receive Onesimus back in good standing not only as a household servant but also as a new brother in Christ.

Paul reminded Philemon of God's sovereign grace even at work in such a messy work situation. "For this perhaps is why he was parted from you for a while, that you might have him back forever, no longer as a slave but more than a slave, as a beloved brother— especially to me, but how much more to you, both in the flesh and in the Lord" (Philem. 15–16). Paul's well-chosen words reflect a needed change of perspective on Philemon's part. No longer was Philemon to view Onesimus as merely a worker, but rather a worker created in the image of God whose identity was now centered in Christ. And as Paul sent Onesimus back to Philemon, he sent him back as a worker—a worker transformed by the gospel of Jesus Christ.

THE TRANSFORMING POWER OF THE GOSPEL

Scripture presents the gospel to us in the broader context of the story line of redemptive history. In the opening chapters of Genesis we read of the one true God who created a good world, but less than three chapters later we see this good world corrupted by Adam and Eve's rebellion against him. Sin and death entered the world. Human beings were alienated from God, no longer able to live in relationship with him as they once did and no longer living according to God's good creation design. Yet as the biblical story line continues, we observe the sovereign God, unfathomable in holiness, perfect in justice, infinite in mercy, and self-sacrificing in love, initiate a costly plan to redeem his fallen world. The one true triune God sends his Son, Jesus, to our fallen planet.

With the opening words of the Gospel of John we see this story continue as John tells us of a new beginning. "In the beginning was the Word.... And the Word became flesh" (John 1:1, 14). The Son of God, the Word, took on human flesh, becoming one of us, coming into the world to redeem us. John says that the Son was active in creation. In fact he says, "All things were made through him, and without him was not anything made that was made" (John 1:3). And as John's story unfolds, we see that the work of God in creation continues through the work of Jesus—a work of new creation that brings deep heart transformation.

This is the good news of the gospel. The apostle Paul tells us of the power of this good news. In his letter to the church in Rome he reminds them that the gospel is "the power of God for salvation to everyone who believes" (Rom. 1:16). There is powerful good news that can transform our lives and our work. This is the power of the gospel!

A NEW CREATION IN CHRIST

The gospel does not wrap us with a thin religious or ethical veneer, but goes to the very core of our sinful minds and hearts.

When we embrace the good news of the gospel, we are transformed from the inside out. In John 3, Jesus described this core gospel transformation as a new spiritual birth to a first-century religious leader by the name of Nicodemus. The apostle Paul describes the spiritual birth in new-creation language. "Therefore, if anyone is in Christ, he is a new creation. The old has passed away; behold, the new has come" (2 Cor. 5:17). Creation is not just something God did long ago in bringing the world into existence; God is still at work creating through the transforming power of the gospel. When we embrace Christ, we experience a new birth. We become a new creation. Old things have passed away; new things have come.

At the center of this work of new creation is the atoning work of Christ on the cross. It is the definitive picture of the love and justice of God. Don Carson writes, "Do you want to see the greatest evidence of the love of God? Go to the cross. Do you want to see the greatest evidence of the justice of God? Go to the cross. It is where wrath and mercy meet. Holiness and peace kiss each other. The climax of redemptive history is the cross."[2] When we pause to look carefully at the cross of Jesus, we see that it is both hideous in its cruel injustice as well as glorious in its sacrificial love. The apostle Paul reminds us of this when he says, "But God shows his love for us in that while we were still sinners, Christ died for us" (Rom. 5:8). On the cross, the one true triune God paid the ultimate price and provided the ultimate swap for your vile sin and mine. As Paul says, "For our sake he [God the Father] made him [God the Son] to be sin who knew no sin, so that in him [Jesus] we might become the righteousness of God" (2 Cor. 5:21).

On that old rugged cross of suffering and shame, God took our sin and placed it on his sinless Son, the innocent and perfect Lamb of God. In doing so, God made available to us, as a gracious gift, the very righteousness of Christ. The gifts of forgiveness of sin, of eternal life, of entering into new-creation life in Jesus's kingdom reign are available here and now to all who embrace Jesus as their Lord and Savior in repentance and faith. The wonderful and glorious news of the gospel is that our standing before and relationship with a holy, righteous God is not based on anything we have done or could possibly do but on what Jesus has already done on our behalf on the cross. It is not by our works but by his stripes that we are healed.

RON'S NEW-CREATION STORY

One of the greatest joys of my life is witnessing the power of the gospel in giving new life to those around me. I remember the very first time I met Ron at a local coffee shop. Although Ron had not done the church thing for a long time, he had been attending our Sunday morning worship services, and to his surprise he had found his church experience meaningful. Ron had many questions about the Christian faith, so we set up a time to get together over a cup of coffee. At first glance, Ron displayed the many appealing attributes of a successful career in sales and marketing. Ron was warm, engaging, and confident. His years of work had hewn his social and relational skills to a razor-sharp competency, but as we talked further, Ron transparently began to reveal more about the turbulent currents swirling under the waterline of his life.

Ron had experienced the pain of two failed marriages and a growing sense of discontentment and disillusionment in his corporate world. Ron was seeking wisdom and guidance on living life well. He wanted to know what the Christian faith was and how it connected to the real world of his messy life and competitive work environment. Over the course of the next couple of months, Ron and I met several times over coffee, and I shared with him the good news of the gospel. We had a very thoughtful conversation about how the gospel transforms us from the inside out. We also interacted about how the gospel reshapes how we view the world as well as how we live and work. Ron and I talked extensively about how the Christian faith permeates all of life and that it seamlessly connects what we profess to believe on Sunday and how we practice our work on Monday.

Ron seemed truly surprised as he began to grasp that the Christian faith, properly understood, brought not only purpose and meaning to one's life, but also an integral coherence to all of life. Like discovering the sequencing code of DNA, discovering the gospel unlocked the sequencing code of reality. The gospel made sense of life. I will never forget the look of joy in Ron's eyes as he contemplated the truth that the Christian faith is not about being good enough to somehow be accepted by God. Throughout his life Ron had thought that Christianity was about being good enough for God to let a person into heaven. Now Ron realized that the gospel called him to place his complete trust in what Jesus had done for him on the cross. There was no way he could earn a right standing before a holy God; salvation was a gift he was to receive in repentance and faith.

One day later, Ron stopped by my office. After some small talk and catching up a bit, Ron told me he now understood the gospel and wanted to become a Christian. I asked him if he was sure about making such an important commitment. Ron nodded. We got down on our knees, and Ron embraced Christ as his personal Lord and Savior. Over the weeks and months that followed, I began to see evidence of the transforming power of the gospel in Ron's life. Ron's love for Christ and the fruit of the Spirit was increasingly evident. Ron's commitment to his marriage strengthened. Though the very real day-to-day challenges of Ron's work and workplace did not immediately change, Ron's attitude toward his work profoundly changed. He now saw that work mattered, and he embraced his work with a renewed passion and creativity. Because things were well at soul level, Ron was more focused at work. He brought a new calm and confidence to the workplace. He viewed his coworkers through the lens of common grace, affirming them and truly seeking their success and betterment. The gospel not only made Ron a more integral person, but it also made him a better employee.

We can find ourselves thinking deeply about our work without thinking deeply about the gospel. But this is something we simply must not do. There is really no good news about our work without the good news of the gospel. For the gospel is the transforming power that changes us. Gustaf Wingren makes this important point. "Only the gospel, not one's vocation, can remove that judgment against the sinful heart and gives peace to the conscience."[3]

THE PRODIGAL SONS

In the Gospel of Luke, Jesus tells a story not of a runaway household servant but of a runaway son. Running away from one's family is no small thing, of course. Before running off to a far country, this prodigal son did the unthinkable. He disgraced his family and demanded from his father his share of the family inheritance. Nevertheless, the son's gracious father granted his son's wishes. Off the young man went, embracing a slothful, self-indulgent, immoral lifestyle. Over time, the foolish son squandered all that his father had worked for, and eventually there was nothing left. Hitting rock bottom, a repentant Prodigal Son made his way back to his father's waiting and loving arms. His father threw a party for him and, with lavish grace, received his runaway son back into the family. But before we celebrate the return of the prodigal, we should remember Jesus's good news story doesn't end here. There is another son in Jesus's story. While the younger son was slothful, the elder son was a hard worker at home. Yet both sons were estranged from their loving father.

The elder brother stayed at home, followed the rules, and dutifully worked hard. Though he had not physically left home, the elder brother had left his father's heart. He had worked hard, but his work was not connected to a loving relationship with his father. The tragedy of Jesus's good news story is that while the younger brother was lost and then found, the lost elder brother didn't realize or refused to admit he was lost and so never was found. Tim Keller reflects on Jesus's heart-arresting story: "Jesus the storyteller deliberately leaves the elder brother in his alienated state. The bad son enters the father's feast but the good son will not. The lover of prostitutes is saved, but the man of moral rectitude is still lost."[4] Hard work, however noble, without a relationship with the Father proves empty, meaningless, and despairing. The elder brother was really only working for himself. What a pitiful and tragic aim. The work we do will not win us favor with our Father. Yet as new creations in Christ, transformed from the inside out, we are able to again do the work we were created for.

REDEEMING WORK

The first-century followers of Jesus in Thessalonica had been profoundly changed by the power of the gospel. Paul reminds them that the gospel had not come to them in word only but "also in power and in the Holy Spirit and with full conviction" (1 Thess. 1:5). The authenticity of their conversion to Christ was evident in that they "turned to God from idols to serve the living and true God, and to wait for his Son from heaven, whom he raised from the dead, Jesus who delivers us from the wrath to come" (1 Thess. 1:9–10).

Having affirmed the gospel's redeeming work in their lives, Paul exhorts these first-century believers regarding the gospel's implications for their work. Reminding them of the Holy Spirit's empowerment and the importance of excelling in true brotherly love for others, Paul calls these Christ followers to aspire to a life of faithfulness in their daily work. Paul writes, "Aspire to live quietly, and to mind your own affairs, and to work with your hands, as we instructed you, so that you may walk properly before outsiders and be dependent on no one" (1 Thess. 4:11–12). An essential aspect of presenting our Christian faith to the world around us is seen in and through the diligence we exhibit in our work.

A FAITHFUL PRESENCE

In his Sermon on the Mount, Jesus speaks to the pervasive influence his transformed followers will have on the world around them. Jesus employs the metaphors of salt and light to communicate the pervasive impact people transformed by the gospel bring to the world. Speaking to his followers, Jesus states, "You are the light of the world. A city set on a hill cannot be hidden. Nor do people light a lamp and put it under a basket, but on a stand, and it gives light to all in the house. In the same way, let your light shine before others, so that they may see your good works and give glory to your Father who is in heaven" (Matt. 5:14–16). In all aspects of our lives, including our workplaces, we display to those around us the light of the glory of Christ who indwells us. Jesus emphasizes that we shine his light in our good works. Our good works take on many dimensions, and we must see that our daily work is a significant part of the good works that glorify God.

One of the ways that we are salt and light and act as redemptive agents in this broken world is to live out a faithful presence in the workplace. Woody Allen once observed that 90 percent of life is simply showing up. These words reveal some instructive wisdom for us. Sociologist James Hunter has thought a great deal about cultural change and the Christian's faithfulness in the late modern world. Hunter reminds us that, first and foremost, Christ is faithfully present to us. He then makes a very important point when he writes, "Faithful presence in the world means that Christians are fully present and committed in their spheres of influence, whatever they may be: their families, neighborhoods, voluntary activities and places of work."[5] As followers of Jesus, we are called to a mission of engagement in, not withdrawal from, the broader world. To faithfully engage the world means we must be fully present within it.

A large stewardship of our calling in the workplace is faithfully showing up every day and demonstrating to others around us our good in and through our work. Seeking to live out a faithful presence in our workplaces means that we incarnate the gospel by doing good work and being exemplary workers. It means that we extend common grace to our coworkers and our customers and seek their good. As image-bearers of God, who is a worker, we must remember that our work has intrinsic value in itself and is to be an act of worship. We also must grasp that our work has instrumental value in that it provides for our economic needs, allows us to care for the needs of others, and creates a sphere of influence for the gospel to be lived out and shared.

BRINGING OUR FAITH TO WORK

For many of us, when we think of bringing our Christian faith to work, our thoughts turn toward a kind of ethical behavior or even bowing our head and saying a silent prayer before we eat lunch. Of course these are good things. Yet when Dave and Demi Kiersznowski embraced the gospel and later began their very successful and innovative Kansas City-based gift company DEMDACO, they desired to allow the biblical story of work and the broad redemptive implications of the gospel to shape their entire organizational culture. Dave and Demi would be the first to say that DEMDACO is not a Christian company; but called by God to be business leaders, they are committed to modeling a faithful presence in the workplace. Many of their work colleagues do not profess the Christian faith; some do not profess any religious faith at all. But DEMDACO is highly intentional about nurturing a corporate culture that holds up the high value of each person, the intrinsic value of work itself, the importance of seeking the common good, and bringing a redemptive influence to work, the worker, and the workplace. A relentless commitment to pursue work as it ought to be reflects the biblical storyline of work and makes its way into the very purpose of the company. DEMDACO's purpose is stated this way: *to lift the spirit by providing products that help people connect in a meaningful way and by pursuing business as it ought to be.* As business leaders who are also devoted followers of Jesus, Dave and Demi have given me, and many others who have the delightful privilege of knowing them, an ongoing glimpse of the multifaceted influence the gospel is to have on our work and the workplaces we indwell. Observing the rich theology of vocation and work that permeates Dave and Demi's calling as business leaders, I have been given a hopeful glimpse of what work was originally designed to be, and I find myself savoring an appetizer of what our work and our workplaces will one day be in the future.

Without knowing Christ, you and I will never experience the life for which we were created. Without knowing Christ, your work will never be all that God intended for it to be. Without knowing the One who created work, your work will never be ultimately fulfilling. The good news of work is that we can be transformed—that our work can be transformed.

A Prayer of Thanks

Heavenly Father, I thank you for the glorious good news of the gospel. May the rich truths of the gospel press more deeply into the depths of who I am and the work I am called to do. Holy Spirit, guide and empower me to live the new life you have called me to live.

Discussion Questions:

- How does understanding what work can be in light of the gospel change the way you inhabit your workplace?

- How is the gospel transforming the way you do your work?

- What are some ways you can be faithfully present in your spheres of influence?

JAY > ATTORNEY

Over the past several years I have been fortunate to gain greater insight into what my Christian faith says about my vocation. As a young lawyer, I worked diligently and tried to be a good witness for Christ, honoring him in all that I did. I always assumed I had a healthy view toward work and the proper motivation as a Christian in the workplace. I was willing to share my faith with others and tried to be salt and light in my office. As both my family and my legal practice matured, I became more motivated to work hard to provide for my family, to earn money in order to give generously, and to provide good service to my clients in order to increase and sustain my business.

While my thoughts and motivations were honorable, I have recently learned so much more about how God views vocation, and I am experiencing more freedom and joy through a more biblical view of work. In short, God is helping me to see my vocation as part of my calling to bear his image and to repair a broken and fallen world. God designed us for work and has gifted each of us in a unique way to have dominion, to create, and to make a better world.

I think God wants our vocations to be in sync with our desires to redeem a broken world. As a business transaction lawyer, I am called to improve how people make promises to each other, to help people honor their promises, to help people better understand their obligations, to help people resolve conflicts, and to help people realize the best of their dreams and aspirations. I am called to use my position to foster healthy relationships in my office and to create a place where employees feel loved and cared for. My vocation is not just a means to make money, nor is my office just a convenient place to have an audience with whom to share Christ. My vocation is to improve the world around me. My work is not "secular," but rather an opportunity to bear God's image and to live within the freedom offered by obedience to God's perfect design. My work is part of my spiritual calling. God has gifted me in a unique way to work within my sphere of influence to participate in the restoration of people's lives and of God's good creation, just as an architect is uniquely gifted to create beautiful spaces and places where people can flourish together or as a teacher has the ability to help kids better understand our complex and awesome created order so that they can discover how they are gifted by God.

Learning that my vocation is part of my calling has allowed me to see more clearly how the gospel unfolds each day in the lives of people around me. Clearly, God had a perfect design of how things ought to be, but sin entered the world and corrupted the "ought." As a follower of Christ, I can help repair the brokenness through my vocation and help the world inch closer to the way things were meant to be until that day when things are once again made whole.

4

WORK NOW AND LATER

The created order, which God has begun to redeem in the resurrection of Jesus, is a world in which heaven and earth are designed not be separated but to come together. In that coming together, the "very good" that God spoke over creation at the beginning will be enhanced, not abolished.[1]

N. T. WRIGHT

Greensburg, Kansas, was once best known for being home to the world's largest hand-dug well. But that all changed on the evening of May 4, 2007. At 9:25 p.m., tornado sirens alerted the sleepy small town of 1,500 residents that big trouble was on its way. The hardy folks of Greensburg rushed to their storm shelters and basements as the 205 mile-an-hour winds of an F5 tornado transformed their town into scattered piles of rubble. In the course of just a few minutes, the fast-moving twister laid down a destructive path twenty-two miles long and almost two miles wide.

The aftermath of the tornado and its devastation is hard to describe. Greensburg looked as if a megaton bomb had been dropped on it. Ninety-five percent of the town of Greensburg was destroyed. Eleven residents lost their lives. The entire town was homeless. All businesses and social services were gone. This historic and quintessential small midwestern town had been completely wiped off the map. Greensburg would never be the same again.

But the town of Greensburg would rise again. The Greensburg community never lost hope in a better future. Almost immediately, massive clean-up efforts began. In some ways the architecture of the new Greensburg would reflect its past history, but in other ways it would be vastly different. A bold plan to create a better and more environmentally conscious and sustainable Greensburg was conceived and implemented. The Greensburg city council passed a resolution stating that all city buildings would be built to the highest green standards, making it the first city in the nation to do so. Powered by wind turbines, the new and better Greensburg would be rebuilt as a "green" town. A nonprofit organization called GreenTown was formed for the purpose of helping Greensburg residents embrace and implement the community's new green-living initiative. Though devastated by a killer tornado that disrupted their lives and altered the landscape of their town, a greener Greensburg is now flourishing. Greensburg, Kansas, is back on the map.

In many ways the devastation and restoration of Greensburg, Kansas, speaks to a broader story line of redemption and redemptive work in our world. The Bible places work within the literary framework of an unfolding progression in God's redemption of the physical world. God created a good world where our work once was what it ought to be. But because of sin and death, God's good world and our good work experienced a ravaging devastation. It is as if a killer F5 twister left a path of destruction altering the topography of our work. Now our work is often toilsome, aggravating, and painfully difficult.

Yet there is good news for us and our work both now and in the future. God took the initiative to conceive and implement a plan of redeeming us as workers as well as our work when he sent his Son to this sin-scarred planet. In and through the glorious gospel, our gracious Lord and Savior Jesus called us to himself. We are adopted into his family, and he has invited us to join him in his redemptive rebuilding project. The totality of Jesus's redemptive enterprise is in one sense already occurring but in another sense is not yet fully accomplished. We live in an already-but-not-yet moment of redemptive history. Not only do we have the promise of future eternal life, but also we have a new eternal life here and now.

Jesus framed eternal life not merely within the time constructs of a yet future reality, but within a never-ending relationship with himself that is available to us now. In his high priestly intercession, Jesus prayed, "And this is eternal life, that they know you the only true God, and Jesus Christ whom you have sent" (John 17:3). Knowing Christ in this already-but-not-yet moment of redemptive history, our work can be more of what it was originally designed to be. In the power of the Holy Spirit we can have a redemptive influence on our work and our workplaces, yet our ultimate hope looks to Christ and to a glorious future. As we go to work every day, we must realize that while our work will never be all it was intended to be in this fallen world, a new and better world is coming. Your work will one day be like God designed it to be in a pristine garden long ago. Your work in the new creation will be even better than it was in the old creation. God has a great future in store for his image-bearing workers, and how you do your work not only matters now, but it also matters for the future.

THE FUTURE OF WORK

We all have a curiosity about the future, and Jesus's first-century disciples were no exception. Steeped in the Old Testament

Scriptures, Jesus's disciples understood that history was not a series of meaningless, random events. They believed that history was being skillfully guided by the hand of a good and sovereign God. History was moving somewhere, but where? How would the future unfold? Overcome by their curiosity, the Gospel writer Matthew informs us that the disciples asked Jesus about the future.

JESUS'S PARABLE OF THE TALENTS

Responding to his disciples, Jesus paints a compelling picture of unfolding future events and the consummation of all things. His aim is not to give every detail, but rather to urge the disciples to live with discernment and expectancy, always being prepared for the Son of Man's future return to this earth and the coming day of future judgment. To drive his point home, Jesus tells his disciples a story often referred to as the parable of the talents. Sometimes we overlook that Jesus sets this parable about the future in the context of work and the workplace. Matthew 25 contains this story:

> For it will be like a man going on a journey, who called his servants and entrusted to them his property. To one he gave five talents, to another two, to another one, to each according to his ability. Then he went away. He who had received the five talents went at once and traded with them, and he made five talents more. So also he who had the two talents made two talents more. But he who had received the one talent went and dug in the ground and hid his master's money. Now after a long time the master of those servants came and settled accounts with them. And he who had received the five talents came forward, bringing five talents more, saying, "Master, you delivered to me five talents; here I have made five talents more." His master said to him, "Well done, good and faithful servant. You have been faithful over a little; I will set you over much. Enter into the joy of your master." And he also who had the two talents came forward, saying, "Master, you delivered to me two talents; here I have made two talents more." His master said to him, "Well done,

good and faithful servant. You have been faithful over a little; I will set you over much. Enter into the joy of your master." He also who had received the one talent came forward, saying, "Master, I knew you to be a hard man, reaping where you did not sow, and gathering where you scattered no seed, so I was afraid, and I went and hid your talent in the ground. Here you have what is yours." But his master answered him, "You wicked and slothful servant! You knew that I reap where I have not sown and gather where I scattered no seed? Then you ought to have invested my money with the bankers, and at my coming I should have received what was my own with interest. So take the talent from him and give it to him who has the ten talents. For to everyone who has will more be given, and he will have an abundance. But from the one who has not, even what he has will be taken away. And cast the worthless servant into the outer darkness. In that place there will be weeping and gnashing of teeth." (Matt. 25:14–30)

Jesus's parable introduces us to three workers. In our modern context we might refer to them as investment portfolio managers who have been given the charge by the owner to manage and grow his wealth and expand his net worth. Two of the three workers demonstrate diligence by investing the financial resources well. But one worker demonstrates slothfulness and does not invest the owner's financial resources. We might say he stuffed the owner's cash in his mattress rather than investing it in the market.

The owner's response to the three workers is telling. The two portfolio managers who demonstrate diligence in their work not only receive great commendation, but they are also promised greater responsibility and opportunity in their future work. The owner says to the two diligent workers, "You have been faithful over a little; I will set you over much." The clear implication is that the owner has more work and greater responsibility in mind for his faithful workers to do in the future. The slothful worker, however, receives a strong, heart-stopping rebuke. The investment portfolio that had been entrusted to him by the owner is taken away from him and given to another, and the slothful worker's future work is not greater responsibility and opportunity, but rather a hellish destiny in "outer darkness," where there is "weeping and gnashing of teeth."

In light of his future return to earth, Jesus calls his followers to lives of gospel readiness and faithfulness. Jesus makes the important connection that Christian faithfulness now, in this already-but-not-yet moment in redemptive history, will in the future be rewarded. I don't believe it is a small thing that Jesus's clarion call to faithfulness is set in the context of work. Let's remember that as God's image-bearers, we were created with work in mind.

SEAMLESSLY CONNECTING FAITH AND WORK

I believe Jesus's parable of the talents not only encourages us to gospel readiness but also encourages us to more seamlessly connect our Sunday faith with our Monday work. Diligent stewardship with all that has been entrusted to us is an authenticating mark of any true follower of Jesus and an essential component of a life well-lived. The writer of Ecclesiastes concludes his quest for life's purpose and meaning with the bottom-line reality of our unavoidable accountability to our Creator. The writer ends with this sobering reminder: "God will bring every deed into judgment, with every secret thing, whether good or evil" (Eccles. 12:14). Each one of us will one day give a full accounting to God for our life. This is a game-changing truth that ought to shape how we live and work. Since such a large proportion of our time is devoted to our work, much of our accounting before God will be answering for the stewardship of the work we have been called to do.

In the parable of the talents, Jesus paints for us an enticing and hopeful picture of a future that brings with it great reward for diligence and faithfulness. Our future reward involves a joyful intimacy with God. We will "enter into the joy of our Master," but we will also be given greater work to do in the future. In many ways we are training now for reigning later with Jesus. The work you do now matters more than you often realize. A biblical understanding of the future of work suggests to us that heaven is much more than merely a beautiful place to eternally chill out. The all-too-common notion of heaven being a place of unending leisure, of playing harps on fluffy clouds, needs some careful reconsideration and theological reassessment.

RETHINKING HEAVEN

As a kid growing up, I was intrigued and very curious about heaven. I was told that heaven was a place far away where loved ones who had died had gone, and that I, too, would join them one day. That sounded pretty cool to me. I remember lying on the cool green grass in my backyard watching the puffy cumulus clouds lazily float by. As I stared upward into the seemingly endless blue sky, I wondered exactly where heaven was and what people did there. Since I loved ice cream with a passion, I found myself imagining heaven as a place where you could eat ice cream all the time. The ice cream would be the best, and it would never run out. And guess what? You would never get full; you could just keep eating banana split after banana split and then start in on some other delicious ice cream treat. I guess you could say my idea of heaven at that time in my life was a never-ending, gluttonous eating frenzy—eating ice cream with reckless abandon and utter indulgence.

Thankfully, as I got older, my conception of heaven became less personally indulgent. Yet what I thought about this future place and what I understood about my present home on this sin-scarred earth seemed universes apart. The earth was merely my present home. I did not realize that it was to be my future home as well. I perceived Scripture to teach that heaven was in a far-off place and that this world we live in would one day be abolished, completely destroyed by fire. It was all going to burn. But was my understanding in line with what the Bible really taught?

71

IS IT ALL GOING TO BURN?

The apostle Peter devotes a considerable time to the future con-summation of redemptive history. Peering down the corridor of time, Peter describes a day of future judgment he along with the Old Testament prophets refer to as the "day of the Lord." Peter writes, "But the day of the Lord will come like a thief, and then the heavens will pass away with a roar, and the heavenly bodies will be burned up and dissolved, and the earth and the works that are done on it will be exposed" (2 Pet. 3:10). Many translations of this text emphasize the earth being "burned up." While this translation can be supported, this particular linguistic rendering tends to project the idea of a fiery judgment of complete annihila-tion and destruction rather than one of purification and healing.

As he peers into the future, Peter does not see a complete discontinuity with the past as we so often tend to think. He does not suggest an infinite chasm between the old creation and the new creation. Rather, Peter says that the unfolding future will have a significant degree of continuity with the present earth and the heavens. With hopefulness anchored firmly in the promise of God, Peter looks ahead to the future and writes, "But according to his promise we are waiting for new heavens and a new earth in which righteousness dwells" (2 Pet. 3:13).

Peter's point is that the present earth and heavens will be puri-fied from the ravaging effects of sin. Like fire and its purifying effect on precious metals such as gold or silver, so too will God's original creation be purified. The apostle Paul also saw the fire of future judgment through the lens of purification rather than annihilation. Writing to the church at Corinth, Paul applies the imagery of fiery judgment to individual human works done in the name of God. Paul writes, "Each one's work will become manifest, for the Day will disclose it, because it will be revealed by fire, and the fire will test what sort of work each one has done" (1 Cor. 3:13). The fiery future judgment of our world, as well as our individual works, seems to suggest there will be a considerable carryover from God's original creation to his new creation of the new heavens and

72

the new earth. God's original creation will not be wasted, it will be purified. N. T. Wright emphasizes this continuity between God's original creation and the new creation. "The transition from the present world to the new one would be a matter not of destruction of the present space-time universe but of its radical healing."[2]

RADICALLY HEALED WORK

When we begin to grasp the transforming truth that the future destiny of our work and our world is not complete annihilation but radical healing, it changes how we view our daily work. If we believe that the earth—everything about it and everything we do on it—is simply going to one day be abolished and disappear, then the logical conclusion is that our work is virtually meaningless. Why should we work hard, make a tasty meal, learn a new skill, run a business, write a piece of music, or design a building if everything will one day be consumed by fire? It would make sense to work only enough to survive and to simply get by. But if our daily work, done for the glory of God and the common good of others, in some way carries over to the new heavens and new earth, then our present work itself is overflowing with immeasurable value and eternal significance.

SAYING GOOD-BYE TO LIFEBOAT THEOLOGY

If we are going to fully embrace the work God has called us to do, then we will need to say goodbye to what Paul Marshall aptly describes as "lifeboat theology." Lifeboat theology views this world as if it were the *Titanic*. God's good world has hit the iceberg of sin and is irrevocably doomed. There is nothing much left for us to do. It is time to abandon ship and get as many people in as many lifeboats as we can. In this theological perspective, God's lifeboat plan of redemption is concerned only with the survival of his people. However noble and well-meaning our efforts to salvage God's creation may be, at the end of the day, our work here on this doomed earth really amounts only to rearranging deck chairs on the *Titanic*. While God is deeply concerned with the crown of his fallen creation and has initiated a glorious plan of redemption through his Son Jesus, God has not abandoned his once-good world.

Paul Marshall wisely calls us to abandon a lifeboat theology for what he refers to as an ark theology. The Genesis writer tells of humankind's deep dark plunge into sin. The corruption of God's good creation and the wickedness of sin were so unimaginably horrific that God seriously considered wiping out his creation. In Genesis chapter 6 we read, "So the LORD said, 'I will blot out man whom I have created from the face of the land, man and animals and creeping things and birds of the heavens, for I am sorry that I have made them" (Gen. 6:7). But rather than annihilating what he had made and starting completely over, God extends gracious favor to a man named Noah. God makes a covenant with Noah and commissions him to build an ark. Rather than blotting out all of creation, Noah and his family and a host of living creatures are rescued and preserved in the ark from the destruction of the flood. God remains committed to restore the earth and to continue on with his original creation. After Noah exits the ark, God makes a covenant with him, promising to never destroy the earth with a flood again.

The story of Noah and the ark reminds us that God has not given up on his good world even though it has been ravaged by sin and death. In a burst of rapturous praise, the psalmist in Psalm 24 declares that the whole earth, and everything in it, belongs to the Lord. God still loves his world. He hasn't given up on his once-good creation. A glorious future awaits the earth. Hymn writer Maltbie Babcock beautifully captures this truth:

> *This is my Father's world, O let me ne'er forget*
> *That though the wrong seems oft so strong, God is the ruler yet.*
> *This is my Father's world: the battle is not done;*
> *Jesus who died shall be satisfied, and earth and heaven be one.*[3]

The fallen world we now inhabit is still our Father's world. It is of high worth and immensely important to God. C. S. Lewis speaks of God's new creation as not unmaking but remaking. He writes, "The old field of space, time, matter, and the senses is to be weeded, dug, and sown for a new crop. We may be tired of that old field: God is not. . . . We live amid all the anomalies, inconveniences, hopes, and excitements of a house that is being rebuilt. Something is being pulled down and something going up in its place."[4] Does your daily work reflect that you and your work are a part of God's new-creation redemptive rebuilding project? Do you grasp this world's future destiny, and have you thought about your important place in it?

Much of our daily work is caring for our Father's world and those who call it home. We make things. We fix things. We care for things. We serve others. What you do here is not a waste. The skills and abilities you are developing now in your workplace will not be wasted; they will be utilized and further developed in the future work God has for you to do in the new heavens and new earth. Your time here in our Father's fallen world is a preparation for an eternity of activity and creativity in the new heavens and new earth. Your work matters not only now but also for the future.

THE NEW HEAVEN AND THE NEW EARTH

So often we think of our future destiny as way outside the realm of the earth. Heaven is often way out there and not anywhere near here. But is this how we should think of our heavenly home? Just prior to his death and resurrection, Jesus told his disciples that he was going away to prepare a place for them and that he would come again (see John 14:1–3). What future place did Jesus have in mind? As the Bible winds to a close, we are given a stunning glimpse of a future new heaven and a new earth. In Revelation 19, we encounter a great homecoming. There is a grand wedding of the Lamb and the bride with a lavish and joyful marriage banquet. In Revelation 21, the new home for Jesus and his bride, the church, is unveiled. The apostle John writes, "Then I saw a new heaven and a new earth, for the first heaven and the first earth had passed away, and the sea was no more. And I saw the holy city, new Jerusalem, coming down out of heaven from God, prepared as a bride adorned for her husband" (Rev. 21:1–2).

CONTINUITY AND DISCONTINUITY

John's vision of our future home reveals both a very real continuity with our present home as well as a good deal of discontinuity. John describes a new earthly city that "comes down" out of heaven. He gives us the name of the city, the New Jerusalem. Throughout Revelation 21, John's language brings with it a continuity that is very earthy. For example, the New Jerusalem is built with walls and gates utilizing "earthly" precious metals such as gold, jasper, and pearls. Yet while this future new home has a kind of earthiness, it is also very different than our present home. There is delightful and mysterious discontinuity. This new earthy home will be a place where there will be no more tears, death, crying, or pain. As God was with Adam and Eve in the garden before their rebellion against him, now God will be with his redeemed people in New Jerusalem. John describes the dazzling beauty of this new earth city whose light is not the sun but God himself. John writes, "And night will be no more. They will need no light of lamp or sun, for the Lord God will be their light, and they will reign forever and ever" (Rev. 22:5).

Rather than thinking of heaven as something way out there, a completely foreign and different reality, the biblical writers present our heavenly home as something "closer" to our earthly home. Paul Marshall points out the transforming significance of what the Bible teaches regarding our future destiny: "It is also an unbiblical idea that the earth doesn't matter because we are going to go to heaven when we die. The Bible teaches that there will be a 'new heaven and a new earth.' Our destiny is an earthly one: a new earth, an earth redeemed and transfigured. An earth reunited with heaven, but an earth, nevertheless."[5]

OUR WORK IS NOT A WASTE

If we are going to do God-honoring work, if we are going to be a faithful presence in our workplaces, then we must grasp in a compelling way that our present work fits into the future that awaits us. So often I hear from well-meaning people in the marketplace that their daily work seems so boring or to be such a waste of time. I am not minimizing the seemingly inefficient and mundane aspects that can be part of our work. Every job has a host of tasks that don't really excite us or unleash our creative energies. But if we will look at our work through the lens of Holy Scripture, our work, no matter what we have been called to do, is imbued with great meaning and significance.

A robust theology of work both now and in the future brings fresh perspective to our lives. Our vocational callings become rich with meaning. Our attitude toward work is transformed. A new creativity and diligence emerges. A sense of anticipation of a glorious future in the new heavens and new earth fills our souls. Tim Keller breathes some very hopeful wind into our sails when he writes, "At the end of history the whole earth has become the Garden of God again. Death and decay and suffering are gone. . . . Jesus will make the world our perfect home again. We will no longer be living 'east of Eden,' always wandering and never arriving. We will come, and the father will meet us and embrace us, and we will be brought into the feast."[6]

MEET ME AT HOME

Her name was Delight, and the day she died the planet seemed to shift for me. On that blustery March day, the tornado of death blew through our family and altered the landscape of our lives. Seeing my mom breathe her last breath, a host of thoughts bombarded my mind and a myriad of feelings suffocated my soul. Though she had lived a long and full life, her death and its profound implications were still hard for me to grapple with.

"Meet me at home," were the last written words Mom had left behind. Words scribbled on a crumpled piece of paper reflecting her hope of a glorious future reunion in our heavenly home.

My mom's Christian faith was the central and most important reality in her life. As a single mother much of her life, she had worked very long and hard hours both as a teacher and a homemaker. My mom was bright, curious, and gifted in so many ways. Always the idealistic romantic, she was a poet, an artist with words. She excelled in the art of hospitality. Her kitchen was always open and her well-worn hands always eager and ready to serve what she described as a "home-burnt" meal. Mom knew no strangers; she only met new friends. Not only was her death an immeasurable loss to many, but also in those dark hours of personal grief it all seemed to me like such a colossal waste. All of her gifts, experiences, and talents seemed to be indifferently swallowed up in death.

At my mother's memorial service, many words were spoken, a fitting tribute for such a life well lived. Yet it was not what was said that parted the veil of grief for me as much as what was observed. At the front of the church sanctuary was not a coffin, but a kitchen table—her kitchen table. Surrounding the kitchen table were the tools of food preparation and hospitality she was so skilled at using. Mom's kitchen things were a tribute to the past, but they were much more. They were a reminder of a glorious future of her resurrected body and her work in the new heaven and new earth—a future where I know my mother will hear the words that each one of us who have also embraced Christ will hear, "Well done, good and faithful servant. You have been faithful over a little; I will set you over much. Enter into the joy of your Master." God will have much work for us to do.

In his great hymn "Amazing Grace," John Newton looked to the future and penned these words,

> When we've been there ten thousand years,
> Bright shining as the sun,
> We've no less days to sing God's praise
> Than when we'd first begun.[7]

78

In the new heaven and new earth we will sing God's praises with our lips in our resurrected bodies. And as glorious as that will be, we will have the privilege to also sing God's praises with our work. For we have been created with work in mind. Your work is anything but a waste. Your work matters now and it matters for the future.

When Earth's Last Picture Is Painted

When Earth's last picture is painted,
And the tubes are twisted and dried,
When the oldest colors have faded,
And the youngest critic has died,
We shall rest, and faith, we shall need it,
Lie down for an aeon or two,
'Till the Master of All Good Workmen
Shall put us to work anew. . . .
And no one shall work for the money,
And no one shall work for fame.
But each for the joy of the working,
And each, in his separate star,
Shall draw the Thing as he sees It
For the God of Things as They are![8]

Questions for Reflection and Discussion:

- Do you see your daily work with an eternal vantage point in mind?

- What might it mean for us that the resurrected Jesus not only cooked breakfast for his disciples but also ate some fish with them (John 21:9–14)?

- How does a glimpse of the future, of living and working in the new heaven and new earth, motivate you to develop greater skills and competencies in and through your work?

- How does gaining a greater understanding of the future reframe your perspective of your fellow workers and the work they do?

PEGGY > STUDENT

My vocation has changed many times. My secondary calling has been different at different stages and seasons. Looking back over my life, I realize that identifying your vocational calling is not a once-for-all, what-will-I-be-when-I grow-up, lifetime decision. Preparing for the next season, deciding what you will be in the next phase of growing up, may become ever more necessary as people are living longer and the world is changing faster. Fluctuations in the economy, increasing globalization, and new technologies making some jobs obsolete require flexibility. Planning for the empty nest and retirement are necessary for most of us. Radical change produced by unexpected success or tragedy requires a new look at vocation. And what, after all, requires more faith than change? Perhaps only the dailyness of ordinary life.

As life circumstances required, I have worked for companies and stayed home with my kids. I have been in catering, designed restaurants, run political campaigns, managed my own show horse business, become a master gardener, and have been a student. Sometimes I have been paid; often I have not. But work, after all, is not defined by getting paid. Much of the work we do in life is outside our paying jobs. Lawn mowing, child care, home schooling, meal preparation, laundry, bill paying, errands, driving kids to baseball practice, shopping, washing the car, cleaning the gutters—work that makes life bearable and beautiful—are things we usually aren't paid to do.

Let's face it—most of life is work of some sort, and the routines of daily life require faith. Sometimes I have said that cooking a meal day after day requires every bit of faith I have. Even sleep can be seen as appropriate work and requires faith—faith to let go of the day and let go of tomorrow. Even vacations involve the work of planning and traveling and packing and the work of having fun. What is the value of the mundane things we do? How do they give our lives significance? It's the company we keep. It's walking through life with Jesus by faith that makes everything we do have eternal value.

Right now I am a seminary student. People ask me what I'm going to do with my degree. The real answer is that I am preparing for eternity. I may never become Dr. Mom in this life, but this work will not be in vain. I will take my learning, as well as the character that has been developed in all the work I have done in this life, into the future—into the new heavens and new earth—into the next phase of life.

5

EXTRAORDINARY ORDINARY WORK

*If it falls to your lot to be a street sweeper, sweep
the streets like Michelangelo painted pictures, like
Shakespeare wrote poetry, like Beethoven composed
music; sweep streets so well that all the host of Heaven
and earth will have to pause and say, "Here lived a
great street sweeper, who swept his job well."*[1]
MARTIN LUTHER KING JR.

I met John at a favorite coffee shop. After ordering our lattes, we sat down and he shared with me his story. John grew up in a Christian home and had gone to a Christian college, yet he had always struggled with how mundane and meaningless his work seemed. Hunkering down in his cubicle, John's day consisted mostly in writing and answering e-mails and processing loans for commercial and residential property. Throughout his life, the Sunday messages he had heard in his faith community were that really committed Christians went into "full-time Christian work," as a pastor, parachurch worker, or a cross-cultural missionary of some kind. Having not pursued these vocational paths, he had always felt a tinge of guilt. What really seemed to matter most at his church were the Bible and people's souls, for they lasted for all eternity, and the rest of this world was going to eventually burn up in a future day of judgment.

John could still recall one particular message by a very impassioned parachurch worker appealing for young leaders to join his organization rather than pursuing a business career, which would in essence be like wasting their time rearranging furniture on the deck of the *Titanic*. John remembered how this message had left him feeling rather confused and empty inside. The thought that he had missed God's will for his life lingered in his discouraged soul. John also shared that recently he had gone to a Christian seminar on moving from success to significance. At the seminar he had heard joyful testimonies of successful businesspeople who had made a midlife career change. Now they were using their business gifts in Christian organizations and were fully investing their talents for the kingdom. He left the seminar feeling his current work of processing loans simply didn't add up to a very significant life. I could not help but empathize with the gnawing ache in John's soul.

WHY THE FOG?

It was easy to see that a thick blanket of fog covered John's thinking about faith and work. With these kinds of faith messages about work dancing around in John's mind as he processed residential and commercial loans every day in his corporate cubicle, is it any wonder that he felt such a disconnect between his Sunday church experience and his Monday work experience as well as such a discontentment with his everyday work? Viewing what most of us do every day in our workplaces as rearranging furniture on the deck of the *Titanic* doesn't bring with it a great sense of significance. And this thinking is too often perpetuated by sincere Christian leaders delivering impassioned sermons about the ultimate futility of our work. David Miller speaks with compelling clarity when he writes, "Whether conscious or unintended, the pulpit all too frequently sends the signal that work in the church matters but work in the world does not. It is perhaps no surprise, then, that workers, businesspeople, and other professionals often feel unsupported by the Sunday church in their Monday marketplace vocations."[2]

For pastors to preach, and for us to conclude, that using our gifts within the context of a Christian organization is the only way we can truly invest our talents in the kingdom widely misses the mark of what the Bible truly teaches in its robust theology of vocation. Tragically, I find John's story an all-too-common one among sincere people of faith. Embedded in many of the messages playing in our minds as we work are some very distorted and unbiblical ideas about our work that we need to think our way through. It is a jungle out there, and we need a razor-sharp theological machete to clear away a whole lot of dense, overgrown vocational brush. Thinking that somehow certain kinds of work are more "full-time Christian" than other kinds; or that only some kinds of work have eternal value, while others do not; or that somewhere in life as we get older, we change our work so we can move from success to significance, are unbiblical distortions we must confront in our own lives and in our faith communities.

Why has that which God designed to be so majestic often become so mundane, so meaningless? Why all the foggy thinking about our work? Whatever our work is, no matter how ordinary it seems, it can be extraordinary work brimming with God-honoring importance and significance if it is done well and for the glory of God. If we are discovering the rich and robust doctrine of vocation for the first time, we might be tempted to see it as merely a passing Christian fad. In our more cynical moments, we might wonder whether all this talk about work is merely the latest hype in an often shallow, populist Christian faith. Most of us would agree that we probably don't need another mass-marketed WWJD bracelet to put around our wrists. Though this kind of thinking about work may be newer to you, let me assure you that the language and doctrine of Christian vocation is not faddish but foundational to an integral Christian faith. A right understanding of vocation has been a transforming truth in the day-to-day ordinary lives of faithful followers of Jesus for many centuries. Vocation is a robust theology of ordinary, everyday life.

VOCATION IN CHURCH HISTORY

The sixteenth-century Protestant Reformers recognized the compelling need to get back to a truly biblically centered faith. Over the centuries, the gospel of faith alone in Jesus Christ alone had became shrouded in church hierarchies, sacramental systems, and monastic movements. Martin Luther, whose soul had suffocated in this stifling religious context, was used by God to point the church back to its biblical authority and to once again emphasize the priesthood of all believers in Christ. This doctrine, which held that every believer had equal access to God through Jesus Christ, profoundly altered the landscape of spiritual formation for followers of Christ who had languished under the distorted view that the calling to the priesthood, to a monastic community, or to service of the church was a higher, a more sacred, a more spiritual calling than to be a farmer or a merchant. The Protestant Reformers wisely reconnected Sunday faith to Monday work.

One of the things I really enjoy doing is reading books on history. Stephen Ambrose is well known for his writings on the Lewis and Clark expedition, yet one of his books that I have found most fascinating is on the building of the Transcontinental Railroad. In his book *Nothing Like It in the World*, Stephen Ambrose unveils before the reader's eyes the tremendous courage and challenges that occupied our nation between the years 1863–1869.[3] When we think of this time period in our nation's history, we often think about President Lincoln's courageous leadership in freeing our nation from the hideous scourge of slavery. Lincoln's legacy is clearly stellar here, but through Ambrose's book, I realized for the first time that another lasting legacy of President Abraham Lincoln's, one that is often missed, was his force of courageous leadership in building the Transcontinental Railroad. This massive building project connected our continent and paved the way for an economically developing and politically unified nation.

In a similar way, the courageous Protestant Reformers of the sixteenth century, in their restoration of the biblical doctrine of vocation, laid down the theological tracks that reconnected Christian faith with the ordinary life of work. And one of the biblical banners that they heralded was the apostle Paul's inspired words to the local church at Corinth: "So, brothers, in whatever condition each was called, there let him remain with God" (1 Cor. 7:24). The Protestant Reformers rightly pointed out that the apostle Paul promoted the ordinary callings and stations of life, of marriage and singleness, and of work and vocation.

The Protestant Reformers understood that our calling to follow Christ was to be fully lived out through the conduits of our vocations and stations of life arranged for us under the providence of God. For those who became apprentices of Jesus, the *missio Dei* (the mission of God in the world) was to bloom vocationally where they were providentially planted. It was in our ordinary day-to-day lives of work, rest, and play that we were to flourish, to be salt and light, to be spiritually formed, and to be God's redemptive agents in the world. Along with the apostle Paul, the Protestant Reformers taught that Christian vocation calls each of us to indwell an extraordinary ordinary life. For this is what Jesus himself modeled.

MORE, BUT NOT LESS, THAN A CARPENTER

I don't know why I didn't see it for so long, but one day as I was reading through the Gospel of Mark, I stumbled across a verse that stopped me dead in my tracks. In Mark 6 we are told that Jesus, who was spending his time as an itinerant rabbi, came back to his hometown of Nazareth. The hometown crowd listened to Jesus teach in the synagogue, and they were stunned by their hometown boy who was displaying such extraordinary wisdom and power. In their eyes Jesus, was first and foremost a carpenter from Nazareth. Mark records the hometown crowd exclaiming with a tone of incredulity, " 'Is not this the carpenter, the son of Mary and brother of James and Joses and Judas and Simon? And are not his sisters here with us?' And they took offense at him" (Mark 6:3).

As I slowly pondered these words, I began to reflect on the significance of Jesus spending so much of his time on earth working with his hands in a carpentry shop. Here was the Son of God sent to earth on a redemptive mission of seeking and saving the lost, of proclaiming the gospel, yet he spent the vast majority of his years on earth making things in an obscure carpentry shop. We know from Luke's Gospel that even at the age of twelve, Jesus was demonstrating his amazing rabbinical brilliance to the brightest and best in Jerusalem (Luke 2:47). How did Jesus's brilliance fit in with a carpentry career? At first glance this doesn't seem to be a very strategic use of the Son of God's extraordinary gifts or his important messianic mission. Why was it the Father's will for Jesus to spend so much time in the carpentry shop instead of gracing the Palestinian countryside, proclaiming the gospel and healing the multitudes?

The New Testament records Jesus spending only about three years in itinerant ministry, what we might refer to as full-time vocational ministry. But for the many years before that, Jesus worked as a carpenter. Speaking of Jesus as a carpenter, Dallas Willard brings a refreshing perspective.

> If he were to come today as he did then, he could carry out his mission through most any decent and useful occupation. He could be a clerk or accountant in a hardware store, a computer repairman, a banker, an editor, doctor, waiter, teacher, farmhand, lab technician, or construction worker. He could run a housecleaning service or repair automobiles. In other words, if he were to come today he could very well do what you do. He could very well live in your apartment or house, hold down your

job, have your education and life prospects, and live within your family surroundings and time. None of this would be the least hindrance to the eternal kind of life that was his by nature and becomes available to us through him.[4]

Several years ago I remember reading a fine book that was winsomely titled *More Than a Carpenter*. In this book, the author points out a great deal of convincing evidence that supports the deity of Jesus. This is essential to understanding the person and work of Jesus. Yet in no way should we conclude that because Jesus was more than a carpenter, his vocational calling to work as a carpenter was somehow less than important. Clearly the Son of God was much more, but not less, than a carpenter. This incarnational pattern of Jesus's earthly life speaks volumes about the importance of our day-to-day vocational work.

INCARNATION AND WORK

When we contemplate who Jesus really is, his joyful content-ment to work with his hands day after day constructing things, making useful farm implements and household furniture in an obscure Nazareth carpentry shop, we find him truly stunning. Jesus's work life tells us that he did not think being a carpenter was somehow below him or a poor use of his many gifts. Here is the very One whose hands not only created the world but also the very wood he was crafting in a carpentry shop. The apostle Paul gives us a glorious description of this carpenter from Naza-reth: "He is the image of the invisible God, the firstborn of all creation. For by him all things were created, in heaven and on earth, visible and invisible, whether thrones or dominions or rulers or authorities—all things were created through him and for him. And he is before all things, and in him all things hold together" (Col. 1:15–17).

Think about it for a moment. The very One who was the mas-ter craftsman of the universe spent a great deal of time during his thirty-three years on earth crafting things with his hands. The One who had masterfully fashioned humans from the dust of the earth was making chairs for people to sit on in their houses. No doubt Jesus had strong, well-worn, callused hands. It is all too easy for us to overlook the fact that Jesus knew what it meant to get up and go to work every day. Jesus experienced both the exhilaration and exhaustion of putting in a hard day's work. Jesus faced work and a workplace profoundly affected by sin. I am sure Jesus dealt with difficult and demanding people in the workplace who complained about this and that. I am also confident that the sinless Son of Man not only modeled humility in the workplace, but also maintained a teachable spirit as he served under the tutelage of Joseph, his human guardian father. I doubt if Joseph was the perfect boss. I have yet to meet a perfect boss, and when I look into my mirror each morning, I see anything but a perfect boss.

We are rightly in awe of Jesus, who shockingly ignores cultural convention by picking up a ,basin and towel and washing his disciples' dirty, stinky feet. Yet we tend to forget that Jesus had been modeling a basin-and-towel kind of servanthood in a carpentry shop for years. Jesus's humble service in the workplace was the training ground for that glorious display of servanthood in an upper room in Jerusalem.

Working with his hands day in and day out in a carpentry shop was not below Jesus. Jesus did not see his carpentry work as mundane or meaningless, for it was the work his Father had called him to do. I have a good hunch that Jesus was a top-notch carpenter and did top-notch work. Even before Jesus entered his itinerant rabbinical ministry, Matthew reminds his readers of the Father's good pleasure in his Son. Following Jesus's baptism, the Spirit of God descended as a dove, and a voice out of heaven declared, "This is my beloved Son, with whom I am well pleased" (Matt. 3:17). I am sure there were many things that made the Father well pleased, but one important aspect of Jesus's well-pleasing life that we must not overlook was his well-pleasing work as a carpenter.

JESUS'S GREAT INVITATION

Jesus invites us to become his apprentice and learn from him a whole new way of living. Jesus said, "Come to me, all who labor and are heavy laden, and I will give you rest. Take my yoke upon you, and learn from me, for I am gentle and lowly in heart, and you will find rest for your souls. For my yoke is easy, and my burden is light" (Matt. 11:28–30). In this great invitation to be yoked with Master Jesus, we are invited to experience life as God originally intended way back in the garden of Eden, before sin and corruption entered the world. The path to "rest," this life as God originally designed for us to live, is made possible because of the gospel and is found in Jesus's yoke. In Jesus's yoke we learn to live our new-creation life of submission and obedience.

The word *rest* is not necessarily kicking back in our recliner or chilling out in some way, but rather a joyous ease in our work as we wear the yoke that has been tailor-made just for us. When we enter the yoke of Christ, we press into God's design for our lives and we learn from Jesus how he would live our lives if he were us. A vital part of our learning from Jesus, of being yoked with him, is learning the path of vocational faithfulness. Brilliantly, Jesus teaches us not only how to live but also how to work. Writing to the local church at Colossae, the apostle Paul places vocational faithfulness at the heart of apprenticeship with Jesus and a 24/7 life of God-honoring worship. "Whatever you do, work heartily, as for the Lord and not for men, knowing that from the Lord you will receive the inheritance as your reward. You are serving the Lord Christ" (Col. 3:23–24). We are to be learning from Jesus how to do our work, and living and working each day as unto the Lord.

Our ordinary day-to-day work life is designed by God to be extraordinary. As we go to work day in and day out, it seems as though our lives are filled with many ordinary days. It is what we do on these ordinary days that makes our work and our lives extraordinary. As pointed out earlier, the Hebrew word *avodah* recorded in the Old Testament presents to us a seamless understanding of work and worship, thereby eliminating any compartmentalization of a worshipful life whether it is Sunday or Monday. Not only do we worship God in and through our work, but one of the primary ways we love our neighbor is in and through our vocation. In his Great Commandment, Jesus calls us to love the Lord our God with all our heart, soul, mind, and strength, and our neighbor as our self (Luke 10:27). A proper understanding of Christian vocation puts flesh and feet on this commandment.

INCARNATING THE GREAT COMMANDMENT

Recently I was the recipient of neighborly love expressed through vocation. On a flight from Kansas City to Los Angeles, many individuals knowingly or unknowingly honored the Great Commandment through their work. When I arrived at the Kansas City airport, the baggage handlers assisted me with my luggage. At the gate, security personnel served me. Then a gate agent facilitated my getting on the plane. On the plane, the pilots charted the course and readied us for flight. A maintenance team filled the plane with jet fuel and even fixed an ailing plane toilet. Once we were airborne, a flight attendant brought me a cup of coffee. It was in and through many individuals' diligent work that I was able to get to my destination and be ready for my meetings.

One of the primary ways we tangibly love our neighbors is to do excellent, God-honoring work in our various vocations. When we look at our work through a proper biblical lens, we can see vocation's close connection with loving our neighbor. Your vocational work is your specific and invaluable contribution to God's ongoing creation and an essential aspect of God's Great Commandment to love your neighbor as yourself. Martin Luther reminds us that it is not God who needs our good works, but it is our neighbor who needs our good works. A transforming truth we must firmly grab onto is that God is very much at work in our work. God is transforming us in our work and transforming the world through our work.

SHIFTING WORKPLACE PARADIGMS

When we begin to grasp the rich biblical truths of vocation, we see our work and the workplace where it occurs through a different lens. A friend of mine who has spent a great deal of time looking at his work as a CEO through a vocational lens, often reminds me of how this paradigm shift radically changed his approach to work. Previously he had understood that his primary goal as a CEO who happened to be a Christian was to make a lot of money and then give that money to charitable causes that were making a difference in the world. As a very generous person, he gave sizable amounts to Christian missionaries and other philanthropic causes. As he put it, "I wanted to support Jesus's Great Commission as much as I could." Though my friend continues to give generously to his church and other causes, the game-changer for him was when he began seeing his work as having intrinsic value and not merely instrumental value. He recognized his work as valuable in itself—God-honoring and good. Work was not just valuable because of its economic benefits or as a platform for Christian ministry. Of course, work's economic benefits and the opportunity it provides for Christian ministry can be good things, but they are not work's main goal. Work's main goal is worship through a lifestyle of God-honoring vocational faithfulness.

CULTIVATING A NEW ATTITUDE IN OUR WORK

Every day when you arrive at your workplace, an attitude arrives with you. Our attitudes are like the perfume or cologne we are wearing; we smell the fragrance when we first put it on, but others smell it throughout the day. The fragrance you are wearing at work, others are picking up. So what are those around you smelling? The apostle Paul reminds us that as apprentices of Jesus, we have the fragrance of Christ. The attitudes we wear to our workplaces should remind others of Jesus. The fruit of the

Spirit—love, joy, peace, patience, kindness, goodness, faithful-ness, gentleness, and self-control—should make up a great deal of our attitudinal fragrance. Yet for me, Paul's inspired words to the followers of Jesus at Thessalonica are most helpful in cultivating a new attitude about my work and my workplace. After urging the Thessalonian believers to seek the common good of all, Paul lays out three attitudinal adjustments that powerfully transform the workplaces we have been called to inhabit. Paul says, "Rejoice always, pray without ceasing, give thanks in all circumstances; for this is the will of God in Christ Jesus for you" (1 Thess. 5:16–18).

In these power-packed verses Paul encourages us to cultivate attitudes of joy, of prayer, and of gratitude. Though our work and workplaces can be very frustrating at times and we often deal with some very difficult and demanding people, we are empowered by the Holy Spirit to positively influence a workplace culture that better promotes human flourishing, synergistic teamwork, and the common good. If we will take the time to commit Paul's inspired words to memory we can take them to work with us. Perhaps it would be helpful to write out Paul's words and put them somewhere in your workspace as a reminder. In my workplace, I often review Paul's words and make the necessary attitudinal adjustments throughout the workday.

It is also helpful for me to regularly remember who my ultimate audience is at work. Living and working before an Audience of One is amazingly transforming in both the good times and the bad. In my own workplace, I am particularly encouraged by the truths of Proverbs 16:3, "Commit your work to the LORD, and your plans will be established." When we live before an Audience of One, we have nothing to fear, nothing to hide, and nothing to prove. We can devote our complete energy to doing good work. Having an Audience of One means we can practice the presence of God as we work and enjoy an ongoing conversation with him. As an overflow of our walk with Christ, we have the wonderful opportunity to bring a positive, joyful outlook to our daily work. No matter what our circumstances, our steadfast hope remains firmly tethered to the good news of the gospel. Because of our Christian faith and our understanding of Christian vocation, we can give a warm smile to all of our coworkers, even those who at times rub us the wrong way. We can look for the good in others and praise them. We can truly celebrate when others are recognized for their achievement. We can express our appreciation through kind words and handwritten notes. Our attitudes can be the sweet aroma of Christ to those around us.

PURSUING EXCELLENCE IN OUR WORK

As I have interacted with business leaders over the years, I have heard negative words about the shabbiness and shadiness of Christians in the workplace more times than I can count. Whether the stories I hear are exaggerated for effect, I do not know, but I do believe that many times the reputation of Christians and their work is a sobering indictment on our inadequate understanding, as well as our day-to-day application, of the transforming truths of vocation. Sadly, a great deal of the shabbiness and shadiness of many Christians' work is directly related to an inadequate and often distorted theology of vocation.

I once heard the story of the legendary Alexander the Great who, in a rather serendipitous way, encountered one of his soldiers who was, to put it charitably, a pitiful sight. The soldier was dressed sloppily, seemed disheveled, and clearly reeked of a long night of drinking and debauchery. When asked by his great military commander what his name was, the soldier replied, "Alexander, sir." Alexander the Great glared back at the solider and said, "Soldier, either change your name or change your behavior."

I fear that many of us who call ourselves Christians do not live up to that name in our work. Perhaps we need a fresh reminder that those who call themselves Christians are to behave differently. The apostle Paul makes an important connection between the name of Jesus and our day-to-day behavior. Writing to followers of Jesus at Colossae, Paul says, "Whatever you do, in word or deed, do everything in the name of the Lord Jesus, giving thanks to God the Father though him" (Col. 3:17). When we embrace Jesus as our Lord and Savior, by his grace we work and behave differently in the workplace. Like our Master, Jesus, who modeled excellent carpentry work, in his grace we, too, labor with diligence and strive for excellence in whatever work God has called us to do.

THE WITNESS OF OUR WORK

Though we are called to verbally profess our faith to others, to give an account for the hope within us, we are also called to practice our faith before others. Yes, we witness by our words, but we also witness by our work. The excellence of our work often gives us the credibility to speak of the excellence of our Lord Jesus and to share the good news of the gospel with our coworkers. When you stop to think about it, the sheer amount of time you work each week means you witness much more by your work than you do by your words. Come to think of it, God designed it that way.

Steve Sample has been described as the greatest university president of his generation. For nineteen years, by his capable leadership, Sample led the University of Southern California to new heights of growth and to a worldwide educational influence never imagined. At his last commencement address, he spoke to forty thousand members and friends of the Trojan family who had gathered to celebrate the academic achievement of some of America's most gifted leaders of tomorrow.

Looking out over the crowd, Steve Sample urged the graduates to think about life's biggest issues and not just their future careers. His commencement address raised three questions which would in large measure set the trajectory of the graduates' lives. First, how did they feel about money? Second, how did they feel about children? Third, how did they feel about God? As Steve Sample raised his third question, there was pin-drop silence. Respectfully but courageously, USC's outstanding president challenged all who had gathered to carefully consider spiritual reality and the profound implications it had for their lives and our world.

As I listened to Sample's courageous words, I was struck by the reality that the integrity of his life and the excellence of his work for nineteen years had given him a credible platform and the gravitas to speak boldly of the God he loved and served. His integral life and excellent work made his courageous words persuasive and compelling. Our God-honoring work is often one of the greatest apologetics for our God-focused words.

YOUR WORK MATTERS

A couple of months slipped by, and I caught up with John for another cup of coffee. Since our first conversation, John had done some study on his own, probing the rich truths about vocation found in Scripture. I asked John what he was learning. He said, "Tom, I still struggle at times, wondering if my work is making much of a difference in the world, but now when I go to work, I don't go with a sense of emptiness lingering in my soul. I go with a sense of expectation that I am honoring God in my work. And my understanding of what it means to take Jesus with me to work has totally changed." As I pressed John a bit further on the changes occurring in his work world, he commented, "Being Jesus's apprentice at work has positively changed my attitude, and I am doing more excellent work."

Your work matters a great deal to God, to others, and to our world. There is no ordinary work. The work God has called you to do is extraordinary. Don't miss out on God's best by taking an ordinary approach to it. Dorothy Sayers was right, "The only Christian work is good work well done."

A Prayer of Faithful Presence

Lord Jesus, in your incarnation you were faithfully present in a Nazareth carpentry shop. You honored the Father not only by your redemptive work on the cross but also by making excellent tables. As your apprentice, may I, too, be faithfully present in my workplace. Help me to grasp that there is no ordinary work, only extraordinary work done in your name and for your glory. May the quality of my work honor you, and may my work witness to the glory of the gospel and your unimaginable excellence. Amen.

Questions for Reflection and Discussion:

- What kind of fragrance is wafting through your workplace these days?

- How would your coworkers describe you as a worker?

- What does the doctrine of the priesthood of all believers have to say about how you do your work?

- How does Jesus's work as a carpenter change the way you view your work?

DEBBIE > STAY-AT-HOME MOM

After attending a lecture at an inner-city Christian shelter on "Economic Crisis and the Heart of God," I fell into a conversation with a gentleman sitting near me. I shared that I am a stay-at-home mom, to which the gentleman responded that I was not contributing to the economy and implied that I was a drain on our collective economic resources. He cited several biblical passages to affirm his conclusion, and I realized Christians clearly have differing opinions on work!

Prior to having children, I earned an MBA and worked for an international management consulting firm. I worked with Fortune 500 companies and felt as though I was making a positive contribution to the world. I was a manager in my company when my husband and I bought a house in anticipation of starting our family. We were elated when we learned that we were going to be parents, but our joy quickly turned to concern when we were told that I had tested positive for Down Syndrome. We had planned for me to work part time after the baby arrived, but this news required us to rethink our approach. We made significant changes in our lives, moving to a new city where we had more family support, and I planned a career change—full-time at-home mom. A few months later we were miraculously blessed with a healthy baby girl who did not have Down Syndrome, and I was again forced to rethink my work.

I wrestled mightily with the assumptions that I would not feel intellectually challenged or fulfilled if I did not return to work at least part time. I cringed at the thought of checking the "homemaker" box on various forms I would have to fill out over time. And I knew as an extrovert that being home alone with a baby all day would not be easy for me. When it was all said and done, I decided to stay home. Emotionally, I couldn't bear to leave my baby with anyone else. Intellectually, I concluded that I had a husband and a child who needed me more than any company possibly could. I decided I could find other ways to meet my cerebral needs. In the absence of God's clear call or economic need to work, being home was the right decision for me.

I have two wonderful daughters now, and I have been a stay-at-home mom (not a homemaker!) for twelve years. I am amazed at the ways that God has allowed me to use some of the gifts and talents he has loaned me. Opportunities for leadership and teaching have been extensive for me. I have had the privilege to serve in many capacities at our church, in our girls' schools, in our neighborhood, and in our wider community. I have felt tremendously blessed to be home with my daughters, and if I had to do it over again, I would make the same choice without a moment's hesitation.

6

THE TRANSFORMING POWER
OF WORK

In short, fidelity to the highest practices of vocation
before God is consecrated and itself transformational
in its effects.[1]
JAMES HUNTER

T hough not the typical career path one might expect after receiving a PhD in philosophy from a prestigious university, Matthew Crawford found himself owner and operator of Shockoe Moto, an independent motorcycle repair shop in Richmond, Virginia. Working with his hands as a motorcycle mechanic, Matthew Crawford has become a strong advocate of manual work, the coherent manner of life it fosters, and its relationship to human flourishing.

In his book *Shop Class as Soulcraft*, Matthew Crawford speaks to the transformational effect our work and the workplaces we inhabit have in shaping us. Crawford writes, "To begin with, we are accustomed to think of the business world as ruled by an amoral bottom-line mentality, but in fact it is impossible to make sense of the office without noticing that it has become a place of moral education, where souls are formed and a particular ideal of what it means to be a good person is urged upon us."[2] When we think about work, our tendency is to reflect on how we, as free moral agents, shape our work, yet we must not overlook how the work we do profoundly forms us as individuals within a community. The work we do affects the contours of our thinking, develops our competencies, and contributes to our manner of feeling and well-being in the world. We shape our work and our work shapes us.

OUR WORK SHAPES US

Growing up in a rural farming community, it didn't take me long to grasp the powerful effect work had on the individuals I encountered. I remember as a young boy shaking hands with a neighboring farmer. I politely and respectfully placed my small, smooth hand into his massive hand. With his gentle squeeze, I felt a rush of extraordinary strength. Without saying a word, his rough skin and strong calluses spoke volumes to me about the work he did and the person he had become. Framing his warm and friendly smile was a tanned, windburned face that reflected many hours toiling beneath the summer sun, diligently caring for farm animals and tilling the rocky earth. As a young boy, I was enraptured listening to a close-knit group of farmers chatting at the local co-op store. The conversation I heard echoed a particular down-to-earth vocabulary tied to the unpredictable weather patterns where a timely rain meant the difference between crop success and crop failure. Farmers are people of the land indwelling a way of life that ebbs and flows with the seeming whims of nature and the ever-changing seasons. They are adventurous risk takers. When a seed is planted, there are heartfelt hopes but no certainty of a future harvest. The work farmers do shapes their life competencies, their hearts, minds, and souls, as well as their broader perspectives about life itself and their particular place in the world. This is also true for each one of us regardless of the work we are called to do.

A professional dancer's body and mind will be formed in a way that is distinct from a surgeon or a schoolteacher. The dancer's workplace and the people she works with every day will speak into her life in transforming and enduring ways. Perhaps she will meet her spouse in the context of her work. Many of her closest human friendships will be birthed and sustained in her workplace. She will increasingly see and experience the world through a dancer's eyes. A teacher's work is spent exploring the world of ideas. His competencies are directed toward informing and shaping others' minds. As he influences his students, he, too, is influenced by the very ideas he conveys—often in a multitude of ways he himself cannot verbally articulate. On an assembly line a worker will develop a specialized vocabulary, particular relationships, and mental and physical skills that are vastly differ-ent than a company CEO who spends the majority of her time in a corner office or on an airplane going from city to city conduct-ing strategic meetings in preparation for an impending merger.

An advertisement for an automobile company has described work's transforming power with these well-chosen words, "*The things we make, make us.*" In a multitude of ways, our work defines who we are, what we are becoming, and how we are contributing to the world. Miroslav Volf notes, "Human work is ultimately significant not only because it contributes to the future environ-ment of human beings, but also because it leaves an indelible imprint on their personalities."[3] To a large extent, what we do forms who we are.

When we meet someone for the very first time, the initial question we ask is, "What is your name?" Inquiring as to some-one's name is not only an act of love and proper respect, but it also affirms the person's individuality and intrinsic worth. After

103

we have learned a person's name, the second question usually out of our mouth is, "What do you do?" When we ask this question, we are affirming that work is essential, an integral part of being human. We also are seeking to get some idea of what an individual's life is all about. We gain a greater familiarity and understanding about the unique contours of the person we are meeting by immediately learning something about that person's work. Intuitively we know that the work someone chooses not only reflects a certain human disposition, but it also tells us much about the person and the life experiences encountered by that person.

Our work is a gift. Like the good gifts of education, marriage, friendship, leisure, and family, our work influences in great measure the persons we are and the persons we are becoming. Daily we are being formed by the work we do, the people we rub shoulders with, and the skills we acquire. Work is one of the providential arrangements through which we are spiritually formed. The Protestant Reformer Martin Luther affirmed the central importance of vocation in spiritual formation when he asserted, "God's complete work is set in motion through vocation."[4] Rather than being an obstacle or impediment to God's work in our lives, Martin Luther understood vocation to be the primary pathway God uses to transform our lives. Luther saw vocation as encompassing a broader theology of the everyday common life where God-honoring worship and spiritual maturation were most desired outcomes. Whether you recognize it, your work is shaping you.

OUR CULTURAL CONTEXT SHAPES US

While the specific work we do forms us, the broader cultural and social context in which our work takes place also shapes us. *WIRED* magazine, noted for its reporting on cutting-edge technology, published the results of a study done by UCLA professor Gary Small on how the Internet is literally rewiring our brains.

In his study, Small compared the brain activity of novice and experienced web surfers using a magnetic resonance imager. What he discovered was that the experienced web surfers had developed distinctive neural pathways because of their extensive Internet use. The novice surfers, who had agreed to surf the web for an hour a day, displayed almost immediate changes in their brains. What is truly stunning is that only five hours of Internet use had already rewired their brains. Small's research points out that the current explosion in digital technology is not only altering the way we communicate, it is quite literally altering our brains.

Nicholas Carr, who wrote the article for *WIRED*, wonders if this is a good thing. He writes:

> What kind of brain is the Web giving us? That question will no doubt be the subject of a great deal of research in the years ahead. Already, though, there is much we know or can surmise—and the news is quite disturbing. Dozens of studies by psychologists, neurobiologists, and educators point to the same conclusion: When we go online, we enter an environment that promotes cursory reading, hurried and distracted thinking, and superficial learning. Even as the Internet grants us easy access to vast amounts of information, it is turning us into shallower thinkers, literally changing the structure of our brain.[5]

The workplaces we inhabit in our late modern world possess a very cozy relationship with technology. In many ways technology is a good gift, but what is largely lacking is the critical thinking needed to see the unintended consequences as they relate to human community and human flourishing. Like many other aspects of contemporary life, technology has a numbing effect on us. We must not minimize or overlook the effect on the body, mind, and soul that is taking place in what is now a highly wired and closely connected online global workplace. As workers immersed in a nanosecond information age, a discriminating utilization of technology will be important for each one of us if we are to be rightly spiritually formed and flourish as God designed us. In addition to the vast technological changes, the cultural water we swim in brings with it a plurality of worldviews, faith commitments, and ethical frameworks, all of which make the marketplace more complex and challenging.

OUR PRESENT CULTURAL ETHOS

We live, work, and breathe in a particular cultural ethos. It is the cultural water we swim in every day. Sociologist James Hunter points out that we live in a time in human history marked by two strong and fast-flowing cultural currents: dissolution and difference. The radical skepticism that permeates our society, Hunter refers to as dissolution. We question deeply whether our words have any objective meaning and whether truth can be known. We also find ourselves immersed in a social context that is highly pluralistic. This is what Hunter describes as difference. The flattened globalized world we live and work in confronts us with a myriad of worldviews, cultures, ethnicities, and faith commitments that deeply challenge the Christian faith's claim to objective historical truth and exclusivity. The neighbor living next door or the coworker in the office cubicle adjacent to us is just as likely to be a Buddhist or a Mormon or even an atheist as they are a confessing Christian. Both the strong currents of dissolution and difference bring significant challenges to our faith in the marketplace, often playing an adverse role in our spiritual formation.[6]

We also need to realize that the very plausibility structures, those institutions and cultural supports that provide a consistency and coherence to a faith-informed life, have largely been eroded away. It is as if we are culturally adrift, not sure of where we have been and even more unsure of where we are heading. As followers of Jesus who are called to be a faithful presence in our workplaces, we need to be attentive to the fast-moving currents of our times and become intentional about the spiritual formation of our lives. In some cases this will require swimming upstream. It is not a question of whether we are being formed spiritually, but rather, are we being spiritually formed in the inexhaustible riches of the gospel as we live and work in the already-but-not-fully-yet kingdom reign of Christ. If we are to incarnate lives of grace and truth in our workplaces, we must make the important lifestyle commitments to resist the mindless conformity to the spirit of our age and instead have our minds renewed in and through the timeless truths of God's Word.

CONFORMITY OR TRANSFORMATION?

After articulating the glorious truths of the gospel to followers of Jesus in Rome, the apostle Paul calls those who have experienced transforming grace to a new way of thinking and a new way of grace-filled living. Paul writes, "I appeal to you therefore, brothers, by the mercies of God, to present your bodies as a living sacrifice, holy and acceptable to God, which is your spiritual worship. Do not be conformed to this world, but be transformed by the renewal of your mind, that by testing you may discern what is the will of God, what is good and acceptable and perfect" (Rom. 12:1–2). Paul wants us to grasp the vital importance of our physicality—for we are embodied creatures. Our physical bodies offered in submission to God and daily aligned with his will are to be instruments of God-honoring worship. This is not just about a posture of worship we assume when we arrive at church on Sunday but one we also assume when we enter our workplace on Monday.

If we reflect back at creation design as it is expressed in Genesis 1, we observe that for six out of seven days our physical bodies were designed to work. During these six days of the week our bodies are to be worshiping God as much as they are on the seventh day of Sabbath rest. All seven days of the week are to be days of God-honoring, Christ-exalting worship. When we embrace the gospel and experience the new birth of regeneration, our physical bodies become indwelling places for the Holy Spirit and are temples of God (1 Cor. 6:19–20). As a result, when we go to work every day, we bring a temple of God with us.

While Paul emphasizes the importance of our physical bodies being in submission to God, he also speaks to the high importance of our minds in spiritual formation. In Romans 12, Paul calls us to avoid mindless conformity to the world. Broadly speaking, Paul is referring to the spirit for our age that in many cases is in opposition to the gospel and Christ's kingdom reign. If we are going to effectively navigate the fast-moving currents of our cultural context and thrive as followers of Jesus in our workplaces, we will need to make the ongoing renewing of our minds a top priority in our lives. There are simply no spiritual-growth shortcuts.

RENEWING OUR MINDS

If we are going to avoid a mindless and perilous conformity to the spirit of our age, we must be actively engaged in the renewal of our minds. Only then will we have the discernment and attentiveness to discover God's will and honor him in our lives and our work. As yoked apprentices of Jesus, we not only take the indwelling presence of God's Spirit with us to work, but we also take the truths of Scripture with us as well. Writing to the church at Corinth, Paul reminds these first-century followers of Jesus that they have been given the mind of Christ (1 Cor. 2:16). When we embrace the gospel, we are given a new capacity for spiritual discernment and understanding. In our new-creation life we have a new way of thinking and seeing the world, and it is something we are called to intentionally cultivate through a disciplined life of reading, studying, memorizing, and meditating on the rich and transforming truths of Scripture. Paul emphasizes this very point. "Let the word of Christ dwell in you richly, teaching and admonishing one another in all wisdom, singing psalms and hymns and spiritual songs, with thankfulness in your hearts to God" (Col. 3:16). Immediately following this verse, Paul broadly applies our new way of thinking and our new lifestyle of thanksgiving to "whatever [we] do, in word or deed" (Col. 3:17). Though the immediate context is geared to life in the new covenant community of faith, Paul quickly expands the application of his main point to our work when, just a few verses later, he specifically addresses the topic of the Christian and work (Col. 3:22–4:1). At the heart of Christian maturation and spiritual formation is a mind that is being continually renewed in, through, and by the rich truths of Scripture.

TAKING GOD'S WORD WITH US TO WORK

All too often we get up in the morning and take a few moments to have a short devotional when we read God's Word and then rush off to work. Maybe we even listen to a Christian radio station on our way to work or review a sermon we heard on Sunday. Yet our tendency is to compartmentalize our minds, leaving God's Word behind when we enter our workplaces. As we do our work, thoughts of cultivating God's presence, of communing with him in prayer and meditating on the truths of his Word, seldom if ever enter our minds. While we may reflect on God's Word as we hear it taught on Sunday morning, it is as if we have a kind of spiritual amnesia that accompanies us when we go to work. This kind of compartmentalization is a great impediment to our spiritual growth and must be addressed by the thoughtful follower of Jesus. If we fail to meditate on Scripture and nurture our intimacy with God at work, where we spend the vast majority of our time, then our spiritual growth, Christian maturity, and spiritual formation will be greatly hindered. Would it not make sense that God not only wants to join us in our work but to increasingly conform us into greater Christlikeness while we work? What we choose for our minds to dwell on while we are working matters a great deal.

In Psalm 1, we are given a picture of human flourishing that is tied to the ongoing discipline of meditating on the truths of

God's revealed Word. Comparing the blessed life of the righteous person to a fruitful tree, the psalmist notes that "his delight is in the law of the LORD, and on his law he meditates day and night" (Ps. 1:2). The truths of the Holy Scriptures richly dwelled within the psalmist both when he worked and when he rested. The psalmist emphasizes that the God-honoring person meditates on the law of the Lord both day and night. It continually accompanies his thoughts wherever he is and whatever he is doing.

If you will embrace the spiritual discipline of the careful study and consistent memorization of God's Word and hide it in your heart, then meditating on God's Word in your workplace as you work will be transformational in your life. Bill Hull speaks with helpful clarity on the primacy of God's Word in spiritual formation: "There is no other path to Christian spiritual transformation than through meaningful interaction with the Word of God. Many Christians have tried to change without its penetrating analysis, but they have failed. . . . True thoughts find their rightful home in the Scriptures, and they find their way into the disciple's mind through reading and prayerful reflection"[7] One of God's primary places where he desires your mind to be renewed is your workplace—for your thoughts, words, and behavior to be changed while you work. Your workplace is to be a place of spiritual formation.

MEDITATION AND MULTITASKING

Multitasking is a big thing these days. We talk on our cell phones as we make dinner. We eat our lunches as we drive to our next appointment. We keep track of the stock market as we respond to e-mails. Our brains have the amazing capacity to do several things at once. Sometimes our multitasking can be a distraction and even dangerous, but it also can be a helpful skill. Because of our multitasking ability, we can concentrate on our work and at the same time allow the words of Christ to richly dwell within us. While we do good work, we can foster a close and intimate communion with our heavenly Father. Even while doing the most mundane tasks, we can enjoy fellowship with God and practice his presence.

As a pastor I have repeatedly observed that those who not only do good work but flourish spiritually in the workplace have cultivated and continue to practice the spiritual discipline of meditating on God's Word while they work. But this requires us to shift away from what is often our compartmentalized thinking about worship and work. No one is more gifted in multitasking than a stay-at-home mom. A mom running a household with small children juggles several balls in the air at the same time. I was always amazed watching my wife, Liz, as she kept track of so many things at one time and still maintained her sanity while doing it. Yet if you were to ask her today about her demanding work, Liz would say that it was in the crucible of the multitude of demands she experienced every day as a stay-at-home mom that a more robust theology of vocation was forged. Her vocational calling to manage a household and raise two small children paved the way for a more seamless life of work and worship.

A stay-at-home mom in our congregation began to grasp the transforming truth of taking God's Word with her to her workplace. I was delighted to receive an e-mail from her that described her growing seamlessness of work and worship. She wrote,

> A stay-at-home mom doesn't get a lot of accolades or affirmation. No paycheck. No glowing review from their boss. I have been working through these thoughts and feelings and several weeks ago decided I wasn't going to spend any more time feeling like a victim. . . . I have had a new outlook on life over these past few weeks, and I feel so much better. . . . I have never thought of being a mother as an act of worship. I can look at it in a whole new way now. . . . I can now see the contributions I make to my household as what I was uniquely created to do for this season of life.

We must not compartmentalize our work and our worship, but rather we must learn to see our work as an act of worship. Though

God is omnipresent, make it your thoughtful intention to bring God with you to work and mediate on the truths of his Word while you work.

God deeply desires that each one of us grows to maturity in Christ, being continually formed into greater Christlikeness. The work you are doing now and the workplace you indwell are presently God's providential arrangement for you to glorify him and grow spiritually. God desires to use your work context to contribute to his good world and to accomplish your spiritual formation. Your work is not an obstacle to your spiritual growth, but rather a conduit for it. God, in his unfathomable grace, has invested much in your spiritual growth. He has given you the Holy Spirit, who is with you and who empowers you while you work.

WORK IN THE SPIRIT

The Holy Spirit's indwelling presence joins us in our work—guiding us, empowering us, interceding for us, and producing in us character qualities of Christlikeness such as love, humility, submission, servanthood, and sacrifice. In writing to the churches of Galatia, Paul paints a riveting contrast between the character qualities of those who walk in the flesh and those who walk in the Spirit. Paul describes those who walk in the Spirit as manifesting in their everyday lives the beautiful and fragrant fruit of the Spirit. "But the fruit of the Spirit is love, joy, peace, patience, kindness, goodness, faithfulness, gentleness, [and] self-control" (Gal. 5:22–23 NIV). So often we think that the more multifaceted the ministry of the Holy Spirit we are drawn to, the more spectacular the manifestation of miracles. Yet we must recognize the greatest evidence of walking in the Spirit is the fruitfulness of our own lives and the transformation of our own personal character into greater Christlikeness.

As we fill our minds with the truth of God's Word moment by moment, and as we yield our wills to the Holy Spirit, we experience the fruit of the Spirit being produced by his grace in and through us. It is in the fertile soil of the workplace that the fruit of the Spirit can grow and flourish in a robust way, and a large part of how we are to be salt and light in our world is manifesting the fruit of the Spirit in our places of work.

Paul makes this important point: "For the kingdom of God is not a matter of eating and drinking but of righteousness and peace and joy in the Holy Spirit" (Rom. 14:17). Our attitude toward our work, the excellence of our work, and our relationship with our coworkers would dramatically change if we walked in the Spirit at work. If I were to survey those with whom you work, whether that is in a classroom, an office, on an assembly line, or at home, what would they say about you as a person? What would they say about your work? What would they say about your attitude and actions at work? To not walk in the Spirit in the workplace where God has called you is to live a life of spiritual impotence and carnality. But if we walk in the Spirit in our workplace, we can have confidence of his supernatural empowerment as well as our own spiritual formation in Christlikeness. By walking in the Spirit, we cooperate with God in the redemptive work he is doing in the world and contribute to the common good. Walking in the Spirit empowers us to live lives of vocational faithfulness and to experience seamless lives of work and worship.

OBSTACLES OR OPPORTUNITIES?

For many years I worked in a fast-food restaurant. I spent long hours waiting on difficult and demanding customers, dealing with conflict, managing employees, evaluating financial statements, and cleaning clogged toilets. Being young in my faith, I had not yet fully understood the importance of my work in contributing to my own spiritual growth. All too often I viewed my work as an obstacle to my spiritual growth. During those times when my work was a real pain, I thought to myself, *You know, if it wasn't for my work and the difficult people I work with, I could be a better Christian.* I now realize how wrong my thinking was. The people I worked with and the work I did were the providential pathway God had for me to nurture my spiritual growth and not be an impediment to it.

Many times our work seems less than ideal. Who of us cannot relate to country singer Johnny Paycheck's heartfelt words of exasperation, "Take this job and shove it"?[8] But is throwing in the towel on work the answer? We can be treated unfairly at work. We can face workplace prejudice, abuse of power, harassment, and injustice. Merely because of our Christian faith commitment we can be sidestepped for promotions or even lose our jobs. Clearly some of our greatest disappointments, struggles, and suffering in life occur in the context of our work.

Dave is a friend who works in the highly competitive field of sports broadcasting. He is very good at his work and has crafted his vocational skill to a high level. His career has seen both highs and lows. Dave described a low point in his career. He was in the final interview for a job he really wanted. The job would have meant much wider network exposure, a big step in his career, and more generous provision for his family. While he was having dinner with the leaders of the company he was hoping to work for, he was asked what philanthropy he wanted to endorse as part of his broadcasting role in the community. When Dave mentioned his commitment and support for a nationwide nonprofit Christian sports ministry, the interview came to a screeching halt. His interviewers thanked Dave for coming and immediately asked for the dinner check. My friend had a long flight home knowing that the job he had wanted so badly and thought he had secured was now gone.

Difficulties, disappointments, discouragements, and suffering are a part of every work experience, but they need not be seen as obstacles to God's purposes in our lives. For the follower of Jesus, suffering, in whatever its form, is one of God's means for his formative work in our lives. Detours, difficulties, and delays are often some of the most transformative times in our journey

114

of faith. Under the sovereign hand of God, suffering is not senseless; it is purposeful.

In Romans 5, Paul's articulation and understanding of the gospel puts our suffering in proper perspective. God's preferred path of transformation is not a path of ease, but it is one of enduring hope. Paul declares, "More than that, we rejoice in our sufferings, knowing that suffering produces endurance, and endurance produces character, and character produces hope, and hope does not put us to shame, because God's love has been poured into our hearts through the Holy Spirit who has been given to us" (Rom. 5:3–5). We must embed deeply in our hearts and minds that our work, though often difficult and filled with tribulations, is one of God's main means for our spiritual growth and transformation. Work is where perseverance, proven character, and hope are deeply forged in our lives.

When we face the formidable winds of workplace trials, rather than running from them or becoming embittered by them, we would be wise to lean into them with trust and confidence, knowing that God has allowed them in our lives for a reason. Often this reason is not fully known by us. Through the eyes of faith we find contagious joy and enduring hope. If we grasp the truth of God's Word about our work, we can remain hopefully buoyant even in difficult job circumstances.

In *The Message*, Eugene Peterson paraphrases the apostle James's inspired words in a way that I find very helpful: "Consider it a sheer gift, friends, when tests and challenges come at you from all sides." (Does that sound like your workplace?) He continues, "You know that under pressure, your faith-life is forced into the open and shows its true colors. So don't try to get out of anything prematurely. Let it do its work so you become mature and well-developed, not deficient in any way" (James 1:2–3). As I look back at my life and my vocational work, I see the truthfulness of these words. I now realize that some of the times of my greatest personal and leadership growth have been in the most difficult days. When my work has been the most demanding and when my inadequacy has been most inescapable, my spiritual growth has been most evident. As I have had to increasingly trust God for wisdom and strength in my work, my spiritual formation has trickled down into the depths of my heart, mind, and soul.

When we look at our work, we often look through the lens of our own personal fulfillment. Yet the New Testament writers look at it through the lens of our own spiritual formation, an outworking of our salvation and our sanctification. It is a good and desirable thing to have work that fulfills us. There is nothing inherently wrong about pursuing a great job, but we must remember that it is not necessary for God's will to be accomplished in our lives. What is necessary is that we are formed into greater Christlikeness in our work. If you are facing some really tough times in your work right now, don't let the termites of discouragement eat away at your soul. Realize that God wants to use the difficulties you are facing to forge greater Christlikeness and spiritual maturity in your life. Your work is not an obstacle to your spiritual growth; it is a God-sized opportunity for you to grow.

WORKPLACE INFLUENCE

Not only is your workplace an opportunity for personal growth, it is where you can have a significant influence. Throughout Scripture we observe individuals like Joseph, Daniel, Nehemiah, and Esther whose workplaces, though less than ideal, were used by God in very significant ways in moving redemptive history forward, protecting God's covenant people, and contributing to the common good. No work platform is too small or obscure for you not to make a difference.

Over the years I have observed the significant influence Dallas Willard has had on his students as professor of philosophy at the University of Southern California. Both the excellence of his academic work and the Christlikeness of his life have left a lasting impact on his colleagues and students. In an essay entitled "How God Is in Business," Dallas pens these autobiographical words regarding the importance of the workplace and how it has been used by God to form him spiritually.

> The place of discipleship is wherever I am now. It's whatever I am now, and whatever I am doing now. . . . When I go to work at USC and I walk into class, that's my place of discipleship. That's the place where I am learning from Jesus how to do everything in the kingdom of God . . . that's why it's important for me to understand that Jesus is, in fact, the smartest man in my field. He is the smartest man in your field. It doesn't matter what you're doing. If you are running a bank or a mercantile company or a manufacturing plant or a government office or whatever it is. He is the smartest man on the job.[9]

Where has God placed you? Is your workplace your place of discipleship? Are you learning from brilliant Jesus not only how to live, but also how to do your work? If you will begin to see your workplace as your primary place of discipleship, it will be truly life changing. You will do good work. You will grow spiritually, and you will have a significant influence in the world. Your spiritual formation into Christlikeness is best seen not in what you do on Sunday, but how you work on Monday. As followers of Jesus, it's time we take Christ with us to work.

HOSPITALITY AT ITS FINEST

For the upscale traveler who desires to spend the night in Kansas City, the hotel of choice is often the Westin Crown Center Hotel. Built by the Hall family as part of the larger Crown Center complex, the Westin Hotel is known throughout the nation as setting a high standard for service and hospitality. The Westin staff are devoted to giving extraordinary attention to the needs of their guests. When the name Westin comes up in conversation, the thought of hospitality comes to mind.

My wife, Liz, and I were invited to the Westin Hotel for a going-away party for its general manager, John Evans. As members of our congregation, John and his wife, Deborah, have embraced a seamless life of work and worship, bringing their Christian faith to work every day. Over the years I have known this couple, I have observed the fruit of the Spirit increasingly evident in their lives in the gracious Christian hospitality they model. I like to think that our church is a hospitable place, and would love to think that our community alone was able to provide them with this growth and depth of insight into the true nature of hospitality, but I know that it has been their work in the hospitality industry combined with their deep faith nurtured on Sunday in our faith community that has truly shaped them.

During the evening we spent celebrating their good work at the Westin, one of the hotel employees by the name of Connie came up to me. She had worked at this hotel for thirty-one years, which in itself was pretty amazing, but what she said spoke volumes. Connie blurted out, "John is the best GM we have ever had." City leaders also spoke glowingly of John and Deborah Evans. They highlighted the integrity displayed at work, their community involvement and devoted service. Neighbors spoke of John and Deborah with great fondness and genuine warmth. Throughout the evening, a beautiful picture of ordinary lives working in ordinary places in extraordinary ways was painted before my eyes. I found myself marveling at the influence of lives well lived and the transforming power of our work in forming us and in shaping our world. We shape our work and our work shapes us.

A Prayer for the Workplace

Heavenly Father, in your divine and gracious providence you have presently placed me in my workplace. It is my heart's desire that I glorify you in and through my work today. May I do my work well, and may my mind be renewed as I meditate on the truths of your Word. Draw me near to you. Lord Jesus, let my workplace be a place of discipleship where I am learning from you as I work. As I walk in the power of the Holy Spirit, may the character qualities of Christlikeness increasingly be evident in my life. Lord, use my life and my work to further your redemptive purposes in the world and to enhance the common good. Amen.

Questions for Reflection and Discussion:

- How would you describe the culture in which you work?
- How has your workplace culture shaped you as a worker?
- What disappointments have you faced in your workplace? What might God be teaching you through them?
- How might you be conscious to bring God to work with you?

KEVIN > CHIEF FINANCIAL OFFICER

Our faith community has centered on navigating life and faith in a seamless way. Likewise, my work community at Garmin has centered on providing the world with great navigation technology using GPS. The intersection of these two worlds has provided challenging yet incredible experiences for me. Both organizations have recently celebrated two decades since inception. In many ways, the organization at Garmin has allowed an opportunity to put into practice each day what we often speak of on Sunday. The roots of our company began with a vision to create high-quality, lasting work in order to serve the customer and each other, to create and innovate, and to do so with integrity in all our business dealings. Work is not just about great products but about people, relationships, and how we interact together. We do have a great team of committed people at Garmin.

My position within this company has provided an ability to influence and practice the concepts of faith and work, which has been a real joy. At Garmin we often speak of performing meaningful and productive work each day— part of our language is not being pleased or satisfied with the status quo but striving to improve. Leading a workforce that remains motivated and excited to come to work each day is anything but easy, but it is very rewarding when others catch the vision of how work "ought" to be. Knowing that many in our organization feel they contribute significantly to the success of the organization in all aspects of business is an incredible feeling, and one that is too often missing in companies. Celebrating successes after reaching key milestones is another focus that adds to the richness of our experiences and relationships at work.

Perhaps the greatest sense of satisfaction comes from knowing I am right where God has designed me to be. To know that God has gifted each of us with skills and abilities and called us to serve him best with that calling is unbelievable. Looking back over the last twenty-five years as a professional, I can see how many life experiences, both positive and negative, have prepared me for my current position of leadership as CFO of Garmin. Many of those who work on our teams respect the unique culture that has been nurtured over the last twenty years and are proud of the fact that we are different—different in the value we place on each associate, in the respect and service we grant to our customers and suppliers, and in the vision we have to align individual skills with business needs. The work we do is important, and how we perform our various callings through work is even more important.

7

WORK AND THE COMMON GOOD

God doesn't need our good works, but our neighbor does.
MARTIN LUTHER

Jonathan Swartz serves as the CEO of Timberland Company and brings his faith to work every day. Timberland is known in the business world not only for the quality of shoes it sells but also for the quality of the corporate culture it indwells. As a for-profit company, Timberland desires to be a good neighbor in its community and a responsible citizen of the world. One of the ways Timberland puts flesh on its good-neighbor commitment is by inviting employees to participate in Timberland's Path of Service program. Timberland has embraced a generous culture, adopting a policy of granting paid leave for a variety of community service involvements.

In a *Los Angeles Times* article, Jonathan Swartz was asked how he maintained his values as well as profitability in the midst of tough, competitive day-to-day business dealings. His answer reflects a refreshing and welcomed insight: "In order to equip people to make a difference in their world, we must insist that doing well and doing good not be different." Swartz goes on to say, "I haven't found a corporate environment where their people do not want to serve a truth greater than them."[1] Jonathan Swartz, who embraces a Jewish faith, is saying that faith is not merely a private commitment but should also positively influence the work environment. He believes that work's bottom line is more than just an economic one.

RETHINKING WORK'S BOTTOM LINE

The objective of making a profit or increasing stockholder value is a good and integral aspect of our capitalist economic system. I do not want in any way to diminish this important stewardship for any business enterprise. However, Scripture teaches that our work is about more than financial remuneration, making a profit, economic self-interest, or career advancement. We were created with work in mind, but the work God had in mind for us has a communal nature and responsibility. As followers of Jesus, one of our primary stewardships is to be our brother's keeper. One of the most important ways we fulfill this charge is through our vocations. The work we are called to do is a God-ordained means where we, in very tangible ways, care for God's good world, contribute to the needs of others, and foster the common good.

When I travel, I am regularly reminded of my responsibility to and stewardship of the common good. Inevitably when I check into a hotel, one of the first things I encounter as I enter my room is a small but well-placed brochure made of recycled paper. It reminds me of my important role in energy conservation and ecological stewardship. Turning off the lights when I leave and reusing my towels rather than replacing them each day is my opportunity to protect the environment and foster the common good. With many other things on my mind while I am on the road, it is a gentle nudge I need and very much appreciate. As a business enterprise, the hotel management knows that my behavior as an individual traveler will not only significantly affect their cost of doing business, but will also promote a better world for all. Making a profit is an important bottom line, but being a responsible contributor to the common good is also a crucial bottom line as well.

FOSTERING THE COMMON GOOD

When we speak of the common good, we are describing all the various aspects of contemporary life that contribute positively to human flourishing both as individuals and as communities. The Protestant Reformers connected vocation to human flourishing and the common good. Martin Luther's understanding of vocation was deeply embedded in our calling as workers to promote the well-being of others and our world. Anchoring his thoughts in Jesus's Great Commandment to love our neighbor as ourselves, Martin Luther made the seminal point that while God doesn't really need our good works, our neighbor clearly does. Luther's theology of vocation emphasized a primary way we love our neighbor is in and through our work. John Calvin also saw human work through the lens of the common good. Calvin wrote, "It is not enough when one can say, 'Oh I work, I have my trade, I set the pace.' This is not enough; for one must be concerned whether it is good and profitable to the community and if it is able to serve our neighbors."[2]

SEEKING THE WELFARE OF THE CITY

A concern for the well-being of others and the flourishing of the broader society in which we live is strongly affirmed throughout Scripture. The Old Testament prophet Jeremiah spoke to this during a rather bleak time in redemptive history. God's covenant people had been conquered by the Babylonians. Jerusalem had been sacked and burned. Many of the people had been taken into exile. They yearned to get back home soon. Beaten down, brutalized, and displaced, the last thing I am sure God's covenant people wanted to do was to put their roots down and promote the common good of their captors and the city of Babylon. Yet this is precisely what God called them to do.

The prophet Jeremiah delivered a message that I doubt the people were expecting, but one deeply embedded in God's merciful heart.

> Thus says the LORD of hosts, the God of Israel, to all the exiles whom I have sent into exile from Jerusalem to Babylon: Build houses and live in them; plant gardens and eat their produce. Take wives and have sons and daughters; take wives for your sons, and give your daughters in marriage, that they may bear sons and daughters; multiply there, and do not decrease. But seek the welfare of the city where I have sent you into exile, and pray to the LORD on its behalf, for in its welfare you will find your welfare. (Jer. 29:4–7)

Even in a foreign and pagan city, God's covenant people were to go about their normal lives of working hard and raising families. Remarkably, they were also exhorted to pray for the flourishing of Babylon and to seek the common good of all its inhabitants. Lest we miss it, Jeremiah repeats the Hebrew word *shalom* three times. *Shalom*, or peace, conveys not merely the cessation of hostility or war, but the flourishing of all of God's creation. *Shalom* encapsulates God's brilliant design and benevolent desire for his good world. God's heart is that the city of Babylon might flourish and that his covenant people might flourish with it. *Shalom* is also God's desire for the people we work with, the workplaces we inhabit, and the broader society of which we are a part. The good news of the gospel is that true *shalom* is now possible, for the Prince of *Shalom* has come to earth and will one day come again. In and through the gospel we experience *shalom*. Living out the gospel of *shalom* prompts us to foster the common good.

DOING GOOD TO ALL

Like the Old Testament writers, the New Testament writers weave the important thread of the common good in the fabric of faithful living. While the New Testament writers primarily aim to encourage followers of Jesus to lovingly relate to one another in the local church and to proclaim the gospel, they also emphasize the importance of seeking the common good of all, including those outside the community of faith. Writing to the churches of Galatia, Paul builds his thoughts to a kind of impassioned crescendo as he encourages those who have embraced the gospel to be doers of good to all. "So then, as we have opportunity, let us do good to everyone, and especially to those who are of the household of faith" (Gal. 6:10). Caring for brothers and sisters in Christ was important for the apostle Paul, but so was seeking the good of everyone.

Once again Paul emphasizes a broader and far-reaching stewardship of the common good. To the Thessalonians Paul writes, "See that no one repays anyone evil for evil, but always seek to do good to one another and to everyone" (1 Thess. 5:15). In his emotional farewell address to the elders of the church at Ephesus, Paul's final words focus on nurturing a faith community of tangible generosity, particularly to the economically vulnerable. Paul reminds the church leaders at Ephesus of his own hard work as a tent-maker and connects their capacity to foster the common good to their diligent work. "In all things I have shown you that by working hard in this way we must help the weak and remember the words of the Lord Jesus, how he himself said, 'It is more blessed to give than to receive'" (Acts 20:35).

One of the main purposes of our work is that in and through our vocations our own practical needs are met and the common good is fostered. Theologian Miroslav Volf summarizes the Bible's important emphasis on the common good: "In the Bible and in the first centuries of Christian tradition, meeting one's needs and the needs of one's community (especially its underprivileged members) was clearly the most important purpose of work."[3] Though we don't always feel it or see it directly, as we do our work as an act of worship for the glory of God, we can be confident that we are contributing to the important work that our heavenly Father is doing in our world. If we are going to more seamlessly connect our Sunday faith with our Monday work, we will need to indwell a robust theology of everyday life. This will mean embracing a life of common grace for the common good.

COMMON GRACE FOR THE COMMON GOOD

Common grace views all of life in God's good world as a gracious gift.[4] Common grace is integral to our Christian faith and makes possible a coherent understanding of ordinary everyday life. Steven Garber insightfully distinguishes saving grace from common grace while capturing its beauty and wonder. He writes,

> And so the sweet smile of a baby, the tender embrace of a mother, the passion of a kiss, the smell of bread baking and meat grilling, the glories of the sea and the sky, the gift of good work that satisfies and serves, the ordered safety of street lights and speed limits, the wonders of good novels and good music, the miracles of x-rays and dental care, the bright yellow daffodils and the pastels of foxgloves, the steady support of friends and the enduring affection of a spouse, the accountability of justice and the responsibility of citizenship, and on and on and on—each are common graces. They do not save us from our sin, but they are gifts of God and we see them as that.[5]

The doctrine of common grace is a biblical truth grounded in the very character of the triune God, tethered to creation, and reinforced in redemption. Common grace is unmerited favor and goodness extended to all persons made in the image of the triune God regardless of their eternal destiny. Common grace affirms the goodness of God's world and every human being who has been crafted in the image of God. Though fallen and corrupted by sin, every image-bearer has intrinsic value and is to be respected and valued regardless of behavior or belief.

In his masterpiece sermon on the kingdom of God, Jesus emphasizes common grace as it is extended to us and as we are to offer it generously to others. "But I say to you, Love your enemies and pray for those who persecute you, so that you may be sons of your Father who is in heaven. For he makes his sun rise on the evil and on the good, and sends rain on the just and on the unjust" (Matt. 5:44–45). By affirming common grace, Jesus is neither negating saving grace nor is he advocating a kind of universalism. Jesus came to seek and save the lost, shedding his own blood that those who believe in him might not perish but have eternal life. Jesus does not gloss over the very real categories of evil and good, of the righteous and unrighteous. Jesus is saying that both the lives of the righteous and the unrighteous are sustained by common grace, and his good gifts of provision and providential care are enjoyed by all. Jesus's specific language, that the sun rises and the rain falls on the good and the evil, does not in any way lessen the seriousness of sin or the need for saving faith, but rather suggests God's great value and care for all of his creation. God's providential care can be counted on. It is an ever-present reminder to us of his common grace.

We live, work, and play in a God-bathed world. All the goodness in life that we enjoy is a gracious gift from God. The food we eat, the music we enjoy, the chirping of the songbirds we delight in, the afternoon rain shower that soothes a thirsty and parched earth—these are all tangible expressions of God's common grace. By having the sun shine and the rain fall for everyone, God cares for the well-being of all the earth's inhabitants, even his crown of creation that often rejects and opposes him.

In the Gospel of Luke, Jesus calls his followers to love their enemies. This Godlike love entails doing tangible good to them and extending acts of mercy. Jesus tells us that the Most High God "is kind to the ungrateful and the evil" (Luke 6:35). This kindness God extends is also to be extended by us. This is not just the evidence of saving grace but also of common grace that is to be a distinguishing mark of the true follower of Jesus and of a local church community that gathers in his name. Yet common grace is all too often very uncommon. A robust theology and practice of common grace seems to have been deemphasized by many followers of Jesus in our time. Common grace directed toward the common good is more often the welcomed exception rather than the norm. Perhaps an evidence of the lack of common grace is depicted in a bumper sticker that I saw on the back of the car ahead of me as I was going to work. It read, *"Jesus, save me from your followers."* I don't know what this driver's experience had been with Christ followers, but it caused me to pause and reflect. As a follower of Christ, do I lack a lifestyle of common grace in my interactions and dealings with others in day-to-day life?

Shortly after our family moved to a new neighborhood, my daughter, Sarah, met another girl who lived just down the street. Almost immediately they became friends. As they were taking a walk one day, my daughter's new friend asked the dreaded question of any preacher's kid: "What does your dad do?" Sarah responded, "My dad is a pastor, but don't worry, he only acts that way on Sunday." We all got a big laugh out of that one when later on Sarah recounted the conversation. I am not sure of all that Sarah meant by her response. I choose to believe it was Sarah's way of insisting her dad was a real down-to-earth kind of guy, but I was challenged about the importance of a consistent, authentic lifestyle informed by and overflowing with common grace. I am the kind of guy who is passionate about the truth of the gospel, and I believe God is honored by that commitment. Yet I must also be overflowing with a generous grace toward others, even those who at this time reject the gospel I cherish so deeply. Jesus incarnated and modeled both truth and grace, and as his apprentices, we are called to do the same.

We live and work in a society of great political and religious polarization. States are described as being red or blue. Political pundits label us conservative or liberal. Demographers identify us in terms of economic strata: upper, middle, or lower class. The people we encounter in our work every day often see the world very differently than we do. Yet in and through our vocations we have the opportunity to extend common grace to others, and in doing so we foster the common good. In the rich soil of common grace, the common good flourishes and the truths of the gospel are lived out before attentive ears and watchful eyes. John Piper puts things in proper perspective when he states, "Our aim is to joyfully magnify Christ—to make him look great by all we do. Boasting only in the cross, our aim is to enjoy making much of him by the way we work."[6] Our Christian mission in the late modern world is not only to boldly proclaim saving grace, but also to eagerly and joyfully extend common grace to all. It is often in the fertile soil of common grace where the seed of saving grace takes root, and it is often in and through our vocations that we have the opportunity to indwell common grace for the common good.

COMMON GRACE IN THE WORKPLACE

The remarkable Old Testament story of Ruth and Boaz speaks loudly to common grace in the workplace. It would have been unlikely for these two characters to meet. Still, a sovereign God had plans for them to play an important role in moving redemptive history forward. Ruth was a Moabite. Boaz was an Israelite. Moabites and Israelites had little to do with each other. But a family tragedy brought Naomi and Ruth, her daughter-in-law, back to Naomi's people. Widowed and socially vulnerable, Naomi and Ruth arrived in Bethlehem during the barley harvest.

As was custom in those days, owners of land fostered the common good by leaving a portion of their crops in the fields for the poor to harvest as a way for them to work and provide for their needs. Boaz, who was a relative of Naomi's late husband Elimelech, owned a field, and Ruth went to glean there. Though Ruth was a foreigner, Boaz extended kindness to her and lavished her with grace. Scripture captures this moment flowing with common grace in the workplace. "Then Boaz said to Ruth, 'Now, listen, my daughter, do not go to glean in another field or leave this one, but keep close to my young women. Let your eyes be on the field that they are reaping, and go after them. Have I not charged the young men not to touch you? And when you are thirsty, go to the vessels and drink what the young men have drawn'" (Ruth 2:8–9). Ruth's first encounter with Boaz, who will eventually become her kinsman-redeemer, is one that is instructive to us. Boaz goes out of his way to provide for and protect this Moabite woman he knows little about. He has only heard of her loyal commitment to her mother-in-law, Naomi. At the time, I doubt if Boaz had any idea how his many tangible acts of unselfish kindness and common grace offered to Ruth in the workplace would be used by God. Through Boaz and Ruth, the father of King David would be born, and through the line of David, Messiah Jesus would come.

In and through our vocations, we have been given a daily opportunity to be gracious and to serve joyfully the students we teach, the patients we examine, the customers we serve, and the fellow employees we work with. For many of us this will mean a paradigmatic shift in our perspective about the people we encounter in our workplace each day. Yes, people can be difficult to work with and they can quickly get under our skin, but are we able to look past the messes and see the masterpieces God has made them to be? C. S. Lewis struck a resounding chord of common grace when he penned these words: "There are no ordinary people. You have never talked to a mere mortal. Nations, cultures, arts, civilization—these are mortal, and their life is to ours as the life of a gnat. Next to the Blessed Sacrament itself, your neighbor is the holiest object presented to your senses."[7]

Paul reminds Titus that we as followers of Jesus are, "to speak evil of no one, to avoid quarreling, to be gentle, and to show perfect courtesy toward all people" (Titus 3:2). As followers of Jesus who embrace common grace, we are called to be honest and considerate in our workplaces. We should be quick to praise others for their successes and contributions and seek practical ways to be helpful and caring. It may be a dog-eat-dog world where you work, but strive for a greater sensitivity to the hurts and cares of those around you. Be attentive to ways you can express and model Christlike gentleness and servanthood. Be a good neighbor—not just where you live, but also where you work.

BEING A GOOD NEIGHBOR AT WORK

All too often we approach our work with such compartmentalization that we fail to make the important connection of living out Jesus's Great Commandment in the workplace. In response to a query about who our real neighbor is, Jesus told the story of the good Samaritan. We need to keep in mind that while Samaritans and Jews were neighbors geographically, they lived worlds apart. They simply didn't give each other the time of day. Jesus describes how, when encountering a stranger who had been robbed and left for dead along the Jericho road, both the religiously respectable Levite and the priest chose to walk by the crime victim without lifting a finger. Shockingly to any Jewish listener, Jesus then introduces in the story a Samaritan man who happens to be traveling down the same road to Jericho. Unlike the Levite and the priest, the Samaritan stops and cares for the man who had been beaten and left for dead. The Samaritan offers first aid, but he even does more. He takes the crime victim to a local inn and pays the man's bills. In telling the parable of the good Samaritan, Jesus conveys who the good neighbor truly is, and he intentionally blurs the line often drawn between one's enemy and one's neighbor. Jesus greatly expands the horizons of one's neighbor and greatly limits the possibilities of one's enemies. Jesus not only makes the Samaritan a true hero, but he also affirms the Samaritan's compassion and common grace. Surprisingly, it was the Samaritan who truly loved his neighbor while the Jewish priest and Levite clearly did not.

RAISING THE BAR OF TOLERANCE

Jesus's parable of the good Samaritan has profound implications for the workplaces we indwell and the neighborly love we are to incarnate there. We hear much about diversity, sensitivity, and tolerance of others in the workplace, but for the follower of Jesus, merely being tolerant of others who are different than us or rub us the wrong way puts the bar way too low. Neighborly love and the common grace it exhibits toward others is the high bar we are to strive for in our daily work. Christ does not call us to be merely tolerant of those we work with but to roll up our sleeves and demonstrate Christian love, compassion, and common grace.

A friend of mine who serves as a CFO of a transportation company in Kansas City found out that one of his single-parent employees was the new owner of a Habitat for Humanity home our church congregation had recently built for her family. On move-in day, I was delighted to see my friend arrive at his employee's home with his work clothes on, ready to assist in any way he could. Though we are both quite mechanically challenged, we did manage to assemble the beds that had been donated for the new home. My friend did not merely bring a spirit of tolerance to the workplace; he also brought Christian compassion, neighborly love, and common grace.

LETTING GOD BE GOD

Our work can be a context where we are the recipient of ill treatment from others, and the temptation to retaliate through whatever means we can is strong. A boss can treat us unfairly. Customers can take out their frustration and anger on us, even though we have not contributed to what has caused the outburst. In their workplaces people can abuse power. I still remember a landlord who wrongly accused my roommates of apartment damage they didn't cause. We learned later that this was a pattern he had demonstrated repeatedly with others, all as a ruse for keeping security deposits and increasing his personal profits.

How are we to respond when we face ill treatment in the workplace? Turning the other cheek does not mean it is improper to seek appropriate grievance processes and legal procedures when we have been unfairly taken advantage of. However, as followers of Jesus, we must guard our hearts against bitterness toward anyone and grant them grace. Scripture makes clear that we are not to retaliate or take vengeance into our own hands and that we are to overcome evil with good. Writing to believers in Rome, Paul gives this sweeping exhortation:

> Repay no one evil for evil, but give thought to do what is honorable in the sight of all. If possible, so far as it depends on you, live peaceably with all. Beloved, never avenge yourselves, but leave it to the wrath of God, for it is written, "Vengeance is mine, I will repay," says the Lord. To the contrary, "if your enemy is hungry, feed him; if he is thirsty, give him something to drink; for by so doing you will heap burning coals on his head." Do not be overcome by evil, but overcome evil with good. (Rom. 12:17–21)

What strikes me about Paul's words is how all-encompassing they are. I can't find much situational wiggle room that would allow me to take things into my own hands. Paul says we are to never pay back evil for evil or to take our own revenge. We are to let God be God. Vengeance is God's prerogative alone. When we live a life of common grace, we are not soft on sin or apathetic toward wrongdoing, nor are we a doormat of passivity for people to walk over, but we find contentment in our hearts that God is in charge, and he is the one who will settle any scores that need to be settled. If you find yourself harboring a spirit of bitterness toward your boss or a fellow worker, perhaps it is time for some humble repentance. If you have paid back someone with evil for the evil they have sent your way, then it's time to seek their forgiveness for your sin of retaliation. It is very difficult to exude a spirit of common grace when the human heart is suffocating in bitterness and an unforgiving spirit.

AVOIDING AN "US VERSUS THEM" MENTALITY

A Christian lifestyle lived out in the workplace helps us avoid harboring spirits of bitterness and using language that communicates an "us versus them" mentality. When we increasingly view others through the lens of common grace, we look for areas of common ground and build bridges of inclusion rather than walls of exclusion. As fellow sinners in need of the gospel's saving grace, we are called to interact with others in our work settings with humility and a teachable spirit rather than any pharisaical attitude of moral superiority. When I am tempted to put on airs or look down on someone with whom I am working, I am jolted into reality when the truth, *"but for the grace of God there go I,"* knocks on the door of my prideful heart. It is not just a passion for what is right that often fuels an "us versus them" mentality; it is our own hideous spiritual pride and carnal arrogance.

If we are going to avoid bringing an "us versus them" mentality to our workplaces we need to know our real enemy. Scripture repeatedly informs us that a spiritual battle is raging for the hearts and minds of fallen humanity. Though defeated on the cross by our Lord and Savior, the Evil One still is active and wreaking havoc in our world and in our workplaces. In addition to the "lust of the eyes," "the lust of the flesh," and the "boastful pride of life" that woo our hearts and affections away from Christ, we also face a very formidable foe. Immediately following his inspired words regarding the workplace, the apostle Paul exhorts the believers in Ephesus to remember who their adversary is and to proactively prepare for his inevitable opposition. Paul writes, "Put on the whole armor of God, that you may be able to stand against the schemes of the devil" (Eph. 6:11).

Your workplace is not a neutral zone; it is a battle zone. Every day the kingdom of darkness and the kingdom of Christ are coming in conflict. As followers of Jesus we must remember that as we walk in the power of the Holy Spirit, we have powerful spiritual weapons available to us. The apostle Paul reminds us of this, "For though we walk in the flesh, we are not waging war according to the flesh. For the weapons of our warfare are not of the flesh but have divine power to destroy strongholds" (2 Cor. 10:3–4). One of our greatest spiritual weapons is intercessory prayer, and one of the best ways to avoid an "us versus them" mentality in the workplace is to pray regularly for those we work with. I find that when I am praying for others, I am much more inclined to extend common grace to them, exhibiting workplace courtesy, civility, and respect.

PROMOTING WORKPLACE JUSTICE

When we embrace common grace for the common good, we actively promote justice and fairness in the workplace. Writing to the Colossians, Paul calls out those who have authority in the workplace to cultivate fairness. "Masters, treat your slaves justly and fairly, knowing that you also have a Master in heaven" (Col. 4:1). If God has placed you in a position of authority in your workplace, you have a high stewardship before God to foster a fair and safe work environment for all. A fair workplace will ensure fair wages for all. It will address any gender inequality in wages and avoid excessive executive compensation packages that are given at the expense of the well-being of the company and its workers. A fair workplace will have policies and procedures that allow for employee grievances to be heard. Opportunities for personal growth and career advancement will be encouraged. Ongoing fair-trade practices will be required of suppliers and business partners. While maintaining compassion and care for each individual, immigration laws will be respected and enforced. As we promote safe, fair, and just work environments, we contribute to the good of employee morale and to human flourishing.

TEACH FOR AMERICA

Wendy Kopp grew up in the very privileged neighborhood of Highland Park, Texas. After graduating from high school, Wendy headed off to prestigious Princeton University. While a student at Princeton, Wendy became increasingly aware and concerned about the educational inequity in the United States. Birthed in Wendy's senior thesis was an idea of what to do about the sobering educational inequity she uncovered. Wendy proposed the establishment of a national teaching corps devoted to addressing educational inequity. Wendy believed that a whole cadre of America's brightest and best college students would respond to the need by giving at least two years of their lives after college to teach in some of America's most needy public schools. Wendy Kopp was right.

In 1990, Kopp courageously founded Teach for America to address the issue of educational inequity. Since its founding, the success of Teach for America has been breathtaking. Over fourteen thousand Teach for America corps members have invested at least two years of their lives to work for the common good in many under-resourced school systems across the United States. The Teach for America staff have positively impacted over three million students. In a commencement address to Georgetown College, Wendy Kopp passionately described her work for the common good.

> I believed that the inequity in educational outcomes that persists along socioeconomic and racial lines in our country is our nation's greatest social injustice, that the leaders in our generation were searching for something they weren't finding and would jump at the chance to teach in urban and rural public schools, that our energy and idealism would make a difference in the lives of the nation's most disadvantaged kids, and that ultimately our nation would be a different place if as many of

its leaders had taught in low-income communities straight out of college as had worked on Wall Street straight out of college.[8]

God may not call you to address the injustice of educational inequity, but he has called you to do your work in God-honoring ways that enhance the common good and promote human flourishing. He has created, empowered, and gifted you to contribute to his redemptive work in the world.

The Divine Image

For Mercy, Pity, Peace, and Love
Is God, our Father dear,
And Mercy, Pity, Peace, and Love
Is man, His child and care.

And all must love the human form,
In heathen, Turk, or Jew;
Where Mercy, Love, and Pity dwell
There God is dwelling too.[9]

Questions for Reflection and Discussion:

- In your work, are you cultivating common grace for the common good?

- How does your vocation uniquely allow you to work for the common good?

- How do you see the people in your workplace? Are you treating them with courtesy, civility, and respect?

- In what ways do you seek the welfare of the city in which you dwell?

- Are you committed to praying for your boss and those you oversee?

- How might you foster a more just and equitable work environment?

MATT > COLLEGE PROFESSOR

A university, particularly a fairly large public university such as the one at which I get to teach, is to me a wonderful place. Teeming with the big ideas from across the centuries, inventive and practical solutions to meet real needs for now and into the future, and people from across the globe, it is an alive and dynamic environment. As Samuel Johnson said of London in the eighteenth century, "When a man is tired of London he is tired of life; for there is in London all that life can afford,"[10] so I would be inclined to say of the university today.

There is tremendous diversity on many college campuses— racial and ethnic, socioeconomic, linguistic, age and gender, political, philosophical, and religious. And the branches of knowledge covered, from the arts and humanities to the sciences to professional studies and everything in between, sometimes have markedly different ways of knowing, interpreting, and interacting with reality. At times it would seem, except for the fact that we are loosely held together under an institutional identity, there is little common among us, and yet some cohesion remains evident in our university communities. Perhaps this is because one theme that tends to cut across higher education is the *common good*. In higher education we all in one way or another (even if it's only tacitly expressed) are here to serve the common good, to try to make the world around us a better place through the knowledge that we seek to discover, teach, and learn.

Feeling like I can contribute, even in some very small way, to the common good, to making the world a better place, is motivating to me and seems to align with what I could consider my calling. I value being part of a university community that has similar primary motives.

As a college professor, I also appreciate getting to be part of a *faith community* that places high value on a life of service to the common good. To be honest, on some points of theology at this point in my life, I may have more of an agnostic bent. But seeking the common good is one thing that my conscience allows me to endorse and seek without hesitation. Over the past decade or more in our faith community, we have discussed things such as integral and seamless living, wholeness of soul, wariness of sacred/secular dichotomies, and the intrinsic value of work. We have done so in ways that have also allowed me to work together with and learn from people in other fields, including business, politics, engineering, architecture, and law. It has been very valuable to be able to develop, test out, and refine a philosophy of life while connected with an intelligent and compassionate faith community that deeply values work, and in my case, work in the service of the common good as a university faculty member. For this I am deeply grateful.

8

GIFTED FOR WORK

To believe that a wise and good God is in charge of things implies that there is a fit between things that need doing and the person I am meant to be.[1]
FREDERICK BUECHNER

L ike most kids growing up, my imaginative attempts with paper and crayons were prominently displayed on the front of our refrigerator. Gazing at my well-intentioned masterpieces of art, it is a good thing my siblings did not say out loud what they were thinking inside. Perhaps it was divine intervention motivated by a severe mercy that froze their tongues, or maybe it was the fear of severe parental rebuke that spared me from their transparent critique. Thankfully, I was left alone to admire the unremarkable work of my small, stubby hands.

Though none of my refrigerator art survived the wear and tear of the years, it is clear to me now, as it was to my entire family then, that my childhood masterpieces reflected a woeful lack of God-given artistic talent. One look at our refrigerator door told an important story: God's vocational calling for my life was not to make the world more beautiful through my drawing skills. It was evident to all around me that God had not gifted me to contribute in this way. My refrigerator art was to be a different kind of work in the world.

Our work is a gift from God, but we are also gifted by God for our work. How God has created us and gifted us, and the very human dispositions we have been given, shape his vocational will for our lives. We are called, as Dietrich Bonhoeffer points out, to a particular field of activity. Bonhoeffer writes, "The call of Jesus Christ is the call to belong to Christ completely; it is Christ's address and claim at the place at which this call encounters me; vocation comprises work with things and issues as well as personal relations; it requires a definite 'field of activity.'"[2]

Whether a college student pondering his first job offer or an empty-nest mom considering an encore career, one of the questions I am asked most frequently is, "How do I know what I am supposed to do with my life?" In a cultural context where most of us have some degree of choice regarding the work we do, the quest to know God's vocational will for our lives occupies a significant degree of personal reflection, and even at times creates a heartfelt anxiety. At soul level, we long to fulfill the purpose for which we have been created and placed in the world.

Though I would not presume to know specifically what your field of activity ought to be or what kind of refrigerator art you have been designed to create, I am confident that Scripture provides some helpful guidance for your vocational journey. While we must live our lives forward, we often understand them backward. While having a good deal of life mileage under your belt does add helpful perspective, I believe that at any stage of life you can discern and live out your God-honoring vocational contribution in the world.

BEZALEL AND OHOLIAB

Bezalel and Oholiab are not the first names we tend to think of when biblical characters come to mind. Even for a seasoned student of the Bible, they are tough to recall and even more difficult to pronounce. Though Bezalel and Oholiab would be excellent candidates for a difficult Bible trivia question, their lives and vocational callings were anything but trivial. Bezalel and Oholiab lived at the time when Moses received the Ten Commandments on Mount Sinai. These "Ten Words," as they were labeled in the original Hebrew language, were written on two stone tablets and reflected God's moral law. They also laid out God's designed boundaries for human flourishing.

In addition to the Ten Commandments, God gave Moses extensive and specific instructions on how he desired to be worshiped. At this time in redemptive history, God instructed his covenant people to offer blood sacrifices for their sins in a tabernacle, which involved various instruments of worship such as altars and basins. This is where Bezalel and Oholiab found their vital vocational calling as artistic craftsmen. In Exodus 31 we read,

> The LORD said to Moses, "See, I have called by name Bezalel the son of Uri, son of Hur, of the tribe of Judah, and I have filled him with the Spirit of God, with ability and intelligence, with knowledge and all craftsmanship, to devise artistic designs, to work in gold, silver, and bronze, in cutting stones for setting, and in carving wood, to work in every craft. And behold, I have appointed with him Oholiab, the son of Ahisamach, of the tribe of Dan. And I have given to all able men ability, that they may make all that I have commanded you." (Ex. 31:1–6)

We discover here that in giving Moses a specific and very detailed work order, God had already been providentially at work preparing and gifting workers who could excellently accomplish the task at hand.

145

Reflect with me for a moment on some of the gems of truth nestled in this instructive Old Testament text. Exodus 31:2 begins with the phrase, "See, I have called by name Bezalel." In the original language of the Old Testament, the name *Bezalel* means "in the shadow (protection) of God." Though we might be tempted to view Bezalel as an obscure character in this obscure biblical story, his name tells us that he is anything but obscure in God's eyes. God calls Bezalel by name, and his word to Moses affirms three big ideas: (1) Bezalel's vocational call was able to be observed by others around him, (2) Bezalel's vocational call was specific to him as an individual, and (3) God supernaturally empowered and gifted Bezalel for a specific work that needed to be done.

As the story continues, we see that God is at work in this, specifically noted as "the Spirit of God." This is the same language found in Genesis 1, where the Spirit of God powerfully acts in original creation (Gen. 1:2). Looking back through the lens of progressive revelation, Christian theologians understand this language as a Trinitarian reference to the third person of the Trinity, the Holy Spirit. In Exodus 31 the author validates the Holy Spirit's supernatural filling work in and through observable external evidence, namely, Bezalel's vocational work. Four words are carefully strung together to present a compelling picture of Bezalel's supernatural empowerment and gifting for his vocational calling. The Spirit of God had filled Bezalel with "ability and intelligence, with knowledge and all craftsmanship." There is no indication in the biblical text that Bezalel was suddenly zapped with instant artistic ability or that he woke up one morning a master craftsman. Bezalel's craftsmanship and skillful hands had been honed through years of diligent learning and practical experience. Like all skilled workmen, Bezalel had learned from master craftsmen who had gone before him. However, the writer of Exodus has more than this attained human competence in mind. He wants us to know the Spirit of God had supernaturally gifted Bezalel for his particular vocational calling. God had created and supernaturally empowered Bezalel as a gifted architect, craftsman, and builder. These Holy Spirit-anointed hands were something special to behold. The beauty and excellence of their work revealed it. This was not only true of the excellent artistry and craftsmanship of Bezalel and Oholiab; we are told that God gave "to all able men ability" in making the wilderness tabernacle (Ex. 31:6).

These are weighty statements that have profound implications for our lives and our world. Our lives and our vocational callings are woven into the beautiful tapestry of God's often mysterious providence. Through the eyes of faith, we can be confident that God is moving his redemptive story forward and empowering us to participate with his work in the world. In Exodus 31 we see a providential arrangement emerging at the intersection of work that needs to be done and the giftedness to accomplish the task at hand. Frederick Buechner makes this important and insightful observation: "God calls you to the kind of work that you need most to do, and that the world most needs to have done . . . the place God calls you is the place where your deep gladness and the world's deep hunger meet."[3] You were created with work in mind. You have been gifted to do a particular work. As a follower of Christ who has been born from above, you have been equipped and empowered by the Holy Spirit to make an important vocational contribution, a contribution that God has providentially arranged for you to make in this world. There is a place where your deep gladness and the world's deep hunger meet.

A MODERN-DAY BEZALEL

David is a member of our congregation who is a modern-day Bezalel. When meeting David with his quiet and unassuming manner, you would not guess he is a world-class architect who has designed stadiums and convention centers around the globe. As a follower of Jesus, David has, like most of us, wrestled with connecting his Sunday faith with his Monday work. At soul level David has sought to find his place of God-honoring vocational, contribution to the world. He has thought deeply about work and its important implications for a life of Christian faithfulness, human flourishing, and the common good.

As David tells the story, it was the example of Bezalel that proved transformative in his spiritual journey and gave him the green light to pursue his vocational calling as an architect. David wrote these words in an e-mail to me: "Exodus 31 has been so important to me in understanding the work that I do as God given and Spirit filled. This is such a huge insight that I feel the church has overlooked for years when it has had on its institutional blinders—blinders that only 'church work' can be Spirit led or Spirit filled." For David, living a Spirit-filled life is deeply embedded in a robust theology of vocation where his Christian faith is increasingly becoming a seamless experience that connects Sunday to Monday. As an apprentice of Jesus, David has a clear sense of his vocational calling. His work has become his primary place of discipleship to Jesus. As a result, David exudes a disciplined diligence in the workplace, finding confidence, creativity, and contentment as he relies on a supernatural empowerment to work as an architect.

SPIRIT-FILLED WORK

When we, as followers of Christ, speak of the filling of the Spirit, we often think of fruit of the Spirit—of "love, joy, peace, patience, kindness, goodness, faithfulness, gentleness, [and] self-control" (Gal. 5:22–23). Or perhaps we think of gifts of the Spirit like discernment, teaching, exhortation, or mercy. But in Exodus 31 we observe another and very important dynamic of the filling of the Holy Spirit, one that is all too often missed in our day. An important aspect of the filling of the Holy Spirit is the supernatural empowerment mediated in and through our vocational callings. God's glorious plan of redemption points to Spirit-filled lives accomplishing Spirit-filled work even in seemingly small ways. Singer and songwriter Sara Groves rightly reminds us that "redemption comes in strange places and small spaces."[4] Many of those strange places and small spaces are in your workplace and mine, where the Spirit of God, with little fanfare, accomplishes his sovereign purposes for our lives and our world.

The apostle Paul relied on the empowerment of the Holy Spirit not only while he was penning inspired letters to local churches that would eventually end up in the canonical New Testament, but also while he was making tents for average run-of-the-mill people to find shelter and warmth on a cold first-century night. If our understanding of the filling of the Spirit and walking in the Spirit is not buttressed by a strong and robust doctrine of Christian vocation, we have a very impoverished and reductionistic view of the Spirit-filled life. The filling of the Spirit splashes over all of life—our relationships, our leisure, and our work. To walk in the Spirit as a way of life means we will work in the Spirit.

The Holy Spirit brings the power and presence of the triune God with the believer to work every day. The Holy Spirit works in the worker through his or her vocation and permeates the workplace with the fragrance of Christ (2 Cor. 2:14–15). The central importance of the role of the Holy Spirit in our vocational work laid out here in Exodus 31 and then repeated again in Exodus 35–36 must not be overlooked if we are to understand and indwell a robust theology of vocation.

As New Testament Christians we are exhorted to be filled with the Holy Spirit and to walk in the Spirit (Eph. 5:18, Gal. 5:25). The gifts of the Spirit and the fruit of the Spirit, as well as the guidance and empowerment of the Spirit, find great expression in and through our vocations. Though we are increasingly to grow in our vocational competencies, we must not confuse skill attainment with our true adequacy, which is in Christ alone (2 Cor. 3:5). Theologian Miroslav Volf makes a vital connection between the empowerment of the Holy Spirit and our vocations—this very real Spirit-given competency and capacity. "There is a sense in which all human work is done in the power of the Spirit. . . . When human beings work, they work only because God's Spirit

149

has given them the power and the talents to work."[5] Your vocational calling is not only a gift from God but also equips and supernaturally gifts you for work. If God has providentially called us to make a contribution and has empowered us to do so, how do we discern the vocational field of activity we are to pursue?

DISCOVERING YOUR OCCUPATIONAL CALLING

For several years my wife, Liz, and I worked with an organization whose mission was nurturing college students' spiritual lives. College students are not only fun to hang out with, but they are also overflowing with endless energy and never-ending curiosity. As college students enter their senior year, a kind of urgency sets in. Going on to graduate school or getting a job moves to center stage, and with it comes the challenge of discovering their vocational callings. Times of thoughtful self-reflection around four diagnostic questions proved to be most helpful in a student's vocational discovery. I have also found these four diagnostic questions very helpful for vocational direction at any stage of life. We need to ask ourselves: (1) How has God designed me? (2) What life experiences have shaped me? (3) What circumstances surround me? and (4) What do my wise counselors say?

HOW HAS GOD DESIGNED YOU?

In calling Jeremiah as a prophet, God told him that before he had been formed in his mother's womb, he was known intimately. Before Jeremiah arrived in the world, God had appointed a task for him to do in the world (Jer. 1:5). King David simply marvels at the fact that God had carefully fashioned him in his mother's womb. How amazing that the very days of his life were ordained prior to his birth (Ps. 139:13–16). Though each of us has been deeply affected by sin and its corruption, God's specific work in fashioning us as unique individuals is still apparent in our intellectual capabilities, the contours of personalities, the way we are wired, the things that spark our interests, and our overall human dispositions. Like a glove that is properly shaped to a particular hand, or a shoe that fits a certain-sized foot, our unique design fits best with a vocational calling. Some work that we do fits. Other work that we do simply gives us fits. Wise vocational decisions often reflect very practical realities.

WORK THAT FITS OR GIVES US FITS

I learned early in life that when it comes to working with my hands, I am a klutz. Though I have worked hard at gaining some degree of competency in fixing things around the house, Mr. Fix-It I will never be. Recently, I was painfully reminded of my carpentry shortcomings. Right after we had our wood floors redone, an intense rainstorm battered our house. Unfortunately, a buckling board near our patio door indicated that some water had mischievously snuck in uninvited. A closer inspection of the patio door revealed the culprit. Strategically placed wood rot had created a small channel through which the rainwater had made its unwelcomed entrance into our home, and it called for someone to fix our patio door before the next rainstorm hit. Mustering up the courage, I consulted our local hardware store experts, bought the necessary tools and materials to make the repairs, and started the project. From beginning to end, my work was a comedy of errors, fumbling fingers, and the spewing of words under my breath that pastors are not supposed to say (at least not within earshot of others). Through sheer willpower and bulldog tenacity I eventually completed the project, but it took much longer than it should have. One glance at our patio door tells the trained eye that no real carpenter ever touched that door. Every time it rains we hold our breath, wondering whether my well-intentioned efforts did the job or if a true professional will still need to be called.

There are times when out of economic necessity or the need to simply serve, we do work that doesn't fit us very well. Yet if we are going to pursue paths where we can make our best long-term vocational contribution, we need to grow in self-awareness of what we are good at doing. For most of us, the best course of action is to experiment with different kinds of work and see how we do. Do we seem to enjoy the work? Are we pretty good at doing the work? Do others around us affirm our work? There are also many personality assessment tools available that help us get a better read on how we have been designed.[6]

SPIRITUAL GIFTS

The kind of spiritual gift or gifts we have been given by the Holy Spirit when we come to Christ also play a role in discerning our vocational calling. Oftentimes particular spiritual gifts such as teaching, leadership, administration, or mercy dovetail beautifully and seamlessly in our vocational calling. For example, I have often observed that the vocational calling of a Christian to the work of nursing also has a spiritual gift of mercy. An individual who has been entrusted with the gift of teaching is many times vocationally called to the academy or to some teaching profession. Those with the spiritual gifts of leadership and administration commonly find their vocational calling in business, commerce, and industry. Like your God-given design, your spiritual gifting can be discerned by the affirmation of others. Your local church community is designed to be helpful in ascertaining and employing your spiritual giftedness.

INTERESTS AND MOTIVATIONS

Another consideration in discerning how God has designed us as individuals is to assess what interests and motivates us. One of the ways I like to think of my motivational patterns is to raise the reflective question: *What work would I do even if I wasn't paid for it?* Another way to discover our interests and motivations is to reflect on work we have done when time seemed to really fly by and when our energy and creativity was most unleashed. Carving out some time to jot down on paper what we were doing during those times in our lives when we were most motivated and felt the most fulfilled is a helpful way to identify our primary motivational patterns. In most cases our competencies and intellectual curiosity flow out of what most interests and motivates us. I believe God designed the affections of our hearts not only to be first and foremost directed toward him, but also to be directed toward the work he has called us to do. The kind of work we *like* to do is an indicator of the kind of work we were *created* to do.

To get a better grasp on how God has designed us, it is also helpful to recall those times when the work we have done has emotionally drained us. Of course, all work is in some sense draining, but there is a degree of draining that proves detrimental both to the person and to the workplace. A person whom God has wired with a strongly introverted personality will inevitably find a job that demands constant extroversion to be very draining. Those individuals designed to be brilliant in sales are likely to find the job of a research librarian to be anything but appealing. People who are wired to be big-picture thinkers will blow an emotional circuit if they are in a job that demands constant attention to a myriad of administrative details. Gaining an increased awareness and understanding of how God has designed you is helpful in discerning God's vocational trajectory in your life.

WHAT EXPERIENCES HAVE SHAPED YOU?

God not only designs us in a particular way with a particular contribution in mind, he also providentially allows many experiences to shape our lives. Our family of origin, parental dynamics, and birth order influence our human dispositions much more than we often realize. As we grow older and gaze in the mirror, we shockingly discover that we look more and more like our parents. We also increasingly see how much we have become like our parents. Over the years, I have observed that our family of origin often grooms us for our vocational calling.

A friend of mine who has found his vocational calling as a professional baseball player not only grew up with a dad who was a baseball player, but the woman he eventually married also grew up in a baseball family. The vocational calling of a professional athlete may seem glamorous, and clearly there are many perks that come with it, but it is very difficult on family life. Yet my friend and his wife are nourishing a good marriage and raising a beautiful family. Their collective skills in navigating the challenges of the professional baseball world were honed growing up in baseball families. God does not always call us to the same vocation as our parents, but often he uses our family of origin in profound and lasting ways to equip us for our vocational callings.

CULTURAL CONTEXT AND LIFE EXPERIENCE

The broader cultural context we grew up in also greatly affects how we see the world and navigate life. Stan is a friend of mine who grew up in urban Kansas City. After working for a decade in corporate America, he now pastors a vibrant inner-city church. Growing up in "the hood," as Stan likes to refer to his neighborhood, has given him a deep rootedness. Being groomed in a largely majority culture of a Fortune 500 telecommunications company has also forged in Stan strong leadership abilities, excellent problem-solving skills, undaunted courage, and a remarkable resilience to adversity. Stan has an amazing emotional intelligence and is at ease moving between the different cultures in our city. When I am with Stan, I often marvel at how God has used his life experiences to so perfectly fit him for his vocational calling as a pastor whose passion for the gospel and community advocacy is not only an inspiration, but is also making a big difference in our world.

It is not just our cultural context that shapes us. The educational experiences we have had, the people we have rubbed shoulders with, the spouse we chose to marry, the single life we chose to live, and the places we have visited are all part of an experiential map of our lives. Both the joyful experiences and the tragic experiences that come into our lives leave an indelible mark on us. As a young boy, the unexpected loss of my dad to an untimely death set my life on a very different trajectory than it would have been had my father lived a more normal life span. When I take the time to evaluate my life experiences map, many of my strengths, weaknesses, joys, and fears find an uncanny connection to this great loss early in my life. The deep valleys we walk through, as well as the exhilarating mountain-top experiences we have, play a key role in God shaping us for a vocational calling.

WHAT CIRCUMSTANCES PRESENTLY SURROUND YOU?

As we discover and pursue our vocational calling, we must also be astutely aware of the circumstances that presently surround us. Under the broad banner of God's providence, and within the permissible will of God, our present circumstances are often signposts in vocational discovery or vocational redirection.

When people come to faith in Jesus Christ, they often somehow feel God wants them to change vocations. Though this is a possibility, particularly when the work they do may have strong immoral implications, in most cases new Christians should remain in the stations of life and the vocations God has already providentially arranged for them. Writing to new believers in Corinth, the apostle Paul makes this very point. "Only let each person lead the life that the Lord has assigned to him, and to which God has called him. This is my rule in all the churches. . . . Each one should remain in the condition in which he was called" (1 Cor. 7:17, 20). While it is often good for people to remain in their vocations, when the prompting of God is clearly leading in a different vocational direction, the implications of that change should not be taken lightly. In seeking vocational direction, relational and economic circumstances should carefully be considered.

RELATIONAL CIRCUMSTANCES

We often find our vocational calling through relational networks that are already part of our lives. Each one of us has a wide range of individuals who we have personally encountered and who also know many other people. We have all had the experience of meeting someone at a party or in a business context in another city who knows someone we know. How many times have we marveled at what a small world it is? God has providentially given you a wide-ranging network of people who, in most cases, are more than willing to interact with you about their work and may even be eager to open doors for you in their extensive vocational network.

In preparing for my vocational calling as a pastor, I faced the challenge of funding an expensive graduate school education. One course of graduate study that I felt would be most helpful to my vocational calling was a class that was actually offered during the summer on location in Israel. I wasn't sure whether I should pursue this educational experience, and I was sure I didn't have the sizable funding needed. As I considered what to do, the thought occurred to me that in Dallas, where I was attending seminary at the time, I knew some business leaders who had affirmed my giftedness and vocational direction to the pastorate. One morning over coffee, I shared with one of these business leaders about the graduate program in Israel that was being offered. He quickly affirmed that I should take the course and offered to assist me in acquiring the necessary funding. The warm relationship that I had been given with this business leader was an important part of the providential circumstances God used to prepare me vocationally.

ECONOMIC CIRCUMSTANCES

In addition to the relationships God uses to direct us, we often find that God uses our economic circumstances to guide us vocationally. Though we can view money as an impediment to our desires and dreams, economic realities are a part of God's providential arrangement for our lives and the times in which we live. Modern global economies go through times of job growth as well as job decline. Sometimes jobs are plentiful, and other times they are difficult to find. Bull markets and bear markets and stagnating markets are all part of the cyclical, modern economic landscape. Inflation can raise its ugly head, and there are times when deflationary pressures emerge. Changing technologies eliminate jobs. New technologies add new jobs that require new skills and new job training.

In addition to the broader economic currents, each one of us faces unique economic realities in our own financial situations. We may have sizable financial resources, or we may be living virtually paycheck to paycheck. We may be saddled with debt from a failed business, medical bills, school loans, or consumer debt, or we may have the financial freedom of being debt-free. The vocational work we do at any particular place and time is often guided by taking close stock of our own financial situation. There are times when both broader economic realities and our own personal financial situation dictate the work we do. We do not need to see these as vocational detours, but rather what God has for us to do in this particular stage of our life journeys.

OPEN AND CLOSED DOORS

As we seek to discover and pursue our vocational calling, we are wise to take into account the circumstantial open and closed doors that we confront. Making decisions based on open and closed doors can be a bit tricky, and prayerful wisdom is needed. Sometimes in our vocational pursuits several doors open at the same time, requiring us to make the wisest choice we can. Other times we encounter a seemingly closed door that is quick to open when we knock on it. Yet I think our tendency is to keep knocking on a closed door rather than taking no for an answer and moving on or being content where God has us vocationally right now.

I am reminded of the young man who was convinced a particular young lady was the one for him. Mustering up the courage, he blurted out to the young lady that God had told him she was to be his wife. A bit stunned and clearly unimpressed with his blunt proposal, she responded that God hadn't communicated this to her, and if he did, she would be the first to tell him. Clearly the young man encountered a closed door, but I wonder if he just kept knocking or took the hint. As we seek God's direction regarding the work we are called to do, a wise course of action is to focus our prayerful attention not on a closed door but on any door that might be opening for us at a particular time.

It has been said that God answers our prayers in one of three ways. Sometimes God says an immediate yes. Other times God gives us an immediate no. And there are times when God's answer to our prayer is simply "not now." Open and closed doors often swing on the hinges of God's providential timing. Again, not all circumstantial closed doors indicate a vocational redirection, but a primary focus should be on the doors of opportunity that seem to be opening to us.[7]

WHO ARE YOUR WISE COUNSELORS?

When we are seeking vocational guidance, it is important to carefully read and prayerfully reflect on the guiding truths of Scripture. It is also important to seek out wise counsel from others who are very knowledgeable in our vocational fields of activity and are known to be mature individuals brimming with understanding and wisdom. The writer of Proverbs tells us, "Where there is no guidance, a people falls, but in an abundance of counselors there is safety" (Prov. 11:14). It is not uncommon for us to seek out wise counsel when it comes to financial or legal matters. We may even seek out professional counsel in dealing with a difficult issue in our lives or our marriages. Yet we often do not seek out wise counsel when it comes to what we do with the majority of our week. I am often asked the question: "How do I know this is the right job for me?" My initial response to this is simply to find out who the person knows who can help in wisely answering this important vocational question. A wise vocational counselor will help a person identify his or her vocational sweet spot.

FINDING YOUR VOCATIONAL SWEET SPOT

A tennis player knows that there is a particular place on the racquet that is the sweet spot. Unlike the other areas on the racquet, the sweet spot offers the maximum recoil, allowing for the most power to be unleashed on the ball. A wise tennis player lives in the sweet spot. In a similar way, a wise person works in the sweet spot. Your vocational sweet spot is that place where your creativity is most unleashed, your passions are most engaged, and your work makes the greatest contribution to advancing the mission of the organization or business you serve. Identifying your vocational sweet spot is an ongoing process, requiring growing self-awareness through a good conscience and the coaching of wise counselors in your life. Like on a tennis racquet, you learn to feel your work sweet spot before you observe its influential effect.

Keep in mind that under the umbrella of God's perfect providence your vocational sweet spot may or may not be connected directly to your economic engine. When your work sweet spot adequately provides for your economic needs, that is an ideal situation. Many of us do not have this ideal situation for a multitude of reasons, but that does not mean we cannot press into our vocational sweet spot in a significant way. With discipline and grace we can work in our sweet spot, but we will most likely need to do other work as well to pay the bills. The entrepreneurial tug often occurs when a person is in this situation. I have observed many entrepreneurial adventures that have been birthed following the discovery of someone's vocational sweet spot.

The movie *August Rush* tells the fictional story of a young boy with an extraordinary musical talent. Early on in his life, August Rush hears the music of his vocational calling and pursues the music with great courage and commitment. On the cinematic screen, *August Rush* not only tells a cute story with a feel-good ending, it also speaks to both the heart and the mind and tells of the mysterious reality that each of us is created and gifted to make a contribution in the world. A large part of that contribution is the vocation to which we are called. If you listen carefully, you, too, can hear the music of the One who calls you to do a good work.

A Prayer for Vocational Guidance

Heavenly Father, I thank you for uniquely creating me and gifting me. Holy Spirit, guide and empower me in my vocational pursuits. Grant that I might have contentment to be fully present in the workplace you have called me to be in at this time. Lead me with your wisdom, and give me the courage to make the necessary changes that I might more fully embrace my vocational calling. In Jesus's name I pray. Amen.

Questions for Reflection and Discussion:

- How has God designed and gifted you?
- What do your life experiences tell about you?
- How has God arranged your present circumstances?
- Who are the wise counselors who are speaking into your life?

GAYLN > PHYSICIAN

Like most college freshmen clueless about a major, I opted to take classes in my areas of strengths: math and science. Surrounded by premed students, I began to consider medicine as a career as it integrated the hard and soft sciences that I loved. After encouragement from mentors and family, I entered medical school.

Medicine brought many challenges, spiritually, academically, and physically. Spiritually, I was blessed with several committed believers who had chosen medicine as a means of opening the door to closed mission fields. My love for science, and now medicine, caused me to question my decision to practice medicine rather than follow my friends overseas. Academically, I struggled with the first two years of "book learning," but I sensed a real giftedness as I began applying medicine in the clinical setting with patients. Physically, one-hundred–hour work weeks resulted in lack of church involvement and Christian fellowship. Had God really meant for me to be a doctor? I simply wanted what God wanted for me. After much prayer and reflection, I finally concluded that God delighted in me delighting in being a doctor!

It became apparent to me very early on that relationships with patients develop very quickly due to the patient's need for my competence, confidentiality, and compassion. The best thing I could offer my patients was excellence in my profession, but beyond that, I was called to serve them. The prayer I offered over my class at graduation was that we would be instruments to serve our patients and be advocates for life, not just professionals in sterile white coats. In reality, this meant walking our sick patients to and from the restroom, getting them a drink, or tying their shoelaces in clinic if they could not bend over. Caring for them meant listening well, which was often more important than a prescription. Spiritual struggles came as I learned that God controlled the eternal destiny of my patients and did not place that sole burden on me to share the gospel with every dying patient. The role of servant and advocate came so naturally for me that it reinforced the conviction of my calling.

I found myself finished with medical training before I was able to experience what I believe is my second calling—being a wife and a mother of three children. I have an even deeper conviction about my family calling than I do medicine. Over the years, wise women in medicine have encouraged me to train in areas that I love and then tailor my lifestyle to meet the needs of my family. God has honored me with a very supportive husband and provided me with part-time positions throughout my career in order to nurture my family. What an honor to serve him in such a great capacity. My two greatest joys in life have been helping my patients and holding my own children in the middle of the night. When I'm doing these two things, the satisfaction is indescribable—honestly!

9

FACING CHALLENGES IN OUR WORK

*All at once a secret, smoldering fire is kindled. The
flesh burns and is in flames. It makes no difference
whether it is a sexual desire or ambition or vanity or
desire for revenge or love of fame and power or greed for
money. . . . At this moment God is quite unreal to us.*[1]
DIETRICH BONHOEFFER

Prominent investment manager Bernie Madoff had a big
secret. When the financial meltdown of 2008 occurred,
Bernie's big lie simply couldn't be hidden any more. With
$7 billion of investors' redemption requests quickly flooding Ascot
Partners, Bernie Madoff's massive Ponzi scheme came crashing
down. No one seemed to suspect any wrongdoing of one of New
York's most well-known and highly esteemed citizens. Bernie, as
he was called by many, had become a Wall Street icon, and his
philanthropic work was well known around the globe. Any questions of concern regarding the consistent high rate of returns that

might have been normally raised by investors and those entrusted with financial oversight were quickly dismissed. Bernie Madoff had convinced many that he had the magic investment touch. His common persuasive angle was to pitch to the investment community his secret "black box" model that timed the market, signaling when to buy and when to sell. It was just too good to be true, and all of it eventually proved to be one big lie.

On December 11, 2008, seventy-year-old Bernie Madoff found himself handcuffed and arrested for securities fraud. On March 12, 2009, Madoff pled guilty to eleven federal offenses including securities fraud, wire fraud, mail fraud, money laundering, making false statements, perjury, theft from an employee benefit plan, and making false filings with the Securities and Exchange Commission. The amount missing from client accounts used to support Bernie Madoff's lavish lifestyle and philanthropic causes was discovered by investigators to be almost $65 billion. Thousands of individual and institutional investors lost millions of dollars. Many of Madoff's victims lost their entire life savings.

After his arrest and conviction, Bernie Madoff sputtered out an apology to his victims, saying, "I have left a legacy of shame, as some of my victims have pointed out, to my family and my grandchildren. This is something I will live in for the rest of my life. I'm sorry." Madoff then added this pitiful postscript, "I know that doesn't help you."[2] When the scandalous dust finally settled, Bernie Madoff's giant scam would prove to be the greatest act of investment fraud in American history.

The tragic story of Bernie Madoff is a vivid and sobering reminder of the evil that lurks within the human heart. We may not bilk billions from people, but we all have a penchant for deceiving ourselves as well as others. We are only one step away from personal and ethical compromises that can lead to personal disgrace and unleash a torrent of devastation on others. The Bernie Madoff story speaks to how our work and the workplaces we indwell can be used not only to foster the common good but also to wreak havoc on others. Our work is not only where life often makes up its mind, it is also where the daily decisions we make have lasting consequences to ourselves, to others, and to our world. If we are going to connect our Sunday faith with our Monday work, then we will need to recognize and prepare for the formidable challenges that the workplace brings. One of the greatest challenges we face every day in our workplaces is living a life of personal integrity.

MAINTAINING PERSONAL INTEGRITY

It has been said that personal integrity is what we do when no one is looking. While there is a great deal of truth to this definition, the biblical idea of personal integrity is not merely one of ethical conformity to a moral code, but rather a life of internal coherence and wholeness. The integral life is made possible in and through the power of the gospel and increasingly reflects God's design for human flourishing in a seamless experience of work and worship. Personal integrity is observed in a person of good conscience where belief and behavior are growing in consistency. Maintaining this consistency in the workplace can be a formidable challenge, and in many cases wisdom and courage are needed.

DARE TO BE A DANIEL

One biblical character in whom we see this integral life play out at work is Daniel. Along with other promising Jewish young men, Daniel was taken from his home city of Jerusalem to the foreign city of Babylon. It was King Nebuchadnezzar's plan to train the Jewish nation's brightest and best to work in his opulent palace. A three–year, fast-track work training program was put in place for Daniel, including the best educational tutors and a training table fit for the king. After this training course, Daniel's hiring would come down to a personal interview with King Nebuchadnezzar.

For such a young man, Daniel's career opportunity was truly extraordinary, yet almost immediately he faced a big workplace challenge that tested his personal integrity. While many would view a training table with every imaginable food and wine a coveted palace perk, Daniel's kosher conscience saw it as a violation of his personal integrity. In Daniel 1 we read, "But Daniel resolved that he would not defile himself with the king's food, or with the wine that he drank. Therefore he asked the chief of the eunuchs to allow him not to defile himself" (v. 8). The courage Daniel exhibited in the workplace is truly remarkable and sets off a chain reaction of high-stakes drama. Daniel's boss looks on Daniel with favor but finds himself in a very tight spot. If he grants Daniel special circumstances, it will potentially affect the morale of the rest of his trainees, and worst of all, if any of his trainees show a lack of vibrant health and physical well-being, it will reflect negatively on his own supervisory responsibilities. Daniel's boss minces no words with his work trainee: withholding the king's food might very well mean not just the loss of his job but the loss of his head.

Recognizing the difficult situation they are both in, Daniel does not intractably dig in his ethical heels. Rather, he wisely proposes a possible win-win solution. Daniel proposes a ten–day dietary test for himself and his three friends. This will allow Daniel to maintain his personal integrity as well as address his boss's legitimate and heartfelt concern. Daniel says, "Test your servants for ten days; let us be given vegetables to eat and water to drink. Then let our appearance and the appearance of the youths who eat the king's food be observed by you, and deal with your servants according to what you see" (Dan. 1:12–13). Amazingly, Daniel's boss agrees to the test.

At the end of the ten days, Daniel and his friends display greater physical health and vitality than those who had been indulging in the king's diet. Daniel and his friends are then given the green light to continue their kosher diet, allowing their personal integrity to remain intact. At the end of the three-year training program, Daniel and his friends are at the top of their class. With flying colors they pass the final interview with

Nebuchadnezzar and are entrusted with jobs of great importance and influence. Daniel 1 ends with these words, "And Daniel was there until the first year of King Cyrus" (v. 21) The biblical writer does not want us to miss that for over sixty years Daniel had a distinguished government career where he served his God and his king with impeccable personal integrity. We are told later on in the book of Daniel that when Daniel is unfairly targeted by his jealous peers, they cannot find any political or moral dirt on him at all. Daniel is morally and ethically untarnished (Dan. 6:3–5).

In contrast to the scandalous headlines we all too often read in our time, the remarkable story of Daniel serves as a true inspiration for maintaining our personal integrity in the workplace. God's gracious favor clearly rested on Daniel's life. Yet we must not miss that Daniel's distinguished government career and his faithful service before several kings pivoted on a courageous decision he made early on in his career. As a young man, Daniel made a commitment to maintain his personal integrity in the workplace. Daniel "resolved that he would not defile himself."

Your personal integrity is the most important asset you bring to your workplace. If your personal integrity is compromised at work, your life is inevitably comprised. The pressure to compromise our core beliefs and ethical values as Christians is a regular temptation in many workplaces today. You may be told to look away and pretend that nothing ever happened. You may be asked to fudge a bid or a sales number. You may feel pressure to ignore a worker's immigration papers, to sleep with your boss, to put a good spin on a financial statement, to spy on a competitor, or to overlook a shoddy product. You may be handsomely rewarded for doing so, and you may be severely punished for not complying, but you must make up your mind ahead of time what workplace boundaries you simply cannot cross as a disciple of Jesus, making a commitment to do what is right no matter the cost or the consequences.

Maintaining personal integrity in the workplace requires ongoing vigilance at the heart level. Like an iceberg, which may seem small floating on the water but is truly measured by what is below the waterline, the true weight of personal integrity is much more about what is really below the surface of our lives. It is defined by the unseen places in our lives where our true motives lurk and our ethical decisions are made. The writer of Proverbs looks below the waterline and wisely calls us to diligent self-reflection in those unseen places of the soul: "Keep your heart with all vigilance, for from it flow the springs of life" (Prov. 4:23). Watching over our hearts in the workplace will require a growing self-awareness of what is below the waterline of our lives and an increased sensitivity to the ever-present danger of cutting corners and making small ethical compromises.

SMALL COMPROMISES

It wasn't long after Liz and I purchased our first house that a sump pump adjacent to our finished basement had the presence of mind to refuse to work. After an evening of heavy rain, I walked down the stairs to our basement, only to be greeted by a soaked carpet. Feeling a sense of panic coming over me, I called a trusted friend who was a veteran homeowner and all-around handyman. He told me that I needed to rent a shop vacuum, suck up as much water as possible, then pull up the carpet and allow it to dry with the circulating air of strategically placed fans. I dutifully followed his directions.

When I pulled the carpet and saw the pad hidden beneath, I was stunned and angry. The carpet pad was an inferior patchwork of builder's-grade remnants, carefully taped together to give the impression of a normal-quality installation. The only thing I could figure out was that the workers who had originally installed the carpet had cut some corners in order to enhance their profits. Figuring the carpet pad was invisible to the naked eye and that the plush carpet would remain for a long time, it must have seemed a safe bet that their carefully crafted deception would go uncovered for a long time.

It is easy to convince ourselves that small deceptions, little white lies, and cutting some corners in our work won't hurt anyone and that no one will find out. Yet even tiny cracks in our character can develop into deeper fissures of moral and ethical compromise. As you think through small cracks that can become big fissures, how are you doing? Are you making small ethical compromises and cutting corners? Do your expense reports accurately portray your actual expenses? Are you using office supplies for personal use? Are you calling in sick when you are not sick? Are you stealing time from your employer by using company time for personal projects? Large ethical fissures often begin as small cracks of compromise. Doing what is right matters a great deal, even if it is in what seems to be the smallest of matters.

WORK OVERLOAD AND BURNOUT

A very real challenge to our personal integrity and personal well-being is work overload and burnout. Cost-cutting measures and staff reductions often contribute to a greater workload for those who are still employed. Greater work efficiencies have been realized through the use of technology, yet a smaller workforce is confronted with doing more work. The work pile continues to grow, and there is too little time in the day to get everything done. Our initial response to a greater workload is simply to work longer hours, which can have detrimental effects on our physical and emotional health as well as on our family. We have all been given a finite amount of time and energy, and we must seek to be wise stewards of this gift from God. If we are not careful, our work can become a black hole that eventually sucks the life out of us and hinders our relationship with God and others.

A FATHER-IN-LAW'S WISE ADVICE

Moses was a hard worker and an amazing leader used by God to shepherd his covenant people from the bondage of Egypt and take them to the Land of promise. Leading God's covenant people was not only very challenging and exhausting work, but also caused Moses to fall into an unwise work pattern that was unsustainable. Rather than delegating wisely, Moses simply tried to do too much himself. Moses didn't see it, but Jethro, his father-in-law, did. In Exodus 18 we read, "Moses' father-in-law said to him, 'What you are doing is not good. You and the people with you will certainly wear yourselves out, for the thing is too heavy for you. You are not able to do it alone'" (vv. 17–18). To Moses's credit, he listened to his father-in-law, who advised a wiser approach to his workload that included systemic restructuring and wise delegation (Ex. 18:19–27).

ADDRESSING UNHEALTHY WORK PATTERNS

What do we do when we find ourselves in an unsustainable work pattern and on the road to burnout? Like Moses, we need to be open to wise counsel from others and take the time to do some important personal assessment. God created you to flourish in a rhythm of work and rest modeled by God with six days of work and one day of rest. The Sabbath day was not a mere afterthought of creation; it was the capstone of the week of creation. If your work is crowding out a weekly Sabbath rest, it is time for you to make changes. This may mean reducing your economic lifestyle requirements and embracing a greater simplicity of life, or it might require changing jobs or reducing your current workload.

Recently I saw a bumper sticker that spoke to the freedom of a simpler lifestyle. It read, "Debt is normal, be weird." The ongoing daily pressure of being financially overextended by a consumptive lifestyle is a recipe for a host of stress-related physical maladies and has a detrimental effect on our spiritual formation as well as our interpersonal relationships. The chronic fatigue and irritability that an overextended lifestyle and work overload often bring lessens workplace morale and creativity and leads us to make poor decisions that contribute to the poor choices that undermine our personal integrity. Fatigue not only makes cowards of us all, it makes us more vulnerable to a host of temptations that confront us in the workplace. When I get into work overload mode, I am spurred on to make changes by a wise proverb: "A bow that is always bent will break."

If you are in an unsustainable work pattern, it is time to make some wise changes in your life. You didn't get into this mess overnight, and it will probably take you some time to get out of it as well, but if you are caught in an unsustainable rhythm, it is time to ask some important questions to begin moving toward vocational health. Ask yourself the question, "What do I need to concentrate on, and what can I possibly eliminate?" Is there work you are currently doing that someone else can do? In other words, are there some possibilities of wise delegation or job restructuring that will allow you to concentrate your work energies doing fewer things well? Another important consideration is to evaluate whether some work can be done at a later time. This evaluative exercise will force you to greater organization and prioritization of your work. Sometimes our work overload is due to our poor planning and management of our work. An exercise that I have found helpful is to regularly make a to-do list as well as a stop-doing list. Sometimes in my workplace I find myself doing things I really do not need to do—things that are not leveraging my workplace calling and contribution to the mission of the organization I serve. Maintaining your personal integrity and personal well-being in your workplace is a formidable challenge, but with wisdom and Holy Spirit empowerment, you can be a healthy and integral worker.

ANTICIPATING WORKPLACE TEMPTATION

Our work world brings with it the formidable challenge of many personal temptations. We can be tempted to abuse our power, to manipulate others for our own gain, to plagiarize someone else's creative work, to steal from our employer, or to engage in premarital sex or extramarital affairs. Whether we are single or married, the workplace is often where we are most tempted to cross the boundaries God has for us in regard to our sexual purity. The workplace forges healthy friendships, but it also affords many opportunities to pursue more intimate relationships. How are we to address the sexual temptations that often greet us in the workplace?

LOOKING TO JOSEPH

It didn't take long for Potiphar's wife to notice what a fine physical specimen their new household employee was. The problem was that Potiphar's wife not only noticed Joseph's good looks, but also she lustfully wanted Joseph sexually. While Joseph faithfully did his work, Potiphar's wife repeatedly tried to get him to sleep with her. As a young man committed to honoring God, his employer, and his own personal purity, Joseph repeatedly refused this powerful woman's sexual advances. One day, sexual temptation not only knocked on Joseph's door, it barged in. Potiphar's wife had set and baited a temptation trap for Joseph. What happened next is recorded in Genesis 39. "But one day, when he went into the house to do his work and none of the men of the house was there in the house, she caught him by his garment, saying, 'Lie with me.' But he left his garment in her hand and fled and got out of the house" (vv. 11–12).

In his workplace, a young and single Joseph in the prime of his virility and sexual desire faces great sexual temptation. Joseph could have seen this as an opportunity to enjoy the pleasure of sex with a powerful and beautiful woman, as well as a means to greater job security and promotion. Yet Joseph's moral compass guides him in a very different direction. Joseph flees from sexual compromise. Scorned and enraged by Joseph's refusal, Potiphar's wife abuses her power and accuses him of attempted rape. With no witnesses to clear Joseph, Potiphar has no choice but to imprison him. In doing what is right, Joseph honors not only his employer, but also his God. As a result Joseph, suffers the indignity of false accusation and is unjustly thrown into prison.

Joseph's story reminds us that the immediate consequences of God-honoring obedience are not always what we desire, yet the long-term result far exceeds any short-term pain we encounter. When it comes to sexual temptation in the workplace, we don't have to go out of our way to look for it; it often finds us. Joseph's wise response to sexual temptation in the workplace is a model for us to emulate. Joseph didn't cozy up to sexual temptation, he fled from it. If we are not going to fall to sexual temptation, then we will need to understand how temptation works and learn to flee from it as well.

HOW TEMPTATION WORKS

I sat down on an old log crossing a dry streambed. Out of the corner of my eye, I saw a large spider web glistening in the morning sun, sparkling with droplets of dew. It was an extraordinary work of art and a picture of great beauty. The architect of this masterpiece, a large black spider, emerged from the shadows and began to touch up the web. I watched in awe as the spider skillfully wove new strands into the web and then, with a look of what I must assume was great satisfaction, moved back to the shadows, patiently and confidently awaiting its morning victim.

I sat there in stillness and silence, in absolute awe of this spider's stealth and skill. In just a few minutes, a small butterfly came flitting by. Attracted by the glistening sight and the sweet smell of the web, this little creature made a bank turn and came in for a closer look. A bit leery at first, the butterfly kept at a relatively safe distance, but the appeal of the web began to lure the butterfly in for a closer look. Convincing itself that the danger was minimal, the beautiful little butterfly got closer and closer to the web. With great grace and passion, the little butterfly began to do a couple of touch-and-go landings on the very edge of the web. The dance was graceful and aerodynamic, but I wondered if the butterfly realized what it was doing. Did it know it was dancing the dance of death?

I watched as the little butterfly got closer and closer with its touch-and-go landings. Suddenly the tip of her wing touched down and stuck fast to the web. With heroic effort, the little butterfly struggled to extricate herself from the web, only to get more and more immersed in its sticky net. I kept thinking that the spider would soon appear, but it didn't. More and more encumbered in the web, the butterfly's futile struggle began to weaken. Having exhausted all strength and hope, the butterfly lay motionless. Then a movement from the shadows shattered the deathly stillness. The spider slowly made its way to the victim. Death was sudden, swift, and sure. The little butterfly's dance of death was over.

Observing this dance of death, I was reminded of the tragedy of dancing on the edge of sexual temptation's envelope. In many ways we are a lot like that little butterfly. As we journey through life, and particularly in our workplaces, we often encounter temptation's alluring webs. We live and work in a sex-saturated society. Just a mouse click on the Internet avails us of a vast array of pornographic sites. With an unfulfilling marriage and an interested person at work, we can find ourselves dancing on temptation's web of an extramarital affair. As a single person, embers of passion are flamed in a warm and affirming relationship at work, and we find ourselves on temptation's web of premarital sexual involvement.

At the opportune time, presented with the right bait, each one of us is vulnerable and capable of dancing the dance of death on temptation's web. Few things are more important to our spiritual vitality than gaining wisdom about temptation. The New Testament writer James gives us some profound and compelling wisdom into how temptation works. James writes, "Let no one say when he is tempted, 'I am being tempted by God,' for God cannot be tempted with evil, and he himself tempts no one. But each person is tempted when he is lured and enticed by his own desire. Then desire when it has conceived gives birth to sin, and sin when it is fully grown brings forth death" (1:13–15). According to James, when temptation greets us, our minds quickly begin to play games on us. A hungering lust grabs us. We succumb to temptation's invitation and the taste of sin gratifies us. Yet with the exhilaration of gratification there inevitably comes consequences. Sin tightens its death grip on us. This is how James says the slippery slope of temptation works. Dietrich Bonhoeffer makes an insightful observation regarding temptation as well, noting that at the point of temptation God becomes unreal to us.[3] In other words, if we allow temptation to get a foothold, getting to the point of intense desire, the reality of God fades into the background of our consciousness. Once desire has seized our minds, we have an amazing capacity to rationalize sinful behavior and give a green light forward.

FACING SEXUAL TEMPTATION

As a pastor I have repeatedly observed the lasting carnage arising from sexual temptation in the workplace. Extramarital affairs that originate in the workplace indiscriminately send deeply wounding shrapnel in many directions, often leading to personal scars, divorce, and the breakup of a family. Workplace productivity and synergy is also detrimentally impacted, and in some cases employees are terminated or demoted. Sexual harassment lawsuits are increasingly common, often having a negative effect on workplace morale and productivity, and are devastating to the careers of the individuals involved.

When it comes to facing the challenge of sexual temptation, there are several important things to keep at the forefront of our minds. First, know that God has empowered you to resist temptation. Paul writes, "No temptation has overtaken you that is not common to man. God is faithful, and he will not let you be tempted beyond your ability, but with the temptation he will also provide the way of escape, that you may be able to endure it" (1 Cor. 10:13). Second, the way to escape sexual temptation is to flee it. If you nip temptation in the bud decisively and early, you are less likely to succumb to its gravitational pull. Pointing out that our bodies are temples of the Holy Spirit, Paul calls us to flee sexual temptation: "Flee from sexual immorality. Every other sin a person commits is outside the body, but the sexually immoral person sins against his own body" (1 Cor. 6:18). God created sex as a good thing, but he designed it to be enjoyed, cherished, and protected within the context of marriage. Finally, establish wise boundaries within your workplace. The way we speak to one another shapes how we think. As you relate to others in your workplace, avoid using any language that brings with it a sexual connotation. Making sure you have strong pornography filters on your work computer is another way to reduce temptation and create helpful boundaries at work.

FREQUENT FLYER, FREQUENT TEMPTATION

Take extra care if your work involves out-of-town business travel. Frequent flyer means frequent temptation. Max Lucado writes,

I'm away from home. Away from people who know me. Away from family members who love me. Voices that encourage and affirm are distant. But voices that tantalize and entice are near. Although the room is quiet, if I listen, their voices are crystal clear. A placard on my nightstand invites me to a lounge in the lobby, where I can "make new friends in a relaxing atmosphere." An advertisement on top of the television promises me that with the request of a late-night adult movie my "fantasies will come true." In the phone book, several columns of escort services offer "love away from home." An attractive, gold-lettered volume in the drawer of the nightstand beckons: *The Book of Mormon—Another Testament of Jesus Christ*. On television, a talk-show host discusses the day's topic: "How to succeed at sex in the office." Voices. Some for pleasure. Some for power.

176

Facing Challenges in Our Work

Some promise acceptance. Some promise tenderness. But all promise something.[4]

When I travel, I have strict guidelines about working with and being alone with the opposite sex. In hotel rooms, I avoid watching things I shouldn't watch by simply having a personal policy of unplugging the television while I am on the road. I maintain a pattern of discipline in regard to eating and exercise when I travel. Your boundaries may be somewhat different than mine, but it is important to establish workplace boundaries that are designed for your protection from sexual temptation. Temptation is less alluring when you are nurturing your own spiritual life. A soul that is feasting on the goodness of God and intimacy with Christ finds temptation less appealing, regardless of its form and approach. If you are married, cultivate your marriage. Keep in touch with your spouse while you travel. If you have succumbed to sexual temptation, repent of your sin and seek God's forgiveness. Talk to your pastor. Be accountable to others and to your local church community. A winning athletic team has a good offense, a good defense, and a good game plan. Wisely facing the ubiquitous presence of sexual temptation in our sex-saturated society means we need to adopt the same approach.

MAKING THE MOST OF UNEMPLOYMENT

Another formidable challenge we can face in our work is unemployment. Being out of a job may have been precipitated by broader economic circumstances or by our own lack of productivity and workplace fit. We may find ourselves out of work because we resigned, were terminated, or because we received a pink slip from a job reduction decision by our company. However unemployment strikes us, it has an immediate impact on our emotional and financial well-being. Our work is often closely tied to our sense of self-worth, and when our work disappears we can feel a great deal of worthlessness and self-doubt. Fear and worry can rob us of a good night's sleep. We also can find ourselves in an energy-zapping black hole of bitterness and discouragement. We may even blame God for what has happened to us. When we find ourselves unemployed, how do we make the most of it?

MOVING FORWARD

While looking back and assessing what we can learn from our previous job experiences may be helpful, our primary energy should be focused on wisely navigating the road ahead of us. We can have confidence that a sovereign God is in control of our lives and circumstances and that he will guide and provide for us as we walk in faith. Writing to believers in Rome, Paul reminds them of God's steadfast love and gives a bedrock promise to securely anchor their lives when he writes, "And we know that for those who love God all things work together for good" (Rom. 8:28).

Trusting God and his promises, we can take positive steps in moving forward. First, create a working-type schedule for your life. In many cases, securing employment is a full-time job in itself, so structure your day and week accordingly. Manage your new workplace like you would in a full-time job context. Second, get in a disciplined life rhythm that includes good eating practices, physical exercise habits, and spiritual formation activities. Though your finances may be limited, include some fun times and recreation opportunities as well. Also look for opportunities to volunteer and help others. Perhaps give a few hours each week to volunteer at a local Habitat for Humanity project, assist the hungry and the homeless in your city, or serve your local church in some way. Third, don't put off making the practical financial adjustments in your budget that are prudent with your reduction of income. In many cases this will mean a significant reduction in your spending and will provide the opportunity to experience greater simplicity in your lifestyle. Avoid taking on credit card or consumer debt if at all possible. Fourth, find a support group of others who are also looking for a job. Not only will you find encouragement that you are not the only one facing the challenges of unemployment, but also new friendships are often forged and new job search ideas emerge. Finally, get out of the house and meet with as many people as possible who may be able to open a door for you or expand your job-hunting network. Pray hard. Do your homework. Network extensively. Take the initiative. Keep asking, keep knocking, keep seeking, and a door will open.

LOOKING FOR NEW OPPORTUNITIES

As a pastor I interact regularly with many who face unexpected unemployment. Though it is a challenging time in life, I often see that it is also a positive time of spiritual and personal growth. Many times new work ideas and new opportunities never considered before present themselves. A time of unemployment provides a unique time of personal evaluation and career exploration seldom possible while working a full-time job. God often allows one door to be closed in order to guide us to another open door that is a better fit for our vocational calling.

STAYING HOPEFUL

Any extended period of unemployment can be very stressful and challenging. It can easily lead to feelings of discouragement and isolation. What do we do when the embers of hope in our hearts seem to be fading? Memorizing and meditating on God's Word fans the flame of hope in our hearts. As a pastor, I often write out a prescription for those who come to me and are struggling to stay hopeful in the midst of bleak circumstances. On a pad of paper I write a text of Scripture that is to be memorized and meditated on three times a day. My primary prescription for a buoyant hope is Psalm 121. I commend it to you.

179

I lift up my eyes to the hills.
From where does my help come?
My help comes from the LORD,
who made heaven and earth.
He will not let your foot be moved;
he who keeps you will not slumber.
Behold, he who keeps Israel
will neither slumber nor sleep.
The LORD is your keeper;
the LORD is your shade on your right hand.
The sun shall not strike you by day,
nor the moon by night.
The LORD will keep you from all evil;
he will keep your life.
The LORD will keep
your going out and your coming in
from this time forth and forevermore.

LEARNING VOCATIONAL CONTENTMENT

A final challenge we all face at one time or another in our vocations is a gnawing discontentment with our job. Every job brings with it the good, the not-so-good, and at times, the ugly. You may not like your present job at all. You may find the people you work with to be difficult and demanding. With a stack of bills to pay each month, you may feel economically trapped in a dead-end job. Wherever you find yourself in your vocational journey, it is important to cultivate a deep sense of contentment. Scripture tells us that true contentment is not found in the accumulation of financial wealth or a fulfilling career, but in a fulfilling and intimate relationship with Christ. Writing to Timothy, his protégé in the faith, the apostle Paul gives us an important and helpful perspective on true contentment. Paul writes, "Now there is great gain in godliness with contentment, for we brought nothing into the world, and we cannot take anything out of the world. But if we have food and clothing, with these we will be content" (1 Tim. 6:6–8).

180

An important aspect of our spiritual growth and spiritual formation is the cultivation of a contentment that is not tied to our job, life circumstance, or even physical limitations, but to an increasing Christlikeness in our lives. One of the marks of Christian maturity is a growing sense of joyous contentment wherever God has us and in whatever he has called us to do. Paul will tell followers of Christ at Philippi that contentment was not something he woke up and discovered one day but something he learned. With refreshing transparency Paul declares, "Not that I am speaking of being in need, for I have learned in whatever situation I am to be content" (Phil. 4:11). We may never have the job of our dreams or the vocational success we had hoped for, but this does not mean we have somehow missed God's will for our lives or that true contentment is out of our reach. Contentment was learned by Paul and can be learned by us in whatever vocational circumstances we find ourselves.

If you are wrestling with job contentment, there is nothing wrong with praying about and seeking another job that perhaps would be a better vocational fit. However, I believe that our present vocational stewardship ought to be our primary focus of faithfulness. Perhaps God will transplant us to a new workplace, but it is important that we bloom where we are presently planted.

BLOOMING WHERE WE ARE PLANTED

If we are going to be faithfully present in our current workplace, we need to cultivate a spirit of contentment and not of complacency. A growing familiarity with a job can dull us into a passive complacency where we do not bring our A game to work every day. While a soul-suffocating complacency leads to job ruts, a God-honoring contentment unleashes increasing creativity, synergistic teamwork, and overall productivity in our work. When we are fully and faithfully present in our workplaces, we remain teachable and are continually looking to grow as people. One of the things I look for in hiring someone is not only character, competency, and chemistry with our staff and organization, but also curiosity. I know of few areas in our lives where the possibility for unleashing creativity and innovation is greater than in our vocations. You honor God and your fellow workers when you bring your A game to work every day.

The greatest challenge we face with our work is not what happens to us in the workplace but what happens within us at soul level. As the writer of Proverbs reminds us, we must *keep our hearts with all diligence* (24:12). The greatest opportunity our vocation affords us is not the reward it brings or the important contribution we can make to the common good, as significant as these are, but rather the glorious conduit it becomes in conforming us to greater Christlikeness.

For several decades, John Stott has been a tall tree on the landscape of evangelical Christian faith. His well-lived life and the many insightful volumes he has written have spoken loudly to a robust Christian faith of mind and heart. In his latest written work, aptly entitled *The Radical Disciple*, Stott raises this important question: "What is God's purpose for his people?" Stott's answer gets to the heart of the matter: "It is this: God wants his people to become like Christ, for Christlikeness is the will of God for the people of God."[5] Consider your workplace challenges not as obstacles in your life but as opportunities to grow in greater Christlikeness.

A Prayer for Faithfulness

Heavenly Father, I place my life and my work in your loving hands. Protect me from evil and strengthen me with your grace that I may resist the many temptations that confront me daily. Lord Jesus, help me to be fully present in the workplace where you have called me to honor you and to faithfully serve the common good. Holy Spirit, empower me to live a life of integrity, to be a faithful presence in my workplace, and to learn contentment. In and through the vocation you have called me to, conform me to greater Christlikeness of life. In Jesus's name, I pray. Amen.

Questions for Reflection and Discussion:

- Which of the workplace challenges discussed in this chapter do you most resonate with? How are you addressing that challenge and seeking to be faithful in your vocation?

- Who are your wise vocational counselors? How have you allowed them to speak into your work life?

- What steps have you taken to remove temptations in your workplace? What further steps do you need to take?

- Are you content in the place where God has you today? If not, how might you learn contentment?

DAVID > ARCHITECT

As a result of some deep reflection in our congregation about how our faith intersects our work, I was led to consider how better to integrate my faith and my work as an architect. Seeking that integration is the motivation behind the name of my architecture firm, Convergence Design, and it has set me on a quest upon which I expect to spend the rest of my life.

This quest, redeeming architecture, has two components, depending on which word you emphasize. *Redeeming* architecture has set me on a journey to discover how to design buildings that contribute to human flourishing. Although it is intuitively easy to pick out buildings that are cherished components of a community, as a practical matter, design for human flourishing is very difficult. Patterns of American culture over the past sixty years have not been conducive to human flourishing. And architects are called in after most of the decisions about roads, parking, and floor plates have already been made, giving architects little scope in the overall process of creating our cities. And while protecting the public health, safety, and welfare is supposed to be of primary concern to architects, human flourishing is a harder concept to get a handle on, and our profession does little to promote it. Also, because of its close proximity to the world of fine arts, the profession itself inclines *away* from thinking of human flourishing and toward the art world's ethos of alienation and despair.

There are obstacles, yet I find myself constantly asking, how can this building contribute to human flourishing? Do its components (say, doors and windows) have a human scale? Are there even doors and windows? Does it create a sense of shelter or vulnerability? Does it promote healthy behaviors like walking and using stairs instead of the use of cars and elevators? Is there access to nature or are there at least views of nature? These questions may seem obvious, but browsing any architectural magazine will show that they are often not asked.

This quest also means that I am redeeming *architecture.* This is the more ambitious part of my quest as I seek to redeem the architectural profession as a whole. Of course I can never do this alone, but I can be a voice for redemptive thought in a profession where thoughtless conformity is the norm.

I realized that as a frequent speaker at our profession's national convention, I had an ideal platform from which to raise questions of architecture's moral impact. A crucial part of using this platform is employing redemptive language like "human flourishing" without using explicitly Christian terminology that would be unwelcome in a professional setting. I have raised these questions with convention seminars such as "Architecture as Moral Art: Designing as If People Mattered," and "A Matter of Life and Death: Architecture for Human Flourishing." I believe there is value in getting my colleagues to think about such issues even if the answers they ultimately arrive at are different than mine.

10

THE CHURCH AT WORK

*The congregation has to be a place where its members
are trained, supported, and nourished in the exercise
of their parts of the priestly ministry in the world.
The preaching and teaching of the local church has
to be such that it enables members to think out the
problems that face them in their secular work in light
of their Christian faith.*[1]

L<small>ESSLIE</small> N<small>EWBIGIN</small>

Over the years I had gotten quite comfortable with the home our family lived in. It was warm and cozy, but increasingly it began showing signs of wear and tear. The walls had absorbed lots of laughter and witnessed many memories. Every square foot had collected smudges of dirt, revealing scratches and other mysterious residues, all bearing the marks of our English Springer and the busy life of two active teenagers. Whenever my wife, Liz, and I visited friends whose houses were about the same age as ours, we began to notice many of them had recently undergone major remodeling efforts. Particularly striking were the remodeled kitchens with new high-efficiency appliances, shiny light fixtures, sparkling granite countertops, and freshly stained wood floors. Getting a glimpse of what our kitchen could be, we decided to take the remodeling plunge and bring a brand-new look to our home.

After consulting with some of her friends, my wife, Liz, created a carefully thought-out kitchen makeover plan. An amazing thing began to happen to me. Wherever we went, I found myself looking at people's kitchens and seeing things I had never previously observed before. It was like buying a different car and then all of a sudden noticing on the road all those who were driving the same make of car. As I immersed myself in the kitchen remodeling world, I gained some new vocabulary and entered a world of suppliers, materials, and contractors that was new to me. I even looked at kitchen remodeling websites and print magazines, something I never had done before. Our kitchen remodeling project opened a whole new world to me.

With the skill of a very conscientious contractor, our home now has a completely new feel to it. Our first-floor living space seamlessly flows together with purpose, harmony, beauty, and aesthetic warmth. When I walk in the door, the contours of our living space are familiar, yet the environment where I spend so much of my time is now both more functional and inviting. Friends now comment on the beauty and warmth of our home, and we have been encouraged at how our remodeled kitchen enhances hospitality. Comparing the "before" and "after" pictures of our kitchen, I now wish we had not waited so long to do a major makeover. More importantly, I can't imagine ever going back to living in our old kitchen. In the past we got by, but our newly designed kitchen is much more the way it ought to be.

In many ways my experience with our kitchen makeover parallels my own journey with work. For many years I simply got by living with a flawed theology of work. I lived a compartmentalized Christian faith that misguidedly separated secular work and spiritual worship. I not only lived with a sizable Sunday-to-Monday gap, I also perpetuated this faith-and-work gap through my pastoral teaching and local church leadership. At the time, it was the only work "kitchen" I knew. By the grace of God, the study of Scripture, the leading of the Holy Spirit, and the guidance of wise counselors, I have been undergoing a major remodeling project of my own. I have come to a more integral understanding in my thinking about work itself as well as the centrality of vocation in a local church's gospel mission. Gene Veith speaks with welcomed insight regarding the comprehensive and life-transforming effect that a robust theology of vocation brings. Gene writes, "The doctrine of vocation is not just a teaching about the value of work. It comprises a theology of the Christian life."[2]

The doctrine of vocation properly understood weaves together a seamless life of true Christian discipleship in all facets of life. Vocation is the path of daily life where we are called to be a faithful presence in our world. Yet living a seamless faith that connects Sunday faith with Monday work is not easy and will require disciplined intentionality. I still struggle at times, falling into old patterns of compartmentalized thinking and fragmented living. Integrating a robust theology of vocation into my life is a daily challenge, but one well worth the effort. When it comes to my work, I am still very much a work in progress. Still, I find myself living now in a new vocational "kitchen" that is so much better than what I knew before. I simply can't imagine going back to the old "kitchen" I once lived and worked in for so long.

EMBRACING A NEW VOCATIONAL PARADIGM

Perhaps in our conversation on vocation, you, too, realize that you have been living with an inadequate understanding of your work. A cloudy perspective and foggy thinking has led you to live a distorted Christian faith, one that is deeply dissatisfying, often fragmented, compartmentalized, and privatized. Maybe you have been courageously gutting it out and just getting by. With the burden of a pastor's heart, one that longs for you to flourish, let me encourage you that Jesus wants more for you. True life is about more than just getting by. Jesus desires and has made it possible for you to live and work as he designed you. Jesus wants you, as his yoked apprentice, to make your unique contribution to his good world. In and through the gospel, Jesus's abundant, resurrected kingdom life is now available to you. If you are awkwardly straddling a large Sunday-to-Monday gap in your Christian faith, it is time to put your past behind you and embrace some new thinking about your work.

Embracing a more robust theology of vocation is not just about what you do on Monday; it requires changing how you speak, think, and act on Sunday. As an apprentice of Jesus, each one of us has the privilege and responsibility to make the local church more beautiful in its expression and more effective in its mission. Whether you are called to exercise leadership in your local congregation as a layperson or as a pastor, cultivating an integral theology of vocation is at the heart of your church's gospel mission. We must not miss an important biblical truth. A primary work of the church is the church at work. Our work not only forms us spiritually; in and through our work, Christ's gospel mission is advanced in the world.

THE LOCAL CHURCH AT WORK

In many ways the local church at Thessalonica was the apple of the apostle Paul's eye. In no other New Testament letter does Paul exuberantly declare, "For you are our glory and joy" (1 Thess. 2:20). So what was it about this local church that set it apart from others for Paul? I am sure we could garner many plausible answers to this question, but I see two primary motivations bubbling up to the surface. First, the church at Thessalonica was set apart for its flourishing gospel mission. And secondly, the Thessalonian church manifested a vibrant spiritual formation in Christlikeness of life. A closer look at this inspired letter reveals that one of the connecting threads of thought flowing from Paul's inspired pen is a robust understanding and affirmation of Christian vocation. In fact, vocational diligence is one of his main literary themes of this letter. Paul's robust doctrine of vocation inextricably links the church's vibrant spiritual formation with its flourishing gospel mission (1 Thess. 4:11–12; 5:12–15; see also 2 Thess. 3:6–15).

Paul's introductory words to the Thessalonian believers immediately strike a vocational tone. Paul writes, "We give thanks to God always for all of you, constantly mentioning you in our prayers, remembering before our God and Father your work of faith and labor of love and steadfastness of hope in our Lord Jesus Christ" (1 Thess. 1:2–3). An upbeat Paul affirms three Christian virtues of new-creation life: faith, love, and hope. And these virtues are ensconced in the language of work and labor. The rest of the letter tells us that the *work of faith, labor of love,* and *steadfastness of hope* Paul has in mind was not confined to some other world contemplative spirituality, but rather to real-world vocational life.

Paul utilizes these same work words to describe his own hands-on vocational work as a tentmaker. Paul makes this point: "For you remember, brothers, our labor and toil: we worked night and day, that we might not be a burden to any of you, while we proclaimed to you the gospel of God" (1 Thess. 2:9). Paul does not understand his tent-making efforts as an unwelcomed distraction in his apostolic mission. His tent making work was a primary conduit for gospel incarnation and proclamation. Paul enthusiastically points to his own vocational diligence and gives a hearty commendation for the Thessalonian believers' extraordinary, ordinary lives—faithful lives lived out through the work of their hands in the vocations and providential places where God had put them, lives that were used mightily by the Holy Spirit to spread Christ's gospel mission in the world. Paul writes, "For not only has the word of the Lord sounded forth from you in Macedonia and Achaia, but your faith in God has gone forth everywhere, so that we need not say anything" (1 Thess. 1:8).

Through the Thessalonians, the transforming gospel message of faith in Christ had greatly spread. And this came about through their daily work. The Thessalonian believers did not become a monastic community or pull up stakes and head out en masse as Christian missionaries. These first-century believers saw their gospel stewardship through the lens of their vocations and stations in life. Having embraced the gospel, they were honoring Christ in the various vocations and stations of life they were in when they were called. The gospel was spreading like wildfire throughout the increasingly mobile Roman world, which was brimming with economic activity, imposing military presence, and wide-ranging commerce, as these Christians were faithful to their callings to these arenas. In his insightful book *The Rise of Christianity*, historian Rodney Stark raises this question: "How did a tiny and obscure messianic movement from the edge of the Roman Empire dislodge classical paganism and become the dominant faith of Western civilization?" Stark's answer points, in part, to the early church and its normal, day-to-day living in vocational marketplace networks.[3] The early church did not just gather together for fellowship and teaching on the first day of the week, but it was scattered the rest of the week in various vocational workplaces. It was in these workplaces that the gospel dynamically spread.

VOCATION AND OUR GOSPEL MISSION

Sometimes we wrongly buy into the idea that our gospel mission really advances most when we become a pastor or missionary or parachurch worker, or when we recruit others to do the same. But Paul commends gospel proclamation and incarnation in the primary context of Christian vocation and vocational networks. Our gospel mission really advances when we faithfully embrace our vocations, whatever and wherever that may be. If we are called to be a pastor or missionary, that is a high calling and should be applauded. If we are called to be a business leader, a teacher, a homemaker, or an assembly-line worker, that is also a high calling and should be equally applauded. As God's redeemed people, we are called to live ordinary lives in ordinary places as bold and credible witnesses of the transforming power of the gospel.

I believe much of our foggy thinking about work will clear if we begin to see our gospel mission through a vocational lens. As gospel-centered Christian leaders, we have been entrusted with the stewardship of equipping others to live lives of growing Christian maturity and fruitfulness. Our equipping stewardship goes beyond merely assisting others to do church well. We are called to encourage, equip, and assist others in being the church in the world. Lesslie Newbigin brings into sharper focus the depth and breadth of our gospel-centered mission. He writes,

> If the gospel is to challenge the public life of our society, if Christians are to occupy the "high ground" which they vacated in the noon-time of "modernity," it will not be by forming a Christian political party, or by aggressive propaganda campaigns. . . . It will only be by movements that begin with the local congregation in which the reality of the new creation is present, known, and experienced, and from which men and women will go into every sector of public life to claim it for Christ, to unmask the illusions which have remained hidden and to expose all areas of public life to the illumination of the gospel."[4]

God designed the local church to be a transformed people scattered in their various vocational callings throughout the week. One of the highest stewardships for local church leadership is to encourage and equip apprentices of Jesus for their work. Yet this stewardship rarely gets the attention and commitment it requires.

CLOSING THE SUNDAY-TO-MONDAY GAP

Closing the Sunday-to-Monday gap will require more than hopeful thinking. Honest vocational appraisal is needed to begin doing the important work of equipping others for vocational diligence and faithfulness. Change does not come overnight, but with planning and intentionality we can move beyond the Sunday-to-Monday gap and embrace a more integral theology of work. To move forward, a faith community will need to: (1) become more intentional about teaching a robust theology of vocation, (2) begin celebrating the diversity of vocations, (3) equip for vocational faithfulness, and (4) collaborate with other like-minded local churches that also recognize the church at work as a primary conduit for gospel faithfulness.

TEACHING A ROBUST THEOLOGY OF VOCATION

Becoming a faith community that takes work seriously will require a sustained intentionality in teaching the rich truths of Christian vocation. I am hopeful that this book will serve as an appetizer, enticing you to greater biblical and theological exploration. Weaving a stronger vocational thread into the fabric of your local congregation will alter the preaching and teaching ministry of your local church. This requires those who preach and teach to provide the congregation with a rich and regular diet of biblical truth in regard to vocation, and to also increasingly be sensitive to any residual language that reinforces a Sunday-to-Monday gap. Our local church preaching team is vigilant in avoiding dichotomous or reductionistic words and phrases such as "a secular job," "sacred space," "full-time ministry," "frontlines ministry," or "moving from success to significance." Periodically we take a leadership language inventory to see how we are doing in both our oral and written communication. All too often our theology says one thing and our language communicates another. Our teaching team is becoming more intentional about employing illustrations from the workplace, and we are committed to spending time in workplaces and chatting about work with our parishioners. In my interaction with other pastors, I am often shocked how few regularly spend time in the workplaces of their congregation.

Teaching a rich vocational theology not only involves the preaching and teaching ministry of a local church, it also must become a vital part of the spiritual formation pathways in your faith community. In our faith community we have a two–year small group discipleship pathway where we discuss how faith is integral to all areas of our lives, including our vocations. We include lectures, readings, and small-group interaction around vocation, as well as providing a means for networks to be formed around common vocations that provide mutual support and encouragement for our members. A group of stay-at-home moms may emerge. Another group of lawyers, educators, or artists may form. One of the main goals of each small group is ongoing mutual encouragement in vocational faithfulness. Other small groups in our local congregation often include discussions, mutual encouragement, and inter-cessory prayer focused on vocational challenges and aspirations. We have seen some very encouraging and surprising initiatives emerge from these gatherings.

RENEW EATING DISORDER RECOVERY CENTER

For many years Kori had a growing burden for those who suffered with eating disorders. In a small group context in our local church, Kori transparently shared her sense of vocational calling to begin an eating disorder clinic in Kansas City. Having worked with many individuals and families trying to cope with the devastating effects of anorexia and bulimia, Kori longed to make a greater difference in our community. After much prayer and discussion, the small group of which Kori was a part rolled up their sleeves, put together a business plan, and launched Renew. Renew's mission embraces common grace for the common good. As their mission statement says, Renew desires to *inspire and restore wholeness to those with unhealthy eating habits . . . one soul at a time.* Because of Kori's sense of calling and the vocational support she has received from her small group, hundreds of lives are now experiencing greater wholeness. Kori and her staff often have the opportunity to both incarnate and share the gospel in and through their work.[5]

Desiring to encourage more momentum in this area of vocation, our faith community has hosted a church-wide conference devoted to the subject of work, as well as encouraged our congregation to attend other conferences on vocation. Teaching the rich and transforming truths of vocation is a vital part of your local church's equipping mission. Intentionality is required for stories like Kori's to emerge. Renew arose out of a local church community that, with God's help and by God's grace, chose to be intentional about teaching the transforming truths of vocation in its sermon content and small group curriculum.

CELEBRATING THE DIVERSITY OF VOCATIONS

Over the years I have learned that we celebrate what we truly value. Birthdays are like this. When a friend or family member has a birthday, we throw a party, bake a cake, and sing "Happy Birthday" to show that we value that person. A church family also needs to celebrate what it values. Taking a look at what your faith community celebrates provides a helpful observational window into what is deemed most important. As you look at the list, does vocational diversity appear?

Our local church is becoming more intentional about celebrating the broad diversity of vocations within our congregation. In our Sunday morning services, congregational members periodically give short and timely vocational testimonies, either live or via video, regarding their faith at work. At times the video testimonies will be shot on location at their particular workplaces. We are also intentional about who we highlight. We not only spotlight the commissioning of cross-cultural missionaries our church is sending, but also the commissioning of congregational members in their various workplaces. As the school year approaches in late summer, all our educators stand during a worship service. As a congregation we celebrate these individuals who are gifted and called to train up the next generation of leaders. We verbally affirm their vocational calling, and then a prayer of commissioning is offered by one of our pastoral staff or elders. Our worship liturgy also includes vocational language. The lyrics of the worship songs we sing avoid language that is theologically ill informed. We seek out lyrics with language that reinforces a robust theology of vocational faithfulness. The rich truths of vocation often find their way into our calls to worship, pastoral prayers, holy communion, and benedictions. We have found our benedictions to be particularly meaningful and important as we bless and send out our congregation to their primary places of gospel mission in the world.

EQUIPPING FOR VOCATIONAL FAITHFULNESS

In addition to teaching and celebrating vocational faithfulness, we also take seriously the transformational power of workplace mentoring. The apostle Paul modeled the importance of mentoring others not only spiritually but also vocationally. In writing to Timothy, his young protégé in the faith who was a pastor at the church of Ephesus, Paul urges an ongoing mentoring of others. Paul writes, "You then, my child, be strengthened by the grace that is in Christ Jesus, and what you have heard from me in the presence of many witnesses entrust to faithful men who will be able to teach others also" (2 Tim. 2:1–2). While Paul is strongly endorsing a commitment to spiritual multiplication, embedded in his inspired words is another important stewardship: Who will Timothy prepare to pick up the baton of pastoral leadership when he passes from the scene? What is Pastor Timothy's vocational succession plan? Paul follows this exhortation to Timothy by pointing to three different vocations: the soldier, the athlete, and the farmer. Each vocational calling brings with it a certain requirement of discipline and character, and for each vocation to be done well, a great deal of mentoring must take place. You can't be a good soldier, athlete, or farmer on your own. The good soldier is mentored and trained by more seasoned soldiers, the athlete is mentored and trained by a coach, and the hard-working farmer learns how to farm successfully from other wise and skillful farmers.

Whatever your vocational calling, the workplace you inhabit is a place where life-changing mentoring is designed to take place. Workplaces and organizations flourish in a learning environment where a rich leadership culture is nurtured. Vocational faithfulness is not only doing your job well, but it also is learning from others how to grow as a person and how to do your work better. It is also the intentional mentoring of others. Our vocational workplaces are a rich laboratory for personal growth as well as assisting the growth of others. A vital part of a faith community's vocational stewardship is modeling and encouraging workplace mentoring.

COLLABORATING WITH OTHERS

One of the most helpful things we have discovered in raising the flag of vocational faithfulness in our local church is the value of learning from and collaborating with other like-minded faith communities. Mentoring and cross-pollination is transformational, not only on an individual level but also on an organizational level. Our local church has benefited a great deal in learning from Redeemer Presbyterian Church in New York City. Redeemer has been a pioneer in weaving a strong vocational thread into its mission. Redeemer's Center for Faith and Work has been a catalyst for our leaders to think more intentionally about equipping our congregation in vocational mission.[6] We have also benefited a great deal from other local churches who are attempting to be a faithful presence in our world and have become more intentional about equipping followers of Christ in vocational faithfulness.

MAKING A DIFFERENCE IN YOUR FAITH COMMUNITY

If our exploration of the rich truths of vocation have stretched your mind and stirred your heart, let me encourage you to prayerfully consider being a quiet catalyst for change in your faith community. In a spirit of teachable humility, become an example for others to observe what living a more seamless faith looks like. As the Sunday-to-Monday gap increasingly begins to close in your own experience, seek out ways you can influence your local church community to grow in this important area of gospel mission. God designed the local church to be the primary means through which his gospel mission advances in the world. Nothing can replace the local church, for it is Christ's new-creation community. Lesslie Newbigin says it well, "I am suggesting that to live in this way means to inhabit an alternative plausibility structure to the one in which our society lives. A plausibility structure is not just a body of ideas but is necessarily embodied in an actual community. It cannot exist otherwise."[7] I am well aware that the local church at times falls woefully short of God's design and desire. I am also convinced that it must not be abandoned. Rather, it must be generously supported and continually renewed. A vital ingredient in the church's renewal in our late modern world is the recovery of the transforming truths of vocation.

MR. HOLLAND'S OPUS

The movie *Mr. Holland's Opus*, though made many years ago, is a movie that has left an indelible impression on my mind and heart. It tells the story of a high-school music teacher whose longtime dream was to compose and direct world-class music, wearing a long-tail tuxedo under the shining lights of a prestigious concert hall. Like many of us, Mr. Holland's life dream was never to be realized but would be lived out in obscurity. His ordinary vocational life found its place day in and day out teaching students to play and love music. As Mr. Holland is getting ready to retire from his high-school teaching job, a monumental surprise is waiting. Summoned to the high-school auditorium, Mr. Holland is speechless as he encounters a host of his past music students who have come back to their old school to play his composed music and pay tribute to a life lived well. It is in this music hall that Mr. Holland comes to recognize the masterpiece of his life was not a world-class composition; rather, it was his vocational faithfulness evidenced in the myriad of students he had taught to love and play music. Mr. Holland's true life legacy was the extraordinary way he lived his ordinary vocational life. His *magnum opus* was the many people who he touched so deeply.

The *magnum opus* of most of our lives will not be seen under the bright lights of visibility, but will be the extraordinary impact of our ordinary day-to-day life, faithfully lived in extraordinary ways. It is in and through our vocations that the love of Christ shines bright, and the gospel is winsomely lived out and persuasively proclaimed, and where God desires our good work to be well done. It is where our Sunday faith and our Monday work meet.

A Closing Prayer

So, friends, take a firm stand, feet on the ground and head high. Keep a tight grip on what you were taught. . . . May Jesus himself and God our Father, who reached out in love and surprised you with gifts of unending help and confidence, put a fresh heart in you, invigorate your work, enliven your speech. (2 Thess. 2:15–17, MESSAGE)

Questions for Reflection and Discussion:

- What does your local faith community celebrate? Do you celebrate vocation?

- How might you begin to incorporate vocational faithfulness into your community celebrations?

- Who encourages you in vocational faithfulness? Whom might you encourage?

- What are some ways you might begin equipping others for greater vocational faithfulness?

KORI > COUNSELOR

After years of struggle with an eating disorder, depression, and a complete loss of who I was and why I was here, my life shifted at age eighteen when I received Christ as my Lord and Savior. I dove into learning all about this new life with Christ, and after grad school I set off to become a licensed professional counselor helping those who suffer from mental illness. I thought what mattered most at work was bringing clients to Christ. I did not have categories to recognize that journeying alongside someone, helping them heal, is a way to be the church and to share the gospel, showing the love of our Father to them. I simply did not think that was enough.

Through teaching and studying at my local church, I learned how to see a client, a mental illness, or food through the lens of creation, fall, redemption, and new creation. My eyes became open to new ways of seeing my work as impacting culture more broadly through my vocation.

Because of the journey I have taken in my life, I've always felt zeal when working with ones struggling with an eating disorder. I took a big risk and shared my personal story with my local church and the dream of someday having a counseling center in Kansas City that would provide wholeness for ones who suffer from an eating disorder. Words cannot express the response I received from the church. It was beyond what I ever asked, thought, or imagined (Eph. 3:20). Multiple people volunteered their time, their talents, and their treasure to make this dream a reality. A lawyer drew up the corporation papers, a banker worked on the financial aspects, and one of my pastors worked on marketing and developing this counseling center with excellence. A restaurant owner allowed his workers to build our offices in the location we were going to rent and gave us furniture to start out. Others painted, cleaned, and decorated the offices. Countless people gave generously in multiple forms to make this happen. A group met monthly with me to walk and pray through each step of the process of forming a business that would be God-honoring and a place that someone of any faith would feel safe to walk through the doors and have the opportunity to encounter healing and wholeness of soul. God is the healer of their souls, and whether that individual knows it is God who heals and who sets captives free, I can do my part to offer that healing and wholeness and ask God to show himself to them as they continue their life journeys.

Nine months after sharing my story, Renew opened its doors with four therapists and a dietitian ready to come alongside clients, make a positive impact on culture, and do our part in helping individuals heal. Five years later, we have twelve therapists and a dietitian and have seen over one thousand individuals. I am so grateful to be a part of a local church that dreams, dives into the work God is doing in others, and desires to work together for the bigger story. To God be the glory; great things he has done.

NOTES

Introduction: Connecting Sunday to Monday

1. David Miller, *God at Work: The History and Promise of the Faith and Work Movement* (New York: Oxford University Press, 2006), 9.

2. Os Guinness, *The Call* (Nashville, TN: Thomas Nelson, 2003), 31.

Chapter 1: Created to Work

1. Quoted in William C. Placher, ed., *Callings: Twenty Centuries of Christian Wisdom on Vocation* (Grand Rapids, MI: Eerdmans, 2005), 426.

2. Quoted in Mark R. Schwehn and Dorothy C. Bass, eds., *Leading Lives That Matter* (Grand Rapids, MI: Eerdmans, 2006), 237.

3. Quoted in Gideon Strauss, "Making It New: Andy Crouch Proposes a Different Way for Christians to Engage Culture" *Books & Culture*, September–October 2008.

4. Guinness, *The Call*, 70.

5. Dorothy Sayers, "Why Work?" in Mark R. Schwehn and Dorothy C. Bass, eds., *Leading Lives That Matter: What We Should Do and Who We Should Be* (Grand Rapids, MI: Eerdmans, 2006), 195.

6. Ibid.

Chapter 2: Is Work a Four-Letter Word?

1. Miroslav Volf, *Work in the Spirit: Toward a Theology of Work* (Eugene, OR: Wipf and Stock, 2001), 167.

2. C. S. Lewis, *The Lion, The Witch, and The Wardrobe* (New York: HarperCollins, 1950, 1978), 23.

3. Mick Jagger and Keith Richards, "(I Can't Get No) Satisfaction," *Out of Our Heads*, (RCA Records, 1965, 33 1/3 rpm.).

4. Jim Collins, *Good to Great: Why Some Companies Make the Leap . . . and Others Don't* (New York: HarperCollins, 2001), 85.

5. Henry Thornton, *Devotional Prayers*, ed. James S. Bell Jr., (Chicago, IL: Moody, 1993), 19, 79.

Chapter 3: The Good News of Work

1. Dorothy Sayers, "Vocation in Work," in *Callings: Twenty Centuries of Christian Wisdom on Vocation*, ed. William C. Placher (Grand Rapids, MI: Eerdmans, 2005), 406.

2. Don Carson, *Scandalous: The Cross and Resurrection of Jesus* (Wheaton, IL: Crossway, 2010), 70.

3. Gustaf Wingren, *Luther on Vocation* (Eugene, OR: Wipf and Stock, 2004), 76.

4. Tim Keller, *The Prodigal God* (New York: Dutton, 2008), 34.

5. James Hunter, *To Change the World: The Irony, Tragedy, and Possibility of Christianity in the Late Modern World* (New York: Oxford University Press, 2010), 247.

Chapter 4: Work Now and Later

1. N. T. Wright, *Surprised by Hope: Rethinking Heaven, the Resurrection, and the Mission of the Church* (New York: HarperOne, 2008), 259.

2. N. T. Wright, *Surprised by Hope*, 122.

3. Maltbie Babcock, "This Is My Father's World," 1901.

4. C. S. Lewis, *Miracles* (New York: HarperOne, Reprint 2001), 244, 253.

5. Paul Marshall, *Heaven Is Not My Home* (Nashville, TN: Thomas Nelson, 1999), 11.

6. Keller, *The Prodigal God*, 103.

7. John Newton, "Amazing Grace," 1779.

8. Rudyard Kipling, quoted in Guinness, *The Call*, 192.

Chapter 5: Extraordinary Ordinary Work

1. Quoted in Miller, *God at Work*, 19.

2. Miller, *God at Work*, 10.

3. Stephen Ambrose, *Nothing Like It in the World: The Men Who Built the Transcontinental Railroad* (New York: Simon & Schuster, 2001).

4. Dallas Willard, *The Divine Conspiracy* (New York: HarperCollins, 1998), 14.

Chapter 6: The Transforming Power of Work

1. James Hunter, *To Change the World: The Irony, Tragedy, and Possibility of Christianity in the Late Modern World* (New York: Oxford University Press, 2010), 254.

2. Matthew Crawford, *Shop Class as Soulcraft* (London: Penguin, 2010), 126.

3. Volf, *Work in the Spirit*, 98.

4. Gustaf Wingreen, *Luther on Vocation* (Eugene, OR: Wipf and Stock, 2004), 33.

5. Nicholas Carr, "The Web Shatters Focus, Rewires Brain" *WIRED*, May 2010.

6. For a more exhaustive treatment of the present cultural ethos we find ourselves in and the challenges that come with it, see Hunter, *To Change the World*.

7. Bill Hull, *Christlike: The Pursuit of Uncomplicated Obedience* (Colorado Springs, CO: NavPress, 2010), 104.

8. David Allan Coe, "Take This Job and Shove It," *Family Album*, (Columbia, 1978, 33 1/3 rpm.). Johnny Paycheck famously covered the song on his album *Take This Job and Shove It* (Epic, 1977, 33 1/3 rpm.).

9. Bill Heatley, *The Gift of Work* (Colorado Springs, CO: NavPress 2008), 142.

Chapter 7: Work and the Common Good

1. Quoted in Heatley, *The Gift of Work*, 100.

2. Quoted in Marshall, *Heaven Is Not My Home*, 85.

3. Volf, *Work in the Spirit* , 149.

4. Common grace is a vast topic with many facets. The doctrine of common grace was articulated by nineteenth-century Dutch theologian and prime minister, Abraham Kuyper, who emphasized the importance of common grace in a well-ordered society. Kuyper noted that "the fruits of common grace were evidenced in a society's civic virtue, public conscience, integrity, and mutual loyalty." (Quoted in Richard Mouw, "The Postmodern Maze," *Christian History & Biography* [April 2007], 38.) Corwin Smidt, a contemporary theologian, maintains "the common grace of God is experienced in the ordering of nature, the restraint of evil and the ability of unbelievers to reason and perform acts of civil good. The doctrine of common grace holds that God bestows on humanity a grace that, while not 'saving,'

enables unbelievers to develop many virtues and express many truths." (Corwin Smidt, "The Principled Pluralist Perspective," in P. C. Kemeny, ed., *Church, State and Public Justice: Five Views* [Downers Grove, IL: InterVarsity, 2007], 132). J. Budziszewski, professor of philosophy and government at the University of Texas at Austin, writes about common grace: "The purpose of common grace is to chide, to preserve, and to lead us to the greater grace that saves; its interior witness is conscience, and its requirements are the natural law, which is confirmed and illuminated by Scripture." (J. Budziszewski, *Evangelicals in the Public Square* [Grand Rapids, MI: Baker, 2006], 35.) These and others have written more extensively on common grace than space allows me to do. I commend their thinking to you.

5. Steven Garber, "The Story of a Story: The Vision and Vocation of Dave Kiersznowski," *Comment*, forthcoming.

6. John Piper, *Don't Waste Your Life* (Wheaton, IL: Crossway, 2003), 135.

7. C. S. Lewis, *The Weight of Glory* (New York: Harper One, Reprint 2001), 15.

8. Wendy Kopp, Address given May 17, 2008, *http://explore.georgetown.edu/news/?ID=34121*

9. William Blake, "The Divine Image" in *Songs of Innocence,* (Oxford: Oxford University Press, Reprint 1977).

10. Quoted in William C. Placher, ed., *Callings: Twenty Centuries of Christian Wisdom on Vocation* (Grand Rapids, MI: Eerdmans, 2005), 3.

Chapter 8: Gifted for Work

1. Quoted in Placher, *Callings*, 3.

2. Quoted in Schwehn and Bass, *Leading Lives That Matter*, 109.

3. Frederick Buechner, *Wishful Thinking: A Theological ABC* (New York: Harper and Row, 1973), 95.

4. Sara Groves and Matt Bronleewe, "Add to the Beauty," *Add to the Beauty,* (Sony BMG, 2005, compact disc.).

5. Miroslav Volf, *Work in the Spirit*, pg. 121

6. Some popular tools that I have found helpful include the Myers-Briggs Type Indicator and the DISC Personality Profile Test.

7. For more reflection on God's specific guidance, I commend Gary Friesen's *Decision Making and the Will of God* (Portland, OR: Multnomah, 2004) and Dallas Willard's *Hearing God* (Downers Grove, IL: InterVarsity, 1999).

Chapter 9: Facing Challenges in Our Work

1. Dietrich Bonhoeffer, *Temptation* (London: SCM Press), 33–34.

2. Thomas Zambito, Jose Martinez, and Corky Siemaszko, "Bye, Bye Bernie: Ponzi King Madoff Sentenced to 150 Years," *New York Daily News*, June 12, 2009, http://articles.nydailynews.com/2009-06-29/news/17924560_1_ruth_madoff-ira-sorkin-bernie-madoff.

3. Dietrich Bonhoeffer, *Temptation*.

4. Max Lucado, *In the Eye of the Storm* (Nashville, TN: Thomas Nelson, 2001), 88–89.

5. John Stott, *The Radical Disciple* (Downers Grove, IL: InterVarsity, 2010), 29.

Chapter 10: The Church at Work

1. Lesslie Newbigin, *The Gospel in a Pluralist Society* (Grand Rapids, MI: Eerdmans, 1989), 230.

2. Gene Veith, *God at Work: Your Christian Vocation in All of Life* (Wheaton, IL: Crossway, 2002), 133.

3. Rodney Stark, *The Rise of Christianity: How the Obscure, Marginal, Jesus Movement Became the Dominant Religious Force in the Western World in a Few Centuries* (San Francisco: HarperSanFrancisco, 1997), 3, 203.

4. Newbigin, *The Gospel in a Pluralist Society*, 232–33.

5. For more information about the work Kori does at Renew, visit their website at http://www.renewkc.com.

6. More on Redeemer's work can be found at http://www.faithandwork.org.

7. Newbigin, *The Gospel in a Pluralist Society*, 99.

SELECTED BIBLIOGRAPHY

Ambrose, Stephen. *Nothing Like It in the World: The Men Who Built the Transcontinental Railroad*. New York: Simon & Schuster, 2000.

Bonhoeffer, Dietrich. *Temptation*. London: SCM, 1955.

Budziszewski, J. *Evangelicals in the Public Square: Four Formative Voices on Political Thought and Action*. Grand Rapids, MI: Baker, 2006.

Buechner, Frederick. *Wishful Thinking: A Theological ABC*. New York: Harper & Row, 1973.

Carr, Nicholas. "The Web Shatters Focus, Rewires Brain." *WIRED*, May 2010.

Carson, Don. *Scandalous: The Cross and Resurrection of Jesus*. Wheaton, IL: Crossway, 2010.

Collins, Jim. *Good to Great: Why Some Companies Make the Leap and Others Don't*. New York: Harper Collins, 2001.

Crawford, Matthew. *Shop Class as Soulcraft: An Inquiry into the Value of Work*. Reprint, London: Penguin, 2010.

Friesen, Gary. *Decision Making and the Will of God*. Portland, OR: Multnomah, 2004.

Garber, Steven. "The Story of a Story: The Vision and Vocation of Dave Kiersznowski." *Comment* [forthcoming].

Guinness, Os. *The Call: Finding and Fulfilling the Central Purpose of Your Life*. Nashville, TN: Thomas Nelson, 2003.

Heatley, Bill. *The Gift of Work: Spiritual Disciplines for the Workplace*. Colorado Springs, CO: NavPress, 2008.

Hull, Bill. *Christlike: The Pursuit of Uncomplicated Obedience*. Colorado Springs, CO: NavPress, 2010.

Hunter, James. *To Change the World: The Irony, Tragedy, and Possibility of Christianity in the Late Modern World*. New York: Oxford University Press, 2010.

Keller, Tim. *The Prodigal God: Recovering the Heart of the Christian Faith.* New York: Dutton, 2008.

Kopp, Wendy. Address given at Georgetown University. May 17, 2008. http://explore.georgetown.edu/news/?ID=34121

Lewis, C. S. *Miracles.* Reprint. New York: HarperOne, 2001.

———. *The Weight of Glory.* Reprint. New York: HarperOne, 2001.

Lucado, Max. *In The Eye of the Storm: A Day in the Life of Jesus.* Nashville, TN: Thomas Nelson, 2001.

Marshall, Paul. *Heaven Is Not My Home: Living in the Now of God's Creation.* Nashville, TN: Thomas Nelson, 1999.

Miller, David. *God at Work: The History and Promise of the Faith and Work Movement.* New York: Oxford University Press, 2006.

Mouw, Richard. "The Postmodern Maze." *Christian History & Biography* 14, no. 3 (April 2007).

Newbigin, Lesslie. *The Gospel in a Pluralist Society.* Grand Rapids, MI: Eerdmans, 1989.

Piper, John. *Don't Waste Your Life.* Wheaton, IL: Crossway, 2010.

Placher, William C., ed. *Callings: Twenty Centuries of Christian Wisdom on Vocation.* Grand Rapids, MI: Eerdmans, 2005.

Schwehn, Mark R. and Dorothy C. Bass, eds. *Leading Lives That Matter.* Grand Rapids, MI: Eerdmans, 2006.

Smidt, Corwin. *Church, State, and Public Justice: Five Views.* Downers Grove, IL: InterVarsity, 2007.

Stark, Rodney. *The Rise of Christianity: How the Obscure, Marginal Jesus Movement Became the Dominant Religious Force in the Western World in a Few Centuries.* Reprint. San Francisco: HarperSanFrancisco, 1997.

Stott, John. *Radical Disciple: Some Neglected Aspects of Our Calling.* Downers Grove, IL: InterVarsity, 2010.

Strauss, Gideon. "Making It New: Andy Crouch Proposes a Different Way for Christians to Engage Culture." *Books & Culture*, September–October 2008.

Veith, Gene. *God at Work: Your Christian Vocation in All of Life.* Wheaton, IL: Crossway, 2002.

Volf, Miroslav. *Work in the Spirit: Toward a Theology of Work.* Eugene, OR: Wipf and Stock, 2001.

Wingreen, Gustaf. *Luther on Vocation.* Eugene, OR: Wipf and Stock, 2004.

Willard, Dallas. *The Divine Conspiracy: Rediscovering Our Hidden Life in God.* New York: HarperCollins, 1998.

———. *Hearing God: Developing a Conversationalist Relationship with God.* Downers Grove, IL: InterVarsity, 1999.

Wright, N. T. *Surprised by Hope: Rethinking Heaven, the Resurrection, and the Mission of the Church.* New York: HarperOne, 2008.

Zambito, Thomas, Jose Martinez, and Corky Siemaszko. "Bye, Bye Bernie: Ponzi King Madoff Sentenced to 150 Years." *New York Daily News.* June 12, 2009. Retrieved August 17, 2010.

GENERAL INDEX

SCRIPTURE INDEX

AMERICAN DREAMS

The Imagination of Sam Shepard

Edited by Bonnie Marranca

PAJ Publications
A Division of Performing Arts Journal, Inc.
New York

AMERICAN DREAMS

LIBRARY OF CONGRESS CATALOGING IN PUBLICATION DATA
Library of Congress Catalog Card No.: 80-85348
ISBN: 0-933826-12-15
ISBN: 0-933826-13-3 (paper)

Design: Gautam Dasgupta
Cover design: Steven Hoffman
Printed in the United States of America

Publication of this book has been made possible in part by grants from the National Endowment for the Arts, Washington, D.C., a federal agency, and public funds received from the New York State Council on the Arts.

10 9 8 7 6 5 4 3

ACKNOWLEDGEMENTS

Blumenthal, Eileen: "Speaking in Tongues: Joseph Chaikin and Sam Shepard." Copyright © 1980 by the author. Material appeared in a slightly different form in *The Village Voice* and will appear in its entirety in a forthcoming book on Joseph Chaikin to be published by Cambridge University Press. Reprinted by permission of the author.

Chubb, Kenneth and the Editors of *Theatre Quarterly:* "Metaphors, Mad Dogs, and Old Time Cowboys." From *Theatre Quarterly*, vol. 4, no. 15 (1974). Copyright © 1975 by TQ Publications. Reprinted by permission of TQ Publications.

PREFACE

It will be clear to anyone who reads this book that, rather than being one long monologue in praise of Sam Shepard, *American Dreams* is instead a dialogue among critics, directors, actors, and the author himself on his work. I like, and even encouraged, the way the contributors' points of view reverberate against, criss cross, complement and contradict one another. It makes for a kind of intellectual tension that raises crucial issues about dramatic writing and staging that cannot be solved lightheartedly. And though more than one contributor may write or speak about the same play, each has a different "take" on it. In some cases, the mere passage of time has changed the way the plays are regarded. Since this book includes pieces written as early as 1965 and as recent as 1981, that was to be expected.

Likewise, a long essay on Shepard which I completed in 1978 (*American Contemporary Playwrights: A Critical Survey*, Drama Book Specialists, 1981) initiated many of the ideas which are more fully explored in my Introduction to this book. Having had three more years to think about Shepard's work and its continuing relation to dramatic history and American culture, I was able now to address issues in the plays which remained unresolved or obscured for me at the time of the earlier essay.

The critics tend toward uncovering themes, techniques, and styles, situating the plays in overall contexts, sometimes looking at the work from the notion of "career," a difficult proposition in American theatre. In any case, critics are dealing with a finished work, be it play or production.

Because I wanted *American Dreams* simultaneously to consider Shepard as writer and man of the theatre, I included the views of directors and actors who experience the work in a more practical and necessarily process-oriented relationship: how do the plays get done? Of course, running throughout the book is Shepard's own voice—quoted in articles, in interviews, and in his own writing.

American Dreams is intended to be an open book, certainly not the "final say" on Sam Shepard—only a beginning toward opening up more rigorous dialogue on his work. He has been working in the theatre almost twenty years now, and for at least the last ten he's been considered the most important writer of his generation. Indeed, it is surprising that there are not more books devoted to him.

But Shepard is not an easy writer to write about because he so effortlessly, and without warning, changes the rules about writing for the theatre. No one in America has ever written plays quite like Shepard's, in fact very few American dramatists have been able to unite personal and national consciousness in so startling and intense a manner. Reading or seeing a Shepard play reminds me of what critic Hermann Broch says of the true work of art: "It dazzles you until it blinds you and then gives you back your sight." That sense of being struck by lightning is, for me, the great joy of art—to be confronted by an event or idea that forever changes the way you look at the world. Let me say that even when Shepard is not at his best he opens up the possibilities of what can be done on stage, and when he *is* at his best, he surpasses whatever we thought possible in the theatre.

Still, as many of the pieces in this book (my own included) demonstrate, Shepard provokes critical feelings even from those who admire him because we demand so much of him. Perhaps we want, too desperately, to acknowledge him as the great American playwright of our time. Whichever way you view the man, he cannot be explained by conventional dramatic wisdom, his writing is too renegade for that. Like all original writers his work raises more questions than it answers. If we had all the answers, experiencing Shepard wouldn't be such pleasure.

March 1981   Bonnie Marranca
                                                             New York City

CONTENTS

Introduction

ALPHABETICAL SHEPARD

The Play of Words

Bonnie Marranca

the artist in spite of himself

In the relationship of artist and audience the private I devises strategies to evade the public eye. Like the jazz saxaphonist Niles who commits suicide in B^b—the "key" to the mysterious overture—Shepard wants to disappear into the text, and to leave behind for the critic/detective only his outline. Behind this emotional gesture is the radical ideal of the authorless work and the denial of the Author as Myth.

Bertolt Brecht and Sam Shepard

Brecht developed the concept of character as situated between the actor (I) and the role (you). Character created from the point of view of the third person (he), from outside the event: narrative acting. Shepard, a storyteller like Brecht, elaborates this idea by situating narration in the present, in the equation of character as narrator, and so eliminating gestus in favor of the tone of voice. He substitutes myth for history, experience for theory.

The Brechtian actor narrates from the outside in; it's the other way around—inside out—in Shepard. The Brechtian work sets each unit of the play against the larger background. Shepard, the hedonistic writer, enjoys

13

every dramatic moment for its own sake. He writes as if there is no tomorrow.

character

1. What usually happens in the theatre is that the actor is given the opportunity to be a character. Shepard reverses the practice by giving his characters the chance to be performers.

2. Characters in his plays tell us about themselves rather than having other characters or the author tell us about them. They exist prior to the dramatic action not because of it. When a character does not have to explain a play the play can tell itself: rather than being about something, it is the thing itself.

3. The "realistic" character is created by an actor who must develop an "inner life" for himself in order to play his character in full dimension. Shepard's principal characters already have an inner life. So, in effect, the character takes inner life from the province of the actor for his own. And, Shepard, understanding what it means to be an actor, incorporates what the actor prepares into his composition of character. The actor is then free to play the moment, not the whole play; free to express the quality of being rather than having been. The typical realistic character has to play the line of the dramatic text whereas in Shepard's radical transformation of realism the character plays fragments, gaps, transformations—the breaks in continuity.

4. Generally, character chases the illusory ideal of definition: if during the course of a play one keeps an account of the character's emotional and physical details, his center of self will be revealed. The Shepard character has not simply a self but several selves which are continually changing, closer in composition to the transformational character developed by The Open Theatre (the author's one time relationship with this group needs to be fully examined) than the typical dramatic character. The transformational character has a fluid relationship to changing "realities" whereas a character in realistic drama is fixed in his relationship to reality which is itself fixed.

the dramatic field

Conventional realism is a closed structure of scenes with a definable beginning, middle and end that proceeds in a straight line. Causality dominates the action and motivation the character: the outcome is predictable from the point of view of reason. It is a kind of structure that is only interested in the similarities of things.

Shepard's open realism exists in a dramatic field composed of events not scenes, of explosions and contradictions not causes, of the overall effect, of gestalts. It is characterized by disruption not continuity, by simultaneity not succession; it values anomalies not analogies. In other words, it captures a reality that disregards realism's supposition of the rational. It praises the differences, the irregularites between things, and can accommodate the simultaneity of experiences in expanded time/space. Consciousness as subject matter takes precedence over the machinations of plot. Based on an expressionist view of character, the dramatic field encourages the emotionalization of physical space through the outward expansion of personal, inner space. The text as dramatic field is the space of writing as the gesture of emotion.

Unfortunately, Shepard doesn't take advantage of his own sophisticated technique, preferring simple subject matter and plots, instead of complexly developed material. The scope of his dramatic fields does not live up to their potential as really demanding models of experience.

eat your heart out

1. How many of the plays can you name in which the characters do *not* eat or talk about food? Mostly, it's breakfast, the meal associated with the presence of the mother, the start of the new day, light after the darkness of night. Bacon and eggs. "Home" fries. Fresh coffee. Sometimes Rice Krispies. Speeches about food are often the most luxurious in the plays, yet Shepard is no gourmet and, in fact, has very simple tastes—he doesn't seem to care what he eats as long as he eats.

2. Eating is used as a way to evade emotion: sometimes it's a reaction to anxiety or fear, a response to traumatic external events. Let's not forget the pure pleasure of eating, its physical and spiritual nourishment, the suggestion of companionship. One associates it with a setting—a comfortable home or perhaps a chrome diner. Shepard is fetishistic about food which masks the real spiritual "hunger" only obliquely expressed. Brecht: "Grub first, then ethics."

3. Eating and making love: eating as sublimated sex. Is it any wonder that

the speeches about food are so sensual, so seductive? Eating is about desire and fulfillment, as sex is.

the family that preys together stays together

1. *Curse of the Starving Class, Buried Child* and *True West* go beyond criticizing the moral and physical disintegration of the American family to an earnest investigation of what it means to be a member of a family. One of the more interesting aspects of these plays is, unlike the typical American family play written since the war, they seem more able to integrate highly individualistic, even eccentric behavior, and so are more in tune with the kinds of comedies written in the twenties and thirties than those of today. (Interestingly, California playwrights are now challenging this notion.)

2. The sons are the only normative figures in these domestic dramas. The parents are shown to be comic-pathetic, dreamy figures unable to comprehend or initiate events. They are failures as parent figures, and more troubled and out of control than their children.

3. All three of the plays are structured more around dialogue than the solo (in *Curse* and *Buried Child* the son and grandson/son have one solo each, but there are none in *True West*) which signals an emphatic shift in the pattern of discourse—away from characters who are obsessive and self-absorbed, and toward the development of relationships between characters. In the earlier two plays one could hardly conceive of the dialogue as a "conversational flow" but conversation does flow in *True West* which is perhaps the most conventional play Shepard has ever written.

The fact that dialogue is becoming a strong, integrated force in the plays indicates a new strain in Shepard's work, a shift in subject matter from displacement to roots, and an interest in the continuity of relationships rather than their disintegration, and finally, an emotional broadening of character.

geographies of the spirit

1. In *Angel City* the West is described as the "Looks-Within" place "for looking inside yourself," while the East is "the place of illumination." And, in *Rolling Thunder Logbook* Shepard writes,

    . . . Jesse James, Billy the Kid, Mickey Free, Buffalo Bill. Tales grew around them mostly out of a giant communications gap between the solid intellectual East Coast and the wide-open mysteries of the West.

Further along in the book he asks, "Is Boston all that heavy as the papers make out?" Shepard values the mythical status of places, as if to reinforce William Gass's contention that the only history America can have is a geographic one.

Cody (*Geography of a Horse Dreamer*) can't dream up winning horses because he doesn't know which part of the country he's in; Jeep (*Action*) is having an emotional crisis because he's lost his sense of place.

The axis of this poetics of space is not only East/West. In *Icarus's Mother* the opposition is North/South when the unknown pilot writing in the sky unwittingly creates for the picnickers beneath him a language of the apocalypse: $E=mc^2$. Salvation lay in the direction of the mountains in *Operation Sidewinder*, in the desert in *True West*.

2. The landscape of the body: the shape the character creates when his imagination transforms his body (Kent in *La Turista*); the outline of an identity that wants to hide in anonymity (Niles in *Suicide in B^b*); a character describing what it feels like inside his body (Stu in *Chicago*). In Shepard's non-psychological drama, the bodies do the thinking.

At times the body strains toward the fourth dimension. One of the key points in the plays is that of the soul or "I" as an entity separate from the physical body. Shepard's characters want out-of-the-body experiences. Often the characters seem able to observe themselves from the outside; some want to be free of their bodies, or break through to another level of reality; and still others lament their bodies' rhythm as slower than their mental states.

3. Shepard's most moving portrait of the American experience, *Action*, was written while he was living in England. The distance was not only geographic but emotional, intellectual, political, historical. Curiously, this is the only play, by Shepard's own admission, he had ever read aloud to himself, as if the sound of the voice could echo across the Atlantic as some aural image of the distressed voice of America. In England he would, as a character, live the feeling of displacement and loss of community of the characters in his play. He would know what it means to be surrounded by people who speak a language different from his own, for surely British English is not American English. By reading the play aloud he tells himself a story—in a lean, affective tone—that is his own story. The triumph of *Action* is that it defines Nixonian America in a jagged, constrained structure

that mirrors the very difficulty of finding a language of social communication and a means to express feeling: on a very basic level, *Action* is about the loss of language. The vision of Walt Whitman's America is brutally contrasted with what America had become. And like Whitman, Shepard, in his finest play, was able to link his personal experience to the national experience. *Action* is political in the most subtle sense—because his political feelings have more to do with people than systems Shepard uses metaphors instead of direct address to express himself—and yet it is one of the few American plays of its time to capture the cultural moment with any degree of intensity.

4. Shepard's magnificent obsession is the loss of individualism through control by unnameable, outside forces which is really fear of the loss of personal space. The prolonged reverie of the lyrical voice is an extension of the character's emotional space, his mapping of consciousness; it is also the defense mechanism of the individual that keeps "society" from impinging upon the territory of the imagination.

5. Most of American drama is claustrophobic: it takes place in a cluttered living room, dining room, or kitchen. If you think of plays that are "spacious" only a few examples come to mind, these writers in particular: Thornton Wilder, a mid-Westerner whose great achievement, *Our Town*, defied conventional time and space and made the sense of place a philosophical concern and subject matter. And Gertrude Stein who based many of her ideas about drama on the plays she saw in San Francisco—who but a Californian (even if she lived there briefly) could conceive of a play as a "landscape"? Neither of them was interested in psychology (as Shepard himself is not) which can only contain the spirit, make it definable, regulate its situation in time and space.

Shepard's work should be viewed in this context of a larger, non-urban scale. His feeling of space (and nature) is of a vastness that seems unfathomable, generous, still, triumphant, even religious (his transcendental heritage)—simply there. Space that draws consciousness in on itself because next to it the physical scale of the individual is trivial; a space that looks from the Pacific clear across America, and across deserts, unflinching in their refusal to adapt to changing times. In this world people can afford to be talkers and dreamers because the space they inhabit is lyrical. Only Southerners and Westerners, people who understand attachment to the land, retain the gift of gab and the tall tale, even the art of conversation; wᵉ in the Northeast have lost it to the urban language of the concrete phrase. Shepard is the only American dramatist writing today to evoke a new sense of space in drama, and he transfers the values of the American West and its ideals into the emotional landscapes of his plays, highlighting the function of *space as myth*. This is where the discussion of regionalism in drama can begin.

the horizontal and the vertical

The solo is vertical: it finds an image to start with and soars through layer upon layer of physical and emotional detail. However, only the male voice moves on this vertical, rhythmic trajectory. The women in the plays rarely have these personal solos, though *Red Cross* is an exception, and even so it doesn't detail a uniquely female experience of the world. Female discourse is horizontal, circumscribed by its orientation toward the others in the play: harmonic.

the rhythm of imagery

1. The solo carries Charles Olson's idea of "projective verse" into drama: ONE PERCEPTION MUST IMMEDIATELY LEAD TO A FURTHER PERCEPTION. Olson equated speech (the poet's) with performance but he didn't follow the implications of his own manifesto far enough into theatre where it finds a logical application: here the author's breath span is actually translated to the performer as a voice in the theatrical experience. Perversely, one can say that theatre aestheticizes the notion of artificial respiration.

What Shepard does in his best work is to open up the emotional terrain of a character so he can project his feelings OUT THERE. The emotions of the character are the projections of his personal imagery, beginning usually with a single perception and building into a long string of images (verbal, visual, aural) that embroider the initial perception or image beyond the immediate situation of the character to an area of his imagination.

2. Shepard's frequent difficulty in ending his plays (for examples, *La Turista*, *Angel City*, *Curse of the Starving Class*) is directly related to the explosion of images that accumulate in strength and autonomy throughout each play. He seems to run away from the energy he unleashes in his characters, unable to confront and control the rhythms of imagery he himself has set in motion.

3. Imagery vs. symbol: imagery is dynamic ("meaning" is not fixed), non-psychological because it is not tied to motivation; theatrical because it

outlines its own space. The symbol is static (it generally has the same repertoire of meaning wherever it appears), psychological because it reflects literal states of mind; literary because it speaks a familiar language. (For example, the airplane in *Icarus's Mother* is imagery whereas the vegetables in the garden in *Buried Child* are symbolic.) The symbol is a fairly literal transposition of a certain thematic aspect of a play; representational in attitude it simply reinforces what is already there. Imagery is metaphoric, it has more possibilites, it is presentational; it functions simultaneously on several different levels. Imagery subsumes symbols in a larger meaning. To the extent that Shepard's plays remain in the realm of the trope they highlight their feeling for imagery. Plays such as *Seduced, Buried Child* and *True West* are less provocative than Shepard's metaphoric work because their symbolic language is familiar.

4. In its most destructive frame the image can lead to aestheticized feeling—the absence of real feeling—or the substitution of a picture of something for the real thing. If American culture is moving more and more toward the production and consumption of imagery, it has to do with the aestheticizing of feeling, of history, of the self, of politics, of personal relations; our fragmented world has lost the means to express itself in a unified symbology. The contemporary way of expressing the world and the self is through imagery. The symbol reflects a wholeness, a shared system of values and experience that is largely absent from contemporary life which is dominated by the images of things, not the things themselves. Shepard's use of realism as a form reflects the preponderance of images as opposed to symbols which as a unifying element have always dominated realism in its most traditional examples.

jazz

Shepard prefaces *Angel City* with this "Note to the Actors":

> Instead of the idea of a "whole character" with logical motives behind his behavior which the actor submerges himself into, he should consider himself a fractured whole with bits and pieces of character flying off the central theme. In other words, more in terms of collage construction or jazz improvisation.

Characterization in the play follows the structural make-up of improvisation to the point of building into a musical finale of Act I that has the actors (or are they performers?) jamming. The appeal of jazz is more than structural. As an approach to composition it embodies an attitude that is at the heart of Shepard's work: spontaneity of expression. Not chance, but improvisation.

Angel City is Shepard's big jazz ensemble piece; elsewhere jazz is reflected in the free association of long solos (particularly in the early plays) which seem to make themselves up as they go along. They follow the same principle as jazz improvisation—composition by digression. For Shepard it means being able to go with the flow of words, as his literary big brother Jack Kerouac described it, in more sensual terms, writing whatever "comes into your head as it comes."

The jazz artist teases the audience into following his rhythm for as long as he can keep it going, lifting them to a tantalizing high, taking them down, bringing them up again, one tempo to another, a little bit at a time as if they were caught in a sexual embrace with music that continually forestalls the orgasmic response of applause and shouts. The most powerful solo parts in Shepard's plays have that same erotic effect which is what makes his writing sexy though there's no actual sex in them: it's the rhythm of sex not the representation of it. Shepard's seduction is linguistic—a coming to language than to speech.

kitsch as myth

Vintage Chevys, old Packards, chrome diners, and Hudson Hornets are objects turned subjects in a nostalgia for pop artifacts. Kitsch as romanticized attachment to the mass-culture object, turning common imagery into art. ("Romanticism is the mother of kitsch": Hermann Broch.) In a society which easily discards old products and artifacts in a frantic race to produce new ones, the discarded object as setting quickly attains special status. The outmoded consumer object—in its nostalgic setting—is America's historical ruin.

"land of the free"

The spirit of the American West, its triumph of individualism, unlimited potential, transcendant beauty, and disdain of regulation is the soul of Shepard's work. It is also the same philosophy that put Ronald Reagan in the White House. There is nothing wrong in loving your country, which Shepard does—and Reagan does, too—but the frontier ethic turns ugly when set in global, even national perspective.

What's problematic in Shepard's thinking is his overly Romantic, self-satisfied view of the historical past (even as a presence in the plays) and his inability to examine the implications of this position in broad terms.

Side by side with Shepard's glorification of the frontier ethic, and its concomitant isolationism, oppressive view of women, retreat from group concerns, is his sixties-style radical politics with its dread of the "system," its pastoral ideals, and persistent criticism of the American way of life. There's always been this tug-of-war between radical ideals—however more emotionally felt than politically reasoned—and a deeply-felt conservatism that is never fully resolved in the plays and, in fact, is the source of their political tension. This duality which, sadly, history has shown resolves itself to the right, embodies all that is good and bad in the conscience of the American people, it is its promise and failure, and, more significantly, the basis of its doctrine of rebirth. It is the mark of Shepard's provincialism and his essential Americanness.

the melodramatic imagination

1. The Shepard mystique is grounded in the image of a cool, laid back cowboy, an outsider, a man in control of things. Yet, if you look at the plays they suggest an author given to hysteria, even paranoia, an author who views life melodramatically by magnifying an ordinary event until it attains the proportions of a disaster. What's true in part is made to define the whole perspective. The figurative devices of metaphor and metonymy that dominate Shepard's writing are easily linked to melodrama: they make what is absent from a text seem more important that what is present in it.

2. Shepard the moralist. Melodrama equals a drama of opppositions: hero vs. villain, individual vs. system, intellect vs. emotion, artist vs. public, East vs. West, inside vs. outside. Shepard's plays are always communicating the loss, and the corruption of ideals without offering solutions, and without actually dealing with moral issues. His morality is hidden in form.

3. Melodrama and American drama. Unlike European drama in which irony and cynicism have dominated since the modern period, American drama is predominantly melodrama—it is idealistic, moralistic, emotional, it simplifies issues. Characters generally say what they mean, believing in language as means of communication. If the response to the void for most of modern drama is silence, for Shepard's characters it is talking as a way of coping with emotional stress. His characters have not lost faith in the pro-

mise of a return to innocence, they still mourn their fall from grace. Nietz-sche: "I fear we are not getting rid of God because we still believe in grammar." American drama refuses to believe the European position: that God is dead.

narration

1. By American standards of dramaturgy the speeches of Shepard's characters are too long and too narrative. Much of the background of the plays is narrated; events which don't occur on stage are narrated; narration is used as a purely informational device; the solo itself breaks apart the structure by reconstituting the narrative line as a rejection of dialogue and an act of imagination. The movement of the plays, in general, subverts discourse, character, dramatic action, and setting, all of the elements by which the "puzzle" of a play is traditionally fitted together. The plays are always coming apart at the seams because they are constructed out of pieces, and even so, many of the plays refuse to end. The plays mitigate against the ideal of conceiving work as a totality, on a unified scale, offering instead only a sampling of feelings and events that have to be experienced in segments. The structure of the narratives reflects the way Americans experience everyday life—in fits and spurts, and surface impressions, suffering the loss of extended conversation as a way of communicating feeling. Through his revitalization of realism Shepard has been able remarkably to show changes in the structure of experience in America. His plays change the contours of speech and, therefore, communication in realism.

2. The breakdown of dialogue. Reliance on narration instigates the devaluation of dialogue. The plays can hardly be said to have a conversational flow when characters are often unaware of what each other is saying, or they ignore it, and rarely do they comment on what has been said. Extended dialogue is occasional, as if conversation were pre-empted by the other languages of the stage, imagery for one.

Conversational dialogue has come increasingly to be disvalued in American theatre, almost exclusively by avant-garde groups from The Living Theatre to the present whose work has reflected new psychoanalytic theories and a general drift toward narrative, presentational modes of acting rather than motivational, representational acting. Before writer-directors such as Richard Foreman, Robert Wilson and Lee Breuer were writing texts that broke down the structure of dialogue and elevated the solo voice—taking consciousness as subject matter—Shepard had already moved in this direction in his early plays. Of *American* playwrights, only Gertrude Stein had preceded him.

The disavowal of dialogue as the prime mover of the dramatic line suggests a drama that is not exclusively rooted in the manifestation of conflict between characters, but one that is more internalized in the self. (For example, much of the drama written today by women is simply the stringing together of monologues, as if there is first the need to tell all of oneself rather than a story; on the other hand, black drama has always been based on dialogue, conflict between characters, and behavior rooted in relationships.) Spalding Gray's solo, autobiographical talking pieces—pure narrative—in which he constructs his personal history for an audience, is the evolutionary end product of the breakdown of dialogue in theatre.

3. The current rejection of dialogue, and Shepard's plays up to his most recent few reflect this, signals a presentation of character that owes less to Freudian psychology than to the development of the narcissistic personality which is increasingly defining the individual of today—in cultural, sociological and psychological terms. The implications of this change are undeniable: the breakdown of dialogue reflects in its dramatic form the overly analytical exploration of the self and the inability to sustain relationships that characterize behavior today. To the extent that they emphasize the narrative aspect of the lone voice and the lack of interaction with other individuals in their world, Shepard's characters illustrate the contemporary malaise. To the extent that they refuse to give up the uniqueness of the individual imagination to group psychology they are a mode of survival in an institutionalized world.

ontology of the sentence

How the rhythm of speech evolves from the emotional line of the moment:

When Wesley describes the drunken return of his father (*Curse of the Starving Class*) he begins in a leisurely, joyous, personal mood ("I could feel myself in my bed in my room in this house in this town in this state in this country") then moves to a quick rush of incomplete sentences. Images are set in short phrases whose staccato rhythm echoes his heart beating ("Man throwing wood. Man throwing up. Mom calling cops. Dad crashing away. Back down driveway. Car door slamming. Ignition grinding. Wheels screaming"). The dangling participle used to recall the past event pushes it along as if it were happening now.

Howard's imagination takes flight like the plane overhead (*Icarus's*

Mother); he needs conjunctions to do it:

> Lake after lake with river after river running away from the lake and going to the ocean. House after house turning into city after city and town after town.

His topographical essay is narrated from the point of view of the pilot.

The style match of *The Tooth of Crime*, one of the author's many plays about the artist and his relation to society, calls for poetry: Hoss's rhythm and blues truth ("You lost the barrelhouse you lost the honkey-tonk") vying with Crow's superficial punchline ("Talkin' sock it to it, get the image in line"). This talking rock piece has a syntax like good guitar licks—all rhythm and no harmony.

In the meta-language world of *Tooth*, two different (musical) languages confront each other in a fusillade of metaphors. *Tooth* is about making up language and using it to manipulate reality. Hoss eventually commits suicide because he can't adopt Crow's "language" (verbal or gestural)—in Shepard's conception of character speech is so integrated with individual being that for any character to imitate someone else and transform his way of speaking (that is, his way of thinking) is to give up his identity.

In "Rhythm" (*Hawk Moon*) the more than page long catalogue of images is all percussion, run-on incomplete sentences isolating a single aural or visual rhythm.

> Dog claws clicking on hardwood floors. Clocks. Piston rhythms. Dripping faucets. Tin hitting tin in the wind. Water slapping rocks. Flesh slapping flesh. Boxing rhythms. Racing rhythms. Rushing brooks. . . .

play/pretend/performance

1. The Pirandellian character wears a mask which allows him to reflect the philosophical viewpoint of the playwright, formalized in the "play-within-the-play" structure. Shepard's characters, having been influenced by both Pirandellian theatricalism and the narrative acting of the Brechtian character, though not Genet's social perspective, is free to remove his mask. He knows he is a performer, and takes the opportunity whenever he wants to, to leave, mentally and in another time frame, the play and verbalize or act out his emotional responses to events around him. There is no such

thing as illusion vs. reality, only shifting realities. In Shepard's work there is not the play-within-the-play but *play within the play*. His plays are written from the point of view of the actor, and so incorporate the notion of performance.

2. Instead of thinking of the character as an actor who is playing a role, it seems more appropriate in the case of Shepard to think of the character as a performer—not acting a role, but improvising, in public, aspects of his private, imaginative life. Pirandello's characters were conceived at a time when the individual was believed to have both a public side and a private side. Since then, however, cultural, social and technological forces have conspired to eclipse the individual's private side; in effect, the public side has emerged, in the last twenty years, to be the measure of the individual.

The contemporary individual is less interested in playing several roles than in conceptualizing (creating images of) a whole new self: it's today's recycled notion of what was formerly called "upward mobility." In role-playing the situation sets the scene, but in "performance" the individual sets up the situation. (Sociologist Erving Goffman's theories seem irrelevant vis à vis Shepard. Goffman, who is interested in defining the self in relation to social roles, regards performance as an attitude toward *communication*. Shepard's characters do not relate to society, there is no world outside, they often cannot see beyond their own mental states. They react, they do not interact.)

3. Since the sixties the culture has tended increasingly to define all aspects of human interaction—politics, law, business, psychoanalysis, sexuality, work—in terms of performance (the term used to mean "behavior" or "accomplishment" unless, of course, one was speaking of the theatre). Now, life is viewed in terms of spectacle. The very make-up of Shepard's characters reflects the author's belief in performance—that is, the spontaneous creation of other scenarios within the main storyline of the play—as a technique for dealing with the "reality" of a given moment. His characters make spectacles of themselves.

In a country where the non-fatalistic, fluid concept of self supercedes class, professional and ideological formalities, the notion of human potential—the potential for changing into someone else (making yourself up)—predominates. The great irony in all of this is that an actor is now president, politics having united with entertainment as the current great performance opportunities. In an America that has become more and more self-conscious of its forms, and the parody of them, performance style is all.

4. There are no "performances" in *Operation Sidewinder, Curse of the Star-*

ving Class, Buried Child and *True West* because the characters are caught up in the world of Fate, Necessity. Performance is an ironic attitude, not a tragic one.

quotations without quotation marks

Everybody's got a language. Shepard writes American regional speech, contemporary slang, cowboy dialect; the jargon of sports, car racing, gangsters; the doublespeak of disk jockeys, high tech and science fiction; the platitudes of Republican America, quasi-militants and Hollywood; the talking music of old bluesmen, young punks and rock and rollers.

Quotation is a natural critique of language but it rarely functions in the plays philosophically (cf. Peter Handke's *Sprechstücke*) or politically (cf. Heathcote Williams's *AC/DC*). Because he is more interested in talking than language per se, Shepard focuses on the idea of *speech as myth*. Quotation in its American usage (Ronald Tavel, Lee Breuer, Robert Wilson) is more poetic than political in its orientation because the American voice is classless.

varieties of religious experience

Christian symbolism and the development of Christian themes is an aspect of the plays that profoundly describes the context of Shepard's output. Corruption and its physical manifestation organizes the symbolism of *Angel City's* slimy green ooze and the power-grabbing hands of Hackamore in *Seduced*. The return of the prodigal son Vince in *Buried Child* is also a fairly obvious interpretation of character. With great brio Weston, the buffoonish father in *Curse of the Starving Class*, is born again after being baptized in his own dirty bath water.

While these plays easily allude to Christian themes, *Operation Sidewinder* develops an elaborate repertoire of symbols out of the contradictory sources of the Bible, technological manuals and Indian ritual to demonstrate the Origin and the Fall, as dramatized by American life. The snake/computer in the desert/Eden is the dominant image in the play, doubling as a symbolism of evil that is transvalued into an Indian spirit of salvation.

Even more poignantly The Young Man, whose lost soul is eventually redeemed, is cleansed of Original Sin—loss of his spiritual values—in a baptism of fire at the apocalypse. His symbolic reenactment of confession is individualized in a language dominated by traditional symbols of evil:

> I devour the planet . . . I came to infect the continent . . . To spread
> my disease . . . To cut down the trees, to dig out the gold, to shoot
> down the deer, to capture the wind. . . .

Shepard's plays are acts of faith, and his emotional response to being an American reflects the characteristic American pursuit of rebirth, and its opposite, the denial of history.

Gertrude Stein and the American experience

G.S.: "The business of art is to live in the actual present, that is the complete actual present, and to express that complete actual present."

Stein and Shepard seem at first an unlikely pair but they are quintessential American writers who have understood at once the American preference for the spontaneous and experiential grasp of a phenomenon. Both are obsessed with examining the immediacy of the present, and in minute detail. Description becomes a function of consciousness, a way to convey the fullness and fluidity of the moment; only then can the event of the past be present in the memory of the one speaking. Language creates reality. The personal experience of time is valued over conventional dramatic time, and personal expression is valued over the etiquette of narrative form. Shepard's characters corroborate the continuing truth of Stein's observation that "sentences are not emotional, and paragraphs are." It's the only way obsessive talkers can communicate.

Stein and Shepard: They've produced narcissistic characters who will tell you more than you want to know about them.

talking/telling stories

1. Characters who talk are different from characters who speak. In plays dominated by dialogue characters speak lines, and when the solo dominates a character can be said to talk. Talking comes from the performer (I) whereas speaking comes from the role player (he).

2. The virtuosic soloists in the plays are great talkers. The solo (performative) as opposed to the monologue (literary) stands apart from the action around or behind it and creates a life of its own, for as long as it desires. The

soloist inhabits a different space temporarily; an inner, emotional space that others cannot enter because it is a personal space. It's the talking out of feelings that dominates the characters' lives, very rarely the direct expression of emotion in relation to another person.

3. Much of the solos consists of story-telling bits. Little stories, self-contained—they're about the speaker or an event he makes up or describes, not the story of the play itself. Shepard's characters are accomplished storytellers because they'd rather talk than act. Since their colleagues on stage are rarely listening to them they speak for themselves and for the audience. What Shepard has done is to link the oral tradition of poetry to the dramatic tradition, erasing the difference (momentarily) between drama (literature) and theatre (literature performed).

4. The Romantic poet thinks in the breathtaking/breathgiving line of poetry. The rhapsodic solo is the "song of myself" that was sung by the first beat poet, Walt Whitman, then by Kerouac and Ginsburg, and now by Shepard's characters, who carry the beat legacy into dramatic form.

urban cowboy

1. The contemporary counterpart of the cowboy is the rock star, also a man who stands outside the system—the would-be rock-and-roll Jesus with a cowboy mouth. The metaphoric translation of the cowboy showdown appears in *Tooth of Crime* when two rock stars compete for territory and status in a style match that spits words instead of bullets; the groupie Becky is a contemporary version of the gun moll. *Tooth of Crime* exorcises the spirit of cowboy mouth—in real rock terms, look what the new rock star, Crow, promises for the future.

2. Cowboys, too. The image of the cowboy helps Shepard bring the ideal of play into adult life, it establishes a continuity of imagination. The cowboy represents a longing after heroes and heroic deeds which is often at the center of Shepard's plays, and is the heart of American West mythology. Even Henry Kissinger couldn't resist comparing himself to a cowboy: "This amazing, romantic character suits me precisely because to be alone has always been part of my style or, if you like, my technique."

voices

How to read Shepard: don't look at the name of the character—you will know who is talking from the rhythm and tone of his voice.

Individualism finds its truest manifestation in the way each character uniquely shapes language. It is always the character you hear, not the author, and as many characters as he creates there are distinct speech patterns.

Shepard's characters love to hear themselves talk, they may even repeat a line of dialogue or a cliché or phrase in a few different ways, as if a voice talking, or imagining out loud, could, if only momentarily, control or create reality.

the zero gravity of women

1. One of the most problematic aspects of the plays is Shepard's consistent refusal or inability, whichever the case may be, to create female characters whose imaginative range matches that of the males. Women are the background of the plays: they hang out and make themselves useful for chores while the men make the decisions, take risks, face challenges, experience existential crises. Women are frequently abused, and always treated as subservient to men, their potential for growth and change restricted.

For a young man Shepard's portrayal of women is as outdated as the frontier ethic he celebrates: men have their showdowns or face the proverbial abyss while the women are absorbed in simple activities and simplistic thoughts. They are wives, girlfriends, mothers or some sort of servile worker (maid, secretary); in other words, always connected to someone or something, never simply women whose consciousness might be revealed with the degree of intensity a man's is. There is no expression of a female point of view in any of Shepard's plays. Even the stage directions can be used to indicate a woman's lack of individuation (Honey in *Operation Sidewinder*), and some women are interchangeable (Mom in *True West* is just the leftover Halie from *Buried Child*).

The heroism and strength of the cowboy is revered by Shepard but in actuality the men he creates are ineffectual, fearful, and emotionally immature. They show no strength or character or will, yet they are allowed to dominate because it is their due as men.

2. Shepard has no apparent interest in the relations of men and women, preferring instead to write about male experience. He writes as if he is

unaware of what has been happening between men and women in the last decade. Though he has opened up whole new areas of exploration in the form of dramatic realism developed by his literary forefathers, he has not radicalized the way women interact in dramatic form, neither has he given them a new language, and, in fact, his female characters are much less independent and intelligent that many of those created by these forefathers a hundred years ago.

It cannot be ignored that Shepard, who is in some ways an idol of his young audiences, is not simply traditional in his view of women, but downright oppressive. One of the reasons why the lyrical solo is not characteristic of female expression is that the women are rarely given anything to say that can stand alone. The voice—of consciousness, of the emotions, of reason, of triumph, and of failure, too—and finally, of America— is a man's voice.

3. The only truly dominant, autonomous female character in the plays is Cavale in *Cowboy Mouth*, and it took a Patti Smith, ironically an artist who had molded herself in the Romantic tradition of the male artist/outlaw, to write her part for herself. The one character written by Shepard who comes close to rebelling against female stereotypes is Emma in *Curse of the Starving Class* but she is written as a tomboy—a tough high school kid who tears up a local bar, and plans to work her way to Mexico hauling in barracuda, fixing four-wheel drives, learning how to be a short order cook while writing novels on the side . . . something along the lines of a Jack Kerouac. Rebellion and individuality are given a specifically male character. When Emma's own female "curse" is linked poetically to the fall of her class, it makes one ask if Shepard isn't cursing women for their powers of reproduction.

4. Shepard conceives of space—emotional, intellectual, physical—as a male domain, a territorial imperative, as it were. The landscape of the female body has yet to appear, but when a language of the sexes and a female language are added to all the other "languages" he has mastered, the silent voices in the plays will tell their stories.

X: known and unknown

The object of closed, conventional dramaturgy: to make known every factor. It operates on the principle of subtraction: environment minus character minus gesture equals meaning. The open text as dramatic field multiplies each of its autonomous elements to generate unforeseeable sets of possibilities as its algebra of emotion.

"You act yourself out"

1. In *Action*—a play that centers on the experience of entropy—the isolated characters view themselves from the outside. Jeep: "I can even imagine how horrifying it could be to be doing all this, and it doesn't touch me. It's like I'm dismissed." Shooter literally acts himself out (as a dancing bear, a turtle, a father in a comfortable chair): these moments of acting out function for him as a survival mechanism. They are the only emotional responses he is capable of.

The flip side of keeping in control is getting caught in the image of yourself which you are acting out. "I made myself up," Henry Hackamore boasts, having been seduced by the images of power he himself has fabricated. "I was taken by the dream and all the time I thought I was taking it."

Kent acts himself right out of his body and out of *La Turista*'s plot as he creates a Frankenstein fantasy, an existential horror scenario in which man and beast engage in the ultimate confrontation.

(If performance is an ironic and comic attitude toward the self, acting yourself out is its existential, tragic opposite.)

2. The endings of the plays mentioned above are essentially the same: Jeep, Henry and Kent confront their terror of losing control by attempting to transcend physical space—Jeep by moving around the stage as if "he's attempting his own escape from the space he's playing in," Henry by pretending he's flying, Kent by lunging through the upstage wall of the set. These plays have to end because the major characters have left metaphorically, even literally, the space the other characters inhabit. When all else fails you act yourself out. For Shepard space is more than setting—it develops its own thematics rather than remaining decorative, functional or symbolic.

3. One of the most interesting usages of this mode of behavior is in *The Tooth of Crime* in a dialogue Hoss, about to meet his challenger, Crow, devises. The voice of "Yer old Dad" intrudes to offer some reassuring words to a frightened son. In therapeutic terms, the acting out helps Hoss objectify and get a grasp on the situation.

the zone of myth

The theatre experience exists in the space between what is there in the performing space and what is not there. The power of Shepard's plays is in what is absent from the event, that space he leaves for the spectator's imagination to play in. The Shepard play is a metaphoric model of the American experience, localized in fictional characters. The empty space in the contemporary mind is the space from which myth has absented itself: Shepard tries to fill that space. And by being so generous with his feelings, another myth is outlined—that of the artist, in spite of himself.

Commentary

THE TRANSFORMATIONS OF SAM SHEPARD

Gerald Weales

"I would have like a picture, and just start from there." The voice is that of Sam Shepard explaining in an interview with the editors of *Theatre Quarterly* how he went about writing his early plays. An ugly sentence from a playwright justly celebrated for his theatrical eloquence (the poet trapped in the tape recorder), it seems as good a way to get into an essay as it does to begin a play. My picture is not in my head, however; it is lying on my desk. The dust jacket of *Five Plays* offers Sam Shepard in quintuplicate, comic-strip balloons rising from his many mouths to announce the title, the author, the contents of his first book. A joke? Certainly. A symbol? Well, perhaps, but almost accidentally, as though the physical presence of Shepard—the self as metaphor—already knew something the young man only suspected. At first glance, it is the changing expressions—from wide grin to quizzical bemusement—that catch the eye, but finally it is those five figures, feet firmly planted on a black line that cuts the bottom of the jacket, which command attention, which say, "Well, we're/I'm here." And so he was.

Shepard made his debut as a playwright with the double bill, *Cowboys* and *The Rock Garden*, at Theatre Genesis, October 10, 1964, and quickly became one of the handful of off-off-Broadway playwrights who were at once avant-garde experimentalists and show-business celebrities. Since he was only twenty at the time, Shepard became the most visible of the lot. It was a case of that old American theatrical tune, "Barefoot Boy on Broadway," played in a new key. Not that Shepard ever made it to Broadway, unless the 1970 production of *Operation Sidewinder* at Lincoln Center can be said to fill that bill.

Instead he played the best of the off-off-Broadway houses (Genesis, La Mama, Caffe Cino, Judson Poets' Theatre) and then moved on to the American Place Theatre, Princeton's McCarter Theatre, The Performance Group, Joseph Papp's operation, the Yale Repertory, the best advertised non-commercial theatres in the country. He scooped up writing grants and Obie awards as though they were jelly beans, and edged into the art-glamor market by writing the first version of Antonioni's *Zabriskie Point* and letting *Oh, Calcutta!* present one scene of *The Rock Garden* as genteel porn. As late as 1975, he was on the road with Bob Dylan's *Rolling Thunder Revue*, as observer and scriptwriter not as musician (although he had played briefly with the Holy Modal Rounders in the late 1960s), and in 1978 he emerged as a film star in Terrence Malick's *Days of Heaven*. That was the year that *Buried Child* opened, first in San Francisco and then in New York, and went on to win the 1979 Pulitzer Prize, a very institutional blessing for a never quite domesticated dramatist.

"The minute an avant-garde artist becomes a household word he stops being avant-garde," Michael Kahn, who was then directing the Princeton production of *Angel City*, said in a Philadelphia *Bulletin* interview (March 20, 1977). "I think Shepard is always going to be a renegade in the theatre and I think that is fine." Kahn's words have a nice old-fashioned ring to them, for in the United States in the 1970s renegades had a way of turning into culture heroes and then into big business, the "new version of chic" as Shepard said of the Dylan company in *Rolling Thunder Logbook*. Shepard seems to understand the phenomenon in his own career as well. His tendency to change roles and locations; his need to cut and run to London in the early 1970s, to the West Coast later in the decade; his being "extra horny for a car" in metaphorical ways that that line in *Logbook* barely suggests, all these reflect the recurrent themes of his plays—the invention of the self, its transformation under pressure through release, the need to escape, the threat or attraction of real or symbolic death.

The critic with a fondness for fiction as biography could have as much fun with Shepard as his colleagues have had with Chaplin or Hemingway, could use Shepard's thirty-odd plays as a kind of disguised roadmap which, once the code was broken, could explain how Shepard moved from the confident boy on the cover of *Five Plays* to the thirty-five-year-old whose strong but vulnerable face was seen so often closeup in *Days of Heaven*. The critical pleasure would be increased if *Suicide in B^b* were taken—as I suspect it should be—as the author's attempt, like Edward Albee's in *Box-Mao-Box*, to do in some of his earlier aesthetic selves. For me, however, a play is a public act, and whatever autobiographical impulses helped to shape it, it is the play itself, its ability to hold, to inform, to inspirit an audience that counts.

From the beginning of his career, it has been evident that Shepard is a bona fide playwright, a man who can animate images on stage and, however unusual or obscure they seem to be, make audiences—some at least—respond to them. Not that he ever lacked dissenters. Particularly after he moved beyond the family audience of off-off-Broadway's halcyon days, he hit playgoers who resisted his art, who insisted that he was being willfully difficult. There were always—there still are—drama reviewers prominent in the latter group. Glenne Currie of UPI dismissed *Seduced* (February 10, 1979) as not having "much to say, though anything Shepard writes is liable to seduce the listener into thinking it means more than it says." Characteristic of Currie's uneasy response to most of Shepard's work, the review managed to admit Shepard's theatrical power even as it denied his play's importance.

The difficulty from the beginning was that Shepard's plays resist analysis. Traditionally, reviewers have found it congenial to handle plays by talking about what they are about and that is the least valuable way of approaching Shepard's work. Michael Smith, the first reviewer to recognize Shepard's talent, the director of *Icarus's Mother*, said in his director's notes in *Five Plays*, "It's always hard to tell what, if anything, Sam's plays are 'about'—although they are unmistakably alive." His production failed, he said, because he began by concentrating on the play's "content and overall meaning" and because he spent too much time trying to make his actors understand the language instead of simply playing it.

The unanchored meaning of the early Shepard plays can be seen in *Up to Thursday*, a play that Shepard later rightly dismissed as "a bad exercise in absurdity . . . a terrible play, really," one that he chose never to have published. The play was described in *The Best Plays of 1964-1965* as "About a sleepy youth who waits for clean underwear while two couples play games," a statement that seems as accurate and probably more useful than that of Edward Albee, whose Theater 1965 produced the play, that it "was about a boy about to be drafted." (*Village Voice*, November 25, 1965). What I remember most about *Up to Thursday* is that, despite its general sense of incoherence, it was more intriguing than the more conventional, more sentimental refugees from off-off-Broadway with which it shared the bill—Lanford Wilson's *Home Free!* and Paul Foster's *Balls*.

It was Elizabeth Hardwick who first tried to define the Shepard method in the larger context of modern literature. When she defied the author's ban on critics to review *La Turista* for the *New York Review of Books* in 1967 (*pace*: the review became the introduction to the published play), she said: "The episodic, the obscurely related, the collection of images, moods: connections in fiction and also in drama have become like those of poetry." Characteristically (old critical habits die hard), she found or suggested specific meanings in the process of definition. "To me, that's really a dangerous area," Shepard was to say later (*Village Voice*, October 27, 1975), "because then it goes away from the very simple reality of the play. . . . Once it goes off into the so-called *meaning* of it, then it's lost, it's gone away."

Shepard said in the *Theatre Quarterly* interview that "the so-called originality of the early work just comes from ignorance," that he began writing plays without knowing what a play was. It was a seminal ignorance, as it turned out, because it allowed Shepard to discover his two important theatrical talents, both still evident in recent works like *Seduced* and *Buried Child*. The one that has been most widely celebrated is his verbal facility, his manipulation of a wide variety of American voices from the dryly factual to the lyrical, not simply to produce playable dialogue but to create set monologues, the dramatic power of which depends much more on verbal substance than on dramatic context.

Stu's train speech in *Chicago* is a good example. It begins very positively, almost joyfully, but the description becomes uglier, more tired as it goes on as though the speech itself were the train ride, and the imagined riders who started out in high spirits unravel in the process. The speech is clearly Stu's reaction to Joy's impending departure and it presumably gains some dramatic force from an implied relationship between the characters, but its effectiveness is self-contained.

It would be a natural as an exercise in an elocution class if that American phenomenon had not disappeared back in the 1940s. Shepard's other obvious skill is the stock-in-trade of the traditional dramatist, the creation of tension between characters. Where Shepard differs from the traditionalist in these early plays is that we are given no biographical or psychological information to explain the attachments and confrontations, and the relations shift abruptly, operate for only a few sentences sometimes, alter as the characters adopt new personalities or assume borrowed roles. The result is a series of constantly changing dramatic images, each of them carrying at least the promise of emotional content—audience empathy as *coitus interruptus.*

The most effective of the early plays, so far as I am concerned, is *Red Cross.* Unlike so many of the Shepard plays of that period, in which the elements seem often to be in business for themselves, *Red Cross* manages a kind of unity without recourse to connectives like plot or verifiable theme. The balance between the skiing accident (Carol's monologue) and the swimming sequence (Jim's scene with the Maid), between verbal image and visual one (Carol's "little red splotch of blood" on the snow and the actual blood on Jim's forehead at the curtain), between character and character (the transfer of Jim's crabs to Carol) give the play a sense of completeness that even the best of the other plays—*Chicago, Icarus's Mother*—somehow lack.

Red Cross, more obviously than the other early plays, is also reaching forward to the longer plays—*La Turista, The Unseen Hand, Operation Sidewinder*—in which Shepard's themes begin to emerge more clearly. The plays of the late 1960s and early 1970s are often thought of in terms of the recurrent mythical figures—the cowboy, the rock star, the Indian, the enforcer—and of the popular genres—movies, comic books, science fiction—which feed them vocabulary and imagery. Plot and overt satire invade the work, but these plays are more interesting for the view of life that informs their fables, their myths, their images. "Everybody's caught up in a fraction world that they can't even see," Shepard said in a note to the English edition of *The Unseen Hand,* and he ended "Back in the 1970's" in *Hawk Moon* with "And far off you could hear the sound of America cracking open and crashing into the sea."

Shepard's dramatic response to this feeling of a battered and broken society has been a series of escape images, transformation finishes that are sometimes obviously comfort-of-death endings. *Red Cross* has two—Carol's skiing accident in which she is finally only that touch of red on the white snow, and the Maid's imagined transformation into a fish, lying immobile, forgotten, staring at the frozen lake. In *La Turista*, Salem and Kent use and enrich the language of tourism. "You came here to disappear?" she asks Kent and, when she wants to know what he would "do if you did disappear," he answers, "Nothing. I'd be gone." At the end of the play, after a long dual monologue based on the film chase in monster movies in which the alien force has to be captured, destroyed, rendered harmless, Kent swings on a rope from the back of the theatre, across the heads of the audience and the other characters, and crashes through the set leaving just his outline. He disappears in fact.

The connection between disappearance and escape stayed with Shepard long past 1970, led to his use of B. Traven and Howard Hughes—the latter as the original of Henry Hackamore in *Seduced*, the former in Emma's lines in *Curse of the Starving Class*: "That guy who wrote *Treasure of Sierra Madre* . . . And he disappeared. Nobody knew where to send his royalties. He escaped."

There is a wide variety in the escape/transformation endings. *Operation Sidewinder* borrows from Hopi legend, lets some of the characters experience "the Emergence to the Fifth" world as the corrupt Fourth comes to final destruction. *The Mad Dog Blues* closes in a Fellini-like dance as the mythical characters, from Mae West to Captain Kidd, join hands and exit through the audience. In *Seduced* (the published ending differs from the versions performed in Providence and in New York), Henry Hackamore becomes invulnerable to the bullets fired into him and turns into his own myth. These are fantasies not solutions, of course, as the end of *Shaved Splits* indicates. Geez's final speech conjures a perfect jam session amid the ruins of revolutionary violence, but since the speech is constructed on the analogy of Cherry's opening pornography reading, using the same kind of offstage recorded voice, it is clearly imaginary. Other such endings carry the ambivalence within the image—the transformation to beasts at the end of *Back Bog Beast Bait*, Sycamore's assuming Blue's role in *The Unseen Hand*, the fire at the end of *The Holy Ghostly*.

The Western-movie rescue in *Geography of a Horse Dreamer*, "the Sam Peckinpah sequence," as Shepard calls it in *Logbook*, belongs with these other endings. Even Hoss's replacement by Crow can be said to fit the general pattern, but *The Tooth of Crime*, like *Geography* a product of Shepard's stay in London, is far too rich a play to be limited in that way. In the *Theatre Quarterly* interview Shepard said "maybe *Geography* was playing for more modest stakes than *Tooth of Crime*." No *maybe* about it; *Tooth* is his *Master Builder* while *Geography* is his *Three Men on a Horse*. In *Tooth* most of Shepard's imagery sources come together to create a world in which the poet-hero (Hoss) is number one in a profession which crosses rock stardom with killing in a literal sense, decking him out with guns, knives, fast cars, sustaining dope and songs (words and music by Sam Shepard) which raise the character to mythic proportions. Hoss's success is his destruction, locking him into the system ("We're punk chumps cowering under the Keepers and the Refs and the critics and the public eye"), making him ripe for attack from a Gypsy Killer. The battle, when Crow comes to challenge him, turns out to be a contest of style which Crow wins partly because he has allies—Hoss's own doubt and Hoss's entourage, orchestrating his defeat in preparation for the new hero. Often taken as a comment on American artistic-commercial life, *Tooth* is much more universal. After all, without Hilde Wangel's enthusiasm, the master builder would never have had occasion to fall from that steeple. Generations will replace one another, as Ice shows his father in *The Holy Ghostly* when he shoots him.

"Is this that generation stuff that you hear about all the time?" asks Shepard in *Logbook*, after leaving the cozy comfort of the Bob Dylan music to visit a punk-rock club. "Am I a part of the old folks now?" He already knew the inevitable answer to that question when he wrote *The Tooth of Crime*. He knew it earlier still, way back in *The Rock Garden*, which he says "is about leaving my mom and dad," in the dressing-undressing switch that identifies the boy with the man, more abstractly but just as clearly as the costume exchange in *Curse of the Starving Class*.

"I'd like to try a whole different way of writing now," Shepard said before he left England. "Well, it could be called realism, but not the kind of realism where husbands and wives squabble and that kind of stuff." After he returned to this country and allied himself with the Magic Theatre in San Francisco, Shepard continued to write plays that recalled the themes, the images, the non-realistic devices of his earlier work—*Angel City*, *Suicide in B♭*, *Seduced*, *The Sad Lament of Pecos Bill on the Eve of Killing His Wife*. He even returned, in *Inacoma*, to the kind of company-created work which he had a hand in when he worked with The Open Theater early in the decade; in *Tongues*, two monologues done in collaboration with Chaikin, who performed them, Shepard extended his experiments with the supportive juxtaposition of text and music/sound.

Yet, in at least two of his recent plays—*Curse of the Starving Class* and *Buried Child*—he seems to have found his "different way." He has even presented husbands and wives squabbling in the first family plays he has written since *The Rock Garden*. The plays, in setting and even in language, are much closer to traditional American realism than anything Shepard has ever written, but it is a realism that is regularly invaded by Shepard caricature (the enforcers in *Curse*), by symbols (the dead lamb in *Curse*, the child's corpse in *Child*), by Shepard monologues (Wesley's speech at the beginning of *Curse*, Dodge's catalogue of his belongings in *Child*), by visual images which are as powerful as the verbal ones Shepard created in the early plays. The marvelous scene in *Child* in which Tilden cleans the corn and then gently covers his sleeping father with the shucks, as it was played in the New York production, is one of the most remarkable scenes that I can remember having seen on stage.

The settings of the two plays—the unproductive avocado ranch in *Curse*, the barren Midwestern farm in *Child*—are clearly situated in the "America cracking open" of the *Hawk Moon* quotation above. Shepard, for all his distrust of message, of meaning, has become much more specific in his social criticism. In *Curse*, for instance, Weston gives a speech on American debt culture which seems to explain the particular nature of his ruin. That play, with its phantom realtors hovering on the edge of the action ready to devour the family home, is the most explicit social drama Shepard has written. It would be misleading, however, simply to define the play in those terms. Both plays are about the disintegration of the family—at least they present disintegrated families—and the cause is within as much as without. When Emma warns off the prissy con-man in Act I of *Curse* with her account of her family's inherited nitroglycerine in the blood, the scene is comic, but in Act II the family "poison" becomes more serious; in the end, Wesley becomes his father. The family is destroyed (Weston on the lam, Emma dead, the ranch lost) and the fault is as much human as social.

Buried Child is also about inheritance, about Vince's taking over his grandfather's farm. The melodrama plot—the dead baby, the presumed incest between Tilden and his mother—is only a contributary element in a family situation which is already clear as we watch the dying Dodge, the foolish, philandering Halie, their sons, the crippled Bradley and the mentally defective Tilden, and the violent Vince as stranger and then as inheritor.

There is no place in Shepard's realism for the escapes of the fantasy plays. In *Curse*, both Weston and Emma imagine that they might disappear, like B. Traven, in Mexico, and Ella thinks she can get away to Europe. She cannot, but, even if she could, as her daughter tells her, "It'd be the same as it is here." There may be more ambiguity in the end of *Child*, but I do not think so. Conventionally, in the theatre a kind of purification takes place when the secret is uncovered, and life is presumed to go on in a different, a healthier way. When Tilden enters carrying the corpse of the buried child, it could be the sign of a new beginning. After all, he has brought in corn, then carrots, although nothing grows on the property, and at the end Halie's off-stage voice proclaims a miracle, the crops bursting from the ground. "Maybe it's the sun. Maybe that's it. Maybe it's the sun." Even if we do not remember Dodge's earlier words ("Now you think everything's gonna be different. Just 'cause the sun comes out"), our last image is of Dodge, dead on the floor, and Vince, stretched out on the couch, staring at the ceiling, his body having assumed the posture of his dead grandfather.

With these two plays, Shepard seems to be working a theatrical vein more accessible to a larger audience than the one he reached before, as the imprimatur of the Pulitzer implies. What that portends for his work is difficult to guess. He is obviously no longer the boy on the *Five Plays* book jacket, the young man who could simply sit down and write *Chicago* in a single day. "The stuff would just come out," he said in *Theatre Quarterly*, "and I wasn't really trying to shape it or make it into any big thing." As Cody says in *Geography of a Horse Dreamer*, "At first it's all instinct. Now it's work." The best of Shepard is so good and even the worst of Shepard is so provocative that anyone who cares about American theatre will happily settle for work over instinct. And Shepard? He has finished shooting another movie. Does that mean a transformation ending—playwright into movie star? A new disappearance? A fresh escape?

THE PLAYWRIGHT AS SHAMAN

Jack Gelber

I've been told more than once that plays, modern plays in particular, are difficult to read. Faced with the spare printed page with its scanty stage directions and elliptical dialogue, the reader must summon an intense and vivifying concentration if he is to get anything out of the experience. Often in our best plays there is as much happening below the lines of dialogue as there is action implied in them. Dialogue is the air in the bubbles breaking sea surface from the very deep, highly condensed, poetically charged experience intended by the author. Asked to read and project an ideal performance of a new play without benefit of the weeks of rehearsal where actors, director, and playwright confront and clarify the text, many readers abandon the effort and read a novel or get out of the house and see a movie.

No wonder then that introductions are commissioned to guide the reader. Unfortunately, I am all too aware of the tendency in our society to substitute the guide for the thing itself: the critic as star. The following is not meant to be a substitute for Sam Shepard's work, nor is it meant to assign a number showing where he stands on someone's hit parade. It is an all too fallible approach intended to aid the reader in getting into the plays. And "getting into" or immersing oneself within the depths of the text is what it's all about.

Since plays are meant to be complete, I try to get a sense of the whole before I attempt to decipher any specific bit of dialogue. I skim. I flip through the pages of the play searching for hints of the playwright's design. I try to get a sense of the characters, of the story and of the place, but I do not stop the

45

forward momentum in the face of the stumbling blocks of inexact appreciation or less than satisfactory understanding. I push on to the end, for as Kenneth Burke has said, whether we consider life a dream, a pilgrimage, a labyrinth, or a carnival makes all the difference in the world.

What's going on? And is it happening on one set or many? Twentieth-century playwrights have been obsessed with the livingroom, so it should come as no surprise to meet one of the many variations of this theatrical metaphor in *Cowboy Mouth* or *Action*. All but one of Shepard's plays in this collection [*Angel City & Other Plays*, Urizen Books] call for one set, a condition to which I will return. Whether we are in a Hollywood office in *Angel City* or the stage itself in *Mad Dog Blues* I am interested in any event which binds together the characters: a daily ritual, a meal, a particular kind of language. Does the playwright stress the interpersonal relationships as in *Cowboy Mouth*? Or pageantry as in *Mad Dog Blues*? These are the kinds of questions which are held open in order to sniff out a working hypothesis as to what constitutes the moving spirit of the whole.

Are playwrights conscious of this "moving spirit?" The answer is: only dimly while at the writing desk.

Applying this method to Sam Shepard's plays, it takes a glance to recognize that they are trips. Not only are the characters in them on trips, for they tell us as much, but also the shapes of the plays themselves are in the form of trips, quests, adventures. Many of the characters are high on drugs, some are high on music, still others are flying on their own words. These characters speak directly to us or to each other or to their visions, the likes of Mae West, Paul Bunyon, Jesse James, or Lobster Man. These visionary beings are in search of gold, fame, or love, as indeed are the principals. Along the way we see cures, clairvoyance, the finding of lost objects, and the foretelling of the future. And all of this action takes place in play after play on a bare or nearly bare stage accompanied by spell-binding music and trance-inducing monologues.

Anthropologists define the shaman as an expert in a primitive society who, in a trance state induced by drugs or music or other techniques, directly confronts the supernatural for the purposes of cures, clairvoyance, the finding of lost objects, and the foretelling of the future. Sam Shepard, my working hypothesis runs, is a shaman—a New World shaman. There are no witches on broomsticks within these pages. That's the Old World. Sam is as American as peyote, magic mushrooms, Rock and Roll, and medicine bundles.

North and South American Indian shamans regularly use drugs to induce trancelike states which carry them on their trips to the spirit world. The primitivist in Shepard parallels this experience (*Mad Dog Blues, Cowboy Mouth*) with certain characters in his plays who actually take drugs, go on trips, and live out what they hear and see. The emphasis is on the trip, the personal visions, the shamanistic goals fulfilled along the way—in short, the metaphysical. It is not important for Shepard to examine the social, economic, or political implications of drug taking. One must not ask him to answer questions he hasn't asked. Drugs are one technique in altering the conception of space-time between audience and actor. This alteration is essential if anything remotely resembling the metaphysical is to occur. Shepard's design is to promote a theatrical condition between audience and actor similar to an ecstatic state which will allow him to fulfill his shaman's role within the play and between audience and actor.

Even when a particular play does not have a character altering his consciousness with a chemical substance, the trance strategy remains. The sound of the cricket in *Cowboys # 2* and the saxophone in *Angel City* would be mesmerizing in production. The reader ought to make an effort to keep them alive in the background of his mind, for Shepard's obsessively minute instructions regarding music and off-stage dialogue are the expert's choices to invoke another world.

One effect of the volcanic monologue, which is one of Shepard's favorite forms of address, is the near hypnotic state it promotes. These riffs, these poetic ejaculations are incantatory. They reaffirm the contiguous time between audience and actor without which the playwright as shaman could not function.

Still another element in the preparation of the audience in accepting the metaphysical nature of the evening is the matter of the bare or open stage. The open stage theatrically forces the audience to concentrate on a few suggestible props and use its imagination to provide the rest. The playwright need not depend on expensive stage machinery to move his characters from place to place because the audience makes the necessary mental adjustments. In Shepard's plays the abstract quality of the open stage lends credibility to the mythical figures in *Mad Dog Blues* and *Cowboy Mouth*. Having everything happen in one set with the audience doing the mental traveling also reinforces the continuity with the actors. Combined with the time element, which is usually left unbroken, the use of one set, the open stage, solidifies the sense of immediacy.

This sense of "nowness" celebrates in a personal way the human scale of the theatrical experience. Of course, if Shepard is to make the world of the spirit palpable he must have the cooperation of the audience. How else is he to effect a cure or find a lost love?

One exception to the shaman theory is the earliest play included here, *The Rock Garden*. The presentation of the man and woman as endlessly mouthing boring American claptrap goes beyond boring into irritation, and as irritation reaches its apex the young man in the play erupts in a monologue designed to shock a puritanical old man with its sexual explosiveness. It literally knocks him over and kills him.

Despite the hilarious table dance and bear imitation, *Action* resonates a

European sensibility which appears to be set off by visions of a holocaust. Although the four young people in the play have their counterparts in his other work, here they are isolated, trying to survive apart from society.

There is a definite movement in Shepard's work to center shamanism in one character rather than spreading it around. That character is the artist, the poet-visionary. In the latest Shepard play, *Angel City*, the character "Rabbit" has been called for to help doctor a disaster movie which is in great danger of becoming a disaster itself. Rabbit shows up with his medicine bundles and does his stuff. It is when I begin to describe this play that I begin to sense how inadequate this introduction is. It is here that the content of Shepard's work blinks on and off like a neon sign at Hollywood and Vine, and my text touches content hardly at all, which means that it must be time for me to stop and for you to get the message yourself.

SPECTACLE OF DISINTEGRATION
Operation Sidewinder

John Lahr

Operation Sidewinder begins with an image of strangulation. The lights come up on a desert. A mammoth snake, its eyes blinking like red beacons, is poised to strike. Two tourists—Honey and her husband, Dukie—stop to photograph the curiosity. While Dukie sets up his tripod, Honey gets too close to the snake. The snake leaps; she is caught in its powerful coil. Dukie photographs the event while barking orders to her, and then runs for help. The image sets the tone of the play: grotesque, horrific, and darkly comic. Things are out of joint, and people, surrounded by images of disintegration and death, are so numb to them as is Dukie, who is photographing the preposterous embrace. Shepard strings his play out in episodes which counterpoint the country rock music played by the Holy Modal Rounders. Each scene is like a panel in a medieval triptych (a small mystery which is clarified only after one experiences the entire event). The theatrical experience is deepened by the musical one which, like print in medieval illuminated manuscripts, is for a modern audience an explicit but less familiar language than the stage image.

The characters react to death and the threat of it in an aloof, absurd way. Shepard's central figure, the Young Man, is waiting nervously for his car to be fixed at a desert garage. The car has a mysterious ailment—its lights blink uncontrollably. Dukie races in for help. The Young Man wants his car. The mechanic tries to calm Dukie down. The Young Man draws a gun and demands that the mechanic get on with the work. Dukie makes a panic-striken move. The gun goes off, almost by surprise, and Dukie is dead. Seconds later, the mechanic is shot, and he somersaults backward in a parody of a gun-duel death.

The Young Man is obsessed with carrying out a crackpot, radical scheme to seize Air Force planes on the desert by dropping dope into a military reservoir. He is delivering guns for Mickey Free, the Indian renegade who will actually make the drop to his contact, an old prospector. Their meeting place is the spot where Honey has been attacked. She is still writhing with the snake. The prospector gabbles on to Honey as if he were daydreaming. He talks about the decay of the old mining towns, but not of her danger. The Young Man arrives but pays no attention to Honey. The prospector points her out to him. "She's got nothing to do with me," the Young Man says, handing over the gun and leaving. In order to survive, the Young Man cannot permit himself to feel for others. Death surrounds him and he acts as though his emotions are frozen.

The Air Force officers are introduced into *Operation Sidewinder* in an oblique, alcoholic discussion about hunting dogs. The military men are literally numb from drinking; they too are cut off from themselves and the world. They are debating remedies, not for society but for their animals. They talk about them as people to justify loving them, whereas the reverse process—dehumanizing people and describing them as pigs, dogs, freaks—makes it easier to justify killing humans:

> COLONEL WARNER: Trouble with that bitch, you just didn't get her out in the world enough, Henry. A young bitch like that's gotta come in contact with a whole lotta people and noise. Otherwise, you'll just never get her cured.

Everyone is struggling to survive. Mickey Free, the half-breed, cuts Honey loose from the snake, keeping the gigantic head for himself. The Young Man enters with the dope and the final plans. Again he blocks out Honey's predicament: "I see you're free now. Why don't you split?" But the irony, reiterated continually through the play, is that because of individual obsessions (means of psychically sidestepping death) no one is free. Mickey Free has sold his Indian birthright in order to survive. He has killed his own tribesmen; he has led the white man to the land which is now the military installation he is plotting to destroy. The Young Man makes the final arrangements. Mickey Free leaves. The Young Man is left alone with Honey and the severed body of the snake. He starts to shoot up, but he has no belt. He tries using the snake's massive coil. The extent of his despair is measured by the exaggeration of that gesture. In this barren terrain, anything that will give life or alleviate the sense of decay is acceptable. A song makes the point:

> It doesn't matter what you try it's all about take and give
> It doesn't matter how you die but only how you live

A sense of frenzy builds out of the play's grotesque images of death. The obsession with killing evolves out of the climate of suffocation. "Men are most apt to kill when they feel themselves symbolically dying—that is, overcome by images of stasis, meaninglessness, and the separation from the larger currents of human life." (Robert J. Lifton, *History and Human Survival*.) Even the snake—an escaped Air Force computer invented to trace UFOs—is struggling for its survival. The military has created the snake out of a desire to extend human power to control of the universe. The Air Force wants the snake back because it represents billions of research dollars; the snake's inventor, Dr. Vector, wants it back in order to justify his life's work and to calibrate the superhuman capabilities of his invention. As he explains to the Air Force officers:

> DR. VECTOR: At this stage it became apparent to me that all man-made efforts to produce this type of information were useless and that a much more sophisticated form of intelligence was necessary. A form of intelligence which, being triggered from the mind of man, would eventually, if allowed to exist on its own, transcend the barriers of human thought and penetrate an extraterrestrial consciousness.

The oppressiveness of the society's technology—the death-oriented investment in military research and the military itself—becomes so large a threat that the radical despair turns from revolutionary plans to petty rebellions. The Young Man is a pawn for three black militants. Shepard introduces the audience to the trio as they discuss their plan at a desert hot-dog stand. Their political scheme is as pathetic and futile as the Weathermen's but, like the Young Man, they have lost a sense of their identity in America and they are trying to forge a new one. Revolution gives their lives an immediate focus and destiny. The militants are very conspicuous guerrillas. Dressed in paramilitary fashion, they exist above ground in a daydream of underground activity. The carhop immediately assumes they are Panthers. They want lunch; she wants a soul talk. She too is looking for a sense of power and purpose. She imitates their rhetoric of revolt and imagines a revolutionary unity in a society which, like the snake, has been dramatically divided.

> CARHOP: Like I can really dig this whole unity thing that you guys are into but it seems like we could be doing something to help bind it all together. You know. I mean you people have such a groovy thing going. . . . We're not going to turn on any of those zombies. We gotta find our own people. Turn ourselves on. Make something happen for us.

Her hyperbole is hilarious. In her eyes, the blacks as victims are the only hope of America's spiritual salvation. She sees only the relationship between purity and powerlessness. But when the blacks talk about their plans, the audience sees how deeply the society's oppression has affected them. One crazy scheme is topped by another:

> BLOOD: The pilots get a good taste of supersonic water. They start feel-
> ing funny. They hear voices. They see things in the air. They hear
> music. They get stoned like they never been before in their lives . . . In
> the middle of the night they all get up in unison like Dracula and his sis-
> ters and walk straight into the night. They climb into their sleek F-one-
> elevens and take off. They fly straight for a little island just south of
> Miami whereupon they land and await further instructions.
> DUDE: I don't know, it's like James Bond or something. Why don't we
> just go in and take the thing over?

The blacks' scheme may seem outrageous, but the despair beneath it parallels the Yippie tactics in Chicago:

> The list of Yippie projects, by no means exhaustive, include ten thou-
> sand nude bodies floating in protest in Lake Michigan; the mobilization
> of Yippie "hookers" to seduce delegates and slip LSD into their drinks; a
> squad of 230 "hyperpotent" hippie males assigned to the task of seduc-
> ing the wives and daughters of delegates . . . the insertion of LSD into
> the city's water supply. . . . An emergency guard [of Chicago Police]
> was placed on the city's LSD-threatened water supply, just in case.
> (Lewis Chester, Godfrey Hodgson, Bruce Page, *An American
> Melodrama.*)

The gestures become more preposterous as the society becomes more re-
pressive. The victims become victimizers. In *Operation Sidewinder*, the
ghoulish paradox in the Air Force plot is that there is a lack of humanity in
the rebellion. In the name of life, the revolutionaries will take lives. The
"heroism" of the radicals is not in their plan for society, but in taking *any* action at all. As the targets get larger, the possibilities for success get smaller.
The desperation in the recent bombings that have terrified the nation comes
out of the kind of manic anguish Shepard dramatizes. In both the stage and
the real world, we witness the panic-stricken attempts of the drowning to find
air, to rid themselves of society's death imprint. A terrorist letter (*The New
York Times*, March 13, 1970) contains the pain, the dislocation, the mad
disproportion Shepard evokes through the Young Man and the militant
"cadre":

> This way of "life" is a way of death. To work for the industries of death
> is to murder. To know the torments Amerika inflicts on the Third
> World, but not to sympathize and identify, is to deny our right to
> love—to deny our own humanity. We refuse. In death-directed
> Amerika there is only one way to a life of love and freedom; to attack
> and destroy the forces of death and exploitation and to build a just
> society—revolution.
> —(*Signed*) Revolutionary Force 9

Shepard's Young Man, zonked on drugs and obsessed with his scheme, has tried and failed to find a place for himself in America. He sees his predicament clearly, but he cannot put a stop to historical momentum. Sitting with Honey in the desert, he says, "I am depressed, deranged, dehumanized . . . and damned." His anxiety comes from feeling the innocence and purity ripped from him by the society that betrays even the dreams it foists on its citizens in order to control them. Honey confesses that she and her husband were on their way to get a divorce. She is bored. She can't understand her aimlessness. But as she talks, Honey shows her sense of abandonment by describing dreams of largesse, safety, and hope which have fed the nation's mythology:

> HONEY: . . . my mama said that sometime . . . someday I'd make my living from my hair. That I should come to Hollywood and the very next day, just from walking around the streets and everything, that someone would see my hair and ask me to come and get a screen test. And that before very long I'd be famous and rich and everything.

For Honey and the Young Man, the only experience of America is loss. The play's episodic structure is a dreamlike correlative to the Young Man's sense of America. As one of the songs emphasizes, there is nothing in America to latch on to:

> I came here with my guidebook
> With my license in hand
> But the landing field keeps slipping out of line
> And this ain't what they told me I'd find
> The biggest laugh around here
> Is the changing ground here

When Honey asks the Young Man his name and his origins, he starts to freak out. He is everyman and no man; he is everywhere and nowhere:

> YOUNG MAN: I am from the planet Crypton. No. I am from the Holly-wood Hills. No. I am from Freak City. That's where I was raised any-way . . . I am an American though. Despite what they say. In spite of the scandal. I am truly an American. I was made in America. Born, bred, and raised. I have American scars on my brain. Red, white, and blue. I bleed American blood. I dream American dreams. I fuck American girls. I devour the planet. I'm an earth eater.

The Young Man wants to swallow the world, to hold it within himself. He cannot relate to a life force within America. Like the rest of the people in Shepard's play, he belongs to a country of aliens. A song crystallizes the Young Man's predicament:

> I couldn't go back where I came from
> 'Cause that would just bring me back here
> And this is the place I was born, bred, and raised

And it doesn't seem like I was ever here

The Young Man has witnessed the violence of the government toward peaceful protest. He is haunted by images of political deception and emotional castration:

> YOUNG MAN: . . . The election oppression: Nixon, Wallace, Humphrey. The headline oppression every morning with one of their names on it . . . And I was all set to watch "Mission: Impossible" when Humphrey's flabby face shows up for another hour's alienation session. Oh please say . . . something different, something real, something—so we can believe again. His squirmy little voice answers me, "You can't always have everything your way." And the oppression of my fellow students becoming depressed. Depressed. Despaired. Running out of gas. "We're not going to win. There's nothing we can do to win." This is how it begins, I see. We become so depressed we don't fight any more. We're only losing a little, we say. It could be so much worse. The soldiers are dying, the Blacks are dying, the children are dying. It could be so much worse.

Those bludgeoned and jailed for legally protesting the 1968 Chicago Democratic Convention are the Young Man's ghosts. The government reacts with equal capriciousness to legal or illegal protest. The Young Man's actions are an attempt to deny the lies of government, to mobilize himself with an energy and force he cannot find in the society. He feels invisible; the plot is a means of making his presence felt.

But the Young Man's plan does not work. Mickey Free does not make the drop. Instead, he takes the head of the snake to the Spider Lady, the shaman of the Hopis. She immediately accepts this as an omen of their race's transcendence, the final struggle between the material and the spiritual world:

> SPIDER LADY: . . . once the two halves were joined the people would be swept from the earth by a star, for they were to be saved from the destruction at hand. That soon after the spirit snake would again be pulled in half by the evil ones and the Fourth World would come to an end.

Mickey Free gives up guns and drugs, and awaits his spiritual transformation. Meanwhile, the blacks have sent the Young Man and Honey back into the desert looking for the sidewinder computer, which the blacks want for political leverage. To the military, the snake is property; to the Young Man and Honey, it is a way of getting themselves out of a threatening jam; to Mickey Free, it is a hope of rebirth.

The CIA is brought into the case. Captain Bovine questions the prospector about the identity of the Young Man. Behind Bovine's search for scapegoats is an insistence on national purity, a dream he will not admit has been destroyed. His conspiratorial view of history reflects his own consciousness of the society's deterioration. The Young Man and the other renegades in Shepard's play use sex, revolution, and drugs to get outside their flesh, to imitate the longed-for rebirth. Captain Bovine faces the same problem, but has a different solution. He is also confused about the present, but he wants to return to a past he imagines was secure:

> CAPTAIN BOVINE: . . . Over the past few years there's been a general breakdown of law and order and a complete disrespect for the things we hold sacred since our ancestors founded this country. This country needs you, Billy. It needs your help to help root out these subversive, underground creeps and wipe the slate clean once and for all. . . . Things have stayed the same for too long now. It's time for a change!

Captain Bovine is talking the language of annihilation. Shepard etches the contours of what is emerging in America: a society more afraid of its dissenters than its corruption. Bovine wants a pure society, a nation as pristine as it was when the first settlers came here. Yet he cannot see how far that society has strayed from its original dreams. Richard Harris reports in his book *Justice* that Attorney General Richard G. Kleindienst had "reportedly promised to crack down on 'draft dodgers,' on 'anarchistic kids,' and on 'militants' of all persuasions, and this threat led some high members of the Justice Department to wonder if all dissent was to be stifled on the pretext that it amounted to subversion." Harris quotes from a report in the *Chicago Daily News*:

> Undercover police investigations in Illinois are at an all-time high. In the Chicago area alone, more than 1000 men from the FBI and various other federal, state, county, and city agencies are working on super-secret assignments. "Our growing concern about subversives and militants with their talk of armed revolution has brought us a temporary shift away from organized crime," said Illinois State Police Supt. James T. McGuire. "I've never seen anything like the intensity of the current investigations in all my years in law enforcement. . . ."

Operation Sidewinder dramatizes the yearning for a new history and the search for new symbols to inhabit the world. Like the Young Man, Shepard is fascinated by Indian culture. The apocalyptic vision prophesied by the Spider Lady is acted out on the stage—a fantasy enactment of our cosmic longings and fears, as in a science-fiction thriller. This theatrical tactic reflects Shepard's own desire to have symbols transformed from death-giving to life-giving. The sidewinder begins the play as an evil omen associated with a Christian tradition which has linked the snake with death, and ends as a symbol of rebirth. At first, Honey and the Young Man do not react like Mickey Free when they bring the body of the snake back into the Hopi camp:

> MICKEY: You are the Pahana! You have come! You have brought us

our salvation!

YOUNG MAN: Wait a minute! Wait a minute! That's mine! That belongs to somebody else! Mickey! Cut it out! You can't have that snake! . . . That's a machine, you creep! It's not real. The Air Force cooked it up to trace flying saucers! The spades want it to trace the Air Force. I want it because it means my life if I don't get it back to them.

The Hopi snake dance begins, with the sidewinder incorporated into the ritual. Shepard is interweaving cultures: that of the Indian, with his sense of sacredness in life, with that of a modern society which has lost that reverence. The play's final image brings the outlandish plot to a brilliant epiphany: the world of spirit (the Indians) challenged by the material world (the military). Paratroopers, claiming the sidewinder as their property, interrupt the snake dance just as the snake's head is being reunited with its body, fulfilling the Hopi prophecy of transcendence. Honey and the Young Man have now allied themselves with the Indians, discovering an identity and a sense of spiritual continuity. The radical scheme and the drugs are abandoned for a mystical "grace." To the Indians, Honey and the Young Man are saviors; but they are also saved. Chanting, while the soldiers fire into the crowd, the Indians cling to the snake. No one falls. Finally, a soldier wrestles the snake away. He rips off its head. His victory is the destruction of the world. The Indians, untouched, move toward their salvation; the soldiers twitch in a violent death. Smoke fills the theatre. The final poetic image anticipates the apocalypse and friezes the true believer.

American theatre is threatened by the same *rigor mortis* as the society. For both to survive, a new flexibility must evolve. To achieve this, the playwright and his audience must take risks. Not all theatrical probings will be successful and those that succeed may be flawed as literature. But the theatre needs distinct, ruthless visions like those of Shepard to shock its audiences from their life-sleep, that numbing complacency by which they survive the nation's spiritual decay by pretending it doesn't exist.

IMAGE SHOTS ARE BLOWN

The Rock Plays

Robert Coe

In proclaiming the simultaneous disintegration and triumph of a distinctly American mythology, Sam Shepard has rediscovered, perhaps more completely than any dramatist of his generation, the one transforming American Frontier: "the last horizon of an endlessly retreating vision of innocence" (Leslie Fiedler, *Love and Death in the American Novel*), the *terra nova* of all authentically American writing, past and present.

Shepard's protagonists only indirectly express an interest in the figures of historical time; rather than shape history and discover the names of their desires, they go after adventure, self-discovery and the authentic forms of play. Shepard's theatre incarnates the Cowboy of Interior Plains, the lumpen prole drifter, the shiftless suburban punk, the self-referential jazz artist, the violent and paranoid rocker, the ratiocinating detective, the off-the-wall madman. With his deeply ingrained Western sense of psychological rootlessness and space, Shepard's work is nonetheless prodded by a conflicting urge to make a home in the contemporary wilderness. Appropriately enough, Shepard himself entered the paradoxically open and enclosed space of the theatre not through the urban fastnesses of "literature" but through the ephemera of music, drugs, and the felt needs of an actor working in a decaying Eastern city during a time of intense theatrical experiment and social change. Successfully locating a place in the shattered yet still heroic American landscape, Sherpard's theatre evinces a kind of passage home into the blood truths of second innocence.

In his rock plays of the early '70s—*Cowboy Mouth, Mad Dog Blues*, and *The Tooth of Crime*—Shepard approached rock as the extreme embodiment of his fascination with all theatrical forms. Rock was about much more than cheap thrills and expressionist license. In Shepard's view, America's "temporary culture" had defined and limited the terms of all performance, forcing the Self to act out the fortunes of limited identity in an atmosphere made feverish by the elusiveness of a more substantive freedom; rock offers a countering style of self-assertion, self-command, "full of fuckin' courage . . . flying in the eye of contempt," he writes in *Tooth*. In Shepard's theatre, characters who aren't clinging, paranoid or nostalgic, to some remnant of a real or imagined past attempt vivid projects of self-invention: immediate, exhibitionistic self-projections, an opening of the self to varying styles of risk, violence and escape. Angry and disappointed, seething with thwarted energy and lost patience, they become the wanderers, outlaws, gamblers and musicians—escape artists, seeking a home in the moment, where the heart lies, merging role-playing with iconoclasm, leaping into the void to find themselves on stage. These restless, liberated *personas* overlap in Shepard's imagination: it's the cowboy, Hank Williams (not Little Richard, for instance) who's the Gate Keeper to Shepard's rock 'n' roll heaven, and Bob Dylan, the self-invented Gypsy Cipher of Shepard's *Rolling Thunder Logbook*, who can vanish "like the Lone Ranger."

Just as the Cowboy embodies freedom, self-sufficiency, and a plentitude of interior imagery for theatricalization, the greatest rockers make a music that is "life-infusing, life-transforming," Shepard writes in the *Logbook*. "It's not the kind of energy that drives people off the deep end but the kind that brings courage and hope and above all life pounding into the foreground"—a music that liberates innocence and imagination for performer and audience alike.

The horrors of corporate rock are the subject of Shepard's earliest rock play, *Melodrama Play*, a minor work toying with the barrenness, terror and humiliation of forced creativity and coerced role-playing, a theme Shepard has returned to again and again, most effectively in *Angel City*. Connecting with the traditional American theme of culture's opposition to freedom, Shepard went even further in contending that institutional coercion exposes the ultimate hollowness of the Self: the formalizing tendencies of civilization are not so much oppressive as they are painfully revelatory. Rock music, on the other hand, presented a potentially liberating form. Shepard had a Rousseauesque faith that human freedom isn't a matter of social agreement, tempered with a recognition that freedom comes to those who are prepared to accept its inevitability in formal expression. Consequently, when Dylan tells Shepard that he doesn't want the film of the Rolling Thunder tour to make any "connections," Shepard can let it go, because in his view that's what the tour does by itself through sheer mythic undertow.

There is a danger, however, in the hubristic act of self-creation: it can mask arrogance, self-deception, and emotional poverty, dampening the mythic resonances of the past and present. The pitfalls of performance and the pit-falls of dramatic form are always the same in Shepard's theatre: *Cowboy Mouth*, his collaboration with the poet and soon-to-be rocker Patti Smith, sweeps Slim, Cavale and their audience into the claustrophobic, inflam-matory rhythms of spoken dreams, before surrendering finally in exhaustion to the artificial *coup de theatre* of the Lobster Man/Rock Messiah.

Nonetheless, the need in Shepard's theatre for what might be called an "authentic mask" is overwhelming. When the risks are avoided, as Shepard himself does most clearly in the easy-going, random picaresque *Mad Dog Blues*, then the problem of identity—of the Self, of Acting—is reduced to a matter of pretense and fantasy, a safe and facile copping into roles.

Shepard is best when his characters bleed real blood. Side-stepping the im-perative of self-creation denies Shepard the generative loci of his best work: the notion that performance, as the ritualized act of self-creation, is capable of transforming shattered history into present "nature"; of drawing the displaced thunder of a mythic past into the present to cohere the fragments of the Self. This "communal giving of spirit energy" is the true greatness of both theatre and rock.

Of the rock plays, only *The Tooth of Crime* locates this tension and this promise. The result is one of the most extraordinary plays of the '70s, a sci-fi/primitivist vision uniting language, metaphor, action and intention at a level few American plays have acheived. Shepard begins with the assumption that rock is about violence, a sacred criminal violence with its own standards and values. *Tooth* applies the realization that if denied a living historical base, a continuity of myth, past and present, then such violence is empty, and ultimately self-destructive. Rock was the theatre in which an entire generation enacted precisely the same cultural disillusionment.

Of the many playwrights who've written about rock or rock culture—most notably David Hare, Barrie Keeffe and Thomas Babe—only Shepard has been able to translate the tangible experience of the music to the stage; Shepard in his language has aspired to the condition of rock music itself, connecting his work with a dream revived by the Romantic poets and sur-viving into the post-modern era: language as rhythmic sound, scarcely mediated by the literalness and complexities of linguistic meaning. The result is a poetic, fabulist theatre rather than a naturalistic one.

Tooth, Shepard has written, "started with language—it started with a cer-tain sound which is coming from the voice of this character Hoss." A *sound*—like the musician Niles in *Suicide in B*^{b}, who is "looking for a whole new sound." Sound doesn't exist on what Shepard once called "the boring printed page." In a letter to Daniel Nagrin about their dance/play, *Jacaranda*, Shepard wrote, "My work is not written in granite. It's like playing a piece of music. It goes out in the air and dissolves forever."

Shepard's father was a musician, and Shepard himself plays guitar, piano, and is an accomplished drummer: he performed in his *Operation Sidewinder* at Lincoln Center in 1970 with The Holy Modal Rounders, wrote original scores for *Tooth* and an opera, *Pecos Bill* (1976), and he still sits on San Francisco music productions occasionally. His simple rock compositions depend on strong musicianship and good arrangements for their effectiveness, which is generally dependent on the *mise en scene*; his own musical inclinations tend towards a more improvisatory, looser form than most rock or linear theatre forms permit. (In 1980, Shepard is playing with a free-form jazz group in San Francisco.)

"Ginger Baker's burned down," says Crow in *Tooth*, referring to the flashy power drummer in Cream; in a case of life imitating art, Crow drives the same '58 Impala as the 1975 Rolling Thunder Tour's super drummer, Howie Wyeth. "Get into Danny Richmond," Crow tells Hoss, "Sonny Murray, Tony Williams, one a' them cats. More jazz licks." Shepard seeks a quality of inner listening more generally available in good jazz and only at the highest levels of the rock form.

Shepard's musical training has clearly nurtured the way he writes. "From time to time," Shepard wrote in the December, 1977 *Drama Review*,

> I've practiced Jack Kerouac's discovery of jazz-sketching with words. Following the exact same principles as a musician does when he's jamming. After periods of this kind of practice, I get the haunting sense that something in me writes but it's not necessarily me . . . This identical experience happened to me once when I was playing drums with the Holy Modal Rounders.

Though he insists on the vitality of craft, Shepard remains largely free of literary self-consciousness. "Intellectual probes," Shepard wrote in 1975 (in a position he seems to have softened lately) "are a constant threat to any artist." Shepard is part of an anti-intellectual tradition in American writing dating at least from Whitman, with whom he shares the notion of literacy as somehow at war with spontaneous feeling.

This idea has defined the nature of his accomplishment more than any other artistic choice he's made. As pure wordsmith, Shepard is often sloppy and uneconomical, in the manner of many an American autodidact. He's never exhibited—even when he seemed to need to—a sharply analytical mind, nor has he until recently been at all concerned with self-reflective commentary on creative process within his plays. Like the work of Pinter and McClure, Shepard's plays "translate," he continued in TDR, the daydreams in his head of "characters who appear out of nowhere in three dimensions and speak." In addition to the experience of other media, Shepard has drawn on the gothic melodrama, the detective novels of Raymond Chandler and Dashiell Hammett, old Hollywood films, and the tall tale—elements of

Americana one doesn't necessarily have to study up to use. The very mundanity of these forms open up a space for letting "someone else" take over, so that he, Shepard, might "enter the world behind the form."

His writing usually goes on "halfway in the dark," he claims; he prefers not knowing where he's going. One might argue that he would be a better playwright if he did, but the point is mute: as Balzac might have observed, Shepard's mistakes—mostly of consistency, logic, motivation, and exaggerated facility—sweep all before them, and in practice are elevated to the status of thematic concerns.

Shepard is not being particularly facetious when he writes that he's been influenced by Jackson Pollock, Little Richard, Cajun fiddles and the Southwest; the only playwrights he's publically admired are Beckett, Brecht and Shakespeare. Shepard's unique brilliance and continuing promise must finally be attributed to his negative capability for translating other artistic media into theatrical terms. "Shaping a self out of the materials in which it is immersed," Richard Poirier calls it in *The Performing Self*; "rhythum trade-offs," says Patti Smith, a bit more pointedly. To read Shepard is to renew his ironies and enrich the mythic subtext, but with his often clichéd verbal imagery, unabashed stereotyping, lack of generic decorum, logical contradictions and demotic naiveté, the work remains surprisingly uninvolving on the page: a pretext for performance.

Robert Creeley once observed that a poet doesn't have to "think" anymore than a good musician or a painter has to think. Sam Shepard is evidence that for better or for worse, the same might apply to the playwright, a direction for American dramatists who consider consciously abandoning a literary formalism for an asethetic grounded in experiment and theatrical urgency.

"Words are tools of imagery in motion," Shepard has written. In his rock theatre, he attempted a special kind of violence: rhythmic verbal assault.

A fucked up bed, a dead crow, hubcaps, an old tire, raggedy costumes, a boxful of ribbons, lots of letters, a pink telephone, photographs of Hank Williams and Jimmie Rodgers, stuffed dolls, crucifixes, Southern license plates, a travel poster of Panama, rum, beer, white lightning, a Sears catalogue, drums, guitar and an amp: the junk in the room where Slim and Cavale hold up in *Cowboy Mouth* is the detritus of the western/rock connection, seen through the eyes of Sam Shepard and Patti Smith, holed up together in the Chelsea Hotel in 1970. The play begins with a list or black magic incantation of the terrible powers that hold them enthralled: "Wolves, serpents, lizards, gizzards, bad bladders, typhoons, tarantulas, whipsnakes, bad karma, Rio Bravo, Sister Morphine, go fuck yourself!" cries Slim, thinking about returning to his family in Brooklyn, of all places, but held for the time being in "some border town, some El Paso town," by the decibel dreams and crystal-meth raps of the Circe-like Cavale (meaning "escape"). She's a loser, a cripple, a mystic, a little girl/tough: Patti Smith herself.

Shepard and Smith's poetic strategy is to establish a rhythmic relationship to the use of words through inclusion, incessance, insistence: the modernist delusion of sustaining talk to both create and prop up the world, using the power of myth fired by the tongue to create a timeless present, seeking a salvation in the glory of spoken rhetoric sprayed through an enclosure like visionary Mace.

"The Rock and Roll Savior in the highest state of grace will be the new savior," proclaims Cavale, who wants to transform Slim into the image "of the cowboy mouth . . . somebody [people can] get off on when they can't get off on themselves." This rock star savior is no empty image in which to dump fantasies of power. He is a figure of passion, someone "who'll represent our pain . . . You gotta reach out and grab all the little broken, busted-up pieces of people's frustration," Cavale begs Slim.

> That stuff in them that makes them wanna see God's face. And then you gotta take all that into yourself and pour it back out. Give it to them bigger than life. You gotta be unselfish, Slim.

Shepard and Smith's medium for attempting just that is a black hole of Southwest Indian shamanism, French symbolism, American Western mythology, jazz licks and rock rhythms. Yet *Cowboy Mouth* also finds its life on the margins of a fantastical Christian idealism, with its insistence on future redemption. Johnny Ace is Cavale's early version of the rock messiah, a John the Baptist who died for our sins. Dylan and Mick Jagger are the present-day false messiahs. Interestingly, the mysterious, relatively anonymous Keith Richards, a kind of image model for Crow in *Tooth*, has more appeal for Shepard (and clearly for Smith) than the Stones' glamorous front man.

At any rate, Cavale attaches a disclaimer of sorts to her ambitions: "It don't mean nothing, just play," she tells Slim. Cavale says he's "Mr. Yesterday," but her project also involves a re-visioning of the past, not its extinction: a replacement of the family and a neat little life with the supreme risk of self-sacrifice. She can hardly believe it herself.

"I ain't no rock and roll star," says Slim, who truly hasn't got the chops; despite the banality of his previous life, he can't forget his family and the world outside the room. ("Back to REAL LIFE," Shepard calls it in the *Logbook*.) Cavale fails to make Slim the voice and flesh of her desire. With her crow talisman, she's the Shaman in the Wasteland, daring holy violence; all she does is close down her world. Language has been ignited, desperation momentarily exhausted. With the appearance of the Lobster Man as Rock Messiah (Cavale, who fancies herself as Nerval, must have conjured up the one he walked through the parks of Paris), *Cowboy Mouth*, limited by its fabulist anti-historicism, stumbles into decadent ritual.

> "Most rock plays are just Broadway versions of Rock 'n' Roll. A real rock play would have to be at least as good as The Who. Meaning at

least as overtly violent."

—Sam Shepard in conversation, 1980

As anyone who made it through knows, events of the early '70s struck a hardy blow to the fundamental optimism of the '60s rock culture. A more-or-less naive millenial faith in the ability of society to transform itself was swept away; suppressed anger and violence surfaced from beneath the shattered idealism. Denied a progressive participation in history and an identity as communal sacrament, rock music ceased to galvanize people into broader awareness, devolving for a time into pop or a delusionary hermetics of power.

Mad Dog Blues reflects rather than illuminates the banality of those times, their loss of mission: a corny, undisciplined spectacle, a symptom rather than an insight into the larger cultural disillusionment. While acknowledging white rock's roots in drugs, ambition, street life and the lumpen proletariat, Mad Dog banalizes playfulness—an unfortunate legacy of the playful '60s. As much as Shepard relishes bigness, he has little gift for the kind of broad romp he attempted in Mad Dog. In Tooth, this flaccid, sentimental vision of rock culture—a '60s nostalgia which Shepard thinks "sucks"—will be debunked with devastating power.

At the opening of The Tooth of Crime, a "sound" like the Velvet Underground's "Heroin" segues into Sam Shepard's "The Way Things Are." Hoss, the Star Marker—an established punk criminal—is stuck in oblivion, "fucked up on illusion." The past, present and future have rolled over him, creating an unrecognizable place and time, a blend of the occult, sci-fi futurism, the actual history of rock and rock culture, along with a sadistic criminality capable of taking over entire cities. Crime has displaced rock music in a way that is never described but doesn't need to be: the sub-cultural connections between violence, the white suburban punk, and rock music are convincingly portrayed in the character of Hoss himself.

A vicious loner, a beast of nature, born to kill, Hoss is rising up the charts but anxious nonetheless that his success and stardom are divorcing him from his primitive instincts. His moll, Becky, protests that "the only way to be an individual is in the game," but he senses that his fame has simply gotten him stuck in his image. His astrologer advises "durability," but for Hoss, movement and change are everything; being suicidal is part of his nature, and "the road's what counts."

Hoss has premonitions of a gypsy marker who can take over the game by being outside it—a mark of genius. And despite his belief that turf (space) is both power and freedom, Hoss, Hamlet-like, begins a process of locating himself in time. He wonders what has become of the tradition he feels part of.

> There's no game. It's just back to how it was. Rolling night clubs, strip joints . . . Can't they see where they're going! Without a code it's just a crime. No art involved. No technique, finesse. No sense of mastery.

Anticipating the coming combat, Hoss senses an "emotional field" disturbing the purity of his malice: an empathy with the gypsy marker, based on class and shared history. He tells a story about a fight in the parking lot of the Bob's Big Boy in Pasadena: his friend Moose is being beaten up by crew cut jocks from their own high school.

> Then I saw it. This was a class war. These were rich white kids from Arcadia who got T-birds and deuce coupes for Xmas from Mommy and Daddy. All them cardigan sweaters and chicks with ponytails and pedal pushers and bubble hairdo's. Soon as I saw that I flipped out. I found my strength. I started kickin' shit, man.

Crow makes his awesome second act entrance: this gypsy marker, a pure punk, is a figment at least in part of Hoss's—and Shepard's—ambivalent craving for the liberation of pure violence. The word "Crow" itself is not a symbol; it's a living incantation, Shepard has written. "He speaks in an unheard of tongue . . . He spits words that become his weapons. He doesn't 'mean' anything."

Hoss, who has felt his identity closing in around him, admires and respects Crow at first for not having a role. "Image shots are blown," Crow proclaims, convincing Hoss that he, Crow, is just straight ahead energy, pure style, ahistorical, owing nobody and nothing. A bit more candidly, Crow sings, "I believe in my mask, the man I made up is me," without questioning who does the making up; he tells Hoss that his problem is he "chose ears against tongue."

Not noticing at first that Crow is copping his mannerisms, Hoss is overwhelmed with fascination, curiosity, frankness—innocent emotions which set him up for a fall. Because rather than dueling with "shivs," they settle on something new: a gestalt match, pitting powers of tongue and self-assertion, a battle of style, getting "the image in line with the fantasy rhyme." This macho competition, complete with cheerleaders and a sports referee, will be judged on the basis of "deviation from the neutral field state"; literally, the appearance of pathos or emotion.

Crow's "sound" is an undiluted expression of anger, frustration and cultural poverty, moving him beyond either loathing or confidence. He charts the progress of the punk rocker—"the dumb kid. The loser. The runt. The mutt. The shame kid."—to the discovery of rock.

To Hoss, it's all just phony historicism, history "in the pocket," a fiction, a rationalization, a music in the head, all flash and no heart. But this contest has nothing to do with content. "How can you give points to a liar?" Hoss asks the referee, who awards Crow the round. "I don't," the ref answers. "I give 'em to a winner."

Hoss' "sound" acknowledges roots not in his personal misery but in his music, which is the transcendence of suffering, and more: a music that can actually fend off the oppressor, a music "of something inside that no boss man can touch."

"But you miss the origins, milk face," Hoss tells Crow in black rhythms. "Little Brother Montgomery with the keyboard on his back. The turpentine circuit. Piano ringing through the woods. Back then you get hung you couldn't play the blues." "Bring it to now," Crow protests nervously. "You'd like a free ride on a blackman's back," Hoss retorts. "All you got is yo' poison to call yo' gift."

Hoss has earned his style, and in Shepard's view, this makes him an original—which is to say an innocent, as well as a victim, in this prophetic future, of a bizarre cultural obsolescence. Because of the nature of the game, emotions, even thinking, are retrograde. Crow is triumphant as pure show, flash, violence—in opposition to historical involvement and therefore merely defined by it. Rock is no longer "a technique for giving life," as Ernest Becker once defined all ritual; it has become pure image mongering. The victorious Crow has tricked Hoss: "I give you my style, and I take your turf." As Rene Girard argues convincingly in *Violence and the Sacred*, the kind of violence that breaks down true individuality can only result in martyrdom: ironically, Hoss ends with a pure act of self-definition. He puts a bullet in his mouth.

While Shepard identifies deeply with both Crow and Hoss—each an aspect of what makes his theatre possible—his deeper and more crucial allegiances are with Hoss. Four years after *Tooth*, Shepard writes of an experience at a Tubes concert in Boston the same night Dylan is performing.

> What are all these kids doing watching this shit when they could be hearing good music? What do they care about good music? What do they care about a bunch of West Village folk singers from the sixties? They wanna see some action. They wanna see brains dripping from the ceiling . . . Am I part of the old folks now? Is Dylan? Is Dylan unheard of in certain circles? Like Frank Sinatra? Bing Crosby? Is time flying? Is this time flying right past us on all sides? Can anybody see what's really going on? Not me.

Not Hoss either. He can't learn the new game, so he's got to go; as William Burroughs notes, "The one mark you can never beat is the mark inside."

In the heart of our temporary culture, a culture of almost instant obsolescence, Shepard seeks authentic values to sustain the performing self. These values rest in the ability to trust in the imagination and the heart as a repository of emotional truth, the living myths of the past and present. What Charles Olson (in *Call Me Ishmael*) wrote of Melville is equally true of Shepard and Hoss:

> He had the tradition in him, deep, in his brain, his words . . . his blood . . . History was ritual and repetition when Melville's imagina-

tion was in its own proper beat. It [had] more to do with magic than culture.

Shepard has a similarly conservative desire to sniff "through the past for pieces of evidence that could lead us to a truer picture of the present," as he writes in the *Logbook*. In rock, the risk is that playful self-creation enacted from the depths of historical, mythological memory will be overcome by the darker spirit of sacrifice, which "reveals the whole science of ritual," writes Becker in *Escape from Evil*, "establishing a footing in the invisible dimension of reality." *Tooth* was Shepard's last rock play.

"I tend to run away," Shepard has written of his own processes. "It's scary because I can't answer to it from what I know." The fundamental American myth involves what Huck Finn called "lighting out for the territories." Though perhaps we might also consider the real meaning of the word "history," from the Greek root, *istorin*: to go find out for yourself.

AN INTRODUCTION
La Turista

Elizabeth Hardwick

A few lines, as a prologue to my review of Sam Shepard's *La Turista* which is reprinted here just as it was written immediately after seeing the play. I have, in the months since, thought again and again about this play and the imaginative strength of it. From the moment I entered the American Place Theatre I was caught up in the violent energy of a new work. It is hard to forget the bright, bright yellow and orange set, so hard and brilliant, so open, glaring and aggressive, that announced the bright, glaring, aggressive brilliance of the play.

Some further thoughts about the text occur to me. Nothing is harder to come by than a truly meaningful central image, one that opens out to possibility, encourages invention. For some reason we must, aesthetically, be satisfied with the image, or situation, on the first plane of concreteness. Without that it is hard to give assent to the elaborations that will follow; in a sense you have to enter the structure the author gives you before you are willing to see what is inside. In this play the identity of the person—the tourist—and his affliction, that humbling diarrhea—"la turista"—are signified by a single word. This word and the two things it represents are the bare center of the play, the ruling image. The sickness is a sort of a joke—that kills.

Salem and Kent are literally tourists in Mexico in the first act. In the second, which in point of time takes place before the first, Kent is on another kind of journey—I won't say "trip"— in which American rhetoric is offered for his cure just as the blood of freshly killed chickens had been offered in "primitive" Mexico. Neither works.

Perhaps the characters are not profitably thought of as characters at all. They are actors, parodists. They slip from style to style; they carry a few props around with them as they change their roles; they "freeze" when they want to withdraw from the action on the stage. The essence of their being is energy, verbal energy. In the restless inventiveness of their parodies and tirades, a storm of feeling and experience blows across the stage. The parts are arias. In the last section of Act II Doc and Kent "sing" an extraordinary duet. These arias have to do with death. It is amazing the number of "deaths" that will fit the text: Vietnam, Santo Domingo, racial violence, drop-outs, colonialism.

When I wrote about the play, I gave more attention to the critics than I think it is worth now. And yet that was a part of the scenery in which the first production of the play took place. I would have felt very sorry if I had missed seeing it and I must confess that I hated to see it close. But this play lives on the page, and that is a rare thing nowadays.

La Turista by Sam Shepard, in a dazzling production at the American Place Theatre, is a work of superlative interest. The reviewers have not been invited to submit an evaluation of the play. It is merely there, for a month, appearing for the membership of the American Place and for those who find their way to it. I have no knowledge of the intentions and feelings about the reviewers of those responsible for this play; I went to it of my own free will and write about it under no duress and without asking permission. Still, it appears logical that when a play invites the press it is making a sort of plea or demand that the reviewer, under his contractual obligations to his publication, offer some comment about what he has seen. He may not have wished to go and he may not wish to write; he is a captive, arbitrarily condemned to the formation of an opinion. The production, by its foolhardy solicitations, condemns itself to the recognition of the opinions. Play and critic, thereby, become linked like suspect and detective.

The night I saw La Turista the American Place audience was, for the most part, utterly depressing; middle-aged, middle class and rather aggressively indifferent: a dead weight of alligators, dozing and grunting before muddily sliding away. It felt like nothing so much as those same old evenings in our theatre, evenings with the reviewers spaced about like stop signs. A further step in the liberation of the theatre became evident: not only must the reviewers be freed of their obligation to go to a play, but the audience they have created, their bent twigs, should not be the object of special encouragement. It is hard to imagine anyone acting under the influence of the inchoate homilies of, for instance, Richard Watts who looks after our local and national morals for us, but, even in the case of La Turista, one could *imagine* a line slowly forming outside some box office and the people whispering,

"Walter Kerr sort of liked it a little, and you know *he* never likes anything."
But, indeed, what good does it do a man to go to see something he won't like
just because the reviewers have told him to do so? He would be better off at
home. Our new American theatre cannot play to the old audience; it must
have a new one.

In *La Turista* there is a poignant meeting on some pure level of understanding of playwright, director and actor: the sort of unity that makes the Royal
Shakespeare's production of *The Homecoming* so rare. Jacques Levy, the
director, is a theatrical talent of unremitting inspiration. The actors are all
first-rate, but in Sam Waterston the play has a young actor of such versatility
and charm that one hardly knows how to express the degree of his talents.
With this play, the promise of the lofts of off-off-Broadway, the dedication
and independence, come to the most extraordinary fulfillment. You do not
feel you are being given a package, assembled for a purpose, and in some
ways this is disconcerting to the senses. The audience, accustomed to
ensembles created as a calculation, may feel left out, slow to respond, trapped
by a sluggish metabolism. In the long run, what is so beautiful is the graceful—in spite of the frenzied energy—concentration of the work as a whole,
and for that, if one would take it in, the audience also has to work.

Sam Shepard, the author of *La Turista*, is twenty-three years old and even
so he is not new to the theatre. He is not being "discovered" in this production. His plays have been off-off in the Cafe La Mama repertory; he has been
at the Cherry Lane and will soon be in print. *La Turista* is his most ambitious
play thus far but still it is in the same style and voice as *Chicago* and his other
one-act plays. The scene opens on an electrifying set: a bright, bright formica
yellow hotel room in Mexico. A young American couple—Salem and Kent—
are sitting up in their twin beds. They are covered with a deep bronze suntan
make-up and are holding their arms out stiffly. On the beach, as a part of
their vacation, they have gotten a painful sunburn. They talk of first, second, and third—and *fourth* degree burns.

> "Well, the epidermis is actually cooked, fried like a piece of meat over a
> charcoal fire. The molecular structure of the fatty tissue is partially
> destroyed by the sun rays and so the blood rushes to the surface to
> repair the damage."
>
> ". . . It's just the blood rushing to the surface."

Mock scientific dialogue, inserted merely for itself, delivered in a cool,
matter-of-fact way, but sharply, insistently, is characteristic of the writing.
(Of course, the couple with their expensive, painful sunburns will bring to
mind those other burns of our time.) The players hardly ever look at each
other. There is a feeling of declamation, rather than of conversation or
dialogue. And yet the monologues do not at all suggest that banality of
Broadway—the "failure of communication"—but actually are quite the op-

posite. They are an extreme of communication. Kent, the young man, also has, in addition to his sunburn, "la turista," the intestinal distress that affects Americans when they visit poor countries like Mexico. At this point in the play, a young Mexican enters. He is one of the world's poor, with his American phrases ("I had to follow that cat around with a palm fan while he scored on all the native chicks")—he begs and yet he is intractable, unmanageable. He spits in the young American's face.

As the act progresses, Kent becomes very ill. Two wonderfully absurd witch doctors, Mexican style, are brought in, with live roosters, candles, voodoo and crucifixes. Kent dies, a sacrifice to "la turista"—his lack of resistance to the germs of the country he arrogantly patronizes with his presence. The second act has all the same elements as the first, but they are acted out in a Summit Hotel sort of room in America and the witch doctors are two circuit rider charlatans in Civil War dress. Here Kent dies of sleeping sickness, or perhaps he is on drugs; in any case he has an American disease this time—he doesn't like to be awake. His final monologue is a psychedelic tirade—and he jumps, in his pajamas, through the hotel wall, leaving the print of the outlines of his body in the wallpaper.

George Eliot said that she wrote all her novels out of the belief in "the orderly sequence by which the seed brings forth a crop of its kind." We all have a nostalgia and longing for this order because it has been the heart of European fiction and drama. Incident after incident, each growing out of the other, united in a chain of significant motivation, of cause and effect—moments of human destiny strung out like beads on a string. This is what we mean, perhaps, when we say we "understand" a work of literary art. Yet each decade brings us the conviction that this order is no longer present to the serious writer. It is most appealing to those writers who construct their works for some possibility of the marketplace. The episodic, the obscurely related, the collection of images, moods: connections in fiction and also in drama have become like those of poetry. Tone and style hold the work together, create whatever emotional effect it will have upon us. Out of episodes and images, characters and conflicts are made, but they are of a blurred and complex sort.

Formless images and meaningless happenings are peculiarly oppressive to the spirit, and the inanities of the experimental theatre could make a man commit suicide. Sam Shepard, on the other hand, possesses the most impressive literary talent and dramatic inventiveness. He is voluble, in love with long, passionate, intense monologues (both of the acts end in these spasms of speech) which almost petrify the audience. His play ends with sweating, breathless actors in a state of exhaustion. The characters put on a shawl and begin to declaim like an auctioneer at a slave mart, or a cowboy suit and fall into Texas harangues. They stop in the midst of jokes, for set pieces, some fixed action from childhood, perhaps influenced by the bit in Albee's *Zoo*

Story. Despair and humor, each of a peculiarly expressive kind, are the elements out of which the script of the play is made. The effect is very powerful and if it cannot be reduced to one or two themes it is still clearly about us and our lives. The diction, the acting, the direction, the ideas are completely American and it is our despair and humor Shepard gets onto the stage.

To return to the decision about the critics: it is a sacrificial act of the most serious sort. It means nothing less than, after a fixed short run, if one is lucky enough to have that, the play may suffer simple cessation for want of those and good and bad advertisements combed from the newspapers and television. Perhaps it is only young people, free of deforming ambitions, who would have the courage to submit to such a test. Or perhaps it is the strength of their art that allows them to wait for what will come or not come. There are worse things than silence.

VISIONS OF THE END
The Early Plays

Michael Bloom

Even without being there, one can easily imagine that the first audiences to see Sam Shepard's early one-acts must have been shocked by their strange and novel theatricality. Although by 1964 off-off-Broadway audiences had already been exposed to the European avant-garde as well as to such Americans as Joel Oppenheimer, Al Carmines, and Leonard Melfi, nothing could have prepared them for Shepard's spare, cool, yet explosive short plays; specifically, for a central character in *Chicago* who spent most of the play in a bathtub situated on an otherwise bare stage, and two characters who used a tablecloth and barbecue to send smoke signals to an airplane in *Icarus's Mother*. Even within their contexts these occurrences seemed, to many, to be deliberately mysterious and arbitrary, and Shepard was attacked for being a theatrical provocateur, producing effect for its own sake. But as understanding of non-realistic work has increased and as myth and a transformation of realism have clarified Shepard's intentions, the early one-acts have become more resonant and intelligible.

From *The Rock Garden* through *Red Cross* (1964-68) and beyond, Shepard's one-acts are plotless, without obvious subject matter, and lacking in the complete individuation of character and place. An early director and critic of Shepard, Michael Smith, describes the playwright's early method as "a gestalt theatre which evokes the existence behind behavior." But getting to the meaning of these plays means going beyond this excellent capsule description to the question of the *quality* of the existence behind the behavior, to the *type* of consciousness Shepard chose to dramatize.

The Rock Garden, Shepard's first extant script, conforms nicely to Smith's notion of a "gestalt theatre." Lacking any narrative at all, the play describes in a kind of triptych portrait a single condition of sensation—the utter tedium and boredom of a typical American family situation. In the silent, opening "panel," a Boy and a Girl (probably brother and sister) exchange glances and sip glasses of milk until finally, out of boredom, the Girl drops her glass and spills the milk. The two other panels that follow this comic "blackout" scene elaborate on the same condition. In the second panel a Woman (apparently the children's mother) chatters on about her father, who led an absurdly sedentary existence:

> Sometimes he just stayed in the attic. He'd stay up there for days and never come down . . . He knew a lot of people. They'd stop by to see him but he was always in the attic. I always wondered why they kept coming back.

From time to time she tells the Boy how much he resembles her father, and after each comparison she orders him to fetch her a glass of water or a blanket. Gradually it becomes clear that on some level of consciousness the Woman has been using the memory to suppress the Boy, continuing the static, vapid existence that characterized her father's life. In response to this threat the Boy—who begins the scene in his underwear—covers himself by gradually putting on all his clothes. The scene ends when the Boy hurriedly exits and the Man, dressed only in his underwear, takes the Boy's place opposite the Woman.

With the juxtaposition of similar images—the Boy and the Man dressed in underwear and seated identically—Shepard symbolizes the Man's impotence, the Boy's future, and the continuity of generations in a sterile, empty family. Because it foregoes strong dramatic actions, juxtaposing simple, banal activities to express a single condition or gestalt, this oblique, deliberately static method is the perfect formal equivalent to the family's emptiness.

In the final panel of this family portrait the Man explains to the Boy the enjoyment he gets from working his garden. But instead of living, growing plants, the Man's idea of a garden is an arrangement of rocks. As the Man rambles on, mindlessly praising the rock garden, the Boy continually falls off his chair out of boredom. Finally, in a stunning non-sequitur, the Boy breaks through the malaise by launching into a catalogue of his sexual techniques with women (real or imagined), at the end of which, for a very different reason, the Man falls off his chair. Although it is an obvious shock effect, the Boy's search for what Norman Mailer would have called "an orgasm more apocalyptic than the one that preceded it" is an appropriately desperate effort to transcend a stifling, barren, inert existence. In poetic terms the image of the Boy's ejaculation—his foundation of life—is in perfect antimony to the image of the lifeless rock garden.

If the playwright's technique was strange and unfamiliar, his vision was, in retrospect, poetically consistent, incisive, and sensually alive. In his later "family plays," most notably *Buried Child*, Shepard extends the simple gestalt of *The Rock Garden*, elaborating the petrified nuclear family into a national metaphor.

Chicago, the next extant play, confirmed Shepard's radically pessimistic vision of contemporary reality. Moving beyond the stifling pressures of the family, *Chicago* dramatized the feelings of anomie that threaten all existence in the nuclear age. Although there is more of a narrative here than in the previous play, the intent once again was not to tell a story but to project images that would provoke a visceral awareness of the dislocation and disorientation of contemporary existence.

The layered reality of *Chicago* is far more complicated than that of *The Rock Garden* because its surface action is so playful and casual. In fact most of the play consists of Stu's game-playing, by himself and with his mate, Joy. His fantasies give the play a lazy, improvised quality that neatly belies the underlying tension. But as Joy prepares to leave, an obsessive fear creeps into Stu's musings. Sitting in a bathtub that he imagines to be a boat, he daydreams about a fisherman and his potential catch, focusing on the fish's frozen moment of indecision.

> You're pretty hungry but you're not sure. So you take your time. You're down there moving slowly around this worm, taking your time. And they're up there drinking split pea soup and grinning and pointing at the moon and the pier and all the trees. You're both hung up.

As this imagery of suspension begins to infiltrate Stu's humorous facade, the expression of dislocation intensifies. Gradually the play's single controlling image takes effect. The disorientation contained in the presence of the bathtub—a real object—on an empty stage rather than in a bathroom setting reflects Stu's condition. He is an inert object stranded between two realities, his fantasies and the world outside himself, trapped by an overwhelming fear of activity. As Joy's vacation is enacted expressionistically, Stu imagines her vacation to be the prelude to a mass suicide. Pushing these fantasies to excess, Shepard means to overwhelm the audience with the existential fear that, in our alienating environment, makes even simple activities difficult.

In retrospect *Chicago* seems both too general and overly ambitious. Stu's *angst*, transmitted directly rather than dramatized through conflicting characters, lacks specific causes and a context connected to the rest of the world. Nor is the situation complex enough to express Stu's existential fear of global disaster. Without the context of violence and potential catastrophe that threatened so much of the 1960s, Stu's hallucinations can appear to be the paranoia of an eccentric.

And yet it is exactly this kind of surface behavior, composed mostly of games and fantasies, that Shepard uses so successfully to structure nearly all of the succeeding one-acts. The sheer quantity of these games and fantasies reflects on the emptiness, boredom, and alienation of modern existence. But the most useful aspect of the fantasy/game behavior is, to quote Smith again, as a means of revealing "the existence behind behavior"—the repressed fears and struggles in an "age of genocide."

In *Icarus's Mother* the vision of a traumatic existence is elaborated more fully and more seriously than in the earlier plays. The vision of *The Rock Garden* is limited to the nuclear family, just as the vision of *Chicago* derives only from the rather eccentric fantasies of a single character. But the world of Shepard's third play is wider and more universal. The skywriting plane and the fireworks display are significant as touchstones of a world outside the characters' inner lives. This external world is not articulated in a fully realistic way; it envelops the characters atmospherically. Nevertheless, by setting the characters off against an external reality, Shepard begins to show us a more substantial dramatic vision. Not only is there a sense of the outside world in this play; there is also a pervasive fear that transmits a powerful gestalt to the audience.

Frank, Bill, Howard, and Jill argue with Pat (over whether she should take a walk by herself) as if their lives depended on the outcome. Just as Stu created his own story about Joy's vacation, so these five characters make up different tales about the skywriting pilot in order to "possess" him and thus to have their own way. Using bogus scientific jargon, Howard goes to extraordinary lengths to scare Pat into staying with the group. Underneath the gamesmanship is a desperate need to hold sway over another person. The play gradually reveals that what is at stake for these people runs far deeper than winning an argument. It is exactly this mysterious disparity between the fantastical nature of the stories and the desperation with which they are used that conveys the characters' tenuous grip on an uneasy world.

When the others finally go walking, leaving Bill and Howard alone, it becomes fully evident that a monumental but unspecified fear is at work beneath the power struggles. For an unexplained reason, Bill and Howard become desperate in their need to send smoke signals to the pilot. When they are interrupted they carefully hide their actions from the others, making up lies to get them to leave. When one of their lies—that the plane has crashed—later turns out to be true, they are left virtually paralyzed by the loss of the pilot, the one bit of reality they had been clinging to. In describing the horrors of the crash, Frank has also evoked their vision of the end of the world.

The fear of that possibility is of course the informing psychological principle of *Icarus's Mother*. Even at the play's end we still do not know why the pilot was so important to Bill and Howard. But we do sense the fear that informed the desperate power struggles and the intense need to communicate with the pilot. Instead of unraveling a plot, the play elaborates a gestalt conditioned by the threat of an apocalypse. In *Chicago* that fear was contained entirely in Stu's fantasies. But in *Icarus's Mother* the fact that the plane actually crashes gives credence and significance to the characters' fears. For the first time in Shepard's writing, a real context is provided for the characters, a context which includes explicit resonances of American life, namely the technological failure at what must be a Fourth of July celebration.

In the early plays Shepard does manage to convey the experience—the consciousness—of existence. Instead of dramatizing events, social forces, or heroic actions, he transmits an immediate visceral sensation of contemporary reality. Focusing in on the minutiae of behavior, he records a picture of a nervous obsessive world where feelings of rootlessness and alienation predominate. Yet even within his obsessive, microscopic vision, the actions and images resonate with the experience of contemporary American life. The behavior of these plays, though universally recognizable, is especially characteristic of America in the middle of this century: the conforming to boring social rituals, the obeisance to work, the obsessive game-playing, and of course the emotional repression. When Shepard went on to write *La Turista, Operation Sidewinder,* and *Mad Dog Blues,* it became obvious that his primary interests were the myths and archetypal figures of America; but the focus on America, though not yet full blown, is clearly evident in the early plays.

With its vision of the apocalypse, *Icarus's Mother* is a model for many of Shepard's later one-acts, especially *Fourteen Hundred Thousand* and *Red Cross.* In the former, the giant bookcase that has a life of its own but no function is a hilarious symbol of a society gone out of control. Determined to have a bookcase even though she has no books to fill it, Donna bullies Tom into finishing their project. Similar to the struggles in the earlier plays, this one also takes on a vehemence far too excessive for the issue at hand. But it is Ed who is especially prone to fears of isolation and death. When he tries to abandon their project, Tom and Donna frighten him into staying, telling a story of a catastrophic snowstorm that will bury him in his country house. In an about-face to their obsession with building the bookcase, the characters dismantle the entire stage set in a symbolic enactment of an apocalypse.

But instead of having a cleansing effect, the end of their former world makes way for an even more object-oriented world—the infinite linear city described by Mom and Pop. *Fourteen Hundred Thousand* illuminates the threat of doom in a more specific way by connecting it with the materialistic and technological obsessions of modern society. Unfortunately, the symbolic apocalypse seems imposed by the playwright because the struggle over the bookcase is not allowed to play itself out. Nor is the linear city proposed by Mom and Pop ever linked to that initial struggle. We are bombarded with an array of ideas and concepts that remain unconnected dramatically, making the play an unwieldy theatrical experience.

Red Cross, on the other hand, is a far more subtle evocation of apocalyptic anxiety. Here there are no plane crashes, no tales of mass suicides, no giant self-propelled objects; the threat to Jim, his case of "crabs," seems almost laughably harmless. Yet Jim mysteriously keeps the problem from Carol, even after she complains of tingling sensations, and he refuses to let the Maid change the bedsheets. In order to divert her attention, he gives her a swimming lesson, an imaginary event that is the highlight of the play's comic surface.

But the Maid begins to believe that she is in danger of drowning, the lesson reveals the insecurity beneath Jim's need to dominate the Maid. When Carol returns with the realization that she is literally being eaten alive by bugs, she unleashes a terror that Jim had been trying to suppress. What had seemed like a minor annoyance now becomes a plague that encompasses an almost cosmic fear. In the rarefied world of this three character play, set in a perfectly white box, the trickle of blood down Jim's face signifies the advent of a horror that has the dimension of an apocalypse.

Even without specific references, Red Cross can be seen as an allegory for America's collective behavior in the 1960s. When Carol demands an answer about the blood on Jim's face, his dodging makes clear that the catastrophe has been brought on largely by his failure to confront the problem.

Faced with a society that suppressed the awareness of danger, Shepard, like many other writers, turned to apocalypse as the only way to describe the turmoil of American life in the 1960s. Since Biblical times apocalypse has meant, among other things, social chaos, fruitlessness, war, and worldwide disaster. Writing the early plays when his country was mired in a foreign war, and racial and generational conflicts threatened to destroy the fabric of American life, Shepard justifiably presented pessimistic visions of impending doom. What we see in the one-acts as a "coolness"—an absence of beliefs, affective actions, and strong relationships—actually belies the feeling of betrayal, the grief about America that surfaces completely in the bitterness and hunger for peace in Operation Sidewinder.

Since the prophet's words to a majority that is largely indifferent to their own crises must invoke a non-rational basis of authority (for rationality, overtaken by sophists, can no longer provide the means for reform), it is easy to see why the apocalyptic flourished in the hands of a 1960s playwright. In an address at Columbia University in 1960 entitled "Apocalypse:

The Place of Mystery in the Life of the Mind," Norman O. Brown set the tone for a decade by calling for an end to the reliance on Mind and an embracing of the blessed madness of the Dionysian spirit. As with much of the writing of this time, Shepard's work is itself an attack on the objective, rational apprehension of knowledge. The apocalyptic proceeds by dreams, visions, and hallucinations. Given the anti-rationalist method of the apocalyptic vision, it is clear why realism, with its rational, objective vision of reality, held no interest for Shepard in the early part of his career.

In these short plays where character and relationship are minimal, there is nonetheless a developing vision of external reality. Shepard's introduction to a later play, *The Unseen Hand,* describes a reality that is remarkably similar to that of all the plays prior to it:

> Everybody's caught up in a fractured world that they can't even see. What's happening to them is unfathomable but they have a suspicion. Something unseen is working on them. Using them. They have no power and all the time they believe they're controlling the situation.

What is crucial in the remark is not only the very exact description of the characters' behavior throughout the one-acts but also the delineation of a reality—the "fractured world"—that is external to the characters. Although Shepard was interested more often than not in expressing his characters' strange inner reality, each succeeding play does more to validate their fears. With the relatively ordinary behavior of *Red Cross*, we can feel that these characters are not eccentric but are in touch with a very real danger. Even though we may only glimpse the horror, by the end of this series of plays we realize that the "something unseen" is the advent of the apocalypse and that it is the key to Shepard's vision of reality rather than merely a figment of the characters' imaginations.

In *Forensic and the Navigators* and *The Holy Ghostly* Shepard theatricalizes the apocalypse, as colored smoke and gas consume the theatre at the end of both plays. In *Operation Sidewinder* Shepard finally articulates the entire myth of the apocalypse, presenting on stage not only the destruction of modern civilization but also its regeneration. Looking back from that play and remembering the historical context, the one-acts appear as single shock effects, images of breakdown under the pressures of modern American society, brief visions of the end.

With its prophesy of regeneration, *Operation Sidewinder* can be seen as the appropriate conclusion to a series of plays which, although depicting a universal condition, also possesses an important and distinctive vision of American life. In Shepard's work, "gestalt theatre" does not mean bombarding spectators with sensations so as to produce a like condition in the audience; rather it comes to mean using the sensations to provoke a visceral awareness of the potential chaos that lurks beneath the contemporary scene.

A TRIP THROUGH POPULAR CULTURE
Mad Dog Blues

George Stambolian

Ronald Tavel, Rochelle Owens, Megan Terry, Terence McNally, and Jean-Claude van Itallie are only a few of a large and growing number of new playwrights who over the past decade have injected a strong and much needed dose of fresh talent into the American theatre. Apart from the appellation "off-off-Broadway Theatre" they have so far been fortunate enough to escape a more restricted definition of their work that would place them in some kind of "school." Although they are united in their desire to experiment with new dramatic forms and in their effort to reclaim for the theatre a meaningful role in our psychic and social lives, their works do in fact vary considerably in quality, structure, and subject matter. There is, however, one striking similarity that does emerge. A remarkably large number of these plays treat the condition of modern Americans living in a world saturated by the popular media, and in particular by the clichés, fantasies, and stories of the movies. In *Gorilla Queen*, for example, Tavel uses the camp form of the Hollywood musical and mixes it with philosophy to create a mad portrait of America's cultural insanity. Owens in *Istanboul* satirizes the scenarios of American movies of the thirties and forties, while van Itallie in *T.V.* shows how the viewers of television become the images they see.

The interest in the popular media and their effects is not surprising in a generation nurtured by movies and comic books, surrounded by advertising, and living in the age of television and McLuhanism. Contemporary playwrights share with artists Warhol and Lichtenstein and novelists Barth and Barthelme the knowledge that our own and therefore our country's identity is largely determined by the figures, images, and myths of our popular culture. And like these artists and writers they have in their efforts to modify our consciousness naturally turned to an exploration of those cultural factors that daily alter and mold our consciousness. Through parody, satire, and even cool analysis they held up to America the image of a land in which human presence and truly individual response have been all but crushed and eliminated by the models and structures projected by the media. It is true that some of these plays give the impression of being as confused and as superficial as the world they decry. In other words, the contemporary playwright has not always maintained a firm stylistic control over his material which can show us, as Richard Poirier writes in *The Performing Self*, "how to keep from being smothered by the inherited structuring of things, how to keep within and yet in command of the accumulations of culture that have become part of what he is." Actually, most of the playwrights I have mentioned have long since moved beyond their first and often undisciplined fascination with the media toward the creation of works which deal with them in a more carefully organized manner. A history of the contemporary American theatre will one day be written which will give them the critical assessment they deserve. My purpose here is not to undertake such a history or even attempt an introduction to it, but simply to discuss in the light of this new culture consciousness the work of Sam Shepard, who is in the opinion of many, including myself, the most original and artistically disciplined of the off-off-Broadway playwrights.

In his early plays like *Chicago* and *Red Cross* Shepard attracted attention by the startling way in which he juxtaposed powerful visual and verbal images producing an immediate and often disconcerting impact on the spectator's mind. He has in his more recent plays developed and refined this technique of dramatic collage and has employed it increasingly to create complex and unexpected combinations of cultural elements. In *Operation Sidewinder* Shepard shows a world of mad scientists and military men that recalls the film *Dr. Strangelove*, uses (in the first version of the play) excerpts from a speech by Stokely Carmichael, and recreates a Hopi snake ceremony. In *The Unseen Hand* he presents a cowboy gang styled on Western movies, confronts them with a science fiction character from another planet, and ends by introducing a "typical" all-American boy cheerleader. *The Tooth of Crime*, which describes how one rock singer and life style is replaced by another, forges a new language by drawing on the dissimilar vocabularies and speech patterns of joke books, sportscasters, disk jockeys, rock musicians, hunters, and gangsters.

In *Mad Dog Blues* he again demonstrates his mastery of dramatic collage and treats many of the same themes found in his other plays—the search for innocence, the loss of identity, the tensions and fragility of human relations, and the obsessive presence of death. *Mad Dog Blues* differs from Shepard's other works in that the cultural elements he utilizes to develop these themes are more directly the center of interest. The play is in fact an intricate dramatization of the value and limits of popular culture, our attitudes toward it, and its effects on us.

Shepard calls *Mad Dog Blues* "a two-act adventure show," and its action justifies that description. After a Prologue in which the two main characters, Kosmo, a rock-and-roll star, and Yahoodi, his drug-addicted sidekick, define themselves directly to the audience, Act One begins with Kosmo telling his friend of a musical vision he had that evoked the image of Marlene Dietrich. She immediately appears on the stage, but Kosmo, unable to sing the song, decides to take a trip to San Francisco to get his "head straight." Yahoodi goes off to the jungle where he is joined by Marlene. Kosmo has another vision, this time of Mae West singing the blues like Janis Joplin. Mae also appears and starts flirting with Kosmo. Soon after they meet Paul Bunyon, who is searching for his ox, Babe, and Waco, an old cowboy in whose heart the dead singer Jimmie Rodgers lives.

The "adventure" really starts when Yahoodi decides to hunt for gold and asks Kosmo to stake him out. Captain Kidd appears and tells Yahoodi of a treasure hidden on an island and protected by a "ghost girl." Hungry for gold herself, Mae tries to convince Kosmo that his friend will betray him. At the same time, Kidd and Marlene tell Yahoodi to cut Kosmo out of the deal. Kosmo and his group now follow Yahoodi to the island where in the struggle and confusion Marlene and Waco are abandoned only to fall in love respectively with Bunyon and the ghost girl.

Act Two finds Yahoodi and Kidd making their way through the jungle with two bags of gold. Increasingly mistrustful of Kidd, Yahoodi finally shoots him, but now, alone, his imagination running wild, and driven by the need "to get off," he shoots himself. Realizing that his vision is going out of control, Kosmo also wants to give up the pursuit so he can return home and find his "roots," but Mae forces him to continue. Just when they find Yahoodi, Jesse James enters, agrees to a deal with Mae, and takes her away with the gold. Kosmo asks Yahoodi to get up, telling him that he can't kill himself in the middle of the plot. Wanting only death, Yahoodi refuses, and the two friends decide to separate. Their decision sets off a chain reaction as the other couples also separate and begin wandering around the stage, searching for their former partners, but never meeting them. Meanwhile, Mae and Jesse cross the border with the gold loaded on Babe, only to discover that the bags are filled with bottle caps. They also decide to go home. The play concludes as all the characters join them in a final song that ends: "My spinnin' brain is a failure/With no/Home."

Mad Dog Blues is clearly an American play, and only an imagination that has grown on American movies, radio shows, pulp magazines, and music could have conceived it. Shepard's presentation emphasizes this fact, for each character in his costume, language, gestures, and songs appears as the pure expression of his own image, and each, like saints in a cathedral of American popular culture, carries his identifying attributes. Kosmo the rock star is dressed in a satin cape and velvet pants, has teased hair, and carries a conga drum. Yahoodi is dressed all in black "like a big-city dope dealer" and holds an Indian flute. Marlene has short shorts, lots of makeup, high heels, and a whip. She sings "Jungen mensch" and has a fight with the ghost girl that recalls *Destry Rides Again*. Mae West in an evening gown with a feather boa drops her famous movie lines and is ever the tough and sexy female looking for a man. Paul Bunyon has his ox, and Waco is like a sad Gabby Hayes carrying a broken guitar.

Shepard's collage includes more than just the characters and costumes. There are songs by the author and his friends, Waco sings Rodgers's "The TB Blues," and the dialogue contains lines from rock hits. Even the sound effects are drawn from our cultural memories for Shepard notes that they should be "like those on oldtime radio shows," that a live band should play in a pit "as for a vaudeville show," and that the piano should follow the action as was done with "the old silent movies." There are also literary allusions. When Kosmo goes to San Francisco he calls it "Kerouac country," and Shepard like Kerouac, a writer he admires, describes the rootlessness of American life, an existence of scattered friends, short-term affairs, and separations. Kosmo and Yahoodi, like Sal Paradise and Dean Moriarty, support each other's "inability to function," a condition which is true of most of the couples in Shepard's plays. The road theme associated with the hunt for gold and the finding and losing of friends also recalls *Candide*. Shepard even does a variation of Voltaire's message, for Yahoodi speaks of buying a farm, and Kosmo, tired of traveling, says he wants to "hoe my own garden and plant my own seeds."

But the most pervasive cultural memory in the play is John Huston's film *The Treasure of the Sierra Madre*. When Yahoodi decides to look for gold he says: "If I could just find Humphrey Bogart we'd be in business." Once evoked the action of the film becomes part of the "adventure." Yahoodi talks about buying mules in Nogales, and later his mistrust and paranoia recall Bogart's character. "Hard to sleep and keep your eyes peeled at the same time," he says to Captain Kidd whose gun is trained on him. "Sooner or later you're gonna have to fall asleep. Then it's gonna be my turn." Both the film and the play conclude with a similar message. In one the gold is blown away by the wind, in the other it turns into bottle caps, and in both the characters decide to give up the hunt and return home.

For the spectator the presence of all these cultural figures, images, and allusions produces a definite, if limited, comic effect—an effect that is not, however, based on anything that could accurately be called parody, satire, or camp. Compared to the plays of many of his contemporaries, and especially to the wild dramatic exercises of Ronald Tavel or Charles Ludlam, Shepard's presentation is remarkably straight. The spectator of *Mad Dog Blues* laughs or smiles for the simple reason that the figures he sees on stage, by their very recurrence in yet another work, reaffirm their existence as clichés. He also takes obvious delight in an imagination that is able to draw on such a variety of sources. This delight comes easily because none of the cultural allusions, despite their relative complexity, are hidden or in any way obscure. On the contrary, they are immediately recognizable, if not blatant. The problem Shepard is posing for Kosmo and for the spectator is not that of identifying images and figures already known to everyone, but of finding a way to live and to deal with them.

Shepard's own technique of dealing with popular culture is the key to the play's significance. While *Mad Dog Blues* does have a dazzling and often slick surface that directly strikes the senses, it also forces the spectator to view that surface, so to speak, from behind, from within the imagination that conceived it. In other words, the play is at once a pop-like display and a psychodrama. Also, the surface itself is not uniform, but is broken repeatedly by the characters who momentarily step out of the plot or adventure in order to comment on it and on their own lives. In this way Shepard's collage is not just a combination of different cultural elements but also of different dramatic tones and points of view.

Once Marlene Dietrich appears at the beginning of the play, it is evident that *Mad Dog Blues* is about the American mind or "brain" and the creatures that inhabit it. Indeed, it is less about the American mind than of it, since this inner world is presented directly on stage. The play can also be seen as an allegory about life in America, where the search for gold explains our callousness, mobility, and rootlessness, and where we are, like Shepard's characters, defined by the degree of our corruption. But these characters are more than convenient allegorical figures, for if they do represent different degrees of innocence and corruption, fidelity and fickleness, it is because they are inseparably associated in our minds with certain qualities and traits. *Mad Dog Blues* supports the idea that we see the world through the images provided by the media and myths of our culture. To think of love or infidelity is to see Marlene and Mae, purity and innocence recall Paul Bunyon, gold evokes Captain Kidd and the Sierra Madre, and the old American West is linked to men like Waco and Jesse James.

Shepard knows that these and other figures are so much a part of us that they inform every aspect of our lives, just as all the stories we have seen or heard determine the nature of our own "adventures." Given this situation each of us may well ask of himself, Who am I? Who speaks when I speak? Who acts when I act? Myself or a character I saw on the screen? While

Shepard is not so explicit, he is intent on establishing through a complex dramaturgy the vital relation that exists between our cultural conditioning and the conduct of our personal lives.

Kosmo's visions are, after all, based on pre-existing images and music. His first vision, associated with Marlene, is already a mix: "It was like old rhythm-and-blues and gospel, a cappella, sort of like The Persuasions but with this bitchin' lead line. Like a Hendrix lead line." His next vision, of Mae West singing the blues like Janis Joplin, proves equally frusturating. "If I could just put something together," he says. "I keep feeling like I'm getting closer and closer to the truth." Although Kosmo does not define what this truth is, one supposes that he is trying to create a kind of cultural metaphor in music, a song that will reveal some special quality of voice or of physical presence common to Mae and Joplin. The scene is suddenly interrupted by Yahoodi, who says that ever since he was a little boy he used to watch the subway and wonder "How all those people were just living their lives and couldn't care less about me. About how separate we were."

Apart from the fact that Mae and Kosmo are riding an imaginary trolley in San Francisco, this rather Camusian evocation of the world's indifference seems to have little to do with the action on stage. Then Mae admits that she never heard of Joplin and shows by her words and gestures that, true to her own image, she is infinitely less interested in this dead woman than in the live man before her. The theme of indifference is picked up again in the same scene when Kosmo beautifully describes how he dreamed of Joplin, abandoned and alone, lying dead in her room, and how her voice sailed through the air and was swallowed by Mae who began to sing "When a man loves a woman." Still indifferent to the dream, Mae reacts only to the idea of love. "What do ya say we get us a bottle a hooch," she says, "and find us a nice cozy place."

The entire scene shows that while Shepard is implying the existence of similarities between different cultural elements, he is also suggesting that the problem of "putting something together" is not limited to culture, since culture itself extends far into our lives. Coming to terms with culture means coming to terms with our own indifference, loneliness, need for love, and all the other conflicting emotions and desires that culture has helped to define and that figures like Mae and Joplin represent in our minds. And it is as difficult for Kosmo to free himself from his cultural memories and the emotions associated with them as it is for Mae to be anyone other than herself. She is only an image, but that image is her identity forever fixed in our minds. Unfortunately for us, she does not exist there alone but in the company of countless other figures among whom our own identity is dispersed. This is a curious world in which the creatures of our myths and media have such strong identities that they usurp our own, and we are forced in order to "put ourselves together" to deal with images that can only be "indifferent" to our dilemma.

It is because of this situation that Kosmo's and Yahoodi's confrontation with the images in their minds quickly develops into a confrontation with their own selves. Halfway through the first act, when it is already apparent that their visions are going out of control, they speak to each other in their sleep. "I'm so many different people at once," cries Yahoodi, and Kosmo answers: "I have an awful memory of places I never was." Not only has culture taken full possession of their imagination, memory, and identity, but the proliferation of images produced by the trip through time and space has led to a proliferation of the self, to a kind of multiple schizophrenia. *Mad Dog Blues* reflects a world in which the old collective unconscious has been submerged by a new media-nurtured collective hyper-consciousness. It dramatizes the fact that the myths and images, figures and settings of all our "adventure shows" are now omnipresent and inescapable. We become what we behold, and there is no way to avoid the beholding.

This explains why no artistic presentation of popular media images or their effects can escape a certain blatancy or exaggeration of surface qualities. The media themselves are blatant no matter how insidious their consequences may be. For Kosmo and Yahoodi, their culture-saturated imagination leads to an over-extension and fragmentation of the self. Moving from one creature in their mind to another, they also move from place to place, from New York to San Francisco, to Mexico, to the islands and the jungle. They discover that to be anybody or any place is to be no one and no place, and they are caught in a desperate search for an identity and a place to call home.

Seen in this light the hunt for gold takes on an added significance, for the characters believe that gold will enable them to be someone "different" or to go somewhere else. "We'll be able to go anywhere and do anything and be anyone we want to," says Kosmo. The irony of their search is that it turns on itself, for the roles and places they seek are not just the goal of their searching but also its cause. Who can one be except a figure that culture has already defined for us? Progressively more isolated and lonely, objects first of each other's hunger for love and then victims of each other's rejections and indifference, the characters are, as Waco says, "space travelers" and "driftin' fools" caught "on the road" of American culture.

Art has always had the power to make us travel in time and space, to become different people in different places, but in Shepard's media-charged psychodrama this imaginative mobility takes on the hallucinatory quality of a "trip" on drugs. The very structure of the play creates this effect. The short scenes follow each other in rapid succession, while the action jumps around the stage, moving from group to group, couple to couple, character to character. The "spinning brain" seems to turn faster and faster until near the end of the play the tension approaches the breaking point. Kosmo's vision turns into a nightmare. "I can't hear the music anymore!" he cries. "It's out of control! The whole thing's crashing in on me!"

Things are always going out of control in Shepard's plays—airplanes crash, bookcases collapse, computers run wild, monsters ravage the earth, and even language takes on a violent life of its own. This is particularly the case in the early plays like *Chicago, Red Cross, Icarus's Mother,* and *La Turista,* which are built around great explosions of language variously called "arias," "manic monologues," and "verbal trips." A character begins speaking and almost immediately he is carried away by the words and images that establish their own logic and connections and seem to use the character more than they are used by him. In these plays that so often treat disease, language itself appears as a disease, whose nature is defined less by the function of communication than by the effects of "communicability." The tensions in a Shepard play are not described or analyzed but "caught."

In most of Shepard's plays since *Operation Sidewinder* these verbal trips have given way to rock songs. This is true in *Mad Dog Blues* where the long verbal passages are more in the nature of soliloquies that form breaks in the surface or interludes in the movement of the action during which the characters speak of their desires and anxieties. But in *Mad Dog Blues* the cultural images produce much the same effect as language in the verbal trips. They gain control of the characters, take on a life of their own, and seem to establish their own independent connections. In his plays Shepard is in fact showing to what extent the mind, and particularly the modern American mind, can become entrapped by its own verbal and imaginative creations.

It is not simply that our emotions are imprisoned in myths and media images and automatically call them forth. These same myths and images also have the power to recall each other. Obviously, the author himself has chosen the images and has consciously made connections between such figures as Marlene Dietrich and Paul Bunyon. Yet Shepard's genius is to make these links appear independent of any conscious choice. The impression produced by the play is that the mind is so saturated by popular culture that almost any idea introduced into it acts as a catalyst around which an endless series of other ideas and images immediately crystallize. Gold recalls Captain Kidd, but Mae West also evokes gold and consequently Jesse James. A similar technique is used, for example, in *Chicago* where the eating of biscuits turns into the idea of fishing and being eaten by fish, and from this to boats, sailors, fornication, and the whole history of man's evolution.

If popular culture can be a kind of disease, it also carries with it the danger of death. From the beginning death is present in the names of Jimi Hendrix, Janis Joplin, and Jimmie Rodgers. Shepard has a particular obsession for artists and performers, especially singers, who died at the height of their careeers—Johnny Ace and Buddy Holly, James Dean and Jackson Pollock. He believes that these deaths, whether accidental or the results of suicide, reveal the deep frustrations of life in America that success intensifies by imposing an image on the artist that alienates him from himself and others. Shepard is also aware of the aura of mortality that surrounds most of the popular arts because of their relatively transitory nature and because many of them are tied to performance, to a living act on stage or screen, to a face and a person. Movies that by their very nature capture the detailed reality of a particular time, place, and personality are in this way, and no matter what their subject, meditations on mortality. After killing Captain Kidd and just before he kills himself Yahoodi cries out to the others, "You're all dead and you've come back to haunt me!" And in fact they are—Joplin, Jesse James, and also Marlene and Mae, since the images we retain of them belong to a period, the thirties, long past. But that of course is the obvious paradox. They are all dead, yet they continue to haunt our memories.

Shepard has a real love for the popular myths of our culture and a genuine nostalgia for some lost age of innocence when life was simpler in America. He also knows that this world may never have existed, that even at the time things were not the way the media represented them, and that our memory and imagination may well be based on lies. Waco points to the danger of being entrapped by the past when he says that he feels "just like a ghost. Stuck somewheres between livin' and dyin'." This statement is applicable to all the characters in the play—to the mythic figures who continue to have a half-life in the memory of the living, and to the living who are half caught in the past. Indeed, Mad Dog Blues suggests that all America is a society of ghosts, and that modern American civilization in general has taken on the attributes of its popular culture, has become a country where nothing lasts, where people pursue visions that lead nowhere, and where all relationships are transitory. America, too, carries the taint of mortality. "We're gonna live," the characters cry in their hunt for gold. "We're gonna die," they say when the vision begins slipping away.

In this as in other plays like Icarus's Mother and La Turista, Shepard sees America caught in a death wish, a longing for an apocalypse. Yahoodi himself has a vision of an American eagle who lets the world drop from its talons. But Kosmo reacts violently. "I'm getting fucking tired of apocalypses," he says. "What about something with some hope?" Later, Yahoodi explains his suicide by saying that he is haunted by a "demon," and that he is "struggling with something in me that wants to die!" Kosmo speaks of his "angel," for, he says, "I'm struggling with something that wants to live." Kosmo escapes the temptation of death and chooses hope and life by returning home to his wife and kids. In Shepard's Cowboy Mouth Slim also escapes from Cavale, who want to make him a rock star, to return to his family. Before writing these plays Shepard himself had gotten married and had a child, so there is clearly a strong autobiographical element behind this decision in favor of domesticity. But it is interesting that Shepard's conclusion, "My spinning brain is a failure with no home," can be found in other contemporary works. Poirier notes how the hero of Barth's *Giles Goat-Boy* "decides that perhaps truth can be found only in the loving eye, not in any of the various efforts he has made to fill mythic and allegorical roles." Similarly, Mailer's Rojack in *An American Dream* wants finally to abandon magic and plotting and pleads to "let me love that girl and become a father, and try to be a good man, and do some decent work." "When the imagination manages to push through contrivance and into those areas of irreducible, often inarticulate human need," writes Poirier, "it discovers that these are heartbreakingly simple."

In *Mad Dog Blues* also home is opposed to the vain pursuits, contrivances, and plots of the modern world. "Home is any place you feel like home," sing the characters. "Home got no rules, it's in the heart of a fool." Home, like the heart, is seen as something permanent and real inside us, and that is why the voice each character hears at the end seems like his own voice, "calling me back, back where I belong." The rediscovery of home puts a stop to the proliferation of the self and joins all the characters together. It also ends the confusion between past and present, the dead and the living. "All of us together," says Mae. "What a party we could have . . . Just like the old days. Just like the new days! Just like any old day!" In this world where there is "nothing to find till you find your heart," Jimmie Rodgers lives on because "he had heart" and called forth a love deep within us. "I'm the real Jimmie Rodgers," says Waco. "A man gets into yer soul. Same as a woman or a piece of land. He's alive in me." By addressing themselves to the "heart's truth," by expressing and evoking love in us, singers like Rodgers triumph over and move beyond the confusion of modern culture. "And where does the mind go? All the visions in space. All the things dreamed and seen in the air. Where do they go?" asks Captain Kidd, and laments, "If only I could sing." But one can truly sing, as Kosmo knows, only if one finds one's own "special music," something original and true that is itself not just a contrivance.

The value of *Mad Dog Blues* is in its ambiguity, or rather in the multiplicity of points of view it offers. The audience also is forced to go on a trip through popular culture during which it can feel its own confusion and question its own attitudes. The "little broken busted-up pieces" of our frustration are presented directly on stage in the fragmented dialogues and soliloquies, and particularly in the characters themselves who represent much of the cultural debris that has accumulated in our minds. Kosmo is almost crushed by it all, but where he seems to fail, Shepard succeeds admirably. The quality of his performance can be judged by his ability to give a voice to the cultural confusion without succumbing to it as a playwright.

There is nothing self-indulgent or contrived about his art in *Mad Dog Blues.* On the contrary, the play reveals his total commitment to the problems he is treating, as if he himself were attempting to discover his own identity in the cultural material inherited from the past.

Like many of his fellow playwrights Shepard knows that the old frontier myths of America's youth are no longer a valid expression of our modern anxieties, even though they continue to influence our thoughts. While the "truth" Kosmo is seeking remains vague, it is clear that Shepard is searching for a new mythology that will encompass all the diverse figures of our cultural history together with the psychological and social conditions they represent. But he is acutely aware of the fact that a new mythology also must be firmly based on the "heart's truth," and that an artificially contrived one would defeat its own purpose. His recognition of the difficulty of this task explains at least part of his admiration for those performers whose struggles transformed their own lives into myths. Shepard's greatest contribution to a new American mythology may well be his elaboration of a new myth of the modern artist. Whatever judgment is finally made on his work, it is certain that in a society drifting rapidly into the escapism of a permanent, and often instant, nostalgia, Shepard's plays are a sign of artistic health and awareness and are, therefore, worthy of our attention.

MEN WITHOUT WOMEN
The Shepard Landscape

Florence Falk

The main point . . . Well, yes, I'll tell you. What do I care? The main point arises from the fact that I've always acted alone. Americans like that immensely. Americans like the cowboy who leads the wagon train by riding ahead alone on his horse, the cowboy who rides all alone into the town, the village, with his horse and nothing else . . . This amazing, romantic character suits me precisely . . .

Interview with Henry Kissinger from
Oriana Fallaci's *Interviews with History*

The lone cowboy riding into town moves straight to the heartland fantasy of America. Why else would Henry Kissinger, a naturalized American forever aspiring to be an exemplary American, be captivated by this particular image? And why would he choose to make this disclosure, which he describes in his *Memoirs* as his single worst media mistake in eight years of public life, to an especially provocative woman journalist? Except that this image glorifies the male: costumes him in unfeeling masculinity (his horse, a kind of pedestal) to display virility and hint at imminent violence; places him in the open spaces and tells him they are his (even the sunset he rides into); tells him like an obliging woman, a woman who knows her place (in contrast to Oriana Fallaci who refuses to be so consigned), that the landscape has been swept free of rules, regulations, and commitments.

The cowboy's credo is that the man who shoots first wins—and is thereby right. He holds the proverbial ace in the hole, since no matter which side of the law he is on, his endorsement of violence means ultimately that he stands for the established order. In short, the cowboy sitting tall in the saddle wins battles (and women).

In the plays of Sam Shepard, the cowboy is the reigning male; consequently, *any* female is, perforce, marginalized. An image strong enough to arouse political leaders (Hitler and Stalin both loved cowboys) can tell us something about "the nature of a nation," to borrow Petrone's words in Shepard's *Suicide in B*^{b}. Shepard himself is fascinated (and partly seduced?) by the cowboy's pre-eminent position in American myths and legends. No other figure so successfully sustains, recycles—and condones—the violence this country is bred on; a troublesome thought at a time when America, and the world, veer toward the Apocalypse.

All Shepard characters—rock star, billionaire, or ordinary mortal—are tourists caught in a world that has undergone a cultural landslide, looking through the debris to find images of themselves. What they can't find, they adapt from the storehouse of images that films, TV, rock, science fiction, etc., provide. If what they find doesn't suit them, they unsentimentally steal. Shepard's plays are full of soul-stealers (Duke in *Melodrama Play*, Crow in *The Tooth of Crime*, the Doctor in *Geography of a Horse Dreamer*, Cavale in *Cowboy Mouth*).

There are several reasons for this resort to underhand—and underworld—tactics. First, Shepard's characters have a diminished sense of expectations: life offers little and promises to get worse. Second, naturally suspicious, they ungenerously assume lies, deceit, and hypocrisy from others. Third, the legitimate and bastard offspring of America's cowboy, their jeans, boots, studs, kid gloves, and shades isolate them from the real world as effectively as a medieval knight's suit of armor. Fourth, most are, in the words of Tympani, the drummer from *Angel City*, "locked into the very narrowist part of the dream machine"—that is, the creative imagination. Their most vivid imaginings circulate in a more or less closed system that grants mythic splendor to images of the renegade hero who occupied the pre-civilized, unsettled landscape of the American frontier.

In Shepard's plays, the "frontier" symbolizes those open spaces where law, order, and social restrictions have never invaded and primitive longings for individual power gain prompt release. The "frontier" also represents conquest, the settling of territories by means of violence, and an alien environment where outlaw cowboys stake out the land and claim their victim before he gets them first (as in the land-grab battle between Hoss and Crow in *The Tooth of Crime*). It is the domain of Male Homo Erectus, whose bulging muscles and veins streaked with violence bespeak daring and conceal any trace of vulnerability.

A late-twentieth-century manifestation of the renegade cowboy, guided by a pastoral vision of a distinctly masculine sort, reappears in play after play. His "frontier" is free also from lugubrious domestic commitments. Men roam the land alone or with a male buddy. Resplendently silent and strong, rarely do they admit to any form of weakness. Like wild horses at a stream, they drink at a woman's fountain; then satisfied yet stubbornly unsubdued, they turn away to face the world alone, and shrouded in mystery, disappear over the hills.

Paradigmatic "good guy" adventurer and challenger of tyranny is Jesse James, who turned outlaw to fight the "system" when corrupt railroad men stole the farmers' land. (His more intellectual European cousin, Francois Villon, is eulogized by Cavale in *Cowboy Mouth*.) In *Mad Dog Blues* James and Mae West, talismanic presences from the past, are resurrected in the full dress of caricature to form a temporary twosome. Blue Morphan, a kind of Rip Van Winkle of the West, speaks with some of Jesse's blood in him when he recalls the "good ole days" in *The Unseen Hand:*

> 'Course yer too young to remember the Morphan brothers probably. Cisco, Sycamore and me, Blue. The three of us. 'Course we had us a few more. Not a gang exactly. Not like these teenage hot rodders with their Mercurys and Hudson Hornets. Least ways we wasn't no menace. The people I'm talkin' about. The people people. They helped us out in fact. And vice versa. We'd never go rampant on nobody.

James's antitype is the violence-prone "bad guy." Head shorn of analytical questions, emptied of intellectual curiosity, his square-in-the-saddle mentality presents a kind of psychological blockade against emotional wisdom. The "bad guys" make settlements by conquest and retain them by violence. Traveling as rogues or in packs, they are stoical, repressed, brutal. The "Gypsy" Crow in *The Tooth of Crime* epitomizes these devolved specimens; some of his closest kin from other Shepard plays include Peter in *Melodrama Play* and Ellis, Slater, and Emerson in *Curse of the Starving Class*.

In American mythology the assimilation of violent, stoical, and repressed energy often makes it difficult to distinguish "good guys" from the "bad." The violent hero of the West is an American prototype. And whether or not these "heroes" scorn or support the "system," they nevertheless enshrine it with ritual acts of violence. In his plays Shepard plunders the sensibilities of both "good" and "bad" guys with deadpan irony.

While the Cowboy Family Tree originally sprung seed in the open spaces of the West, the "frontier" shrank quickly, and the Tree was forced to dig its roots in more eclectic soil. But as Crow reminds us in *The Tooth of Crime:* "Time warps don't shift the purpose, just the style." Some of the Cowboy's direct descendants include gangsters (*Melodrama Play, Geography of a Horse Dreamer*), detectives (*Suicide in B♭*), tycoons (*Seduced*), and the military (*Operation Sidewinder*)—all of whom are created in His image. Generally in awe of their ancestry and a past that is lost to them, these second, third, and fourth generations try to relive it, even recycle it.

In *The Unseen Hand* the resurrected Morphan brothers blink their eyes at the late twentieth century; two opt to stay; the third, Sycamore, retreats when he catches the scent of "a certain terrorism in the air." The Doctor in *Geography of a Horse Dreamer*, who looks (and acts) like Sidney Greenstreet, tries to operate on Cody in order to possess the magic bones of a "dreamer." And in *Mad Dog Blues* Kosmo and Yahoodi salve their injured lives by conjuring Mae West and Marlene Dietrich. These loyal "offspring" try to maintain the legendary male toughness that settled the West. Those, like Crow, who are secure and heartless believers in their "Destiny" succeed; the rest squander their energy in bravado (like Chet and Stu in *Cowboys #2*, Hoss in *The Tooth of Crime*, Mazon in *Killer's Head*, or Weston in *Curse of the Starving Class*). Lost in dreams, the world closes in on them. Male prowess is not enough to insulate them against the dry rot of corruption that has invaded the land.

In Shepard's plays the inevitable happens—Cowboy meets Rock Musician and the Family Tree acquires a new branch: "Cowboy Mouth" (also the title of one of Shepard's plays). In Shepard's vision of America, to be a "Cowboy Mouth" is like belonging to the tribe of Levi, favored of the twelve tribes of Israel. "Cowboy Mouth" drives a sleek car instead of riding a horse, takes speed or "meth" instead of drinking booze. In other respects, though, his gear is traditional. He is best represented by Hoss (the good guy) and Crow (the bad guy), who are prototypes for all Shepard males.

The second act of *The Tooth of Crime* recapitulates the evolutionary, and imagery, line from Cowboy to Rock Star. Hoss taunts the black-hearted Crow for disremembering his (musical) "origins." But Crow resists; having internalized the violent male-as-outlaw image, he is a predatory animal, living off the fallen carcass of Hoss. *The Tooth of Crime* is a perverse re-run of John Ford's *The Man Who Shot Liberty Valence* (1962), a film that pays nostalgic tribute to the "lost machismo" of the Old West in the person of John Wayne, who kills the brutish, lawless Valence (played by Lee Marvin). But the outcome is reversed in Shepard's play. "I can't do a Lee Marvin in the late sixties," Hoss exclaims. But Crow (the Liberty Valence/Lee Marvin figure) can and does, decisively winning the match against Hoss (John Wayne).

Hoss, the "Killer's Killer," once worked by the "outside code." ("It was like John Wayne, Robert Mitchum, and Kirk Douglas all in one movie.") Now he is an "inside" code victim, "stuck" in his "image"—impotent—because he reveres the lost days of "honor" and "regrets" that he has become a "fucking industry." Hoss is tainted with the recognition that the ethics of his law-and-order world are shot through with lies; his fatal flaw is that he can't stay "disengaged," as his "chick" Becky advises.

Crow, however, is a loner, the rogue shark who performs "solo" with the kind of nihilistic bravura of Clint Eastwood. He is, in short, Sam Peckinpah's dream male creation come true, a human wasteland, unencumbered by emotions or history. Crow's motto, "I can switch to suit," announces his complete indifference to any moral code whatsoever. But paradoxically, Crow, rather than Hoss, is the true believer whose fundamentalist rock-core faith ("I believe in my mask") allows him to dethrone Hoss. Crow succeeds, in fact, because he is an effective "ghost"— a conflation of "Cowboy" and "Rock-star" images—though without the humanistic resonances of either. Hoss fails because he carries ghosts within him and is impaled on the cross of his own cultural persuasions. Unkinged, he staggers around the stage like Shakespeare's Richard II, dispossessed of followers and land; and like Richard, he, too, is unable to "adapt" to the New World and "plays" at being "nothing." Hoss finally makes the last real gesture his own style leaves open to him—suicide. Like Hedda Gabler or Mishima, he moves to the demands of his own sense of honor:

> A true gesture that won't never cheat on itself 'cause it's the last of its kind. It can't be taught or copied or stolen or sold. It's mine. An original. It's my life and my death in one clean shot.

In *The Tooth of Crime* the *de cassibus* theme, mirrored in the simultaneous fall of the old order and rise of the new, is as classically rendered as any Elizabethan tragedy.

If Shepard must judge and sentence Hoss, his verdict is tinged with nostalgia. Crown exalts the space between the "jungle" and the "radio"; "skipping origins," he moves straight into the "present." But for Hoss the images waver, refuse to stay firm once they are uprooted from memory (the past); thus he falls victim to the victorious present-tense Crow who lives without memory, hence, without heart. The good guy "Cowboy Mouth" is, in fact, Shepard's evolutionary model of salvation. He is the man who possesses a sense of history (and is therefore rooted to the land), but whose music, removed from the mainstream (pledged, in fact, against the system) remains vital and emotionally meaningful, can tell us where we are, and even signify new directions.

In *Cowboy Mouth* Cavale urges Slim to be a great rock and roll star, like "Johnny Ace," the "real cool" cat from Texas who "pledged his love" to the people. Such a star would be the ultimate performer—the super-cool saint, savior of the disenchanted and disaffected, "rocking to Bethlehem to be born." The "most beautiful dream" Kosmo has ever had is his conjuration in *Mad Dog Blues* of Mae West singing with Janis Joplin's voice. But Joplin died of an overdose, and Mae West appears in "visions" only, even if they are more real than life.

Grave dangers, to pun, beset the "Cowboy Mouth." To feel fidelity to the past, both to its traditions and to those breaks with tradition that are cultural imperatives, one must be shatteringly vulnerable, like glass. Indeed, unless one to some extent *dis*possesses the past, one risks being *possessed* by it, as the respective fates of Crow and Hoss indicate. Niles, the composer-musician in *Suicide in B^b*, invites the past in, then gets so beseiged by its "voices" that he can no longer hear his own. But when he tries to "kill" the past, trains guns and bullets, bows and arrows at it, as history taught him to do, he feels only the cold shock of despair. Johnny Ace serenaded the girls and made them cry, then loaded his revolver and blew out his brains.

Both Hoss—and Presley—were called "King" in their day. But Hoss is "shot up" by Doc, just as in "real life" Elvis Presley's private physician provided his client with prescriptions for 5,300 pills during the last months of his life. "Cowboy Mouths," like Niles or Hoss, have too much heart to stay alive. In *Mad Dog Blues* Kosmo shouts the "real life" names of a heavenly choir of country and rock stars who couldn't "disengage" themselves from the system altogether and are some of its true, unclaimed heroes and heroines:

> Jimi Hendrix and Janis Joplin and Buddy Holly and Sam Cooke and Big Bopper and Otis Redding and Brian Jones and Jimmie Rodgers and Blind Lemon Jefferson! They're all in heaven and they've started a band!

The pervasive image distortion that the "Cowboy Mouth" endures to grasp or salvage a marketable identity indicates the immense difficulties simply in *surviving*. To succeed, Shepard's males play at being *Men*, his females at being *Women*; that is, both sexes act out not necessarily what men and women *are* but how they imagine Men and Women *behave*. Their depictions, imagistically indebted to the mass media, are exaggerated, simplified, and codified, since advertising transmits to the culture the commercial, idealized representations of Men and Women that actual men and women rely on to define themselves. Thus to a large extent, they are fashioned images, embodiments of the artificial pose; in effect, to generalize Mailer, advertisements for themselves. Though they hunger for completion, self-discovery is pre-empted by self-preservation. The landscape of the self, if gender specific, is always temporal, tentative, and often rapaciously Hobbesian, for the hidden question, or subtext, is how one acts to preserve the self, if not the species.

How, then, do the female characters in Shepard's plays survive? For there is no question that the surrealistic conglommerate he reconstructs out of bits and pieces of the Old West and the New Age is pervasively a Man's world, run according to a frontier ethic that recruits women as handmaidens. Shepard himself is an unlikely defender of the patriarchal system and sexual asymmetry, and both his males and females are developed with unflinching irony. Nevertheless, men are the energy centers of most Shepard plays, while women take peripheral roles (as, for examples, the Las Vegas show girls in *Seduced*, or girl groupies in *Melodrama Play* and *The Tooth of Crime*).

In the symbolic frontier Shepard constructs, they perform tasks that are subsidiary to the main action. "Go fetch the Rice Krispies, Oolan," Emmet orders her in *Forensic & the Navigators*, and she does. In *Melodrama Play*, Dana, "a girl with long hair, boots, jeans, leather jacket, shades, etc." (the "etc." tells us we've got the picture), runs errands for her rock star boyfriend Duke, just like tall, blonde Becky Lou in "black rock-and-roll gear," who snaps to attention whenever Hoss calls. In *Action* Lupe and Liza cook and serve the turkey dinner and clean up afterward. With few exceptions, women are the domestic caretakers of the plays, their responsibilities ranging from cooking to fucking on command.

Quite a few Shepard plays have all-male casts (*4-H Club*, *The Unseen Hand*, *The Holy Ghostly*, *Killer's Head*, *Cowboys* #2). In plays with mixed casts, males generally outnumber and overwhelm females. Not only do they speak more lines, but they arm themselves with words and tend to dominate the action. In *Icarus's Mother* Howard nearly drowns Pat in Pinter-like waves of exposition. When she doesn't answer, "He shakes Pat more violently. Pat gives no resistance." In *Forensic & the Navigators* conversation between males occurs behind the back of, and sometimes (literally) over the head of Oolan, who is issued commands but seldom directly addressed. Words are weapons—verbal assaults to disable or slay the enemy. In general, women are a straggling group of camp followers, and men treat these "bitches," "broads," and "stupid fucking cunts" as recalcitrant and dangerous possessions.

Males are usually the seekers in Shepard's plays. Inevitably, it is they who undertake mythic journeys, and it is their trials we attend. And while both males and females "dream" (Pat in *Icarus's Mother* or Emma in *Curse of the Starving Class*), men consistently experience "visions" (Cody in *Geography of a Horse Dreamer*, Wheeler in *Angel City*, Shooter in *Action*, and Kosmo and Yahoodi in *Mad Dog Blues*); at best, women are likely to live vicariously through them. In *Angel City* when Miss Scoons, a "typical secretary type," volunteers to be the "guinea pig" (Rabbit's words) and undergo transformation (that is, improvises "character"), she metamorphoses downwards into a scrubwoman and sets about to wash the floor for her boss Wheeler.

Cavale in *Cowboy Mouth* would appear to be a serious candidate as seeker. She kidnaps the reluctant Slim from domesticity and tries to refashion him in her image: "You gotta be like a rock-and-roll Jesus with a cowboy mouth." But for all her assertiveness, Cavale finally seeks only to be a vessel that pours her being into the male: "I was doing the streets looking for a man with nothing so I could give him everything. Everthing it takes to make the world reel like a drunkard." Spider Lady, native American shaman in *Operation Sidewinder*, envisions the post-apocalyptic "Fifth World," though she is more androgynous than feminine. The one serious exception is Honey, who falls into a trance and seeks the "Fifth World."

In Shepard's plays, women usually navigate alone in a sea of males. (Oolan in *Forensic & the Navigators,* Dana in *Melodrama Play,* Becky in *The Tooth of Crime,* Miss Scoons in *Angel City,* Honey in *Operation Sidewinder,* Shelley in *Buried Child.*) The men often affect indifference toward them (Stu in *Chicago,* Forensic and Emmet in *Forensic & the Navigators,* Hoss in *The Tooth of Crime,* Henry Hackamore in *Seduced*), or, alternatively, treat them with mock or real displays of brutality. Symbolic "rape" occurs in *Operation Sidewinder* and *Buried Child*; males attempt to murder females in *Icarus's Mother, Red Cross,* and *Melodrama Play* and succeed in *Curse of the Starving Class.*

Cowboy heroes only occasionally cohabitate with women, usually to aggrandize their male egos and reinforce their claims to masculinity; their preferred world is essentially homoerotic, however, because a buddy can be trusted (the Morphan brothers in *The Unseen Hand,* Howard and Bill in *Icarus's Mother,* Yahoodi and Kosmo in *Mad Dog Blues*), or one in which they travel alone (Crow in *The Tooth of Crime,* or Henry Hackamore in *Seduced*). Henry calls for "his" women, but collapses when one of them tries to seduce him. The impotent Hoss's fondest memories are of the days when he, Moose, and Cruise "ran together." In *Curse of the Starving Class* Weston triumphantly recounts the story of the eagle who watched him castrate lambs:

> He was after those testes. Those fresh little remnants of manlihood.

Finally Weston feeds the eagle:

> And every time I cut a lamb I'd throw those balls up on top a' the shed roof. And every time he'd come down like the Cannonball Express on that roof. And every time I got that feeling.

For Weston, the eagle's ingestion of the lambs' testes represents the infusion of masculine power and he appears to gain strength even in the telling. But the version his wife Ella and son Wesley recall ends in a paroxysm of male violence that spills the seed of all life:

> WESLEY: And that eagle comes down and picks up the cat in his talons and carries him screaming off into the sky.
> ELLA: That's right. And they fight. They fight like crazy in the middle of the sky. The cat's tearing his chest out, and the eagle's trying to drop him, but the cat won't let go because he knows if he falls he'll die.
> WESLEY: And the eagle's being torn apart in midair. The eagle's trying to free himself from the cat, and the cat won't let go.

At the same time that men deem women necessary as erotic messengers and preservers of male potency, they raucously accuse them of obstructing their survival (Slim in *Cowboy Mouth*, Henry Hackamore in *Seduced*, the Young Man in *Operation Sidewinder*). The battle between the sexes is a consistent Shepard theme (*Fourteen Hundred Thousand, Red Cross, Curse of the Starving Class, Buried Child*) and crescendoes in *Angel City*, when the archetypes in the mode Man and Woman (generals) wage the final battle. Flamboyant illumination in the mode of Wagner, or Cecil B. DeMille, occurs, but not until (notably) the Woman plunges her weapon home:

> At last the generals saw their situation. They were one being with two opposing parts. Everything was clear to them. At last they were connected. In that split second they gained and lost their entire lives.

Indeed, survival is the name of the game, and women traversing the male frontier learn strategems to stay out of the crossfire and endure quietly. Their curious passivity (especially Oolan in *Foresic & the Navigators* and Lupe and Liza in *Action*) is genetically encoded, like the palette of camouflage colors that render animals invisible as soon as they sense danger. In fact, beneath the cloak of passivity, these women are desperately alert and responsive to the slightest changes in their environment. For instance, the Maid in *Red Cross* learns instantly "to swim" at Jim's insistence. Adrift, her legs collapse, her side aches, and she starts to scream. Yet a vital transformation occurs:

> But once it's over it isn't bad at all. Once you get used to the shock of having water all around and dragonflies and water lilies floating by and little silver fish flashing around you. Once that's past and you get all used to your flippers and your fins and your new skin, then it comes very easy . . . and before you know it the winter has come and the lake has frozen and you sit on the bank staring at the ice. You don't move at all. You just sit very still staring at the ice *until you don't feel a thing.* (my italics.)

The Maid glides on thin ice to safety, but reaches the shore feeling her life "frozen." Laureen, who plays bass fiddle in *Suicide in B♭* (dressed, incidentally, in a bath robe) stays cool to keep from cracking. Niles says: "Laureen herself is a confirmed basket case and even she agrees. Madness sucks." In *Action* Lupe and Liza silently and ceremoniously hang laundry, remaining, in Shepard's words, "closed off in their activity." This ritual action might be perceived as a preserving, essential act of restoration—one that transcends time, history, and cultural accident, and provides these women at least with the integument of an identity—but from our cultural perspective it is nonetheless demeaning. The same is true for Miss Scoons's floor scrubbing, or Oolan's pancake making.

When women are cornered and "trapped"—that is, when they are starkly visible—they become utterly submissive. To fend off the designs of the male conspirators surrounding her, Oolan alternatively "smiles," "giggles," and acts "stupid." Shepard costumes her in a white hospital gown, "such as is worn by the insane," and her inanition suggests that she is indeed a mental casualty of the "system," her "rescuers" Emmet and Forensic notwithstanding. Recognizing that she can't escape the family nest of avenging males in *Buried Child*, Shelly also "smiles" and submits: "I'll stay and I'll do whatever I have to do *to survive. Just to make it through this.*" (my italics.)

In other words, Oolan and Shelly, like many of Shepard's female characters, behave like "child women," a term used by sociologist Erving Goffman in his pathbreaking *Gender Advertisements*. The "child woman" is *any* woman who employs a set of expressions, gestures, or actions to protect herself from the abuses of male power and prerogative by acting as the obedient child accommodating the demands of an authoritarian parent. Culturally induced and reinforced by the commercial world of advertising, this behavioral syndrome recapitulates the child's survival mechanism to defend itself and to thwart or manipulate the parent. The child of course pays a price for being "saved from seriousness," in Goffman's turn of phrase, and many of Shepard's female characters illustrate the cost.

Like most women in the "real world," they are frequently subject to "nonperson treatment" and often talked about as though absent (*Forensic & the Navigators*); they are teased and taunted (*Icarus's Mother, Red Cross, Cowboy Mouth, Action, Seduced*); their time and territory are treated as expendable (*Melodrama Play, The Tooth of Crime*); and they are subject to verbal or physical forms of abuse (*The Tooth of Crime, Action, Buried Child, Operation Sidewinder*). In *Curse of the Starving Class* Emma (who really is a "child") learns painful lessons about adult manipulation that catapult her into premature rites of sexual initiation to claim adult status.

As the disadvantaged minority, women in Shepard's plays are compelled to adapt themselves as best they can to the exigencies of the male world to survive. One choice is to be alone even while nominally caught in an enduring relationship with a man. Becky's song "Nasty Times," meant to be delivered with the chill of Brechtian alienation, shows that she gets her highs from masturbation. Each stanza ends with some variation on the refrain: "I get stroked out—I get skin popped/On my own." In effect, Becky "masturbates" in public when she later presents a classically Freudian account of early sexual abuse, simultaneously enacting both male and female roles: ("Her hands unzip her skirt and tear it off. One hand tries to get inside her panties while the other hand fights it off.")

Not only child women but the oppressed at any age seeks means to thwart the oppressor. Passivity signals outward compliance with an established regimen. It may, however, conceal treacherous undercurrents of deceit. A Darwinian ethos prevails. Becky easily commits treason by joining the new order the moment she senses that Hoss will be Crow's carrion. In *Curse of the Starving Class* Ella plays sexual politics by mixing sexual and financial games to steal the house away from her alcoholic husband. Both she and Halie (in

Buried Child) are whore-wife-mothers who are grotesque parodies of the abused Emilia's sentiments in Othello: "But I do think it is their husband's faults/If wives do fall." These women consent to enact the male fantasy of feminine perfidy that men feel they are right to fear.

Passivity may also be linked to inner resourcefulness and resilience of more positive merit. Women in Shepard's world are often victims, but they are also hardier than their oppressors, more skilled in survival strategies. Shelly submits to molestation by Tilden (who symbolically strokes her rabbit coat) and rape by Bradley (who symbolically thrusts his fingers into her mouth), but she retaliates by hiding Bradley's dismantled wooden leg (obviously, a symbolic castration) and escapes. Dodge earlier accuses her of optimism:

> Full of faith. Hope. Faith and hope. You're all alike you hopers. If it's not God then it's a man. If it's not a man then it's a woman. If it's not a woman then it's the land or the future of some kind. Some kind of future.

In *Operation Sidewinder* Honey is "raped" by the sidewinder and abused by the Young Man. Yet she nevertheless lives at the "frontier" of her imagination, for she moves out of the path of the apocalypse and toward salvation. Grudgingly, the Young Man follows, not because he is illuminated, but because he is afraid to be alone. Honey is the true survivor, though Shepard's ironic play with nomenclature momentarily deceives us. Whereas the more abstract and threshold designation "Young Man" freely connotes potential, "Honey" is like the label on a jar, telling us its exact contents: "a very sexy chick with long blonde hair and tight pants, high heels, etc."

In Shepard's plays male-female relationships are truncated, and always obscure. With the ambiguous exception of Slim and Cavale, men and women seem interested in one another only as self-reflecting mirrors. Shepard's *Savage/Love*, written in collaboration with Joe Chaikin, documents the performance ritual of a relationship in which the lover regards both self and other: "Now we're acting the partners in love, now we're acting the estrangement, now we're acting the reconciliation, now we're acting that the reconciliation was a success, etc." Unavoidably, one's incapacity to suspend judgment forces the other to perform *out of necessity*, even though performance may end ultimately in some form of what Strindberg termed "psychic murder." In *Action* Jeep steals the "sole," so to speak, out of Lupe's soft shoe dance: "There's something to be said for not being able to do something well." Lupe protests:

> I wasn't trying to be as good as Judy Garland. It started off like it was just for fun you know. And then it turned into murder. It was like being murdered. You know what I mean.

In *Cowboy Mouth* Cavale "goes through a million changes" to attract Slim. She plays dead, looks alluring, hides in a corner, grabs her .45, and finally yells over his drum playing:

> CAVALE: Look, you jive motherfucker, I'm still packing this pistol. I'm still the criminal. I'll fill you with—I'll—Hey, listen to me. I'm threatening your life. You're supposed to be scared. Look, baby, kidnapping is a federal affense. It means I'm a desperate . . .
> SLIM: (Still slamming the drums) It's "Offense," not "affense."
> CAVALE: What? Hey, what do ya mean?
> SLIM: (Stops drumming and sorta slumps over) I mean your grammar stinks. I mean you talk funny. I mean—
> CAVALE: Shit. Goddammit. How could you? How can you bust up my being a hard bitch with that shit? What a lousy thing. You know I'm sensitive abut my talking. Shit. Just when I was really getting mean and violent. Murderous. Just like Francois Villon. You fuck it up. You wreck everything.

Murder takes place at the juncture between self and image. In performance rituals between male and female, one's psyche is taken apart and reassembled by and usually for the sake of the other; evaluation can swiftly lead to execution. The formula of loving includes minute particles of wanting and desiring the other, but above all, *wanting to be loved and desired*. The extraordinary self-consciousness of Shepard's males and females not only defends against love but, paradoxically, requires *continual* performance.

There is no doubt that Shepard's characters have been seduced and enslaved by manufactured images that designate "male" and "female," "hero" and "heroine," or even "mom," "dad," and "family." When life energy has been squeezed dry, sapped by a society that spoonfeeds "snap, crack, and popple" lies, violence turns inward. Shepard's more "realistic" plays (*Curse of the Starving Class* and *Buried Child*) portray souls sick with battle fatigue. From his earliest to latest works parents and children are locked in a death struggle (*The Rock Garden, Holy Ghostly, Curse of the Starving Class, Buried Child*).

The nuclear family unit is a war zone where blood (heredity) begets blood (homicide). *Curse of the Starving Class* is dominated by blood imagery; lambs and humans alike are sacrificial victims for the "steak house," Western style, that Ellis wants to erect on the site of Weston and Ella's home. Even familiar and historical landmarks have lost their resonance. In *Buried Child* Shelly's laughter ripens and falls on the Norman Rockwell vision of her boyfriend Vince's home: "Where's the milkman and the little dog? What's the little dog's name? Spot. Spot and Jane. Dick and Jane and Spot." Moments later, this early primer image is metamorphosed into grotesque illuminations of the "happy American family."

Like the quartet of lovers in Shakespeare's *A Midsummer Night's Dream* the four people (two men and two women) in *Action* (two couples?) are possessed of dream-like properties and potentialities, and seem almost indistinct from one another. Their relationships are imprecise, the boundaries blurred. They are seeking, as Shooter says, "for a way of being with everyone. A way of finding out how to behave." Dimly they recall "the days of mass entertainment," when something called "community" existed, except that no one can recall exactly what a "community" is. Nor are they certain of their powers to discriminate between the real and the celluloid self. Jeep's attempt to describe how one might recognize an authentic human being emerges in Pinter-like series of false starts and omissions as words and phrases fall into an endless void. The short sentences he utters are like broken strings of chromosomes. The pronoun "we" becomes a mantra that secures him to existence:

> You'd know. I'd know. I mean with us, we know. We know. We hear each other. We hear our voices. We know each other's voice. We can see. We recognize each other. We have a certain—We can tell who's who. We know our names. We respond. We call each other. We sort of—We—We're not completely stranded like that. I mean—It's not—It's not like that. How that would be.

Who, then, are Shepard's characters? Of what clay are they created? They move past our eyes like figures in a shooting gallery: cowboy, rock star, private eye, Las Vegas floosie. Knock one down, it pops up again. Grace affords them instant resurrection, and they have more than a cat's supply of lives. The reincarnated images of Marlene Dietrich, Mae West, Jesse James, Paul Bunyan *et al.* caricature the past, which is a way of repossessing, recording, reassessing it. In his cautionary "Note to the Actors" for *Angel City*, Shepard urges reevaluation of the term "character":

> Instead of the idea of a "whole character" with logical motives behind his behavior which the actor submerges himself into, he should consider instead a fractured whole with bits and pieces of character flying off the central theme.

In a sense all of Shepard's characters are "bits and pieces"; all are "fractured wholes," because corruption and rot are deep set into Shepard's world, which is, also and significantly, our own. His characters have tasted the same apple and share the same after-effects:

RABBIT: You don't know a thing about creation.
WHEELER: I was created without my knowing. Same as you. Creation's a disease.

In one sense, they suffer from the primal curse of having been born. In another sense, however, the "disease" in its late-twentieth-century American mutation is a particularly virulent form of alienation. Shepard never explicitly says that his vision of an America overrun by a horde of renegade cowboys, and their women, trailing at heel, is a distinctively national pathology or whether it reaches beyond, to tell us something that pertains in general to the human condition. In the end, he leaves us exposed and vulnerable, in the circumstance depicted so concisely by an anonymous Burmese poet:

Disease Unknown
cure unknown.

WHAT PRICE FREEDOM?

Stanley Kauffmann

Sam Shepard is phenomenal. He is the best practicing American play-wright, I think, now that Tennessee Williams is doodling. Since 1964 he has written about thirty plays of differing lengths which have been produced all over the U.S. and in some other countries. He is world-famous in the theatre world. (And this without ever having been produced on Broadway. One play, *Operation Sidewinder*, was done at the Beaumont in 1970 under Jules Irving's management.) Several volumes of his plays have been published. But part of the Shepard phenomenon is that, in a sorry way, he represents the course of U.S. playwriting in the last twenty years. After all this time Shepard continues to "show talent." It's the most dazzling talent we have at the moment, but showing talent is not quite the same as making art. (As Harold Clurman once said, "America is lousy with talent.") Much of Shepard's work is unforgettable, seen or read once. Very little of it is worth another visit, which is surely one valid test of real quality.

Curse of the Starving Class [published by Urizen Books] is another of Shepard's heartbreakers—it contains so much, yet it finally comes to not enough. First produced in London in 1977, it deals with California sheep raisers and thus immediately strikes a distinctive Shepard note. He often deals with non-urban people, often in the West; most of our playwrights are urban in setting and feeling. There's a family of four: the father, a former Air Force pilot, now boozing most of the time; a kooky shiftless mother, scheming to sell the place and scurry off to Europe with her children; a son about twenty, easy and competent but frightened of his father; a daughter, sturdy, frightened of no one.

The play's first virtue, as in most Shepard, is that all the roles are good acting parts. No play survives in the theatre without that virtue and some survive that have no other virtue. Shepard writes dialogue that actors can *use*, in situations that have good rising motion, for characters that leave the audience finally with a high opinion of the actors even though/if the actors have concentrated on the characters.

And beyond this, which might in itself be true of a thin and silly play, Shepard stokes a simmering heat under the whole play, even under the punchy comic sections, a ruthlessness, a kind of anger that makes the essential drama seem to be not in the story but between the writer himself and the world. Once again a Shepard play testifies to the fact that he is a true man of of the theatre: he doesn't see life as material for drama, he sees life *as* drama.

But once again he has plunged, so to speak, into a turbulent pool simply because he knows how to dive and swim in turbulence; and, to finish the figure, he has surfaced some time later only to head for the nearest shore without necessarily having intended to go there. *Starving Class* starts as sweaty, cartoon-character comedy—people living wildly and uncaringly in a poverty they not only don't take very seriously, they use it as a medium for farcical family life. They are something like John Steinbeck's Okies seen by Donald Barthelme. In the opening section the son is cleaning up the fragments of the front door that his drunken father broke down the night before, the mother comes out in a wrapper and is unconcerned to find the refrigerator nearly empty, the daughter comes out in her 4-H uniform carrying charts she made for a demonstration she's going to give at a fair on how to cut up a frying chicken. When she finds that her chicken is missing from the fridge, she gets furious. Her brother puts her charts on the floor and pisses on them. Pretty soon the boozy father comes home, providing for his brood by bringing them a large sack of artichokes.

The opening atmosphere, which persists through a good deal of the play, is hard to reconcile with the conclusion. The play ends as a paean to agrarian values, to those who love Nature and Space and Simple Things and who are being forced off their land by exploitative commercial combines. It becomes a drama of rustic simplicity being strangled by city greed. That ending is simply not in the play's beginning: moralism has been tacked on to a work whose vitality is in its passionate rowdyism and its very oblique social comment.

Shepard is not much of a thinker: when he does think, or feels he needs to, he usually comes up with the same theme—the battle between the pure and the impure in America. And when he needs evil, he usually calls on the movies to supply it: cinematized criminal types of various kinds. This deliberate use of movie types is part of Shepard's general method: the language and music of rock, spaceman fantasies, Wild West fantasies, gangster fantasies—pop-culture forms that he uses as his building blocks, rituals of contemporary religion to heighten communion.

My discomfort with Shepard is not with this symbology, which he often exalts into pungent theatre poetry, but with his careless grabbing at chunks of it to get him out of his dramatic difficulties. The best work of his that I know, *The Tooth of Crime*, which casts the rivalries of rock stars in the mode of a '30s gangster picture and which spits along in wonderfully bitten-out language, completes what it's about through the form in which it is put. But the gangsters at the end of *Starving Class* have just been shoved on stage by the scruffs of their necks, to commit a murder that is grossly disproportionate to the reason given. To heighten the inconsistencies, just previously the son has wandered naked across the stage, put on his sobered-up father's drunk-soaked clothes, and has sat himself down in front of the now-loaded refrigerator to stuff his face—in an orgy less of starved gluttony than of rarefied symbolism.

Shepard is for me the archetypal post-Broadway American playwright: the leader of a generation dating from the early 1960s that grew up without the ambition that had dominated previous writers, serious and otherwise—the ambition toward Broadway. Even though the works of some of these newer writers eventually get to Broadway, they have rejected the constrictions and intents of the commerical theatre for the freedoms of off and off-off-Broadway. But, as with everything else everywhere, they have paid a price.

I do not for the smallest fragment of a second suggest that Shepard would have benefited from the advice of a show-shop wizard like George Abbott, that Shepard should have rewritten this play or any of his plays in New Haven or Boston on the way to New York. I do mean that he is a leader of a group which has used its freedom in order not to grow. I know there are earlier versions of many OB and OOB plays, I know that there are summer and winter and non-seasonal theatre conferences where plays are read and criticized and discussed. I also know the results. I see, for instance, that Shepard is as wonderfully gifted now as he was when he wrote *La Turista* in 1967 but is not notably more in control of his plays as organic works. If I say that one cannot discern in the post-1960 playwrights the increased technical skill discernible through the careers of, say, Robert E. Sherwood and Elmer Rice, the response will of course be that one prefers the freedom and commitment of the post-1960 people to the middle-class tailored seriousness of the former. To which *my* response would be: Why must one choose? Between art and freedom? The reaction to the strictures of Broadway has been an overreaction: *pace* all the latter-day theatre conferences, the away-from-Broadway theatre in New York and elsewhere has functioned more as a conduit than as a sieve. It's too broad a statement but not really untrue to say that the non-Broadway theatre has pushed liberated talent at the expense of refining it, and now we have a group of playwrights on either side of forty—Shepard the best—who are not much better now than when they started. Perhaps it's time for the non-commercial theatre to learn the idea of discipline—*to its own ends*—from that nasty old commercial theatre. [. . .]

PAIRED EXISTENCE MEETS THE MONSTER

Ren Frutkin

Shepard's essential contribution—and I am dealing only with his eight published plays to date [1969]—has been to reclaim for the imagination certain territories lost in a variety of recent cultural floodings. He has brought the word back into a theatre where, since the canonization of Artaud, the word and all that it implies—literacy, literature, imaginative connection—has been silted up with non-verbal, sensory overloads. Total Theatre, Living Theatre, Participatory Theatre, Body Theatre, Orgy Theatre, Assault Theatre, Ritual Theatre, Myth Theatre, Ridiculous Theatre, Game Theatre, Light Theatre—this is the theatrical extension of the cultural milieu in which Shepard has been working out his ideas. But I believe his plays, taken as thought in a dramatic mode, have acquired a rather different, a critical and ironic, purchase on the central subject of recent theatre and drama, including Shepard's—the value of performance. I mean here performance as the shared style of a generation, the theatricalization of everyday life.

The spirit of performance and its widespread cultural appropriation constitutes a new sensibility. Like everything new, it has antecedents; one can trace it from action painting and Happenings and Camp. One finds it most currently and popularly in the ironic growlings of W. C. Fields' imitators, in the flashes of colored stockings that transform clothing into costuming, and in political demonstrations that try to convert city avenues into theatres of ideas.

Camp in the mid-sixties, to detour into one of the antecedents, was a way of making room for oneself among the national attics of cultural junk, of indulging both in reminiscence and hip dismissal of movie, advertising, and TV culture. A hybrid of sentimentality and irony, camp tried to charm inherited cultural artifacts into the furniture of lovability and security and not a very dangerous independence. Gushed or witty, it was a dismissal of politics.

Eventually, camp lost its credibility under the pressure of three major political assassinations, the Vietnam war, the needs of Blacks, and the frustrations of students. But the mode of camp—the mode of performance—remained and was reinforced by the political style of confrontation. The 1968 Convention of the Democratic Party, for instance, and all the odors that now rise from the word Chicago, reflected as much a struggle between styles of performance as between rights in conflict. The performance values of the young had been toughened by this time through the observation and practice of politics. University people in significant numbers began to see clearly the endless petty tyrannies of the American Establishment, and to respond more positively to the street vitality of the aspiring ghetto young. Politics-and-pot constituted a new underground for many, an underground alive with the possibilities of real punishment, but real accomplishment as well. With their shared ideals and shared dangers as powerful social epoxies, they turned camp into confrontation.

Shepard's work participates in this movement towards radicalization in only a slight way. With the exception of *Operation Sidewinder*, his only overtly political play to date (and one classified as a victim of political confusion by the black students who demanded its withdrawal from production at Yale), the bulk of his work is pre-political, if one takes politics in the narrow sense. Taking politics broadly, however, as dealing with the good life in a human community, as the adjustment—personal and social—of desires and realities, Shepard's plays are wholly political, for they deal with value and authenticity.

As such, they stand in moral contrast to some of the theory that has infused recent theatrical celebrations of man the performer. I am thinking of Erving Goffman, for instance, and the use of his ideas by Richard Schechner. This is to state the case before proving it, of course, but the following statement of Goffman's, from his largely intriguing study *The Presentation of Self in Everyday Life*, should at least make his side of it clear:

> The self, then, as a performed character, is not an organic thing that has a specific location, whose fundamental fate is to be born, to mature, and to die; it is a dramatic effect arising diffusely from a scene that is presented, and the characteristic issue, the crucial concern, is whether it will be credited or discredited.

This is not a hypothesis entertained by Goffman, but the conclusion of his study and its operative value. As a vision of man, it sadly reminds one of Peer Gynt's onion—void at the center.

Among the writers involved in the modes and values of performance, Sam Shepard is the most successful at using performance value not as a style, but as a subject. In the same way that Elizabethan writers took rich advantage of the stage convention that boys played women's roles, by endlessly varying the pattern of the boy actor playing a woman "disguised" as a boy, Shepard too has taken full advantage of the shared social convention that today everyone is an actor. His actors play characters who play actors (and sometimes playwrights as well). But his characters largely act and make scenarios for a reason, not only for the sheer celebratory fun of it. And their motives supply the dramatic depth that makes Shepard's play such exciting pieces of action. His characters construct scenarios out of an urge towards power. They are usually in a state of competition with other characters doing the same thing. They have turned their imitative talents into weapons of virtuosity.

Such a subject for dramatic action makes for a kind of total and thrilling theatricality, but the burden of Shepard's thought, I believe, is that such theatricality is not total and is often destructive. Shepard is engaged in a project of theatrically rescuing the imagination from total theatricalization.

Turning to the plays, one of the first things one notices is that, for all Shepard's connections with a theatre overheated by Artaud, ritual, and the exotic, his works are quite domestic in their settings and premises. Some begin like notebook entries on homely tranquility. In *Fourteen Hundred Thousand*, three people are building a bookcase in an apartment. A maid changes a vacationing couple's beds in *Red Cross*. *Forensic and the Navigators* opens on roommates having breakfast. In *Chicago*, a man is bathing and his girl friend is making bisquits. *Melodrama Play* has a rock singer's girl friend reading him a letter from a sofa.

Other plays are set in familiar versions of American pastoral: a suburban backyard, complete with charcoal grill for a Fourth of July picnic, in *Icarus's Mother*; a ranch fence in *Cowboys #2*; hotel rooms for sick vacationers in *La Turista*. Nothing is unfamiliar, everything is engagingly at rest. Shepard does not deal with the merely odd or the overbearingly "relevant."

The sense of domestic or pastoral calm is underlined because Shepard positions his characters in their dramatic terrain with the effect of well-placed outdoor statuary. They are vertical beings around whom the ambiance collects. They become monuments to an effort at mediation and harmony between the world as it naturally occurs—the world which comes to us like a continuing inheritance, challenging us like a complex, unmanageable gift—and the world of objects we work and shape and place our values in. And, recurringly, one notices with Shepard's statues that they are done in pairs. Cowboy buddies, singer brothers, maid and guest, doctor and son, boy and girl, husband and wife, Mommy and Daddy: Shepard deals over and over again in the rich material of one of the basic data of human relationships: paired existence, the difficult act of being one-of-two, or two-as-one.

The initial calm of the plays soon ruptures under the pressure of a force that strains the stability of paired existence, the force of competitive virtuosity. Paired existence is not shared existence, at least not for very long in Shepard. In fact the main dynamism in Shepard's versions of social configurations is not that of union—the dynamism of love—but of displacement—the dynamism of power and, specifically and curiously, of the activities of teaching and learning and of sickening and curing.

The use of pairs, after all, is a way of intensifying subjectively—of using the other as a witness, an audience of one's performance. (Genet sees this as the salvation of the alienated and perverted; to Shepard it is a natural instinct, both more innocent and more immediate.) Paired existence offers the possibility of self-knowledge in the form of reflections from the other. Such knowledge has the possibility, if not often the actuality, of greater truth about the subjectively fascinating question of one's identity, and Shepard's characters go after such knowledge in a variety of ways. One sees the impulse carried out most frighteningly in Peter, the uniformed security guard hired in *Melodrama Play* by the singer's manager to keep him from being disturbed while he sweats out the composition of his next song. Peter is thick-headed, a creature of the club, who eventually knocks out everyone in the room, but his pressing concern is: "Now what am I like when you look in my face?"

Without generalizing too far beyond the facts as Shepard fashions them in his plays, I think one can see the patterns of these concerns—performance value, paired existence—in all of Shepard's works. But I think they occur in *Cowboys #2* most paradigmatically, in *Red Cross* most quintessentially, and in *La Turista* most complexly, and I would like to take up each of these in turn.

Cowboys #2, the shortest of the plays, is the action of two young men trying to top each other in impersonating—or, more accurately, competitively playing with the image of—the wizened, weather-wise cowboy. Dressed in all-purpose, mythic black, they alternately act and watch as each puts on his old man's walk and voice, weathereyes the clouds, and mutters the short, gnarled syllables of fantasized disaster. The play then moves up a notch of meaning as they mourn with dry-humor eulogy the land now buried under luxuries, both useful ones like schools and useless ones like peacocks. They reminisce about breakfast foods and morning hunger, watch the sun rise hotter and hotter, and finally imagine that one of them is dying, tongue split with thirst, as the other fends off the encircling buzzards.

As they lie there at the end, an image of the buddy system culled out of a thousand Westerns, two actors in business suits come out of the wings and *read* the script from the beginning in a monotone. Two beat-up devices—one from the movies, the other from the self-consciously avant-garde theatre— help make the essential contrast between the read word and the enacted word, the one dying in the presence of the other. The real danger—as opposed to imagined ones like Indians, death by thirst, vultures—has moved in not from the play but from the wings. It is an unsuspected, unimagined danger: the death of the imagination. It is danger with a pompous sense of its own presence and it takes over with montonous regularity as soon as the two cowboys, herding their fantasies and giving life to the desert, show signs of even pretended dying.

There is, admittedly, a temptation to make too much of this kind of contemporary mythopoeics, but one's enthusiasm gets driven at high speeds by Shepard's unfailing sense of verbal and visual economy, even in a play with the slight length and form of *Cowboys #2*. His language is so full of specific information for actors as to be worth two directors.

If *Cowboys #2* is somewhat slight, the paradigmatic situation it deals with thickens in *Red Cross*. Jim and Carol are in a cottage. Carol tells Jim a story about a ski disaster she dreamt of. She leaves. The maid comes in to change the beds, and Jim, in need of an audience, tries to get her attention. He shows her a crablouse, real or imagined, trying to shock her. He attempts to give her a swimming lesson which is really a lesson in talking about swimming, a lesson in imagination. The maïd learns the lesson, and, to Jim's surprise, betters him at it. She is the finer, deeper performer, and she leaves Jim looking out the door behind her. Carol returns from the supermarket and tells Jim she is full of lice which began to attack her at the store. Jim, who has been standing in the doorway with his back to Carol, now turns around. Carol sees that blood is streaming from his forehead and down the side of his face.

This takes place in a totally white environment—room, furniture, clothing are all white. The room, as the play's title hints, is a survival station, but contrary to expectations (especially in America where there is an economic stake in the equation that youthful equals beautiful), it is the maid, not the young, affluent Jim and Carol, who is cured. Like the crablouse that Jim pulls off his leg to frighten her, the maid detaches Jim from herself. His bloodied face is the area of his defeat in confrontation. The maid's cure and revenge are one. She travels to it daily:

> JIM : You drive from town all the way into the middle of the forest to change somebody else's beds?
> MAID: That's right.
> JIM : Aren't there any beds in town?
> MAID: I like the drive.

JIM : Me too, it's nice. Calm. Smooth. Relaxing. Comfortable. Leisurely. Pleasureable. Enchanting. Delightful.
MAID: Yes.

Jim's string of clichés is the best he can do to counter the maid's simple
realities in a performance situation which he has engineered from the beginning. He greets her in a way that is quite specific to his needs when she enters
and he is doing pushups in his underwear: "Come in, come in, come in. Have
a seat or something." In other words, come in and watch the show.

The maid's victory at the end and Jim's bloodied face secure a situation for
her that she has hoped for from the beginning, a simple desire that grows out
of her sense of honesty, a feeling that she is being unfairly victimized as an audience and that the performance situation has no value for her at this time,
with this person, doing this thing. She is not interested in Jim's endless theatricalization, for it does not fit her situation:

JIM : Is this the last room you have?
MAID: Yep.
JIM : You save it for last?
MAID: No. I just make a point to come here last. I keep hoping one day
I'll come and you won't be here. All I'll have to do is come into this
room and make the beds and go right back out. One day I'll be able to
do this room in no time at all and just go straight home. What a day
that will be.

Her victory is one of saved time, time unconsumed by the entanglements of
social performance.

The title of *La Turista* literally means the tourist's disease, or dysentery.
But it also promises some connection between cultural transformation,
disease, and loss of innocence: travel as an act of imagination.

Much of the complexity and force of *La Turista* come from the way its second half urges on the viewer comparisons and contrasts with the first half.
Act One is set in a hotel room in Mexico where Kent, a kind of filtered young
American, and his wife Salem, all springtime freshness and edgy optimism,
are lying in their beds coping with "la turista." A Mexican boy, a healthy,
knowing, street opportunist, visits them. He installs himself and plays the
role of cunning house servant, becoming a cultural intermediary when medical help finally arrives in the form of a Mayan witch doctor and his apprentice son.

Experience is connected with disease. Kent himself makes the connection in
explicit medical terms, after he has dressed himself in the mythic costume of
the American cowboy as stud-hero:

Yes, sir! Nothing like a little amoebic dysentery to build up a man's immunity to his environment. That's the trouble with the States you
know. Everything's so clean and pure and immaculate up there that a

man doesn't even have a chance to build up his own immunity. They're breeding a bunch of lily livered weaklings up there simply by not having a little dirty water around to toughen people up. Before you know it them people ain't going to be able to travel nowhere outside their own country on account of their low resistance. An isolated island of purification. That's what I'd call it. Now they got some minds, I'll grant you that. But the mind ain't nothing without the old body tagging along behind to follow things through. And the old body ain't nothing without a little amoeba.

After twirling his philosophical pistols this way, Kent sees the Mexican boy in his bed. Deflated, sexually replaced, Kent faints. The boy is his disease. And the boy, to emphasize his health and power, later puts on Kent's costume.

The second act places Kent and Salem in an American hotel room sometime shortly before their planned vacation. Kent has sleeping sickness and is visited by an American doctor in Civil War dress and *his* apprentice son, both of them easily out of *Gunsmoke*. This doctor knows Western medical science but during his cure transforms Kent into a Frankenstein. The play ends with the doctor leading imaginary villagers in pursuit of the monster. Kent/Frankenstein escapes on a swinging rope and leaves a hole the shape of his body in the upstage portion of the set.

The play is not, however, an allegorical fantasy on a theme of cultural relativism, with Mexicans this time in white hats and Americans in black. It is another working-out of Shepard's continuing concern for the transformation and transferral of power. If in *Red Cross* transferred power was in the relationship of teacher and pupil (the maid learning how to "swim" far deeper than her instructor, Jim), here the exchange is related to diseases and their cures, especially in the second half.

Act One is chiefly about the way the Mexican boy installs himself in the tourists' room, where he proceeds to displace Kent through superior performance. Kent, the traveler, has overextended himself. His body can no longer keep up. The boy, toned in the ways of street life, and tougher imaginatively as well as physically, out-performs Kent, defeats him, puts on his costume, and succeeds him. He does not then, however, with obligatory conventionality, rape the defeated man's wife. He teaches Salem what the witch doctor is doing as he too *performs* his cure over the prostrate Kent. And, in a curious, lovely fantasy in which he imagines meeting his peasant father for the last time, the Boy virtualizes his own escape and cure:

> And we'll sit together and smoke by the side of the road, until a truck come by heading toward my home. And my father will kiss me good-bye and climb on the back and drive off, and I'll wait for another truck going the other way. A pale blue truck with a canvas back, carrying chickens and goats, and a small picture of the Madonna on the dashboard, and green plastic flowers hanging from the rear view mir-

ror, and golden tassels and fringe around the window, and striped tape wrapped around the gear shift and the steering wheel, and a drunk driver with a long black beard, and the radio turned up as loud as it goes and singing Spanish as we drive out into the Gulf of Mexico and float to the other side.

To which Salem responds, "You'll never make it alive," and the act ends as she reaches him and throws on him her burden of disconnectedness and revenge (for rejecting her in favor of his father and freedom).

In the second half of the play, the nature of the real disease is made more explicit. Kent and Salem are in America, their native country. Salem describes Kent's disease to Doc:

> SALEM: . . . We're talking about something. We'll be talking back and forth and we'll be not necessarily deeply involved in what we're saying, but nevertheless talking. And he'll gradually begin to go away.
> DOC: How do you mean?
> SALEM: You'll see a person. Like you're seeing me now, and I'm talking to you, and you're talking to me, and gradually something happens to me while we're talking, until I disappear.

Here, unlike *Red Cross*, the disease is a breakdown of the *healthy* competitiveness of paired existence. The other disappears in its own eyes because it disappears in the eyes of the viewer or audience. Given such an extreme oscillation in the tension that normally keeps the paired relationship in orbit, an equally extreme cure rises out of the underground of Doc's science and works its way to the surface. Doc and his son and Salem have walked Kent around the hotel room to keep him awake, but the required cure is much less expected and comes as a surprise to both Doc and Kent. It is a cure that returns both men (Doc also suffers from sleepiness) to a world of mutuality, although a mutuality of a monstrous sort:

> KENT: Now why in the world—I ask myself why in the world would a doctor from a respectable clinic want to disconnect the phone of a dying man. A man he's supposed to cure. A man who's prepared to pay him two suitcases full of money in exchange for his good health. I ask myself why and come up with only one answer.
> DOC: Now what would that be?
> KENT: That this doctor is up to no good. That this doctor, in cahoots with his fishy son, is planning to perform some strange experiment on this dying man that she don't want to leak out to the outside world. So if this experiment fails no one will be the wiser, and the only one to have lost anything will be the dying man who's dying anyway . . .
> DOC: And I ask myself something too. I ask myself why this dying man who's got nothing to lose but his life accuses the one and only person who could possibly save it of such a silly thing as cutting the wires to his telephone. I ask myself that and come up with only one answer.

KENT : Yes?
DOC : That this dying man isn't dying at all. That this here man is aching
all over for only one thing. And he cunningly puts his idea into the
mind of the doctor, and the doctor then acts it out. The doctor performs
the experiment with his faithful son at his side and transforms the dying
man into a thing of beauty.

The "thing of beauty" is a Frankenstein: the cure amounts to a monstrous
construction. But Kent escapes as Frankenstein, now free and immunized
against all disease and monstrously appetitive. His last action is "pulling and
chomping down on the earth" with his massive teeth. He is the disease of
which he was supposed to be the cure. And he is now grotesquely healthy,
compared to his transformation into the stud-hero in the first act.

The monster is a creation engineered out of artistic energy, the abortive attempts at mutuality that Shepard deals with most fully in *La Turista*. The pattern of overt displacement of one character by another is also present in *Fourteen Hundred Thousand* where Tom, the husband, displaces Ed, his friend, in
building a bookcase for his wife Donna's fourteen hundred thousand books.
And Donna's parents bring the play to a monstrous end with their vision of a
linear city displacing all available coastal space from Maine to Florida. The
process of displacement and monstrous creation is also clear in *Melodrama
Play*, where Drake takes the place of his brother Duke, who has become
famous through a hit song stolen from Drake. Drake has every justification
for replacing his phony brother and the change is a matter of indifference to
the singer's manager as long as a new hit is forthcoming. But Drake learns
that the worst thing in the world, after not getting what you want, is getting
what you want, for he ends up under the club of the guard, Peter, and his
monstrous, violently enforced demand:"Now what am I like when you look
in my face?"

Shepard's plays deal with the disasters mutuality is heir to by making his
dramatic subject the character as performer and by confronting the performance principle with the possibility that even the fondest of our celebrations
is limited. His plays are imaginative in Northrop Frye's sense of imagination
as "the power of constructing possible models of human experience." There is
a momentum towards disaster, a destruct system, inherent in the model. And
when Shepard treats this in the most complex and ironic way, he uncovers
the truth that this momentum is bound up with wayward, derailed
creativity—the fashioning of monsters of mutuality. As visions that extend
imaginatively into a moral order, Shepard's plays offer a view of human personality that, on the surface, resembles Goffman's but, upon reflection, is
seen as deeply different from that of theorists who tend to theatricalize the
center out of man. [. . .]

WORSE THAN BEING HOMELESS
True West and The Divided Self

William Kleb

San Francisco's Magic Theatre continued its six-year association with Sam Shepard, its playwright-in-residence, by bracketing its 1979-80 season between two recent Shepard works—*Suicide in B^b* written in 1976, but never before done in the Bay Area, and *True West*, which had its world premiere on July 10, 1980. The two plays provided a striking contrast: compared to the surreal and somewhat obfuscating *Suicide in B^b*, *True West* appeared remarkably realistic and accessible to both audiences and reviewers. Under Robert Woodruff's direction, the comic elements in *True West* were stressed, the pace kept fast and intense. If the acting seemed excessively physical at times, lacking subtlety and modulation (especially on the Magic's cramped proscenium stage), the characters were boldly differentiated and delineated. The narrative line was also clearly traced and sustained despite structural rough spots and improbabilities, and, unlike *Suicide in B^b*, the story of *True West* can be easily told.

Set in Southern California, in a suburban kitchen and breakfast nook, the action focuses on the relationship of two brothers, Austin and Lee. Austin actually lives "up north" with his family, but he has come to the south to "develop" a film script for Hollywood producer Saul Kimmer. The house belongs to his "Mom" and Austin is taking care of her plants while she is in Alaska on vacation. In his mid-thirties, Austin is neatly dressed in sweater, slacks and clean, white tennis shoes; he has a full head of hair but a thin, rather frail physique. Lee looks ten years older and seems huge by comparison. Balding, scruffy, he speaks with a thick western twang and looks like a bum. His past is mysterious but he tells Austin that recently he has been living in the Mojave Desert with a "pit bull." The exact reasons for Lee's sudden return to Mom's are unclear. The play begins at night and he is simply there—wearing an old overcoat, drinking a Coors, prowling the kitchen like a caged coyote, and questioning Austin, who is seated at an old typewriter trying to concentrate on his writing. At first Austin tries to be patient with Lee's intrusion, but as his brother's attitude turns increasingly sarcastic and aggressive, Austin becomes reticent, frustrated, even a little afraid.

The conflict that develops between the two is clearly territorial. Lee resents Austin's "ivy league diploma," his middle class status, his job as a writer. Realizing that an overt challenge would be useless or worse, Austin allows Lee to say and do what he wants, but quietly insists on his own authority in the house, his professionalism, and above all, his self-control. Austin's strategy fails. First Lee takes over the physical space, the kitchen, destroying Austin's concentration by his demanding presence. He then forces Austin to loan him his car, although Austin knows that Lee is a petty thief and intends to use it to rob Mom's neighbors. Finally Lee breaks in on Austin's conference with Saul Kimmer (carrying a huge, stolen, color TV) and badgers Kimmer into agreeing to consider an idea Lee himself has for a "true-to-life western." The first act ends (again at night, four scenes and twenty four hours after Lee's arrival) with Austin, increasingly desperate, at his brother's "service," typing up an outline of Lee's story as Lee tells it to him. Act II begins the next morning, just after Lee has returned from a (rather improbable) golf game with Kimmer. Austin's anxiety turns to near hysteria as Lee tells him that Kimmer has decided to develop and produce Lee's project instead of Austin's, adding that Austin will be hired to write up Lee's idea.

By this point, Shepard's major structural principle—character reversal—becomes apparent. Lee had admitted earlier that he actually hates his rootless life, longs for Mom's suburban "paradise," and even wants to "turn myself inside out." Now Austin, unable to reach Kimmer by telephone, begins to expose *his* secret self. He demands his car keys back, he wants to get out of the house: "I might just take a drive out to the desert for a while." In the following scene, this personality transference becomes explicit; the spirit of each brother actually seems to possess the other. Lee becomes a screenwriter trying to concentrate at the typewriter, while Austin gets roaring drunk and threatens to "make a little tour" through Mom's neighborhood, perhaps committing "bigger crimes" than Lee "ever dreamed of." Even Austin's voice changes—now he talks Western, like Lee—or, as Lee says, like "the old man." (Mom and the Old Man are no longer together; in contrast to Mom's conventional suburban life, the Old Man seems to be a drunk who lives precariously down south, in the desert. His identification with Lee is as obvious as Austin's with Mom.)

In the second half of *True West*, the Old Man's spirit seems to take over not only Austin but the house itself. Even Lee is unable to break free. Without Austin's "thoughts," Lee's screenwriting attempts fail. He ends up getting drunk with Austin, attacking the typewriter with a golf club, burning his manuscript in a hibachi, and virtually demolishing Mom's kitchen. Austin, for his part, staggers out into the night and steals every toaster in the neighborhood. When he returns, he lines them up on the kitchen counter and makes toast in all of them simultaneously while he and Lee stagger about the kitchen like kids on their first drunk. As dawn approaches (the second since Lee's arrival), the yapping of coyotes reaches a crescendo outside.

At this point, significantly, Austin abandons his old life entirely and decides that he wants to move to the desert with Lee. Lee tells him he wouldn't last a day "out there," but Austin begs. In desperation, he offers to write Lee's screenplay if Lee will take him along. Lee at first refuses. The two confront one another silently. Then Austin offers Lee a stack of buttered toast on a plate. Lee smashes it to the floor. After a pause, Austin drops to his knees and slowly begins to pick up the toast at his brother's feet. As Austin performs it, the task seems a mortification ritual, a final submission to Lee's power and authority. Then with a sly smile, Lee agrees to Austin's deal. As if to seal the bargain, Lee picks up a piece of toast and takes a bite.

The last scene opens later that morning with Austin, a nervous wreck, trying to get Lee's chaotic dialogue down on paper. Lee stalks back and forth in the kitchen shouting and complaining. The collaboration is a precarious one, and just at that moment, Mom enters. Alaska was unsettling and she has decided to return home early. Mom is a bizarre creature, to say the least: wearing a white suit, a silver wig and huge mother-of-pearl earrings, she has scarlet lips and a matching red suitcase. In a daze, she walks through her littered kitchen and inspects the now dead plants hanging in the windows. The effect is chilling and the two brothers react, at first, like kids about to be spanked. Then Austin stammers out that he and Lee are going to live in the desert, but Lee, it seems, has changed his mind about that. With a paper bag full of Mom's antique plates, he heads for the door alone. Suddenly Austin grabs a telephone cord and throttles Lee from behind. The two crash to the floor as Austin, at last, gains the upper hand. He threatens to strangle Lee with the cord, saying that he will go to the desert by himself if he must. As Lee's body goes limp, Mom walks out of the kitchen, still dazed and remote; she has decided to check into a motel.

The brothers are again alone. Lee remains motionless. Austin bargains: if Lee will just give him a "head start," Austin will let him up. Lee doesn't answer. He might be dead. Slowly, warily, Austin stands up and backs away, afraid and concerned. Suddenly Lee jumps to his feet and blocks the door, crouching like a cat about to spring, his face twisted into a snarling smile. Austin jumps back, then makes a stand; he smiles too, but only slightly. *True West* ends as the two brothers face off in Mom's ruined kitchen; they might be two wrestlers ready to begin another fall, or two wild animals about to fight to the death.

The ending of *True West* is startling and abrupt. It clicks off the dramatic action like a light and leaves the basic conflict unresolved. Such a culminating freeze-frame has almost become a commonplace in modern drama; unlike the traditional *tableau*, the point is not what will or might happen but what *has* happened. The device summarizes the central dramatic (or existential) situation of the play and, in the case of *True West*, at any rate, focuses attention on its fundamental ambiguity. For despite its concrete presence, its superficial accessibility, Shepard's play, in retrospect, tergiversates on every level. That is its ultimate impact, and its message.

True West seems to be Shepard's most realistic work to date: the dialogue is natural and colloquial; the characters, with the exception of Mom, psychologically motivated; the action, linear and causal. Despite certain structural strains, the play avoids the obvious surrealistic dislocations common in Shepard's earlier work, while his distinctive aria-like monologues are likewise virtually absent. Even the setting of *True West* seems intentionally mundane: in a manuscript "note," Shepard specifically warns against "grafting" a "concept" onto the set and insists that it be constructed realistically with no attempt to "distort its dimensions, shapes, objects or colors." In short, it is as if Shepard were stressing the reality of his play in the same way that the magazine *True West* used to certify on its cover that the tales contained inside were "non-fiction."

Reality is a slippery fish, as Shepard has demonstrated more than once, and such disclaimers usually arouse more doubts and questions than they allay. Indeed, even with its realistic skin *True West* has, from the beginning, a strange, obsessive, dream-like quality. The play opens at night, to the sound of crickets; Austin is illuminated by a small, kerosene lamp, while Lee's presence in Mom's small, dimly-lighted kitchen seems jarring, threatening, somehow irrational—he could almost be a figment of Austin's imagination, a nightmare. As the power struggle between the two brothers intensifies, this surrealistic undertone becomes stronger until, in the chaotic last scenes, it takes over the stage entirely. As the rational, self-controlled Austin crumbles, the realistic surface of the play itself seems to peel away, to disintegrate. Lee batters the typewriter, there's a fire on stage, Mom's counters fill up with toasters, the telephone is ripped off the wall, the kitchen drawers are emptied all over the floor. Finally Mom materializes at the door, an archetype and a parody, a kind of satiric *deus ex machina* without the will or power to restore order in her world—a mom without a country.

Of course, it is typical of Shepard to mix the real and the surreal in his work. Unlike *The Curse of the Starving Class*, however, a play which it resembles in several ways, *True West* does not oscillate between fantasy and reality. Rather, the two levels co-exist: the one seems to displace the other even while the basic realistic framework of the play remains, more or less, intact. In other words, objective and subjective realities are not juxtaposed, they are superimposed; the "real" world is not simply challenged or questioned by "alternative levels of consciousness," it is suffused by them. (Shepard attempted this technique less successfully or subtly in both *Suicide in B^b* and *Buried Child*.) As a result, the reality of the play begins to vibrate with subjective energy and meaning: objects becomes symbols; characters, archetypes; actions, allegories.

This formal ambiguity is reflected on the level of signification. The conflict between Austin and Lee clearly has meaning beyond a study of sibling rivalry. Indeed, as Shepard describes them and as they appeared on stage at the Magic, the *reality* of their relationship is questionable: they couldn't look less alike; they seem to be, at the beginning at least, physical and psychological opposites. That is Shepard's point, of course. Although "brothers," Austin and Lee actually represent opposing styles, attitudes and values in Shepard's scheme. The most obvious reading of this opposition has to do with their major point of conflict—the film scripts that they each try to write. The creation of these scripts is a metaphor for the creative act; at issue is the nature of creativity.

Shepard's dialectic on this point is neither very original nor profound. Austin represents obectivity, self-control and self-discipline, form and order, the intellect, reason. Lee stands for subjectivity, anarchy, adventure, excess and exaggeration, intuition and imagination. Only when Austin abandons his professional project and pose and gets drunk is his repressed, imaginative side released. Then he creates the most inventive and startling (if unrealistic) image in the play, his toaster performance, and tells the play's most amusing and original tale, a story about his father's false teeth. Lee dramatizes the opposite lesson: without self-discipline and technique, he becomes frustrated, his creative energy turns violent and destructive. To sum up Shepard's point, Austin tells Lee, after the two have switched roles, that Kimmer "thinks we're the same person." Metaphorically, they are.

The relationship between order and invention is no news. What is interesting about Shepard's investigation is the manner in which it is resolved—or rather, the manner in which it is *not* resolved. Lee has the vision; Austin the skill and self-discipline. The latter, Shepard seems to be saying, must finally serve the former; even then this collaborative psychic process is a precarious one—a continual, nerve-racking battle. But in *True West*, the battle (work on the script) is abandoned. Mom appears and the work stops. And yet Austin has, apparently, relocated the imaginative root-force and is determined to return to its source—symbolically, his father's country, the desert. But, ironically, it is Lee, the Old Man's surrogate, who blocks his way. Then Mom leaves. Perhaps the struggle with Lee's script will begin again. Or perhaps Lee has, at last, lost control completely. The possibility has been there all along; as he says at one point early on: "What kinda people kill each other most . . . Family people. Brothers."

Moreover, throughout *True West*, the artistic impulse, the role of the artist, the idea of art itself seems dipped in a kind of corrosive contempt. Austin is too embarrassed even to refer to his project as a script, much less a work of art; he calls it "research." Lee, predictably, uses the words "art" and "artist" only with sarcasm and disdain. Art, for both, seems at best a not-very-acceptable or manly way to make money; as an activity, it definitely belongs in the kitchen. Shepard makes this connection obliquely at the end of his play. As Mom wanders through the wreckage, her plants dead, her grown sons squabbling about moving to the desert, somehow she is reminded that "Picasso's in town." Austin tells her that Picasso's dead. No, she says, he's visiting the local museum; she read about it in the newspaper. In short, Mom confuses Picasso's life with his art. To the characters in *True West*, it finally doesn't matter one way or the other: Austin lets the topic drop; Lee, naturally, has never heard of Picasso; Mom goes off to her motel. The artist is irrelevant; his work, a joke. And yet Picasso's name, in this absurd context, shines with another, more positive meaning: in the larger sense, Picasso *is* alive and his name becomes, in effect, a kind of emblem of artistic achievement and the integration of intellect and the imagination. Mom's startling *non sequitur* articulates Shepard's ambivalence on a thematic level.

A second theme in *True West* raises similar questions. It has to do with the nature of the American West. As his title implies, Shepard is asking what is the true, or real, West. Again the two brothers dramatize the metaphor, but, in a sense, they are simply stand-ins for Mom and the Old Man. The Old Man (and Lee) are clearly remnants of what Gary Snyder in *The Old Ways* calls the "first phase" of western "exploitation"—an "epic" or "heroic" period, at least in retrospect, characterized by images of manliness, vigor, mobility, unpredictability, rootlessness, humor and violence. It is a world that stands in direct opposition to the world of Mom (and Austin). These two represent the "new west"—the West of suburbs and freeways; toasters and color TVs; Cocker Spaniels and house plants; Safeway. Shepard's treatment of Mom and her world is harsh: he trashes her kitchen and kills her plants; his portrait of her is satiric. She may seem less vividly "the Terrible Mother" than Hailie in *Buried Child*, but her weird, iconographic presence seems just as threatening and life-denying. Moreover, like Ella, the mother in *The Curse of the Starving Class*, Mom is infected with what Shepard considers the most serious new-western sickness—alienation from the land. No wonder she seems flat, remote, lifeless, unreal. In fact, although at first this non-western landscape appears to be the most *real* world in *True West*—after all, the kitchen, its major symbol, is *really* there, in three dimensions on the stage—it becomes, ironically, a fantasy, a kind of mirage. Austin's metamorphosis makes him aware of this truth and increases his desperation to get to the desert. Initially, he insists that his world (and Mom's) is the only real or true one, and that he, not Lee, is really "in touch" with it: "I drive on the freeway every day! I swallow the smog! I watch the news in color! I shop in the Safeway!" But after this humiliation and transformation, he doesn't "recognize the place" anymore; it reminds him of the "'50s"; it lacks substance and has nothing for him now. A few moments later, Mom echoes Austin's words almost exactly: "I can't stay here," she says, wandering vaguely out of her kitchen. "This is worse than being homeless . . . I don't recognize this place."

On the other hand, Shepard's attitude toward the Old West does not seem, in the final analysis, much more favorable. Lee, its representative, may be the most vital and amusing character in *True West*, but he is also violent and devious, childish and totally self-absorbed; actually he envies Austin and even admits that he lives as he does only because he can't "make it" in Austin's world. And the Old Man seems, ultimately, nothing more than an eccentric drunk. Gary Snyder remarks that the "first phase" West was "in a sense psychologically occupied by boys without fathers and mothers, who are really free to get away with things for a while . . . " In fact, Lee and the Old Man are not adults, fathers, they are old boys (males to be sure). Creation is a kind of play and the artist (as Picasso demonstrated) must remain, in part at least, a child; if a sandbox is necessary to sustain the illusion, then into the sandbox. But in *True West*, Shepard's sandbox, the desert, seems just as immaterial, or unreal, as Mom's suburbs or Lee himself; the Old Man, after all, doesn't even appear on stage—he is a rumor, a ghost, a memory. In *Angel City*, Shepard uses film as a metaphor for the uneasy relationship between illusion and reality (surely an analogy that should be retired by now), and Lee's film script, predictably, makes Shepard's point about the Old West explicit. Lee insists that his is a "true story," yet it seems, in the telling, just another tall tale; it may have what Kimmer calls "the ring of truth" (i.e., archetypic resonance), but it also seems just as fake and contrived as Austin maintains. If it does say "something about the land," that land—that mythic western landscape—is becoming more and more remote, "a dead issue," as Austin puts it before his re-birth. In short, in *True West*, past and present both dissolve; Lee and Austin are left frozen, "stuck" between an empty dream and an insubstantial reality.

This condition is not an unfamiliar one in modern drama—Beckett bases his work on it as does Pinter, to whom *True West* owes a major debt (see Aston in *The Caretaker* and Lenny in *The Homecoming*, for instance). It reflects what R.D. Laing, in a book that seems remarkably apposite to Shepard's play, *The Divided Self*, calls a state of "primary ontological insecurity." In such a state, the individual lacks a firm, central sense of his own and other people's reality and identity; he doubts the permanence of things, the reliability and substantiality of natural processes, even the tangibility of others. As a result, Laing asserts, "there is a rent in his relation with the world," as well as a "disruption of his relation with himself; he does not experience himself as a complete person but rather as split in various ways, perhaps as a mind more or less tenuously linked to a body, or two or more selves and so on." For Laing, an existential psychiatrist, such a condition is "schizoid"; in extreme cases .it can lead to psychotic schizophrenia. For Beckett and Pinter, existential writers, it reflects, quite simply, the psychic state of modern (western) man—homeless, anxious, irresolute, divided. Shepard apparently agrees. However, whereas *Waiting for Godot* or *The Caretaker* both seem to describe this state of mind, *True West* seems to take an *imprint* of it. And Shepard himself encourages such an immediate, even autobiographical reading of his play.

For example, it is well known that Shepard was raised on a small farm in Southern California, east of Los Angeles, and that his mother now lives in a suburb near Pasadena. Shepard's father remains publicly obscure, but it seems significant that the Old Man has points in common with the fathers in both of Shepard's semi-autobiographical plays, *The Curse of the Starving Class* and *Buried Child*—Weston (drunken, irresponsible, violent) and Tilden who has just returned from a mysterious, vagrant life in the Southwest. Further, like Austin (who, as played by Peter Coyote at the Magic, actually resembled Shepard physically), Shepard lives "up north" in a suburb of San Francisco with his wife and son; his literary and film successes (the Pulitzer Prize, starring roles in *Days of Heaven* and *Resurrection*) have presumably brought him securely into the upper-middle class, while he has in the past had several abortive, distasteful experiences as a fledgling screenwriter. Finally, Shepard has *no* brother. To those familiar with his life and legend, however, Lee is just as clearly based on Shepard himself as is Austin—he is Shepard's "cowboy mouth," his own self-dramatization (rock star, farmer, poet, yegg), the "bad boy" Patti Smith glorifies in "Nine Random Years [7+2]." (Shepard even has two nominal identities; he was born Samuel Shepard Rogers II.) Thus, despite its objective reality, and its universal ambiguities and implications, *True West* may, in fact, be Shepard's most subjective, most personal play to date. Like the conflict at its core, the play seems locked in battle with itself; essentially an autodidactic writer, Shepard nevertheless imposes a strict, self-conscious structure on his work; again and again, unaccountably, he tries to pin down his symbols; when he does, they die. And yet the play itself continually rebels, breaks free, comes back to life.

OF LIFE IMMENSE IN PASSION, PULSE, AND POWER

Sam Shepard and the American Literary Tradition

Michael Earley

For close to two decades Sam Shepard has been an anomaly on the American dramatic landscape. Part of the problem in approaching his plays has been the question of just where to place him within a perceivable tradition—be it theatrical or literary. What, after all, does he owe to American drama? Very little, in fact. Rather he seems to have forged a whole new kind of American play that has yet to receive adequate reckoning. But when you step back for a moment and measure Shepard against the deeper wellspring of American literature, particularly the transcendental and romantic traditions, a whole new way of looking at this complex and curious writer is revealed. He is, after all, an intuitive playwright of exhilarating vision who, to paraphrase Ralph Waldo Emerson in "The Poet," sees America as a drama whose ample geography dazzles the imagination. In placing Shepard within this kind of spectrum, you begin to see possibilities for him and his plays that you never thought existed.

If you take the position, as I do, that Shepard is a true American primitive, a literary naif coursing the stage of American drama as if for the first time, asserting a stylistic independence that has become a central dramatic situation for American writers, then what you begin to see in his plays are innocent gestures and fresh associations that resemble the themes, language, and mythic preoccupations of an earlier group of American writers like Hawthorne, Melville, and Whitman. In fact, a substantial case could be made for saying that Whitman is *the* most apparent influence on

Shepard's style. For like the poet in "One's-Self I Sing," Shepard's plays are full of Whitman's "Of Life immense in passion, pulse, and power." And yet while whole sections of his writing seem to resemble that of Whitman—even play titles and characters appear to come from "Song of Myself"—Shepard's passion for dark, ominous visions, and greater abstraction runs a clear course back to Hawthorne and Melville. For what Shepard lacks of Whitman's optimism and deep faith in democracy surfaces in sympathies for the darker and more corrosive side of early American fiction. How this is worked out in the plays and in Shepard's technique is something that needs to be looked at closely, if only briefly.

What you begin to see in Shepard, when viewed through the lens of early American literature, is the sort of pattern that the critic Marius Bewley called the "eccentric design" of American fiction. A design that veers away from observable fact and social manners—a European tradition—and comes into closer contact with abstractions and dialectical tensions that became the core of early American writing. In Shepard those abstractions and tensions come alive in a new way while at the same moment repeating a timeless pattern. The symbolic abstraction of, for instance, Hawthorne's forest, Melville's white whale, or Poe's gothic spaces become echoed in Shepard's desert, sidewinder computer, and farmhouse that hides secrets from the past. *The Scarlett Letter* finds its analogue in the mark of *The Unseen Hand* or the green slime of *Angel City*. These images, and the abstractness of the ideas they represent, gives them the "large and glowing generality" that Bewley attends to their presence in American fiction.

The tension between an American wilderness and a new industrial civilization, a resonant note in American literature, strikes a responsive chord in Shepard, too. His sense of this fundamental conflict is as elementary as anything found in the writing of, say, James Fenimore Cooper. His characters also come as though from an earlier age. Everywhere in his dramatic world there are characters who resemble Natty Bumpo, Ahab, and Huckleberry Finn. For a writer as available to the experience of America as Shepard surely is, such resonances run deep even though they are most certainly unintentional.

A playwright of uncompromising imagination and expressive freedom, Shepard brings to the drama a liberating interplay of word, theme, and image that has always been the hallmark of the romantic impulse. His plays don't work like plays in the traditional sense but more like romances, where the imaginary landscape (his version of America) is so remote and open that it allows for the depiction of legend, adventure, and even the supernatural. Shepard's use of popular iconography is one instance of this impulse at work. But what it allows him to do, and what a similar feat allowed earlier American writers to do, is to transcend normal structures of belief and form. Shepard talks of his idea of drama as an "open ended structure where anything could happen as opposed to a carefully planned regurgitated event which, for me, has always been as painful as pissing nickels." Like the classic American writers that Tony Tanner writes about in *The Reign of Wonder*, Shepard "Thirsts after the primitive, absolute, all pervading truth . . . not content with knowledge of barren insulated facts." Rather than contract experience, Shepard expands it. He takes us to places where experience is fresher to the eye. Even though Shepard is one of our most modernist playwrights—his indulgent surrealism being just one example—what he more keenly resembles is a transcendalist or new romantic whose "innocent eye" wonders at all it surveys and records experience without censure.

A way of linking Shepard to the more imaginatively playful and less philosophical side of transcendentalism is through the innocent and almost adolescent fantasies in such early plays as *Mad Dog Blues, Red Cross,* and *Cowboys #2.* When Shepard says that his plays are extensions of "the sensation of *play* (as in kid)," he is underscoring something akin to what Leslie Fiedler, in *Love and Death in the American Novel,* found operating in our literature at large: "Our novels seem not primitive, perhaps, but innocent, unfallen in a disturbing way, almost juvenile." It's also something that Tony Tanner noted when he speaks of the "unselective childlike wonder" and "cultivated naiveté" of American literature. That Shepard's plays are filled with adolescent-like characters with innocent eyes who approach experience fresh demonstrates the link he has with a specific trait of native literary values.

By retreating from the "carefully planned regurgitated event" and entering forcefully into the world as "play," Shepard cuts himself off from the strict social, economic, and sexual objectification that have always characterized American drama. For him drama is no longer a set of formulaic codes but rather an open field. Like the literature of Cooper, Hawthorne, Melville, Thoreau, Poe, and Whitman, Shepard's plays construct a homemade world where the building of something new is more important than the architecture of the past. In *Fourteen Hundred Thousand* it comes out in the construction of bookshelves and talk about a cabin. In *The Curse of the Starving Class* it is in the construction of an animal pen and a new door frame. The effort is something like Thoreau's retreat to Walden and to the solace of new imaginative space. In order for the world to be new, a new set of boundaries have to be struck. Like so much in early American literature, the effort in so many of Shepard's plays is to create protective environments that will insulate against the wild perils of the frontier. As Henry Hackamore in *Seduced* says: "The world at large! That's what's out there. Wild. Undominated. Ravenous for the likes of us. Ready to gobble us up at the drop of a hat. We can't allow penetration." And yet the frontier is something to be embraced because of the environment of freedom it allows. Both interior worlds and exterior worlds are the dimensions through which Shepard's characters roam.

The wild and sometimes hallucinatory freedom of transcendental vision is not unlike the same seeking after "perception" and "consciousness" that Shepard exhibited best in his plays of the sixties. Here, as before with other American writers, the accent is on removing objective imperatives and stretching the mind into hidden caverns of thought. Just as Henry Hackamore is frightened of exposure, he also delights in flights of fancy: "The mind covers a wide range of territory. Sometimes simultaneously traveling several different hemispheres in a single sweep and then diving suddenly for the prey." It is just this secret fantasy in Icarus-like moments of imaginative flight, something that all of Shepard's best characters share, that is both their release and their peril. Heightened consciousness extorts its own price.

Thematically, Shepard shows all the terror and wonder of being faced with his new continent as earlier American writers did with theirs. The theme of the frontiersman (*Cowboys #2*), the child lost in the wilderness (*Buried Child*), the journey into the unknown (*The Unseen Hand*), the material world as chaos instead of God's order (*Angel City*), possession and dispossession (*The Curse of the Starving Class*), and adventurous travel by sea and land (*Mad Dog Blues*) show that Shepard has never lost intrinsic contact with American literary instincts. As was the case generally for early American writers, his great theme is American expansionism. Only in his mind unlimited possibilities have been reduced to just a few. Verdant growth has been tamed and even virtually annihilated. By locating himself, as the beats did, in "Kerouac country," Shepard tries to stride the expanse and keep the romance alive. And yet there is trouble in paradise. As Capt. Bovine tells the old prospector Bill in *Operation Sidewinder*: "This country's in trouble. Big trouble. Over the past few years there's been a general breakdown of law and order and a complete disrespect for the things we've held sacred since our ancestors founded this country." Despite, and perhaps because of, the gnawing repression that grips most of Shepard's old-style heroes, they retreat into the vast open spaces of consciousness and imagination.

Like so many similar instances in earlier American literature, Shepard's plays examine how specific selves outgrow their environment. Like Huck Finn's escape down the river and disappearance into a newly generated self, Shepard's characters frequently try the same tact. He pits the private self against the national self. As Henry Hackamore says at one point in *Seduced*: "Texas. That's the last time I lived on the earth. Texas. I disappeared in a dream. I dreamed myself into another shape. Another body. I made myself up." The great effort and the great tragedy in American writing has always been the attempt to transform the self into something new; to deny the past. It was true in Hawthorne and Melville and it continued to be true in James and Fitzgerald. In Shepard the dilemma is no less contradictory and dangerous. And yet it's a dream that all his characters attempt in some form or another only to be confronted later with the illusion. Just as Henry Hackamore flies high—"Freer than life"—at the end of *Seduced*, he's still a phantom whose voice fades on the contradictory note, "I'm dead to the world but I never been born."

What Shepard shares with someone like Whitman is an unmediated delight in language as a means of imaginative freedom. Richard Poirier, in *A World Elsewhere*, demonstrates at length how American writers used language as a route to imaginative transports; as "an exultation in the exercise of consciousness momentarily set free." Almost everything that Poirier notes as being true of earlier American writers is true of Shepard as well. Expanding the self through what Poirier calls an "environment of language" is something that Shepard may have learned by way of Whitman. And Whitman learned it first from Emerson. It is refreshing to read Shepard saying with regards to words, "I can't be anything other than an American writer." And when he also says "the power of words for me isn't so much in the delineation of a character's social circumstances as it is in the capacity to evoke visions in the eyes of the audience, " or speaking of "Words as living incantations and not as symbols," Shepard connects himself with Emerson's notion that "Words are also action and actions are a kind of words."

Shepard's *Action* dramatizes this Emersonian dictum. The play is a sustained demonstration of the ways that words can call into being moments of activity and vice versa. And while the play itself might be more correctly linked to the process of action painting or even the experiments of Gertrude Stein to summon through language a continual present, there is still that basic thrust to *Action* which ties into Emerson's notion that "the poet turns the world to glass, and shows us all things in their right series and procession . . . perceives that thought is multiform." *Action* also demonstrates the Emersonian feeling that "All the facts of the animal economy, sex, nutriment, gestation, birth, growth, are symbols of the passage of the world into the soul of man, to suffer there a change, and reappear a new and higher fact." Shepard offers a similar point of view: "Words . . . possess the power to change our chemistry," they "retain the potential of making leaps into the unknown." This essential transcendental belief in the power of language to transform and take us to a higher plane creates the confluence of intentions that link Emerson with Whitman, and Whitman with Shepard.

Beyond the Emersonian impulse to view words as alchemy of a new sort, both Whitman and Shepard share a similar belief in the range and variety of an American idiom: a delight in vernacular, cant, and slang; a strong lyricism that could compose a language of mind, body, and soul; the imagistic and visual values that could be summoned up through the word; and the incredible, almost cinematic, freedom of words leaping from place to place across the page or across the stage. Both poet and playwright express the similar attitude that language can be sly and playful, and that one of its richest resources is its ability to carry a sustained monologue. Whitman's "Song of Myself" is, after all, one continuous monologue from beginning to end. Few American playwrights before or since Shepard have ever attempted, like him, to take the dramatic monologue to similar limits. Almost as if learning from Whitman, Shepard sees in the monologue the large freedoms it could offer his characters, illustrating as Richard Chase says of Whitman, "the fluid, unformed personality exulting alternately in its provisional attempts to define itself and in its sense that it has no definition."

When you move through the competing registers of the language duel in *The Tooth of Crime*, to take just one example, you can see how Shepard's characters float into focus and then out, how the essential perception of self which makes up the conflict of that play lives and dies on the field of language. When you compare almost any speech from *The Tooth of Crime* with "Song of Myself" the associations of technique come into sharp relief:

HOSS: Never catch me with beer in my hand. Never catch me with my pecker out. Never got caught. Never did get caught. Never once. Never, never. Fast on the hoof. Fast on the roof. Fast through the still night. Faster than the headlight. Fast to the move.

(*The Tooth of Crime*)

You there, impotent, loose in the knees,
Open your scarf'd chops till I blow grit within you,
Spread your palms and lift the flap of your pockets,
I am not to be denied, I compel, I have stores plenty to spare,
And any thing I have I bestow.

("Song of Myself")

The intriguing way in which the Whitman passage, by the merest adjustment, could easily become Crow's retort to Hoss demonstrates what a deep kinship there is between Shepard's play and Whitman's poem. The large, multitudinous ways in which the reading of one informs the reading of the other illustrates the ties that bind Shepard to Whitman.

Beyond the use of monologue and an intrinsic identity with rhythms and themes, both Shepard and Whitman find in language the means of expressing the physical self. Just as Whitman had his physiological approach to language ("The smoke on my breath. . . . My respiration and inspiration, the beating of my heart, the passion of blood and air through my lungs"), we continually see that the same holds true for Shepard, sometimes on even a more dramatic level, as in this passage from *Red Cross*:

JIM: You stay down as long as you can until your lungs start to ache.

> They feel like they're going to burst open. Then just at the point you
> can't stand it any more you force yourself to the top. You explode out
> of the water gasping for air. And all this rain hits you in the face.

The fact that language could be physical, that it could contain blood, tissue,
fiber, and bone, is certainly not a new idea. But seeing such a direct correspondence, repeatedly, between Whitman and Shepard on this level alone
leads to just one more way of viewing Shepard's relation to an earlier tradition.

Going beyond the themes and conventions of Transcendentalism and
Romanticism, and the telling verbal associations that link Shepard with
Whitman, one final link needs to be made between Sam Shepard and 19th-
century American literature. And that is his recourse to mythic impulses.
On one level the reading of myth in his plays is quite classical: the agon between characters of huge proportion (*The Tooth of Crime*). On another level
the reading takes a different classical bent: the grievance of son with father
(shown in embryo in *The Rock Garden* and in more maturity in *The Curse
of the Starving Class*). But for a writer like Shepard, imbued with a whole
range of mythic preoccupations that take him as far back as folk and Indian
lore, the correspondences run deeper. Shepard himself says: "Myths speak
to everything at once, especially the emotions. By myths I mean a sense of
mystery and not necessarily a traditional formula. A character is for me a
composite of different mysteries. He's an unknown quantity." In fact, what
Shepard seems to be saying is that his plays spring from the impulse to get
inside this unknown quantity in order to *see* what's there. What's there, of
course, is the play he is writing at any given moment. But through exercising the visual side of his imagination and sketching a scheme towards its
conclusion, which in *The Tooth of Crime* took the form of Crow, a totally
"lethal" and "savage" human who needed a victim, Shepard transforms the
mystery into something approaching a known quantity. And yet only *just*
approaching. For in no sense does Shepard seem to be writing out of some
codified mythopoeic tradition but rather a naive American one that takes its
savagery to heart and finds literary structures to exorcise it. As Hawthorne
and Poe proved, the strategy need not be at all conscious but comes, instead, out of some deep emotional need to show fear in the face of the
unknown and the unseen. In Shepard's dramatic romances and tales fear is a
wilderness with no path leading out.

Like those American writers with whom I've tried to connect him, Sam
Shepard takes it for granted that the mystery is insoluble and will forever
leave its imprint strewn throughout the imaginative landscape of both mind
and body. It is simply another feature of his complex and eccentric design.

LOOKING A GIFT HORSE DREAMER
IN THE MOUTH

Ross Wetzsteon

"At first it's all instinct," says Cody. "Now it's work." And I'm afraid Cody is speaking for Sam Shepard.

At a certain point in their careers writers in a media and celebrity-saturated culture have to come to terms with the relationship between their social roles as artists and the integrity of their work—withdrawing utterly, as J. D. Salinger and Thomas Pynchon have done, or dealing with it directly as part of the very substance of their art, as in the case of Saul Bellow and Vladimir Nabokov. (Though I sometimes feel, in reading works of art about art, a parallel to those affairs in which the two lovers spend so much time talking about their relationship they don't have time to have one.)

Sam Shepard's *Geography of a Horse Dreamer* is an intriguing example of a genre half-way between these extremes—the work of art which ostensibly deals with another subject but which is actually an extended metaphor for the personal dilemma of the artist himself. I think of this kind of work as a translation play. Instead of translating the text from French, say, into English, the audience has to translate the plot into its meaning.

Plot: Cody, a Wyoming cowboy who has the gift of dreaming the winners of horse races, has been kidnapped by gamblers. But he's losing his gift, he can't dream winners any more, and in desperation the gamblers switch to dog racing. Cody's gift immediately returns, but he soon goes mad, and just as the gamblers are about to remove the "dream bone" from his neck, his two cowboy brothers burst into the room, murder the gamblers, and take him back to Wyoming.

Translation: Shepard, whose image of himself is as a cowboy (his first produced play was called *Cowboys*), "dreamed" a number of extraordinary plays in the middle and late sixties, but he was "kidnapped" by the cultural entrepreneurs—first the publicity and awards (Cody was featured in *Life* magazine, while Shepard has won five Obies), then Lincoln Center (*Operation Sidewinder*), and finally Hollywood (*Zabriskie Point*). Torn by the conflict between dreams and power, between talent and its exploitation (Cody's and Shepard's visionary gifts are used to make money), Shepard longs to be rescued, to return to the purity of the Golden West of his youth.

A number of hints and details don't merely suggest but actually enforce this translation.

First, the obvious source of the plot is the '30s comedy, *Three Men on a Horse,* in which Erwin, a writer of greeting cards who has a knack for picking horse race winners, is kidnapped by gamblers—the difference being that while Erwin is the All-American schmuck, Dagwood as artist, his art form the silliest parody, Cody is a true visionary, driven to madness by the dark psychic accuracy of his dreams.

Then there are details from Shepard's own life. *Horse Dreamer* was written while Shepard was in England, when, hardly coincidentally to the plot, his new fascination with dog racing paralleled a resurgence of interest in his work by a new audience. (Suddenly, as in the play, he dreamed "winners" again.) But Shepard was clearly ill at ease in England—in the second act, Cody lapses into an Irish accent (the outsider), and one of his chief tormentors is cast as an effete Englishman.

Furthermore, the text is littered with references to the artistic nature of Cody's dreams (he's called "Mr. Artistic Cowboy" at one point, "Beethoven" at another, and one of his captors says: "I mean maybe his dreamin' does take on a kind of an art form"). The kidnapping is admittedly hyperbolic. (Cody: "I was kidnapped." Beaujo: "Well, not exactly." Cody: "I was wined and dined.") The theme is developed explicitly in terms of the conflict between genius and power. The decision of his captors to remove and store his "dream bone" parallels the way artists are institutionalized. And even the name Cody evokes Buffalo Bill, another western visionary whose dreams were cheapened.

Now while as a theatre critic (and in particular as one who has followed Shepard's work more closely than that of any other American playwright), I find all this intriguing, and while on some level it's gratifying to find oneself in the position of "translating" a play from the apparent stage action into the author's hidden "meaning," still I have the gravest doubts about the aesthetic success of any work of art which requires such extensive mediation between its being and its audience. One of Shepard's greatest gifts as a playwright has always been his ability to skip this process of mediation, to create situations and characters which express his personal obsessions without the necessity for translation, which exist first wholly on their own terms, and which then unfold their broader implications by virtue of their powerful particularity. (I remember Shepard appearing before a class I once taught at CCNY and ruthlessly refusing to admit—to the extent of posing as an inarticulate hick—his plays had any meaning at all.)

But *Horse Dreamer*, like *Operation Sidewinder*, is one of Shepard's self-conscious plays—by which I mean that its "meaning" doesn't emerge from its being, but exists *prior* to its being, which thus becomes merely the vehicle by which it articulates itself. The key, here, is the nature of dramatic metaphor— a successful metaphor, of course, is one in which X does not "stand for" Y, but one in which X first exists on its own terms, and then, through the resonant truth of those terms, *opens up* into Y. The process is not one of pointing at but of unfolding, not one of translation but of evocation.

In a sense, then, I find the unclear ending of *Horse Dreamer* both its major dramatic flaw and its greatest redeeming feature. Among other things, Shepard's plays are remarkable for the stunning impact of their endings (I think in particular of the exhilarating breathing scene of *Chicago* and the running leap through the back wall of the stage in *La Turista*), endings which dramatically open up rich possibilities of release and liberation. In a sense, *Horse Dreamer* has an arbitrarily happy ending—at the last moment, Cody's brothers simply burst on stage, shoot up the place, and drag him away (one misses only the cavalry's bugle call). In terms of Shepard's work as a whole, I'm disturbed by the way in which the rescue is external—usually the liberation is self-generated. And in terms of this particular play, I'm disturbed by the apparent confusion in Shepard's mind as to whether or not Cody is in fact rescued at all—earlier in the play, he's hinted that Cody's brothers had also begun to exploit his gifts, and just consider the pessimism of his final speech: "I was walking in my dream. A great circle. I was walking and I stopped. Even after the smoke cleared I couldn't see my home. Not even a familiar rock. You could tell me it was anywhere and I'd believe ya. You could tell me it was any old where."

In this confusing mixture of rescue and captivity, of gratuitous optimism and trance-like pessimism—as if in his feeling of paralyzed hoplessness he's reaching out desperately for any kind of happy ending—I sense Shepard's despair at resolving the dilemma of art and exploitation. But I also sense that in a way this confusion is redeeming, for in at least confronting it, in trying to come to terms with it, he is not surrendering but continuing the painful struggle of a maturing artist. "His gifts are poison to him now," one of the characters says of Cody, but I feel strongly that Shepard still has the gifts to refute his own thesis, that he still has the strength, the determination, the courage to overcome his despair.

SAM SHEPARD AND JOSEPH CHAIKIN
Speaking in Tongues

Eileen Blumenthal

Joseph Chaikin sits on a high-backed chair, gazing toward the audience. His hands rest on the Mexican blanket covering his lap. Unseen maracas begin a tempo, and Chaikin starts to speak. Occasionally, a bare arm holding the maracas reaches out from behind the chair to accent a beat—the split second image vaguely suggesting a multi-limbed Hindu god. For the next half hour, Chaikin remains nearly motionless, while a dozen voices come through him: the tongues of people dying, giving birth, wrestling with passion and wonder, or just trying to make it through the day.

Tongues is the first of two monologues with music which Chaikin and Sam Shepard created. The second is a biting, affecting, funny piece called *Savage/Love*. Both works came from intensive explorations of language, sound, and the power of an actor to transmit extreme conditions. More basically, they are the fruit of a long term desire by two of the most innovative artists in American theatre to collaborate with each other.

Shepard and Chaikin met at a dinner party in 1964. Shepard, at that point, had written mostly poetry and was just starting to focus on plays; Chaikin had already received recognition as an actor, had directed a little and was the dominant figure in the fledgling Open Theater. "We really had a rapport," Chaikin recalls. "After the dinner, we walked a long distance together along some highway, and we talked. And I told him to come to a workshop at the Open Theater." (Except as noted, all quotations come from my interviews and conversations with Chaikin and Shepard—Chaikin in person, Shepard

via long-distance telephone—in November 1979.) Shepard was around the
edges of the company, then, for the rest of its existence: "I went to a lot of
workshops. Every once in a while, Joe asked me to write something and I
would do it. I was always like in and out, contributing to the work just in
little particles, in little pieces." In 1966, he wrote *Icarus's Mother*, which was
performed by Open Theater actors. Later, he created three monologues for
Terminal, "Cowboy," "Stone Man," and "Teleported Man." (None was finally
used; they are published in Shepard's *Hawk Moon*.) And he wrote several
key speeches and scenes for *Nightwalk*. But, while Chaikin thinks of Shepard
as one of the writers who nourished the Open Theater, Shepard (like all of the
company's writers except, perhaps, Jean-Claude van Itallie) always felt
uneasy, on the periphery:

> I never knew my place in the Open Theater, you know? I didn't have a
> place in the Open Theater. I was hanging out with different people, and
> I would come by. I felt a kinship with Joe. But I didn't know how to
> function as a writer there at all.

After the Open Theater disbanded, Shepard suggested to Chaikin that they
create a piece together, and in the summer of 1978, Chaikin went to San Francisco to work with Shepard for a month. They had decided to proceed
without an ensemble—to make something between the two of them which
Chaikin would then perform. Although they had exchanged letters about the
area they wanted to explore, and Shepard already had suggested the title
Tongues, they had no specific themes and no usable text when Chaikin
arrived—"almost nothing," Shepard says, "but a desire to work together."

After three weeks of intensive conversations, writing, and rehearsals,
Tongues, a piece for voice (Chaikin's) and percussion (played by Shepard),
was ready for an audience. The following summer, after a dozen more letters
back and forth, they worked for three weeks developing *Savage/Love*—this
time using an actor's (Chaikin's) voice, percussion, and horns.

The collaboration periods were so brief, Chaikin explains, because "Sam
has an aversion to New York, and he's terrified of flying, and I couldn't stay
for too long." (New York *Times*, Jan. 13, 1980.) The work could move quickly,
though, "because there was so much water under the bridge between Sam and
me," because of the years they'd known each other both as artists and friends.
The lack of an ensemble also made the process very efficient. Only two people, rather than Chaikin's usual eight to twenty, were exploring each idea.
And since there weren't actors' egos to be protected, sections that seemed barren could be abandoned quickly and ruthlessly.

Despite some specific disagreements, Chaikin and Shepard never found
themselves at odds over the basic nature of the work. At first this seems
strange, because their theatre apart from these collaborations had been very
different from one another's. Shepard's plays had mostly been flashy, kalei-

doscopic trips—chemical, musical, psychological, or literal—through very personal, mid- and western-American terrain. Chaikin's had been intense, distilled collages about mythic-scope themes such as dying and human mutability. Still, Chaikin and Shepard had often been on parallel tracks. Each had tried to express inner territory. And each had explored the relationships between language and music—how words can produce different voices and modes, how musical elements, including structure, can be adapted to the theatre.

A big factor in making the collaboration click was Chaikin and Shepard's mutual respect and affection. Neither their egos nor their sensibilities clashed. Chaikin says he kept expecting to find boundaries beyond which they couldn't relate to each other's experiences, but those obstacles just didn't materialize. There was only one tiny area where an impulse of Shepard's was foreign to him. (*Savage/Love* has a line about wanting to die before one's lover; for Chaikin, who has suffered a critical heart condition since childhood, this was unfamiliar.) Chaikin *wanted* to include that line in the piece, though, to try to enter its realm of emotion. And, he says, "Although it's possible that Sam also had feelings about certain things being very strange, I don't think so. My impression was that he didn't." Asked if he had felt pressed into someone else's way of seeing—particularly since these joint creations are closer in form and mood to Chaikin's work than to his—Shepard said that his enormous respect for Chaikin prevented that from being an issue:

> When you're collaborating with someone who you can learn from, it's very different from collaborating with someone who you're struggling with in some kind of competitive way. Like you're showing each other your chops. Musicians call it chops. If you can play a scale 16 ways, you've got chops—and there are ways of playing together where you show that off. But when you're working with someone who actually has an experience that penetrates deeply, and you know you can learn from it, the relationship isn't that way. I feel like I'm an apprentice to Joe. I don't feel that in any kind of pejorative way, like a servant, but—I feel like he's my elder. So there's no problem with me in terms of feeling like his ideas are infringing on my vision.

Another thing that facilitated the collaboration was that Shepard and Chaikin were accomplished in several areas of theatre. Chaikin was an experienced actor and director as well as a leader of experimental workshops and ensemble creations. Shepard, in addition to writing, had directed, performed in, and composed music for his plays, and had recently acted in a Hollywood film. And although he had mostly written alone, he had contributed to the Open Theater and had collaborated with Patti Smith on *Cowboy Mouth*, so joint playwriting was not new to him.

The functions of playwright, director, and composer melded in the San Francisco work. Shepard says: "The actual material of the thing doesn't break down so easily into who did the words and who did the music; for me, it really was a collaboration in the truest sense. Nobody can really lay claim to any one aspect. The words were both of ours really." Chaikin agrees, though he adds that because Shepard "is a writer the rest of the time, in that sense I feel like he was the custodian of the words." Chaikin credits Shepard with having directed *Savage/Love* and, for the most part, *Tongues*. (Robert Woodruff came in to help direct *Tongues* in San Francisco when Shepard began performing the music and directed both plays for the subsequent productions.) But Shepard says, "In a way, Joe directed from the inside."

Chaikin and Shepard began work on *Tongues* by trying to explore a kind of expression Chaikin could not quite define but called "thought music." In the early stages, they used a simple story as a provisional springboard and structure. Chaikin recalls:

> The first idea, which was thrown away but is in the piece anyway, was "Let's make up this thing about a person who died and had many other lives. And make a fantasy of the lives." So that's where we started from. Although we departed entirely from that idea, it gave a really very nice trampoline for us to play with.

For several weeks they worked in different places around San Francisco: "Sam likes egg foo yung, so we'd go to this Chinese restaurant, or we'd go to the park or to the zoo, or we'd stay in my hotel room." Through conversations, they would focus on an area, a kind of voice that they wanted to include in the work. Then, Chaikin explains:

> We would sit there and make something up. I'd sometimes make up a line, he'd follow it; he'd make up a line, I'd follow it. Or sometimes he would write something and read it back to me, and I would say why I didn't want to go in that direction or why I didn't think it was such an interesting direction or—you know how I like everything to be distilled, how I can't stand anything that spreads—I'd say why it would be better like that.

The resulting texts often mixed Chaikin's and Shepard's impulses. One section, for example, sprang from Chaikin's account of being with a friend who had come out of brain surgery almost totally blind. But Chaikin's manner of description was fused with an image that really was from Shepard's America: "In front of you is a window. About chest level. It's night out . . . On the wall are pictures from your past. One is a photograph. You as a boy. You standing in front of a cactus. You're wearing a red plaid shirt . . . A mosquito races around your ear. The same mosquito you're hearing."

Some voices in the piece came directly from Chaikin and Shepard's experiences during the collaboration. For example, since they worked all over the city, deciding when and where to eat became a daily ritual of almost comic mutual politeness. One day, their talk about eating led to a long discussion about hunger. They generalized, Shepard recalls, "from that particular mundane hunger for food to many aspects of hunger, hunger on different levels. Fat people, for example, want more than just steaks." After that conversation, Chaikin told me, "Sam went home and wrote, and came in the next day with this speech which was, more or less, the way it is in the final piece."

It begins with a dialogue (both voices performed by Chaikin):—"Would you like to go eat? Isn't it time to eat?"—"I don't mind."—"We don't have to. It's up to you." Gradually it switches gears; "I'm famished . . . Nothing I ate could satisfy this hunger I'm having right now." By the end, the person is talking about hunger that can only subside briefly but will return even stronger so that "there'll be nothing left but the hunger itself when it comes back. Nothing left but the hunger eating the hunger when it comes back."

Another section was triggered by a phone conversation Chaikin had with his brother. Chaikin described to Shepard how this brother had developed an oddly businesslike persona that he used now even with his family—and how that image finally encroached on the basically sensitive, socially conscious person who projected it. Chaikin did an imitation of his brother, and Shepard said "It's wonderful. Let's put it in." They developed a spoken letter, performed in a flat, dry tone. What communicated was a stifled, hopeless attempt at caring and contact:

> I'm writing you this today from a very great distance. Everything here is fine. I'm hoping everything there is fine with you. I'm hoping you still miss me as much as you once did. . . .
> Something happened today which you might find amusing. I know I found it amusing at the time. A dog came into the hotel and ran around the lobby. . . .

Although they felt, in Shepard's words, "no urgency to tie these facets [of the developing pieces] together or force them to tell a 'story,'" *Tongues* did wind up with a kind of double-yolked center—not too far removed from the original story idea of the man who dies. One repeating theme is voices, the total inadequacy and the miraculous expressiveness of sounds, especially words. Chaikin, as woman giving birth, in a mixture of agony and awe, says, "Nothing they told me was like this. I don't know whose skin this is." A character tries frantically to find a voice he can recognize as his own, running through an orchestra of vocal timbres and pitches in the search: "That was me. Just then. That was it. Me . . . Must've been. Who else? Why should I doubt it?" And the final segment is about really learning to hear:

> Today the people talked without speaking.
> Tonight I can hear what they're saying.
>
> Today the tree bloomed without a word.
> Tonight I'm learning its language.

Even more central is the theme of death and dying. This focus came partly from the original story idea, partly from Chaikin and Shepard's interest in expressing extreme conditions—and partly from the fact that Chaikin literally was in heart failure. (He underwent emergency open heart surgery days after returning to New York):

> I was very sick when we were working on *Tongues*, extremely sick, and I didn't know it. And I'd work with Sam and then I'd go back to the hotel room, unless we had never left the hotel room, and I'd lie and look at the ceiling. It was in a geriatric hotel; I wanted to be there because of the feeling that I wouldn't ever be old and I might as well just be around oldness on this occasion when I was out of town anyway.

Tongues circles back again and again to death. The opening is about a man who lives "in the middle of a people," is honored, dishonored, married, becomes old, and then one night dreams a voice telling him, "You are entirely dead . . . You are entirely gone from the people"—and "In the next second/He's entirely dead." The theme resurfaces later in a haunting litany:

> Between the space I'm leaving
>   and the space I'm enjoying
>
> The dead one tells me now
>
> Beside the shape I'm leaving
>   and the one I'm becoming
>
> The departed tells me now.

Another voice talks about the "moment where I vanished," leaving "the whole of my body." There is an address to a dead one who is somehow present: "Is this me calling you up/or are you appearing? Volunteering yourself?" And one section near the end is about comforting a dying person, trying to guess what comes at the moment of death.

Shaping the dozen-plus sections of *Tongues* into a performance piece, Chaikin and Shepard used principles drawn more from musical composition than traditional dramaturgy. Rather than looking for a story line, consistent characters, or an Aristotelian beginning, middle, and end, they worked with statement, development, and counterpoint. Although only one character/mode actually repeats in the piece (the person trying to find his voice), themes from the various sections play off, orbit around and build onto one another. Chaikin, whose ensemble creations have mostly been constructed this way, says:

> One of the things which we share, Sam and me, is our intense involvement with music. We're never looking for the dramatic structure. We're looking for [a] . . . shape that's musically tenable.

As the words of *Tongues* became more set, Shepard and Chaikin decided there should be some kind of instrumental accompaniment. The original conception for the piece had included music as an essential part, but they had forgotten about it. Chaikin rekindled the idea about a week before they were to start performing—partly, he claims, because of nervousness about being up on stage all alone: "I think actors are insecure anyway, but in my case I perform at these irregular intervals, so I'm insecure for those reasons as well. And I have so many opinions about acting, more and more and more. And here I am performing!"

He and Shepard each tried to telephone a musician (the two people who later performed *Tongues* and *Savage/Love* in New York). Then Shepard said he'd like to do the sounds himself; "I felt it would be terrific if we could both be in it." So, Chaikin recalls, laughing:

> Since Harry's line was busy and Skip wasn't home, rather than pursue it I said, "Terrific." And I thought 4/5 "terrific" and 1/5 "What if he does music like he sort of slaps against some guitar and thinks that's it?" And then it just was wonderful! Sam's a very good percussionist. He's not only musical as a writer.

Shepard brought a selection of instruments to the theatre (by now they were working in the Magic Theatre, where *Tongues* was first performed), and they started to jam and experiment. They devised a percussion accompaniment on traditional and invented instruments—bongos, cymbals, maracas, an African drum, a tambourine, bells, chains, pipes, brass bowls, kitchenware. The voice addressing the blind one was accompanied by the high, eerie whine of a brass bowl being vibrated by a soft mallet—a sound which suggested the noise of a mosquito. Seeds inside a long, thin drum pittered and rolled as the tube was rotated during the childbirth speech. A section about wanting to change from a job involving noisy, dangerous machinery was accented by the chains being smashed down against metal pipes. A rhythmic jingling of bells undercut the possible morbidity of the long series of guesses about "When you die . . ." The final section, about learning to hear, was said to the low, pastel gong of broiler trays.

Both men wanted to keep the focus on Chaikin while making the music an integral part of the performance. They had already decided that Chaikin would face front in a chair, motionless except for his head, his lap covered with a blanket. Now Shepard sat behind him, back to back, on a low platform, the instruments arranged around him. As he played he periodically held his arms and instruments out so that they could be seen over the top or around the sides of Chaikin's chair. For the opening section, about the man born in the middle of a people, an arm repeatedly reached to the side shaking maracas, punctuating the speech both visually and aurally; the brass bowl and mallet appeared later held on the other side of the chair; the tube with seeds was held high over Chaikin's head. Shepard invented and scored the various gestures (which, of course, neither he nor Chaikin could see) trying to give the sense that his arms, in motion, were "extensions of Joe's static body."

The total stage picture suggested illness and also, somehow, a priest or medium through whom voices come. Chaikin suspects, though, that the show's visual austereness was the result of medical as much as thematic considerations: "I think I furtively got Sam to agree that this would be interesting, even though we didn't want it to be like *Endgame* or something with this guy in a chair. I think I got him to do that because I had no other choice physically." But, Shepard responded when told Chaikin's comment, "It wasn't hard to agree. We originally had said it would just be a voice piece. And that staging put the focus on Joe's voice and face—on that voice and amazing, expressive face."

Before Chaikin had even left San Francisco, he and Shepard were talking about doing another piece as soon as their schedules allowed. During the year, then, Chaikin made *Re-Arrangements* with his Winter Project workshop, and that piece became a kind of bridge between the two California works. It incorporated several sections of *Tongues*—and it moved into an area that neither he nor Shepard had dealt with much in their plays: love. Chaikin suggested that the second San Francisco collaboration continue exploring this theme and Shepard wrote back: "I've been wondering about a dialogue concerning love for over a year now, so it's almost uncanny that you suggest it . . . I can hardly wait to start on this with you."

Although they had exchanged letters about the upcoming work, and Chaikin had suggested several books for Shepard to read (including Simone de Beauvoir's memoirs about her life with Sartre), they once again started their rehearsal period with no form or text. What they did have this time was a theme—and, more important, the experience of the first collaboration:

> Sam met me at the airport, and we dealt with the baggage—and then I said, "We've got three weeks!" We both said it was crazy. I said, "We haven't even begun." Sam said, "I know"—and then he said, "Yes, we have." And he was right.

Shepard explains:

> We had already established certain guidelines in working before. I have the feeling that this collaboration seemed to go much smoother in a way, in terms of being hooked up to each other so that we didn't have to go through a lot of unnecessary dialogue. The last time it was feeling out what would be a method of working together. And we discovered it. But this time was much more fluid.

The theme was a tricky one. First of all, collaboration involves coming together on shared ground—and, superficially at least, Chaikin and Shepard don't have a lot of common ground in their dealings with love. Shepard has a tight, extended-nuclear family—wife, child, in-laws; Chaikin forms deep and lasting relationships, but not longterm, primary ones. Shepard is straight;

Chaikin bisexual. They found, though—contrary to Chaikin's initial apprehensions—that it wasn't hard at all to find terrains of shared experience. Shepard was not surprised: "We were trying to deal with the interior of it. And it doesn't really matter what your exterior circumstances are in relationship to it, because the interior, I think, is where you find the common ground with anything."

The work process on *Savage/Love* was different than on *Tongues* in that, Chaikin explains, "it was a theatrical dialogue rather than conversation." Shepard describes their method:

> We would agree on a particle of the subject, sometimes very small things, and Joe would start to work as an actor, improvising around that particle. Sometimes the language that he used in the improvisation to investigate what the material was became the language of the script. I would take it down and rearrange it and mess with it a little, and then that became the actual text.

Shepard became more and more drawn to Chaikin's feeling for language:

> Joe has a poetic sense without using elaborate or fancy words, without being excessive. The language is stripped in a way that's ordinary, but the ordinariness serves as a kind of jolt. There's something undramatic about a line like "The first moment I saw you in the post office" that makes it have a dramatic impact.

Once again, the delineations of writer versus director broke down. Some sections are mostly Chaikin's words edited by Shepard; some are Shepard's words filtered through Chaikin.

The play came to focus less on the joys and ecstasy of love, though they're included, than on its pain. A recurring them is the lover's paralyzing, tormenting self-consciousness—wondering what the desired one sees and how to shape a self that will be most lovable. A voice says, "When we're tangled up in sleep/Is it my leg you feel your leg against/Or is it Paul Newman's leg?/ . . . /If you could only give me some clue/I could invent the one you'd have me be." In another part, the speaker strikes a pose and asks, "When I sit like this/Do you see me brave/ . . . /Which presentation of myself/Would make you want to touch/What would make you cross the border." Another character watches himself in conversation, trying to make his face and body transmit what he wants them to, unable to make them cooperate.

Several times in *Savage/Love*, Chaikin and Shepard use the image of killing—always metaphorically—to express both the hatred in love and what happens when passion dies. One speech, by someone who's just "killed" his partner, ends, "I saw you thinking of something else/You couldn't see/The thing I'd done to you." Another voice, a person watching a sleeping lover, says, "For one moment I think of the killing/ . . . /I want to strangle your dreams/Inside me."

The most wrenching section of *Savage/Love*, and one of the funniest, is a part Shepard and Chaikin call "The Beggar." They began by writing a monologue of somebody pleading for a crumb, moving from "Could you give me just a small part of yourself" to, finally, "Could I just walk behind you for a little while." When that speech was done, Shepard and Chaikin felt there also should be a part showing the reverse—so they created a monologue that began "Don't think I'm this way with everybody/ . . . /In fact, usually it's the other way around" and, by the end, was "I'm wasting my time right now/Just talking to you." Shepard had the idea, then, to run the two speeches together as segments of one voice. "It seems to be true," he explains, "that one emotion is absolutely connected to its opposite, and the two sides are actually simultaneously happening. You can't show the simultaneousness of it so much, but you can show how they evolve—they don't really evolve, they just flip."

The bleakness of *Savage/Love* is undercut not only by its (relatively few) affirming voices, but especially by its humor. Lots of it is funny, even as it is painful: A lover tries out different terms of endearment to see which will fly; a character declares he's lost fifteen pounds and dyed his hair brown, all for a beloved he has yet to find. "One of the wonderful things about Sam," Chaikin says, "is that he's funny. There has to be a certain proportion of humor in everything he does. It's as clear as that there would have to be pepper on somebody's food or vegetables as part of a casserole. It's very important. Anything without humor at all is very hard to care about."

Because of the briefness of the work period, some areas that Chaikin and Shepard had meant to explore were not worked out. Chaikin told an interviewer:

> On my way to the airport I realized that we had not dealt with the terror of replaceability one can feel with love. Both of us wanted to include it, we both thought it was integral and even central to the whole thing, and it isn't there because we couldn't finish the piece together because we live on different coasts. (New York *Times*, Jan. 13, 1980)

They were satisfied enough with what they had been able to do, though, to give the piece a firm shape. Once again, their approach was more musical than dramaturgical; they worked with shapes, rhythms, and thematic relationships, but did not try at all to mold their material into a story.

Instrumental music also became very important in the piece. "As we were writing," Shepard says, "we were really trying to think in terms of being economical enough with the words so that it left space where music could really make the environment for it." In program notes for the San Francisco production, he wrote "Both of these collaborations are an attempt to find an equal expression between music and the actor."

Two musicians, Harry Mann, who had performed in several Shepard works, and Skip LaPlante, who had been in Chaikin's Winter Project, collaborated on *Savage/Love*. Mann played clarinet, sax, flute, and various whistles in the piece—often honky-tonking humor into Chaikin's monologue. The "I've lost 15 pounds for you" speech, for instance, was counterpointed by a jazzy, syncopated alto sax. When Chaikin, looking placidly at the audience, began to wail a few bars of "The thrill is gone," Mann accentuated the irony by precisely matching his pitch, timing, and mood on the sax.

LaPlante (who also learned Shepard's accompaniment for *Tongues* and performed in the New York and European productions) used mostly home-made instruments constructed from trash—chains, metal strips, kitchenware, fluorescent tubes, wooden planks—as well as a double bass. During the "Beggar" section, he jangled chains in a wicker basket, making a sound vaguely like coins in a tin cup. For an angry, accusing speech—"YOU/who controls me/ ... /YOU/Who leads me to believe we're forever in love"—he used a homemade bull-roarer, a plank of wood whirled on a string to make a noise like a car motor. For a lover's recollection of "days by the water," he created a muted, glubby percussion by tapping the lid of a peanut butter jar partly filled with water.

Often, Chaikin, Mann, and LaPlante played as a trio. While Chaikin spoke of being "haunted by your scent/When I'm talking to someone else," LaPlante made a hollow eerie sound by bowing metal strips, and Mann created a high, quivering dissonance by blowing two penny whistles at once. For the "15 pounds" speech, LaPlante tapped a spunky rhythm on a kitchen bowl.

The physical staging this time was less austere but still extremely spare. Chaikin performed from a niche, about four feet off the ground—six feet high, five feet wide, and two and a half feet deep. He sat, stood, lay down, and squirmed in his little space: once during the "Beggar," he even left it for a few moments to follow behind his loved one. The musicians, their instruments arranged around them, were further downstage to either side of Chaikin, visible yet funnelling focus in to him. The lighting, designed by Beverly Emmons, was full of "specials"—in contrast to her design for *Tongues*, which was subtly modulating white illumination. New voices were marked by light changes, sometimes as extreme as a tight spot from directly above or one side, which helped to punctuate the monologue and define its sections.

Tongues and *Savage/Love* opened at the Public Theater in November 1979 to critical acclaim. Mel Gussow wrote about the program twice, first a daily review then a long Sunday New York *Times* feature. He described the production as "not only an exquisite piece of performance theater," but also "to a great extent, a consolidation, a précis of the work of these two extraordinary theater artists over a span of 15 years." James Leverett wrote in the

Soho News, "What emerges is the pure presence of an extraordinary actor—mature, classic in its economy, consummate in its power." The *Village Voice* made my article on the collaboration the week's lead arts feature.

Both men also are pleased with their collaboration. In fact, they plan to create another theatre piece as soon as their schedules permit—definitely with music, probably with more physical movement (an area they had hoped to explore in *Savage/Love*), and maybe even with one or two actors. "I'd like to do a lot more with Joe," Shepard says: "I'd love to keep working with him over a long period of time." Chaikin agrees: "We don't know what's going to come of it, but we feel that there's a fertility."

Directing the Plays

INTERVIEW WITH ROBERT WOODRUFF

Robert Coe

How did you first become involved with Shepard's work?

San Francisco has a small theatre community. You get to know everyone, and when something feels right it becomes sort of natural for two people to work together. The first play of his I did was *The Sad Lament of Pecos Bill on the Eve of Killing his Wife*. I'd been working at the Eureka Theatre for about three years and Sam had enjoyed my work—it interested him. In 1976, we were organizing the Bay Area Playwright's Festival in San Francisco and I asked him for a piece. He had written this operetta for a huge bicentennial project that the city had authorized in '76, and which was really a mess; they'd spent $100,000 and wound up not using *Pecos*. He said, "I have this piece, so do it," and handed me an eight page manuscript with words and sheet music . . . a wonderful piece, an investigation of myth and his humanity. It's like 45 minutes long, which creates a problem as to where to perform it in New York. I'd like to do it at midnight in a cabaret kind of setting.

What can you say about your relationship with Shepard?

I've learned a great deal from the man with regard to the possibilities of theatre. I think, too, that the form I've given his work has been important to him. I think there's been a trust we are both learning to relax behind. It's been a great gift just watching the productions he's directed.

How does Shepard work as a director?

A strong physicalization of the text. He draws from actors and allows them enormous freedom to come up with what they can, but there's no sense of improvisation for its own sake: there's nothing outside the play. He respects them, gives them room and gets a lot of joy from seeing what they do with his work. There's no sense of sanctity around the words.

And that connected with your own approach?

I think we both share a desire for anarchy. In any production of his, it just bounces off the stage. It's almost frightening. A sense of *gangness*: that the actors are a gang. His production of *Angel City* I think is the best example of that. The poster for that play is so vivid, with the five of them there, Sam in the background with his dark glasses. It's just this street gang. I'm almost tempted to say there's an element of "fuck-youness" about it, because they know so well what they're doing and they're so free with it. There's a great joy in seeing that, for me.

How do you connect personally with Shepard's work?

Easily. This WASP from the Midwest and this Jew from New York and somewhere there's a real compatibility. I don't know why . . . I think the bottom line is that the work is so theatrical and the metaphors so huge. That's what started to work on me. The magic of it, just moving from image to image to image, an incredible journey opening up in the pieces. When you work on the plays enough, you begin to see connections, you see the same sets of rules—dramatic rules, a way of looking at theatre and what theatre should be, as well as another set of rules that are a way of looking at life. When you go through the plays, you synthesize these two sets of rules, and with each new play you see how he's taken those ideas further or moved off them.

Finally, it's about putting a universe on stage, the universe that is in the play; keeping the logic of it and the logic of his body of work, and not imposing much after that. A lot of the work grows from the actor's ability to connect with the way the characters look at the world, with all the inherent contradictions. There are lots of contradictions in the plays, especially *Buried Child*. Sam doesn't think in terms of contradictions, but he reinforces them when he sees them. The contradictions of what people say and what they do, the way people are versus the way they're supposed to be.

Shepard speaks in the introduction to Angel City *of characters shifting identities . . .*

In that play, that was true. Simply changing identities like this (*snaps fingers*). But now I think that for me this has evolved into a need for an actor to be very prismatic, able to play a side or a color of a character very strongly at one moment, and the next play another color or another side of that character. For instance, Halie's monologue in *Buried Child*. She comes down the stairs and she's going through this rap about Catholics and this love of her child and this incredible sanctimonious thing about the church and Father Dewis, and these changes are all happening at breakneck speed, one idea after another after another after another and we're seeing this woman do this evolution where she's committing to a wonderful thought and then committing to this desperation and then committing to this fear and then committing to this almost demonic side of herself, with her wrath about the honeymoon. And then she parachutes out of this swirling dance-like dialogue very gently.

With all due respect, actors have a natural tendency to fight this kind of thing. Their training comes out of a transition/motivation process. Sometimes Sam just asks, in effect, what happens if we don't do it that way? If we skip the *psychological* transitions. I think that's in *Buried Child*.

Is there an ideal actor, then, for Shepard's work?

It's not any different than for any other play. Somebody who's very flexible, very open, in touch with himself, with an outrageous imagination and energy, who can give on the stage, who's receptive on the stage, who can talk and listen and who doesn't have his ego on the line all the time.

What were some of the other problems you faced with Curse *and* Buried Child?

In *Curse*, it was probably just finding how much we could blow up the characters, in terms of giving the actors freedom within the material. How much could you stretch it and still have it be available to the audience. I never thought the play worked on a realistic level. The form of it is, of course, The Great American Melodrama. I got the deed! No, you don't! I got the money! Here comes the cops! And the guy with the black moustache comes on at the end twirling it. The problem was basically seeing how far you could stretch the distance between these people and the audience and still have the play work. I think in the production in New York we took it pretty far. I think we really blew it up and made it mythic in a great American way.

And then *Buried Child*: I guess the contradictions we talked about earlier started out to be problems. Contradictions which create stage tensions, seeming inexplicability, shifts of mood and character. Halie has a line, "You better get this stuff cleaned up before Bradley sees it," and she's kicking the corn all over the room. You've got dialogue in direct opposition to action. The idea is that whatever works, at the moment, for the character, the actor, and the play, creates more oppositions, quick reversals, dramatic tension. Because at one level all these characters are incredible opportunists. Halie and Dodge are fighting like cats and dogs in the first scene, and as soon as Tilden comes in they agree lovingly that there hasn't been any corn out there since 1935. If they work better as a team at that moment, OK. It's not something that's conscious. It just happens. What we discovered was that the actor just has to *commit* and then he's fine.

Another problem we faced was that if *Buried Child* is to be a kind of horror story, how much humor can be kept in the piece without it losing that edge? Because you want a darkness. I remember we had a difficulty in figuring out what kind of play this was. A mystery, a comedy, gothic horror, or what?

Seeing the play again at the Circle Rep, a year after it opened at the Theatre for the New City, I noticed a more consistent high energy running through the thing.

Well, something has to happen when a play runs a year. I think that that's not a bad thing to have happen. I think it became funnier by the end of the run, and that maybe it lost some of the horror. The horror of somebody coming home and nobody recognizing him, the pain of facing a buried past, the desperation of those people: I think that edge was softened a bit. But it was still very alive. *Buried Child* is great material for actors, by the way. The actors said they wished the play could run much longer so other actors could have a chance to do this material, because it's so rare that actors get to stretch out like that.

The portrayals also seemed to have become more grotesque: the characters had in fact become grotesques.

That seemed like a natural evolution. In terms of situation becoming more ingrained, of becoming a way of life for them, the actors living with a character over a length of time . . . It was kind of a nightly explosion for them, coming out of the freedom which is in the text, an anarchy working itself inside and against a necessary economy and discipline: a contradiction again, I realize. Anarchy versus economy equals tension. You realize that Shepard's got nothing there: he mentions seven things in the play. He's got one couch. One TV. This allows everything else to happen, because nothing's in your way. You don't have to deal with minutia and bullshit.

What do you think is still to be found in Shepard's work?

The next play. Or what anybody does with any play at any time. There are no holds barred. In the plays Sam and I have done together, a direction simply evolves. I know we're going *this* way, though I know that in going this way there's always freedom involved. But now for every other person who tackles the material, there's a whole spectrum of what you can do with the plays. Having gotten the Pulitzer Prize, *Buried Child* is going to be done a lot now. It will have many different treatments.

So what's the director's role in this economic anarchy?

To give the actors a situation in which they are free. To goose them and say it's OK. To make a working situation free enough so they can stretch their own limits and stretch the limits of the play. There's another side to this, which is just doing what's there. People want to embellish or give it a style, or if it's not a style they want to give it a motivation. Or if it's not a motivation they want to make it "Pop." They don't need, I think, to do that. Again, whatever "style" *Buried Child* had was not preconcieved. It grew out of a logic and it grew out of an order that was discovered. And rules. It has rules. Perhaps that's the director's primary job: to discover the rules of this universe. In this universe, there's no self pity. That's a rule. In this universe, an idea comes up and when it's dismissed, it's gone. Vince is in the house and they go through 17 pages of "don't you recognize me" and then he leaves. The next line is Shelley's "You really don't recognize him?" and Dodge says, "Recognize who?" There is no past. Whether it came up in the preceding moment or twenty years ago, it's gone. That's a rule too. So Shepard's characters can't indulge their pain. It gives them an incredible dignity. It sort of gets them through the night. It's almost the source of some of their problems: an incredible pride. Another rule then: pain is momentary, and we continue.

Shelley seemed to be a new figure in Shepard's work: someone outside the craziness and looking in.

That was a nice door for the audience, wasn't it? Everybody's talked about that. At the beginning of the run the audience was totally on her side. She would break her cup and say, "Who are you people!" and the audience would go yeah, right, these guys are crazy, you gotta shake this place up! And then two-thirds of the way through the run the audience was saying, "Hey, shut up girl, we're having a good time with these people!" They didn't want her interfering with the way the house was run, which I think is wrong, you know. I suspect it happened when the comedy went too far and the needs of the family and their desperation wasn't there.

Toward the end of the run, they were back on her side, but even then it would switch back and forth. Some nights they would go with the family and exclude her. That was fascinating to watch. And then Mary McDonnell as an actress and Shelley as a character would have to find a way to get the people back on her side.

Perhaps the way she did that was by dropping her hysteria and seriously questioning people, which could have been a directorial decision.

Which is what the audience really wants . . . There are moments all through the play when Sam writes with the audience in mind. There's all this corn, and literally everybody in the audience is going, "Well, you know, the corn, you know what *that's* symbolic of," and then Halie just stops the play and says, "What is the meaning of this corn, Tilden?" The audience has been sitting there for five minutes meditating on the meaning of corn, and why, in essence, dramaturgically, it was brought into the farmhouse. Sam does the same thing in the third act: Bradley sticks his fingers in Shelley's mouth, creating this stunning image to end the second act. During the intermission the audience is debating what the image means. Rape, gynophobia, whatever. Then in Act III, Halie goes, "Bradley, did you stick your fingers in her mouth?" and spanks him. It gets reduced to a child's game. It reduces the great big metaphor to just, well, that's all it is. Which is essentially all you do in the play. You go from image to image to image. Why'd he stick his fingers in her mouth? I don't know. It's just something he does.

Actors have trouble dealing with that. There's something about trying to motivate an action that weakens it, not letting it be what it is itself. Vince's staying at the end is just something he does. It's in his blood. It's in the air. Sam isn't into the psychology of it, I don't think. He's not into working out his problems. He's got a distance. There's always something in the pieces which push the action, and it isn't a conscious thing. "It's bigger than government, bigger than business, it's *bigger*," as Ella says in *Curse*. It's always something intangible. Call it what you will, but it drives the plays. It's inescapable. And Vince is sucked home to deal with that in *Buried Child*. We're not the masters of our fate at every level. There's something that pushes us in directions we might not go otherwise.

We've talked about rules, about admitting to contradictions, and about a way of looking at the world. They give actors choices. The director's role is just reconfirming them. The director has to discover the rules, too.

In talking with Sam these things come up. If I know, if I can observe how Sam sees the world, then I can see it in the plays. And then it becomes just a process of implementing these rules theatrically. When we did *Buried Child* in San Francisco we had the seven actors, me sitting in the second row, and Sam sitting in the fourth, and there was still this sort of circular movement: Sam and I would see what they'd do and there would be this feedback of elation which would be reconfirming, or something would be very wrong, an attitude would be wrong. Then Sam would be very succinct. He would say this scene is about establishing trust between the old man and the girl, with all its implications, and we would just take that idea and play with it.

So Shepard sat in on rehearsals of Buried Child *in San Francisco?*

And he was also shaping the play around the actors. Specifically: the character of Shelley was originally not as universal as she turned out to be. She was more of a hippie type. A jive lady. The actress who played the role there, Betsy Scott, was a very available kind of person, very open, and I think her dialogue was pared down, and a lot of the clichés were gotten rid of to make her more the window on the world that we talked about.

So Shepard did some re-writing during the rehearsal period?

Yes. We went into rehearsal with quite a different third act which, after two readings, was taken away.

What happened in the original third act?

It was a lot headier. It took off into ideas. It was more of a mystery play, with the murderer being unveiled. You don't gain much new knowledge in the third act now. Dodge tells a story that in effect had already been told; while it's embellished, everything but the possibility of incest had already been introduced in Tilden's speech in the second act. I think the idea of just having a mystery play was disturbing to us. It was a lot less clean, too. Halie's religious jag and Shelley's dealing with the *mythos* of America and how hurt she was that it no longer existed were taken much further.

A lot of the contradictions in the play own up to the fact that much of the third act was rewritten seven months after the first two acts and there were no major changes made in them. But it played. It played incredibly well, because the idea of contradictions was built into the play from the beginning. As a result we have different people's perspectives on the same ideas—almost a Rashomon effect. Everything gets revealed, but in different ways. It's not the mystery of who really did what. It's not Agatha Christie.

Let's talk about Suicide in B♭, *which you just directed in San Francisco.*

It was funny going back to that material. I had read it three years ago, but neither Sam nor I had seen the production, so it was new to us. The six performers that we assembled had worked together before, so it was a regrouping. The piece has much in common with *Angel City*, in the sense of characters being able to switch personas. But where *Angel City* is a piece with jazz, this turned into a jazz piece, one very long jam. The music was improvised every night, which created an incredible risk factor—not only for the piano player but for the actors, too. Obviously there had to be a fine sense of listening to make that improvisational element work. Some nights it wasn't there; other nights it soared.

What are the greatest pitfalls in Shepard's work for you?

Too much enthusiasm. When I get a new play I go crazy, I'm so excited about having it in my hands. I come up against all the different problems we've talked about, but usually I don't have a sense of that. I just feel a freedom. The nicest thing is to get incredibly imaginative actors and just let them feast on it, discover the rules. It'll happen. I have the idea that Sam's plays just ask questions. Maybe that sounds simplistic, but that's really the best thing the material can do. People hit some of the plays because there are no resolutions, but I think that's the strength of them, that they just raise things. They allow you to just *look*, in a context which is new. If you can pose the questions in ways that speak to people, that makes them see a reality in a new way, in a way they've not seen before, that's good enough. When the questions become clearer to us, when we can better see what questions are important, we can find out our own answers.

NOTES
Icarus's Mother

Michael Smith

I directed the first production of *Icarus's Mother* (premiere: November 16, 1965) at the Caffe Cino in New York. It was Joe Cino's idea. I didn't know Sam Shepard, but I already had a special feeling about his work. His earliest plays, *Cowboys* and *Rock Garden,* had formed the first production of Theatre Genesis a year before. I was dazzled by them—their immediacy and vitality, the freshness and integrity of the author's voice. I wrote a rave review in the *Village Voice* and felt for ever after as though I'd "discovered" Sam Shepard.

I immediately liked *Icarus's Mother;* and I still think it is the best of Sam's plays to date—the fullest, densest, most disturbing and provocative. But it is terribly difficult to produce. I failed. Maybe I can share the lessons of that failure.

When I read it, I couldn't tell the characters apart—and Sam said he doesn't think about characters. I was struck by the play's smooth, mysterious ascent from cosy reality to high lyricism and symbolism, its debonair plunge into the sharky deeps of resonant meaning. All Sam's plays use the stage to project images: they do not relate to the spectator by reflecting outside reality (they are not psychological or political); rather they relate to reality by operating directly on the spectator's mind and nerves. The imagery is surreal, the method nonrational, the sensibility hunchy. It's always hard to tell what, if anything, Sam's plays are "about"—although they are unmistakably alive. *Icarus's Mother* is exceptionally ambitious, and I think it succeeds in objectifying its impulse, externalizing it in terms of human actions and reactions and stage events.

Icarus's Mother is about fear—specifically, the so-called paranoia of the nuclear present—and its effect on people individually and in community. The plane is a vivid and convincing symbolic threat; its equivocal reality and inexplicable relation to the characters—does it after all have anything to do with them?—are as dis-orienting as the Bomb it may be thought to carry.

As director I approached the play all wrong. I started rehearsals by talking about its content and overall meaning. Trouble. The actors didn't share my interpretation or even care about it. More important, they couldn't use it: it didn't give them anything to do.

Mistake two—language. The play's basic diction is cool, almost unexpressive; then three times it erupts into huge monologues that overflow its token naturalism. (They are in fact the means by which it transcends itself.) I thought of them as arias and looked for the music of the play. Again I was blocking the actors. Our nexus of anxiety was the smoke signals. "What are we doing?" they'd ask. I told them they were making smoke signals. "Why?" Don't think about that, just do it. "What is the motivation?" I could make things up, but they seemed irrelevant. I figured out how to make smoke, I showed the actors how to hold the blanket, gave them gestures and rhythms and sounds. Not enough. They were confused, uncomfortable, floundering. How could I free them from worry? How could I get them simply to *do* it, not to *act* it? They felt foolish just going through the motions, and the results were self-conscious and hollow.

Tardily we got to work on character, at which the actors were expert. It turned out that the characters in *Icarus's Mother* are perfectly distinct, it's just that we're given almost no information about them. Close scrutiny reveals a coherent pattern of reponse for each of them, and it's possible to extrapolate backwards from that pattern to postulate the omitted facts. We decided that Howard and Pat are married. She's depressed and he's fed up with it; she's self-indulgent, he's mean. Jill is Bill's girl friend, a warm cheerful girl who does what she can to distract Pat and keep Howard from tormenting her. Bill is an overage Boy Scout, a little dumb, easily scared by his own fantasies. Frank is older, we decided, an envious outsider to the group, charming enough but clumsy. Bill and Howard retreat into boyhood when frightened; they play with their security blanket, try to control reality with symbolic gestures, shut the girls out, try to turn Frank off.

All this fits fine, although a whole different set of hypotheses might be equally good or better. But at last we had something we could work on.

We were at about this stage on opening night, and for the first week the production was terrible—heavy, unconvincing, obscure, forced. Only then did I realize that the play is about a picnic. That should have been my first concern, the picnic, instead of all the probing into meaning, all the theories about paranoia and politics. And at last the play began to come together. The dialogue isn't Sam being arty, it's people talking, people who know each other and don't have to explain themselves, people who are hot and a little bored and a little too full of food. And so on. Lesson: go for the reality. The meaning is built in. Get the reality, and the meaning takes care of itself.

But it's not that simple, and realism isn't all there is to *Icarus's Mother*. It needs reality in order to transcend reality—and it's the transcending that makes the play extraordinary. The smoke signals are just barely possible as real behavior; finally, essentially, they are the abstract gestures of a formal rite. The long speeches really are more operatic than conversational. The plane transforms from everyday artifact into agent of apocalypse behind a veil of fantasy and deception. And how do you go from real plane to planes of reality? I don't know.

Sam Shepard overreaches the boundaries of the known and possible. Who is Icarus? The play itself is Icarus, and if it fails, then so did Icarus fail. Would you have him heed his father's warning?

THE WRITER AND THE PERFORMANCE GROUP
Rehearsing *The Tooth of Crime*

Richard Schechner

I'm not sure if an ensemble company like The Performance Group would give the play the right feel. I'm not being specific about your group because I've never seen them, but every ensemble group that I've seen always works best from a piece which they originate along with a director and writer. If they attempt plays it always seems that the play takes a back seat to the ensemble and director.

Sam Shepard

We are now ten months into work on Sam Shepard's *The Tooth of Crime*, still very much in the middle of it. But some of my expectations have been ambushed by situations I could not have predicted. I think The Performance Group's work in environmental theatre has changed the way I work on a script, and the way the performers work. And because several of the environmental theatres have indicated that they plan to work from scripts I think TPG's experiences with Shepard's play are worth noting.

TPG has used words in its productions, although this is the first time I've done a "regular play" since the 1967 New Orleans Group production of Ionesco's *Victims of Duty*. Often these words have been pushed, pulled, punched out of shape, transformed into sounds without regard for denotation. Words have been treated *operatically*, except that our criterion for distortion has been not music but the feelings of the performers as revealed through highly disciplined exercises. But the effect is similar to opera: a musical treatment of words.

After reading Shepard's *The Tooth of Crime* I wrote him:

> I want to look at the play nakedly, approach its language not as a dialect but as a way into the heart of the play and a way to uncover things in the performers playing the roles. I can't say what the results will be because our way of working is truly to let the rehearsal process take its own course, uncover what is to be uncovered. We find the style of a production by rehearsing it. . . . Most directors and actors start with a "guiding idea," an "image to be realized," a "preexistent action." I don't, the Group doesn't. We start with only what is there, the barest facts: seven performers and a collection of words organized under role headings.

The Tooth of Crime builds from an identity between the languages of rock music, crime, and big business. A "hit" in one world is the same/different from a "hit" in another; a "big killing" is/isn't murder; a "contract" is a contract is a contract. Shepard is a master of the language of the world he has created. In addition to the languages of rock music, street gangs, the Mafia, and the image-makers, Shepard assembles a language spoken by Crow, the "gypsy killer," and the young punk moving in on the turf of established stars. The meeting between Crow and the old man, Hoss, is a conflict of idioms. At one point Hoss pleads, "Hey, can't you back the language up, man, I'm too old to follow the flash." The song-duel between Hoss and Crow, in fact, has many prototypes—from the once popular "Battle of the Bands" to the ritual combats of certain Eskimo peoples as described by Peter Farb.

> In Alaska and in Greenland all disputes except murder are settled by a song duel. In these areas an Eskimo male is often as acclaimed for his ability to sing insults as for his hunting prowess. The song duel consists of lampoons, insults, and obscenities and the disputants sing to each other and, of course, to their delighted audience. The verses are earthy and very much to the point; they are intended to humiliate, and no physical deformity, personal shame, or family trouble is sacred. As verse after verse is sung in turn by the opponents the audience begins to take sides; it applauds one singer a bit longer and laughs a bit louder at his lampoons. Finally, he is the only one to get applause, and he thereby becomes the winner of a bloodless contest. The loser suffers a great punishment, for disapproval of the community is very difficult to bear in a group as small as that of the Eskimo.

This is exactly the structure of the Hoss-Crow duel. Hoss loses; he is stripped of his authority, his machismo. What is most interesting to me about the duel is what Jerome Rothenberg has called "the belief that language (i.e., poetry) can make-things-present by naming them." Many times in *Tooth* Shepard uses language in the way that M. B. Emenau says Hindus do:

> It is noteworthy and perhaps to be interpreted as a general tendency in Hindu culture to *raise certain aspects of the subliminal to con-*

sciousness, that Hinduism in general and the Tantric sects in particular make extensive use in ritual and religious practice generally, not only of the intrinsically meaningless gestures of the dance and iconography, but also of *intrinsically meaningless vocables*. For example, the famous *om* and *hum* and the not so famous *hrim*, *hram*, *phat*, and many others, are meaningless, religious noises in origin, whatever symbolic meanings are given to them by the developed dogma.

Or in the terms of Ray L. Birdwhistell:

> Since regularities appear in the stream of movement and in the stream of audible behavior around certain syntactic forms, it is possible to state that body motion and spoken "languages" do not constitute independent systems at the level of communication. By a logic, not yet known, they are interinfluencing and probably interdependent.

All this confirms what dancers and theatre performers have known for hundreds of years. But this knowledge is just at this moment being raised to a kind of scientific consciousness characteristic of Western thought. As such it is available as a tool, just like other technologies. Shepard's play uses this tool, and scrutinizes it. In this way, *The Tooth of Crime* is about performing, and about techniques which TPG has helped develop.

Working on the play raises these issues of language—of the concrete essence of the word, of how words are emptied of meaning and filled with new significances. The more we work the more we find that Shepard's words are bound to music, specifically rock music. Shepard is a musician as well as a writer. He composed a score for *Tooth* but we did not want to use his score for several reasons. In my first letter to Shepard I said:

> We start with the belief that music is essential to the play—but without knowing what shape that music will take. We do not play electrified instruments and do not import outsiders into our productions so I would say, probably, we will not use electric music done electrically. We will have to find out how to do electric music with our bodies. The problem becomes for us: How do we make the kind of music necessary for your play without microphones, electric guitars, and so on? I think we can make the necessary music because I don't think rock is a function of mechanics but of some movement within the human spirit. One of the things we have to find out is precisely what that movement is, *what does it sound like?* In other words, the problem isn't how to play rock, but how to find the cause from which rock springs. Then to play that cause.

Shepard wrote:

> The other doubt I have is about the music. Most of it is very simple: rock progressions from Velvet Underground to The Who. It's gotta be electric! No other way for it to work. The songs were all built for elec-

tric guitar, keyboard, bass, and drums. All the music is written down and fits each section of the play according to the emotional line that's going down. It's gotta be played by rock musicians who've got their chops. Actors who aren't musicians just couldn't handle it.

While waiting for Shepard's reply to my letter we went ahead and began work. The first problem was to approach the language concretely. I did not want us to work "around a table" figuring out what the play meant, or even discussing its story. I wanted to start with some actual experience of its very rich, troubling, and difficult language: a poetry as dense as any in the modern theatre. First we sang the play as if it were an opera. Every line was sung, sometimes as recitative, sometimes as aria, sometimes solo, and sometimes in chorus. Then we sang the play as a kind of Jagger-like "talking rock." (Later we saw Jagger's film, *Performance*; I think that the style of the film has influenced our work on *Tooth*.) Then we read the play "naturalistically," as if every scene were taken directly from life. In none of these explorations were we trying to figure out the dialogue from the point of view of characterization. The performers were feeling the language out, weighing it, discovering how it moved, what its possibilities were. The text was treated concretely —not simply as sound nor simply as denotation, but as meaning conditioned by sound. The performers used a "verbo-physical" approach: taking sentences and distorting their usual intonation according to the physical impulses in and among the performers. Once we went through the play speaking the lines as fast as possible. New ways of saying the words were found. Later, while working on the fight scene, I massaged the performer playing Crow while other performers accompanied him on musical instruments as he worked through his lines. As I pushed and pounded his flesh he began to discover new relationships to the language. Some of these soundings were retained for the fight scene.

At the same time performers began making up melodies and trying out rhythms for the songs. A great deal of Shepard's play deals with the different images people wear like masks; and also the contrasts between the styles of one era versus the styles of another. The conflict between Hoss and Crow is aptly described as a "style match." Performers tried to find well-known styles: the vocal mannerisms of a movie star, the beat of a rock musician, the walk of a superstar athlete. These styles were then taken to the extreme, extended, put under a scenic microscope. Barry Klein, TPG technical director, went through Shepard's text and made a list of every song, every musician, and even phrases and words that alluded to music. Then Klein made a three-hour tape of all the music. We played the play to the music. The tape recorder was so loud the performers could not hear each other. Gestures were exaggerated. From where I sat it looked like a silent movie. Next we did an improvisation containing all the main actions of the script as the performers understood them while listening to the Klein tape.

As we were doing this work, Shepard wrote me:

> I got a lot of conflicting feelings and thoughts about the whole thing. First off, it's nice to know that you begin work without any preconceptions. But you gotta understand that this play for *me* is very preconceived. I got exact diagrams and pictures in my head about how it should be done. . . . This play is built like *High Noon,* like a machine Western. It's gotta work with all its insides hanging out. You know what I mean. I'm really not trying to pull artistic priority bullshit because to me the play stands outside me on its own. It's like a kid brother that I wanna protect.

We kept working on *Tooth* while waiting for Shepard's reply to my second letter, which said in part:

> We accept your words as written, and the parts that they are organized into, and the basic flow of the action. But the rest of the scenic activity is our responsibility; we must work long and hard *to find our own places within the world of your script.* Or, to put it another way, we accept your script as *part of an artwork yet to be completed.* . . . Our five years of work entitles us to the claim of creativity, just as your work as a playwright entitles you to the identical claim. We don't want to dismember your work, or to do it against its own grain; but we want to accept it as a living term of an artwork of which we are the other living term; and together to bring the performance into existence.

Until the anti-literary revolution in the theatre—first unsuccessfully fought by the surrealists in the twenties and Artaud in the thirties—and then triumphant in the fifties and sixties—the playwright held sway. Then the writer was out and only now is he being invited back in. But on what basis? Some, of course, want to forgive and forget. Others, following Cocteau's dream, want poets of the theatre not poets in the theatre. I propose that the playwright develop his own particular skills to the highest degree. These skills are literary, poetic, the mastery of language as distinct from the mastery of action.

If one examines the texts of the non-literary theatre one discovers an abundance of literature, *pure* literature, stuff never intended for the theatre. For example, Grotowski's use of Eliot, Dostoevsky, Simone Weil, and the Bible in *Apocalypsis Cum Figuris,* the Open Theater's use of the Bible in *The Serpent,* The Manhattan Project's use of Carroll's *Alice in Wonderland,* Peter Brook's work with Ted Hughes in *Orghast.* What is one to make of this spate of purely literary text in a theatre most noteworthy for its proclaimed anti-literary intentions? What I see is a sharp division made between the *craftsmen of words* and the *craftsmen of actions.* Because the texts do not inherently carry with them intractable associations of actions the directors and performers were able to confront these texts with actions that arose from the associations of the performers rather than from the dictates of the authors. In other words, the performers were free to develop *to the end* their own actions.

Using well-known literary texts not only lets the performers invent their own actions, but it encourages a kind of blasphemy and irony. But these opportunities are also a severe limitation. The classic texts are perhaps too well-known; irony and blasphemy are too easy a response. And the opposite responses of high seriousness and faith are insupportable. Once again theatres are turning to playwrights because the writers can provide a personal and to some degree original vision. But I believe that if playwriting is again to become important to the theatre it will not be because writers master dramatic and theatrical action but because they provide to the masters of that craft a mastery of their own: writing. Without playwrights the theatre is improverished in the direction of irony, fragmentation, and—ironically enough!—exegesis: for the actions of performers taking off from the "great texts" is nothing so much as a further elaboration of what those texts might mean. Now that performers have begun to learn to use words not only as dialogue but song; now that scenes can be exploded to fill whole spaces; now that audiences can watch, collaborate, participate, influence, and even dominate performances—the time is ready to include again in the theatre masters of the literary arts.

Shepard responded to my second letter:

> I've decided to be adventurous and let you go ahead with *Tooth*. Your enthusiasm is hard to deny. I think your group will probably come up with a powerful production although it may be far from what I had in mind. The main reluctance I have is that the play will become over-physicalized and the language will fall into the background. But time will tell.

But a few more thoughts. When we began working, knowing that we would do the play publicly, we searched through the text for whatever personal associations each performer could find. I also contributed some of my associations. The director is not absent from this phase of the work. We began assembling musical instruments, including car parts from junk-yards. Much of the play's imagery concerns automobiles. Slowly some scenic shapes emerged from hours of working in small rooms both in Berkeley, California and Vancouver, Canada. Jerry Rojo came to Vancouver for three weeks and together we designed the environment. It is a modular environment—capable of endless variations like a giant tinker-toy—and it will be used for our entire repertory.

Tooth should stir *associations in the audience* rather than simply presenting incarnations of associations in the performers. It is outer-directed. Meyerhold said it with clarity and finality in his 1936 lecture on Chaplin:

> I have come to regard the *mise en scene* not as something which works
> directly on the spectator but rather as a series of "passes," each intended
> to evoke some association or other in the spectator (some premeditated,
> others outside my control). Your imagination is activated, your fantasy
> stimulated, and a whole chorus of associations is set off. A multitude of
> accumulated associations gives birth to new worlds—whole films which
> have never got beyond the cutting-room. You can no longer distinguish
> between what the director is responsible for and what is inspired by the
> associations which have invaded your imagination.

It is interesting that Meyerhold is talking about film, because the techniques of film—especially montage, quick-cutting, musical back-up, and iconographic gesturing—have heavily influenced *The Tooth of Crime*. In fact, when Rojo and I worked out the environment for *Tooth* we thought it would offer the audience a film-like experience. The environment is a large, centrally situated structure more than thirty feet in diameter, with several towers rising twelve and sixteen feet. No spectator can see everywhere because the environment fills the space. To improve sight-lines somewhat Rojo had the idea of cutting windows in the environment. This had the effect of framing and focusing scenes and scene fragments. Sitting in one part of the environment a spectator could see a hand, a face, or a whole scene through one or more frames. As we worked through August a few people came to watch rehearsals and commented how much the performance felt like a film.

People will work with scripts; people will work without scripts; people will use scripts as material; people will work with the playwright present as part of the theatre group; people will work with a script sent from afar by a living writer, as Shepard sent *The Tooth of Crime*. Each of these ways of working is supportable, and in the same group. A repertory of different kinds of work—classic, contemporary, collage, improvised—is more than possible: it is necessary. The shaman who dances in animal skins is sometimes called Master of Animals though it is not clear who is the master and who the servant. So too the performer, the director, the playwright.

Acting the Plays

CLUES IN A MEMORY

Joyce Aaron

Sam is a recorder of the authentic American voice. He starts from a certain perception of daily life, and then transforms that into a specific voice—a voice with its own rhythms and shifting consciousness, its unique, particular curve or leap. You can track that leap by following the flow of his language. Each voice is different, and speaks from a different place inside you. That is part of the theatrical challenge and wonder of speaking Sam's language.

In most conventional plays, however admirable, there is a certain kind of development—a continuity, some external sense or logic, usually a dialogue of give-and-take, which defines the play's architecture and establishes its focus. You can't look for that, or expect it, in Sam's plays. Very often, he provides you with no transitions. As an actor, you have to live the moment as his plays give it to you—and you have to live it as experience, not as history or chronicle. You have to trust that moment and the language which he has captured in sporadic resonances and reverberations. Unless you trust the reality that he sets up, you can't play him as he demands to be played. And from the very second you enter into one of his moments, you have to give that moment the fullest state it calls for—you can't catch up with it later. You can't impose some linear line on the chain of his moments for your own pleasure or satisfaction, because Sam rarely makes his leaps according to any

171

psychological rules or patterns. If you hang on to the moment, you lose the play—because that one moment has already passed and you are at the edge of another one.

You can't ápproach Sam's plays according to the usual acting terms and conditions—there are no rules, because he has broken them. You might find yourself opening one of his plays as a character who has to deliver a twenty-minute monologue. The character may be in a kind of "tripping-out" state, veering from paranoia to explosion, and the momentum and intensity of the vocal rhythm never lets up, it hounds you. What you have to do is let that rhythm take you instead of you taking it—you have to surrender to the dynamics of that rhythm, let it possess you. That particular originality is one of the things that makes Sam's dramatic voice so different from any I've experienced.

I first met Sam when I was cast as an actress in his play *Up To Thursday*, done at the Cherry Lane Theatre in the mid-1960s. One of the things the role required was that I *not* stop laughing—the character had to go on laughing beyond the limitations of naturalistic convention; the laughter had to hang in the air almost like text. If I had stopped, paused to ask: Why is this character laughing? Why is she laughing so long? Where is it all coming from?—then I would have been at odds with Sam's imaginative process. The conventional logic and rationale an actor asks for was simply not there. The richness lies in the risk-taking.

It is a mistake to play the poetry in Sam's plays. What you are doing then becomes precious, and so does the play—you are then describing a state rather than embodying it. If you don't enact the moment that Sam creates, you will miss it—and it won't come back again. Unless you can make the leap, you're lost.

You make the leap through the imagination. You could compare it to jamming, or improvising on a single note. Or even having a baby. When you're having a baby, you push. Nobody tells you how to push, or when—there's just a certain moment when your whole body says: "Push." Giving birth to one of Sam's monologues is similar.

What happens when you "go with" Sam's world—let the rhythm and dynamics of his language enter you and then literally take off—is, for me, one of the keys to acting Sam's plays. It's also what makes them such a wonderful, mysterious, inexhaustible territory for the actor to explore and to experiment with. It's like stepping from planet to planet—exploring how to find the right voice and how and when to slip in and out of it; experimenting with how much time to allot a certain line before you break it; testing the points at which you enter a character and when you withdraw from that same character. You may find a certain plateau in a speech where your breathing will change, and if you allow that to happen, you'll see that some enormous expansion has taken place. But all of this will reveal itself to you only if you surrender to the language—there is no set "method" for the actor who wants to get at the heart of Sam's plays.

Sam himself—his presence and instinct—was usually the most illuminating element whenever I worked on his plays. I always sensed that he knew his material better than anyone else and that he could probably *act* it better than anyone else, that he really knew what he wanted to happen on the stage, in the theatre—even though in those early days, he was hardly aware of the actor's technique and vocabulary.

Perhaps because we were close during that period, I never knew where our life—where *my* life—was going to turn up on the page, or later on some stage, but inevitably there was always some aspect of our experience together that I would recognize. Yet I never felt exposed by Sam—he transformed whatever he drew on. I watched him write. I traveled with him. I knew where his plays came from, what their sources were. I saw how and where he didn't rewrite, and how and where he did. I read the plays out loud to him. *La Turista*, which grew out of a trip we took together to Mexico, is a good example of that process.

Sam's work can be very difficult for actors because they don't quite know how to approach it. They may be seduced by it, charmed or even moved by it. But when it comes to putting the play itself up there on the stage, they have difficulty finding the direction. That happens especially when they become too involved with Sam's "meanings." Rather than exploring what the language reveals and where it will take them, they start to act, and before they know it, they've fallen into the current traps of actor training.

When you do Sam's plays, it's important to remember—and actually you will *feel* it—that you are enacting some aspect of a particular person: not in the conventional terms of character, but rather as a witness to a moment or condition in American culture; that you are enacting on the stage one experience of one person at a particular moment, in a particular state. Often you discover that the particular aspect you are enacting exists within a much larger whole—it is only one reality within a kind of super-reality. But you can't start from that super-reality as a point of departure. Your enactment of some condition of being-in-the-world is what's important.

Your conscious obligation to Sam's plays should be to their aliveness, to making them come alive on the stage; otherwise, you'll end up acting the metaphor or the poetry. Your job is not to enact feeling or to embody emotion. What you're enacting is the pulse or heartbeat of feeling, the essence of emotion. If you try to play Sam's language "cold," it won't work either.

What you can't do is let yourself be enveloped by the feeling, speak through the tears, say, as you might with Chekhov. Because that way, you're sure to lose the rhythm and the music. There's a tremendous freedom in working this way, because you're not locked into any psychological system that calls for exploring or demonstrating "feeling." It's a mistake, for example, to think of Sam's monologues as an evasion of feeling, when what they really are is an explosion of feeling. It's hard to put this concretely, but when you do Sam's plays, you have to be prepared to bear a kind of witness to yourself—you have to be detached enough to enact yourself. Which is another reason why the tremendous humor in Sam's work is so important—it's a survival technique for his characters, but a survival technique for his actors, too.

There's Sam's imagery, also, which an actor has to accept as part of the whole. You can't compete with it—you have to co-exist with it. The actor must simply accept it being there and work with it. In *Red Cross*, for example, everything on the stage was white: I was dressed in white, I wore white-rimmed glasses, even my shopping-bags were white. When Jim turned around at the end of the play, blood was running down his face. That blood was the only color on the stage. The audience was left with that image.

There's a tremendous joy in acting Sam's plays—a joy that you don't find in many other playwrights. And if you miss that fun—if you can't connect with it at the moment you're working on it—then you probably won't be able to relish the great originality and freedom of the plays. In the early days, I felt their astonishment—it was in the air—even when I did *La Turista* and droves of people walked out. As an actor, I was thrilled to be in the plays. I felt I was on a new front. I felt that from the very beginning.

I had great faith and trust in Sam and his work, in his responses and in the authenticity of what he was doing. I still do. I might say I like one play more than another, but I never doubt what he's trying to make happen on the stage.

I wish he'd write a play for women!

INTERVIEW WITH SPALDING GRAY

Gautam Dasgupta

Why don't we begin by talking about what led you and the Performance Group to do a Sam Shepard play in the first place?

Before we did Shepard's *Tooth of Crime* we did a group evolved piece, *Commune*, and I think we were all very tired from that effort and wanted to relax a little with a script. Richard Schechner had gotten hold of *Tooth of Crime* and he liked it very much. I liked it as a play, I liked the rhythm of the language but I couldn't imagine playing the central role of Hoss because I then had this idea that he had to be a tough character and I would have to extend myself in a typecasting situation. I'd been in *Commune* and I'd really been like Ishmael outside looking in and kind of playing myself. I kept my name in *Commune* and so I was straying away from the idea of playing the extensions of characters I thought were far from me. In the case of Hoss I saw this macho killer image. . . .

What happened when you finally decided to jump in and do this play?

When I began to work on the play in Vancouver at the University of British Columbia, where we first worked on it, I began to realize it was a kind of rock opera and that I could return to what little classical training I'd had at Emerson College doing Shakespeare. I felt I could actually use a combination of my classical voice training and my memory of growing up with a

175

tougher Italian element in Barrington, Rhode Island. It was the image of them that the play evoked but within it I had this terrific language structure that was like living a rock beat, a drum beat, because Sam was a drummer. I felt that of all the plays it was most directly a musical piece. So when I began performing it, it was as though I stepped into a track that was meant for me—because of the language—and it carried me. I didn't have to worry about psychological approaches to character because the language itself and the voice made this kind of music, and then the voice began to take on intonations that were not unlike that exposure to the third world root. Seeing just how fast you could say Sam's lines without mumbling it—the preciseness of language. Certainly that play was sheer contemporary poetry. I could really hook into it much better than, say, Shakespeare. I did feel when I had finished with that play I was finished with theatre, that it would be a long time before something like that came along. Everything after that seemed so diminutive.

But the characters in Tooth of Crime *do retain elements of realism. Hoss, for instance, grows, has real conflict, and develops as a realistic character. I mean it's not just entirely poetry.*

That's not the place I connected to but I think that's the place that came through automatically once I made the connection with the poetry. The fact was that I was costumed—I wasn't wearing my street clothes and saying the lines. But I as a performer wasn't primarily concerned with what my costume was. It was much more the director's and costumer's idea at the University of British Columbia. And then of course my head was shaved for two years and that added a terrific strength, an age to the character. I began to become this character Hoss—I even found I was more intensely alive during the performance than I was when I wasn't performing. There was a great jump—achievement, too.

How did the character strike you when you first read it in terms of what you wanted to do as an actor? Was that the kind of character you were waiting to play in order to effect that "great jump"?

No, in fact when I first read it I felt very alienated toward this kind of hard driving macho figure. It's a kind of contemporary *Macbeth*. Richard said, "Look, I think you're ready to take a jump as an actor and live away from yourself" and I saw that as a challenge to try and get into this element and find an element in me that corresponded to it. Find the toughness in me that corresponded to the toughness in this character. Because I knew the softness in me would play, softness is in my nature, the passivity, but I knew that if I could be very hard and active and physical with my head shaved and in leathers, then the softness would play as a nice contrast. I think the play was best when that dichotomy was working. It did happen. I found that answered a lot of questions for me about the theatre because I saw it as a hazard.

I think that any good play has a psychic power to it like any sacred ritual and I became invested with that macho image of the play because of its rhythms and that fighting, aggressive energy. It would take me hours after the play to shake that. After the play I felt very aggressive and hostile—felt like picking a fight in a bar—things I'd never experienced before. I drank a lot, maybe a six-pack, to relax; after two or three hours I'd be ready to sleep, that play so churned me up. It wasn't as if it was a character, per se, that was getting into me. I already had that character in me. What it was doing was emphasizing that—by the nature of the language, by the nature of the costume, by the nature of the ritual, by the fact that all the performers allowed me to scream at them which was never an element in the Performance Group because I would never get angry at group performance sessions before that. Suddenly, here I was expressing all that—I won't say vague anger—an abstract anger because the anger was in the language. I was really shouting but I wasn't sure as a performer what I was really shouting about because I began to question my direct line motivation. There was no direct line. I began to question why I was in service to this text, how I was doing service to the play, why the text was important outside of it just being good theatre because I wasn't directly connected to the playwright—he hadn't worked with us.

Did you ever find the answers to those questions?

The answer now is that I've been much more interested in working my way back to life through theatre. Some time back I sort of gave up and became very pessimistic about a creative life. I thought I could only work in theatre. Now I'm trying to use theatre as a tool to come back to reexamine my everyday life as Spalding Gray. I was recently in San Francisco and Sam Shepard came to a couple of my solo performances and invited me to go see Lou Reed perform. As we were going in this huge, Bronco Ford truck, with him driving in his cowboy hat, it suddenly hit me that this was a style match between Hoss and Crow. But even that was an abstraction next to the actual encounter between Spalding Gray and Sam Shepard. That encounter was only possible because I had my identity as Spalding Gray, the performer, and he had his as Sam Shepard, the playwright. He said, "Who wants to play pool?" so the drummer of Lou Reed's group said he would and they played a game and Sam Shepard beat him and asked, "Who now?" I got to do it—I got to challenge him. First I broke the balls and then I got a very weird shot—it was fabulous. Sam took a couple of beats and then said,

"That's what you might call a New England style."

Right then I thought it all came home—the play had become right. This was all very exciting to me, the nature of true performance. Then he proceeded to shoot all the balls in and beat me and it was definitely that kind of play between Hoss and Crow. I'm not saying one was Hoss and one was Crow but it was definitely two styles coming together—the Western cowboy man and the East Coast salt-tweed man. It was that kind of image—a real living image that was in the earth, not in the theatre necessarily but within theatre's life. That was exciting for me—I felt that the whole thing had come around again in a full circle.

TPG's production of Tooth of Crime *was done without Sam's collaboration. Now that you've met him, do you think that had he been present your approach to Hoss would have been different?*

Yes, I think his presence would have allowed for another encounter with the play that wouldn't just be my encounter with Richard Schechner and the role. It would add another part in the triangle—playwright, director, actor—that's just a really solid creative triangle, one that rarely happens. But when it does I think it makes, if not good theatre, at least very interesting theatre. Sam's very serious about the characters in *Tooth of Crime*. I don't think he saw them as ironic. Our production had a sense of distance, a Brechtian quality. We would have had to come to terms with the flatter, serious side if he were there. I think there would have been a lot of problems. But I do think our production had that necessary ironic quality. I saw *True West* at the Magic Theatre this summer and I felt it didn't reflect it and it became a kind of television show for me. Certainly well written and I liked the surreal elements in it, but I think one should work in a dialectical situation where the director does have different ideas about the production.

Did the ironic element in the TPG production result from a directorial approach or the manner in which you and the other performers played each individual role?

I see two things. One was directorial and I'll give you an example of that. After I do the long monologue about the fighter, Richard said to just finish that, stand in front of the audience and allow myself to come to a neutral place so I'm no longer the character, and just look at the audience's eyes. That time I could feel the charge that had been building up peel away like an onion and I came to this extremely neutral state. Everything disappeared in the room and the audience and I were one, and from there I went on to the next scene playing the old man, and that was such a wonderful transition. I again began to build up from a low, neutral state. It was a very good direction the director gave.

The other approach was an affected one initiated by me as a performer. I didn't relate directly to this macho character so I think at times I would, in the way I acted, comment on the fact that I was Spalding Gray dealing with this character. I can't really say how that can be read theatrically, except again that I would stop the action and simply come apart. That was the most exciting point for me because it allowed a confrontation with the audience's eyes that I would never forget (it's now connected with my solo work) because I wanted to deal with what my fears were. I was afraid of looking directly at an audience because I thought they'd see I wasn't the character and they would lose the quality of illusion.

Now I don't know that Sam Shepard would have wanted it nor would he have liked that fact or that we changed the music and had our own. We certainly tried to make the play our own and I think it would have been difficult with Sam present to do that. There would have been much more fighting and I don't know if the production ever would have gone on.

It does seem, however, that Shepard writes roles that demand they be enacted by performers. Characters in his plays become virtually synonymous with performers.

I'm not sure about that and I'm not even sure Sam is aware of that, if that is what he is doing. But also, what would you say about a character from a Tennesse Williams play or a Lanford Wilson play—are you saying Sam Shepard's characters seem more developed?

I think it has to do with the flamboyance in Shepard's writing and a certain linear disjunctiveness in the development of his characters.

I'm not sure I experienced that in *Tooth of Crime*.

How does moving from a collaborative role to enacting a given role affect your relationship to the craft of acting?

Because it was such a large role and it was the first big role I'd taken on, it answered a lot of questions for me: if I enjoyed acting, whether I wanted to go with it, what it was saying for me. What happened in *Tooth of Crime*, which gave me two full years of acting, was I went through the process of satisfying the need to be an actor. Afterwards I came out of it and thought, "Now what?—there's *Hamlet* but what else?"

Do you think that if instead of Hoss you'd have played the role of Stanley in A Streetcar Named Desire—*another macho male character—you would have been just as satisfied.?*

You know, it wasn't that big a jump. I think that doing something naturalist would be. I agree, it's something that I still would be interested in doing and those questions aren't answered for me as an actor. But the performance questions were answered through doing Hoss because it wasn't that kind of Stanislavki approach that I was brought up on. But had I done *Uncle Vanya*, and I played Astrov, that would have been a different problem.

You seem to suggest that enacting a Williams or Chekhov character is the province of an "actor" whereas attacking a Shepard character belongs more to the realm of a "performer." Perhaps this is what I was trying to get at earlier.

Because I felt I was saying the role most of the time. I felt I was concerned mainly and finally with the rhythms of the speech, not with how I looked at Joan MacIntosh although she was working very naturalistically and was very concerned with what the nature of my looks were. When she would stretch out her hand to me and sing that song "The Feeling Slips Away" I would hallucinate and imagine seeing a can of beer in her hand because I was trying to decide what kind of beer I was going to buy after the performance. It wasn't necessarily that I was into associating a particular psychological mood. I was interested in first saying the words, then the pauses between the words, and it became music to me—music that I performed with the instrument of my body. Whereas if I was playing Astrov I'm not sure; Chekhov might also be a kind of music. I don't know about that psychological approach anymore.

Within music a performer can think of other things—it becomes a kind of private meditation the same way that Robert Wilson's work is music. The fact that the language was so well constructed allowed me a sort of private self within which to daydream, to have my own associations. Perhaps I could do it if I was playing a naturalistic part, I don't know. I've never worked psychologically, so perhaps I've always been a performer and it's just taken me time to realize it.

I've always been interested in the rhythms of language and I think *Truth of Crime* made me more aware of that. The violin was the role, music was the play, the score, and that gave me terrific built-in rhythms to work with. *Tooth of Crime* is very liberating in that way. It was also liberating in giving me terrific creative and physical energy because that was such a demanding role. Richard Schechner had us dance through the whole script to all the music the play mentions; he said just do it as a movement piece and I found the physical vocabulary that way. We were doing four shows on the weekend, in the summer, and one on Thursday, one on Friday, and by the time we got to the fourth show on Sunday night, my head said no, I can't go on, and yet I would jump in with my body. I had a tight physical and verbal score and it was like getting on a track which carried one physically into the place that Grotowski is always talking about. To go to that extreme, to that highly energized place, and learn something about oneself. I think doing that play for two years liberated me. Also, *Tooth of Crime* was the right play for TPG at that time. It needed Richard's type of director because of the audience movement, my movement, and the rhythms of the language.

One question I was going to ask has to do with the high degree of physicality in Tooth of Crime *and the resulting cinematic quality of the production that many have commented on. Did you ever feel that you were performing for a hidden camera? Was there also anything different from working in such close proximity to an audience?*

What was different was having the audience move in different configurations so you would see different faces in different places. It was never that notion of a camera eye, although the idea was that the audience was seeing three different spaces like a camera. The "filmic angle" was of their own choosing although even that was flexible. The only time I felt I was performing for a camera was when I did.

What was different when you made the film of Tooth of Crime?

I think there's a problem with the film that was made. I always thought it was going to be a film of the production but after the first minute the camera crew stopped me and said, "Let's take that over again," so it broke all rhythms. That's when I realized the problems of film acting because the grace of the play was for me stepping into its rhythm and ending two hours later. I don't think it's good to film plays unless it's being done for documentation. The problem has to do with the camera making selections and manipulating the audience. You were missing the active choices made when you saw the play live.

True, but the TPG production was an environmental one, with the action and the audience constantly on the move. Doesn't that entail a strong element of selectivity? Furthermore, I heard that at some performances audience members refused to be manipulated and just sat in one place. Did that bother you?

Yes, it did because I often felt that it was hostile. I couldn't tell if the person was being hostile to Richard or to TPG's idea of movement or if they actually enjoyed that. Now I think some people may just have enjoyed sitting still.

When we did the play at the University of British Columbia we did it on a huge stage, and I would come on stage as Hoss in my costume and say to the audience sitting in the orchestra, "Come in. Come into my house, I'm Hoss." First they'd stare at me and then someone would get the courage to make the first move and then everyone would follow. They'd sit on stage amidst the set moving around. People would come late to this and think they were the audience and the audience onstage was part of a really large cast. They'd sit and think they were watching this very intricate production and I think that was fascinating—the point of view they must have had from that terrific distance. It was like a terrific macrocosm/microcosm thing. I would love to watch it that way if I were an audience member. In *Tooth of Crime* the audience had a terrific choice to be creative. It was great staging for that reason. I do think that Shepard would be outraged by it, and that's part of the reason he didn't come.

Before we end, I'd like to know what consolidated your status as a performer in Tooth of Crime *that eventually led to your present career as a solo performer. Was there, finally, a disillusionment on your part with scripted, traditionally-oriented dramaturgy?*

It wasn't disillusionment, it was a discovery that there are indeed many different styles. Foremost, I became more and more aware in *Tooth of Crime* of working with an audience because the audience was near me. They were my contact and I knew that every time I was looking out the corner of my eye, they were there and were playing back to me. This was the relationship that turned me on and I felt guilty with it for a long time because we'd been brought up in TPG's production of *Commune* that we interconnected with our fellow performers. Then I had to check it, I had to say, "Wait a minute, I like looking at these different people, the fresh faces, I like the responses from them." This led directly to solo pieces because I had to look back and ask what did I like about performance—the relationship to the audience. So I said, "Sit down at a table, look at them, talk to them." So definitely I found that through *Tooth of Crime.*

Curiously, and in a different way, of course, this also happens in the commercial theatre when the audience awaits the entrance of a star performer. The star knows that there is this immediate connection between him or herself and the audience. So Tooth of Crime *did make you a star, a myth, an image—that's what the play is all about, isn't it?—albeit in the world of downtown performance.*

Definitely. I always wanted to be a star in the finest sense—to be there, to be brilliant. I thought maybe I have the wrong idea—the cultural idea—and

I never can be Mick Jagger. Well, Spalding Gray is no Elvis Presley, right? I began then to think in terms of horizontal stardom rather than vertical and began to spread myself out. I see it as a counter culture thing—not that I'd chose it as that. It means staying with the people and the only way you can become a star in our culture is to enter into the media at large. You have to be a household word. I wanted to be in performance and also be a star. The play, as you correctly pointed out, is about that, too.

Shepard on Shepard

METAPHORS, MAD DOGS AND OLD TIME COWBOYS

Interview with Sam Shepard

Kenneth Chubb
and
The Editors of *Theatre Quarterly*

Born 5 November 1943 at Fort Sheridan, Illinois, say my notes. . . .

They weren't kidding, it was a real fort, where army mothers had their babies. My father was in Italy then, I think, and we moved around, oh, to Rapid City, South Dakota, to Utah, to Florida—then to the Mariana Islands in the South Pacific, where we lived on Guam. There were three of us children.

Do you remember much about living on Guam?

I remember the tin-roofed huts that we lived in, because it used to rain there a lot, and the rain would make this incredible sound on the tin roof. Also there were a lot of Japanese on the island, who had been forced back into living in the caves, and they would come down and steal clothes off the clothes-lines, and food and stuff. All the women were issued army Lugers, and I remember my mother shooting at them. At that time everyone referred to Oriental people or to Philippino people as gooks, and it wasn't until the Vietnam War that I realized that gook was a derogatory term—it had just been part of the army jargon, all the kids called them gooks, too.

You were in Guam until your father left the army?

Yeah, then we went to live with my aunt in South Pasadena, California—she somehow had some money through my mother's family, so we had a place to stay. But then we found a house of our own in South Pasadena, and I started going to high school.

What were your parents doing then?

My dad was still trying to get his degree, after the interruptions of the army, and he had to work for his Bachelor's by going to night school. But my mother already had this qualification for teaching kids, so they were working it out with jobs. He was very strict, my father, very aware of the need for discipline, so-called, very into studying and all that kind of stuff. I couldn't stand it—the whole thing of writing in notebooks, it was really like being jailed.

But you did share your father's liking for music?

Yes, he used to listen to Dixieland music while he was studying, and he had this band—it wasn't really professional, more of a hobby, though they got paid for it. But he was a drummer, and that's how I learned to play, just banging on his set of drums. And then I started getting better than him.

What was the town like?

Oh, one of these white, middle-class, insulated communities—not all that rich, but very proud of the municipal swimming plunge and the ice-skating rink, and all that small-town-America-type stuff.

Did you have many friends?

Yeah, I did. I had one good friend, Ernie Ernshaw—the first guy I started smoking cigarettes with. Later he joined the navy, and I went back to see him about ten years afterwards, and he'd turned into this Hollywood slick-guy with tight pants and a big fancy hair-do. It was fantastic.

But you left South Pasadena—when you were how old?

About eleven or twelve, something like that. We moved to this avocado ranch, it was a real nice place actually. It was like a little greenhouse that had been converted into a house, and it had livestock and horses and chickens and stuff like that. Plus about 65 avocado trees.

Did you like the change from small-town life?

I really liked being in contact with animals and the whole agricultural thing, but it was a bit of a shock leaving the friends I'd made. It was a funny community, divided into three very distinct social groups. There were the very wealthy people, who had ranches up in the mountains with white-faced Hereford cattle roaming around, and swimming-pools and Cadillacs. And then you'd get these very straight middle-class communities, people who sold encyclopedias and stuff like that. It was the first place where I understood what it meant to be born on the wrong side of the tracks, because the railroad tracks cut right down through the middle of this place: and below the tracks were the blacks and Mexicans. . . .

I found that the friends I had were these sort of strange guys. There was one guy who was from British Columbia—the one I wrote about in *Tooth of Crime.* He'd just come down from Canada, and he looked exactly like Elvis Presley. He had this incredible black hair-do and flash clothes, which nobody wore in school except for a few Mexicans—the white kids all wore Ivy League button-down numbers and loafers. So he was immediately ostracized, but he turned out to be a brilliant student—he didn't read any books, just got straight A grades. I got to be really good friends with him. And there were a couple of computer freaks, who were working at this aeronautics plant where they built computers for nose-cones. One guy used to bring in paper bags full of amphetamine and benzedrine from Mexico. I swear to God, those pills—if you took two of them, you were just flying. And these guys would work in the plant on amphetamine, and steal all these parts and sell them. The pay was really good too, and they got something like triple the money if they worked overtime, so they'd buy these incredible cars and go out stealing and looting—all on benzedrine and amphetamine. . . .

I was thinking that I wanted to be a veterinarian. And I had a chance actually to manage a sheep ranch, but I didn't take it. I wanted to do something like that, working with animals. I even had the grand champion yearling ram at the Los Angeles County Fair one year. I did. It was a great ram.

Quite a break from this very pastoral sort of prospect, when you decided to go to New York?

Yeah. At that time the whole beat generation was the big influence. It was just before the time of acid and the big dope freakout, which was then still very much under cover. We talked about Ferlinghetti and Corso and Kerouac and all those guys, and jazz. . . .

But you weren't writing yourself?

No. I mean, I tried poetry and stuff, but it was pretty bad. But I went to

New York with this guy Charles, who was a painter, and really just liked that whole idea of being independent, of being able to do something on your own. I tried to get into the acting scene in New York, though I really very soon dropped out of that. We were living on the Lower East Side, and there were these jazz musicians, Danny Richmond who played drums, and I got into this really exciting music scene. The world I was living in was the most interesting thing to me, and I thought the best thing I could do maybe would be to write about it, so I started writing plays.

Why plays, rather than novels or poetry?

I always liked the idea that plays happened in three dimensions, that here was something that came to life in space rather than in a book. I never liked books, or read very much.

Did you write anything before you started getting performed?

Well, I'd written one very bad play in California—a sort of Tennessee Williams imitation, about some girl who got raped in a barn and her father getting mad at her or something . . . I forget. But the first play I wrote in New York was *Cowboys.*

Cowboys, why cowboys? Cowboys figure largely in lots of your plays. . . .

Cowboys are really interesting to me—these guys, most of them really young, about 16 or 17, who decided they didn't want to have anything to do with the East Coast, with that way of life, and took on this immense country, and didn't have any real rules. Just moving cattle, from Texas to Kansas City, from the North to the South, or wherever it was.

Why Cowboys #2, *not just another title?*

Well, I wrote the original *Cowboys,* and then I rewrote it and called it #2, that's all. The original is lost now—but, anyway, it got done at St. Mark's. And that just happened because Charles and me used to run around the streets playing cowboys in New York. We'd both had the experience of growing up in California, in that special kind of environment, and between the two of us there was a kind of camaraderie, in the midst of all these people who were going to work and riding the buses. In about 1963, anyway—five years or so later it all suddenly broke down.

Had you had much to do with live theatre?

I hardly knew anything about the theatre. I remember once in California I went to this guy's house who was called a beatnik by everybody in the school because he had a beard and he wore sandals. And we were listening to some jazz or something and he sort of shuffled over to me and threw this book on my lap and said, why don't you dig this, you know. I started reading this play he gave me, and it was like nothing I'd ever read before—it was *Waiting for Godot*. And I thought, what's this guy talking about, what is this? And I read it with a very keen interest, but I didn't know anything about what it *was*. I didn't really have any references for the theatre, except for the few plays that I'd acted in. But in a way I think that was better for me, because I didn't have any idea about how to shape an action into what is seen—so the so-called originality of the early work just comes from ignorance. I just didn't know.

You were writing very prolifically around those early years.

Yeah, there was nothing else to do.

So what were you doing for money?

I was working at a place called the Village Gate, which is a big nightclub. Charles had a job there as a waiter, and he got me a job there too, and later I found out that all the waiters there were either actors or directors or painters or something like that who were out of work. It was a nice place to work because I got to see like the *cream* of American jazz, night after night for free. Plus I got paid for working there.

It was at night-time so you were free during the day?

Right. I worked three nights a week, and got about 50 bucks a week for doing hardly anything, except cleaning up dishes and bringing Nina Simone ice, you know. It was fantastic.

All those early plays give the impression that once you'd got the habit you couldn't stop. . . .

Yeah, I used to write very fast, I mean I wrote *Chicago* in one day. The stuff would just come out, and I wasn't really trying to shape it or make it into any big thing.

You wrote without any sort of planning?

Yeah. I would have like a picture, and just start from there. A picture of a guy in a bathtub, or of two guys on stage with a sign blinking—you know, things like that.

How important was it to you when your plays started to get performed?

It was frightening at first. I can remember defending myself against it most-ly. I was really young for one thing, about 19, and I was very uptight about making a whole public thing out of something that you do privately. And I was strongly influenced by Charles—he was very into not selling-out, and keeping himself within his own sphere of reference. I felt that by having the play become public, it was almost like giving it away or something. I was really hard to get along with in those days, actually. I would always bitch a lot during rehearsals and break things up. . . .

How did Cowboys *first come to get on stage?*

The head-waiter at the Village Gate was a guy named Ralph Cook, and he had been given this church, called St. Mark's-in-the-Bouwerie, and he started a theatre there called Theatre Genesis. He said he was looking for new plays to do, and I said I had one. He came up and he read this play, and two of the waiters at the Village Gate were the actors in it. So it was sort of the Village Gate company. Well, Jerry Talmer from the New York *Post* came, and all these guys said it was a bunch of shit, imitated Beckett or something like that. I was ready to pack it in and go back to California. Then Michael Smith from the *Village Voice* came up with this rave review, and people started coming to see it.

Did these early plays change much, between writing and the public perfor-mance?

The writing didn't change, I never changed the words. That's even true now, but depending on the people you have, the performance changes. I was very lucky to have arrived in New York at that time, though, because the whole off-off-Broadway theatre was just starting—like Ellen Stewart with her little café, and Joe Cino, and the Judson Poets' Theatre and all these places. It was just a lucky accident really that I arrived at the same time as that was all starting. This was before they had all become famous, of course—like Ellen just had this little loft, served hot chocolate and coffee, did these plays.

So how much money did you make from those early plays—not very much?

No money. There wasn't any money at all, until the grants started coming in from Ford and Rockefeller and all these places that were supporting the theatres because of the publicity they started getting. Then they began paying the actors and playwrights—but it wasn't much, 100 dollars for five weeks' work or something.

How much did it matter to you that critics like Michael Smith started writing approvingly about your plays?

Well, it changes everything you know, from being something that you do in quite a private way to something that you do publicly. Because no matter how much you don't like the critics, or you don't want them to pass judgment on what you're doing, the fact that they're there reflects the fact that a play's being done in public. It means that you steadily become aware of people going to see your plays—of audiences. Not just critics, but people.

Did you feel part of this developing off-off-Broadway "movement"?

Not in anything to do with stagecraft so much as in the ingredients that go into a play . . . On the Lower East Side there *was* a special sort of culture developing. You were so close to the people who were going to the plays, there was really no difference between you and them—your own experience was their experience, so that you began to develop that consciousness of what was happening . . . I mean nobody knew what was happening, but there was a sense that something was going on. People were arriving from Texas and Arkansas in the middle of New York City, and a community was being established. It was a very exciting time.

Did you begin to think of playwriting as your real job?

Well, I never thought of it as my job, because it was something that made me feel more relaxed, whereas I always thought of jobs as something that made you feel less alive—you know, the thing of working ten hours a day cleaning horseshit out of a stable.

Did the second play, Rock Garden, *also emerge from your experience of New York?*

Rock Garden is about leaving my mom and dad. It happens in two scenes. In the first scene the mother is lying in bed ill while the son is sitting in a chair, and she is talking about this special sort of cookie that she makes, which is marshmallow on salt crackers melted under the oven. It's called angels on horseback, and she has a monologue about it. And then the father arrives in the second scene. The boy doesn't say anything, he's just sitting in this chair, and the father starts to talk about painting the fence around the house, and there's a monologue about that in the course of which the boy keeps dropping asleep and falling off his chair. Finally the boy has a monologue about orgasm that goes on for a couple of pages and ends in him coming all over the place, and then the father falls off the chair. The father also talks about this rock garden, which is his obsession, a garden where he collects all these rocks from different sojourns to the desert.

The orgasm scene was the one used in Oh Calcutta!, *wasn't it?*

Yes—that production was pretty bad, and the play hasn't been done much in its entirety. Theatre Genesis did the first production, but I don't think it's been seen in England.

Then came Up to Thursday?

Yes. *Up to Thursday* was a bad exercise in absurdity, I guess. This kid is sleeping in an American flag, he's only wearing a jockstrap or something, and there's four people on stage who keep shifting their legs and talking. I can't remember it very well—it's only been done once. It was a terrible play, really. It was the first commercial production I'd done, and it was put on with a bunch of other plays, in this off-off-Broadway-moves-off-Broadway kind of bill.

What about Dog *and* Rocking Chair?

Dog was about a black guy—which later I found out it was uncool for a white to write about in America. It was about a black guy on a park bench, a sort of *Zoo Story*-type play. I don't even remember *Rocking Chair*, except it was about somebody in a rocking chair.

How do you feel about those early plays now—a bit vague, it seems?

Yeah, the thing is, I find it hard to remain with a certain attachment to things that I wrote. I've heard that a lot of writers make reams of notes before they even go into the thing, but with me I write plays before I get to another kind of play, and each play may be a sort of evolution to something else. I always feel like leaving behind rather than hanging on to them.

You say the texts don't change much in rehearsal—do you revise much while you're writing?

I hate to rewrite, but I can see the importance of it, mainly because of what it means for an actor to actually meet the task of doing this thing on stage. Just from directing *Geography of a Horse Dreamer* myself, I've found I think I'm too flippant about what I write—it's too easy to dash something off and say, okay, now act it; because when it comes down to the flesh-and-blood thing of making it work, it's a different world. I think that's where rewriting comes in—if it seems that the angle that the actor has to come at is too impossible or too difficult.

So it's revision of the mechanics rather than of the language . . . ?

It may be that there's a hole somewhere that needs to be blocked. Something missing.

Are you concerned at all about how accessible your plays are going to be to an audience? I'm thinking of how you described earlier the common background of experience you shared in those early New York years. But now, obviously, you're going to be writing for wider audiences, who don't necessarily share any similarities of background. How far are you, or aren't you, concerned to give them a way in?

It depends on whether you're writing in social terms, or whether the things that you're taking on can cut through that somehow. You can always start with some sort of social terms, because of being white, or living in England, or whatever the conditions are, but hopefully it can then cut into something that everybody has some touch with—otherwise it just remains a kind of *cosy* accessibility.

Isn't there a change, too, between the exclusive emphasis on private worlds in the very early plays, and the almost political sense of an outside threat in Icarus's Mother?

People talk about political consciousness as though it were a thing that you could decide in your head—that you can shift your ways of thinking and suddenly you have political consciousness. But I found that, especially in America, it came from the emotional context that you were moving in. I mean, people in New York are cutting themselves down every day of the week—from the inside, you know, but the conditions come from the outside. Junk, heroin, and all that stuff is a social condition and it's also an emotional response to the society they're living in. . . . But I don't have any political theories, if that's what you mean.

Around the time we're talking of in the States, it was the peak of the anti-bomb movement in England—were you caught up in anything like that?

I was in a few Civil Rights marches and stuff like that—but it's different.

When you see that on the news it's one thing, but when you're in it it's a whole different thing.

Can you say something about how Icarus's Mother *germinated?*

I was in Wisconsin, in Milwaukee, and for the Fourth of July we have this celebration—fireworks and all that kind of stuff—and I was in this sort of park with these people, with this display going on. You begin to have a feeling of this historical thing being played out in contemporary terms—I didn't even know what the Fourth of July meant, really, but here was this celebration taking place, with explosions. One of the weird things about being in America now, though I haven't been there much lately, is that you don't have any connection with the past, with what history means; so you can be there celebrating the Fourth of July, but all you know is that things are exploding in the sky. And then you've got this emotional thing that goes a long way back, which creates a certain kind of chaos, a kind of terror, you don't know what the fuck's going on. It's really hard to grab the whole out of the experience.

*And that's the circling airplane—*Icarus's mother. . . ?

There's a vague kind of terror going on, the people not really knowing what is happening. . . .

How "real" is the image in 4-H Club *of those four guys in a kitchen killing rats?*

Well, there's a big rat problem in New York, but maybe some of the people who talk about poverty and so on never had a rat in their house. And it's different when you have a rat in your house—doesn't all come down to talk.

Had you experienced that kind of poverty?

Yeah, in New York, sure—unless you have a million dollars lots of people experience that in New York . . .

About your new play Fourteen Hundred Thousand—*I get the feeling that it changes direction two-thirds of the way through—there's this play about building a bookshelf, and this other play about a linear city. . . .*

Yeah, I had a long talk with an architect before I wrote that play, and stuck that into it. I was very interested in the idea of the linear city, because it struck me as being a strong visual conception as opposed to radial cities—the idea of having a whole country, especially like America, with these lines cutting across them. . . .

To go back to what you were saying earlier about your plays developing from images, from mental pictures—was this a case of the image as it was switching half-way through? And how should the switch work theatrically?

When you talk about images, an image can be seen without looking at anything—you can see something in your head, or you can see something on stage, or you can see things that don't appear on stage, you know. The fantastic thing about theatre is that it can make something be seen that's invisible, and that's where my interest in theatre is—that you can be watching this thing happening with actors and costumes and light and set and language, and even plot, and something emerges from beyond that, and that's the image part that I'm looking for, that's the sort of added dimension.

Does Fourteen Hundred Thousand *maybe represent a kind of watershed between those early plays, which were largely concerned with simple . . . well, not really simple, but* single *images, and the plays after this, which start to get very much more complex—and maybe the characters too start moving from the ordinary towards the extraordinary. . . ?*

They're the *same* people, but the situations are different. What I was interested in was, like, you see somebody, and you have an impression of that person from seeing them—the way they talk and behave—but underneath many, many different possibilities could be going on. And the possibilities that I brought out, like in *Icarus*, could have taken a completely different direction. It's not as though you started out with a character who suddenly developed into another character—it's the same character, who's enlivened by animals, or demons, or whatever's inside of him. Everybody's like that. . . .

But I still feel that the plays get more complex—perhaps that the early plays are images, the later plays are more like metaphors—creating not one segment of society through a fairly direct image, but finding another way of representing it—say in The Tooth of Crime. . . .

To me, that's the only thing I can do, because . . . first of all, I don't know what this world is. I mean, look at it. Like when you look at Ted Heath and Harold Wilson giving their opinions and trying to sell people on their programs. If you showed those two guys on stage it would be as boring as watching them on television—it wouldn't have any other dimension to it. Satire is another thing, but there's very few people can do it well—Jules Feiffer, but even he has to create another world to show something about this one. . . .

Well, can we try another tack—clearly the early plays, from what you said about them, have their origins in your childhood and adolescent world, and you're writing about that world. What are you harking back to, where do the images come from, for the later plays?

Well, they come from all kinds of things, they come from the country, they come from that particular part of the country, they come from that particular sort of temporary society that you find in Southern California, where nothing is permanent, where everything could be knocked down and it wouldn't be missed, and the feeling of impermanence that comes from that—that you don't belong to any particular culture. I mean it wasn't until I came to England that I found out what it means to be an American. Nothing really makes sense when you're there, but the more distant you are from it, the more the implications of what you grew up with start to emerge.

Is there a point at which you stopped writing plays about Southern California, say, and started writing plays about New York?

Yeah, but it's very hard to talk about, because . . . obviously, if you were writing in Jamaica, you'd be writing under a different influence, or even if a man wanted to write about the Industrial Revolution in England but went to South Africa to do it, he'd be writing under those conditions. He'd have to take on the conditions of where he's writing, he can't escape that.

But all these things are accumulative, aren't they? You really haven't lost any of the early influences, you've simply put influences on. I mean, Geography of a Horse Dreamer is about dog-racing in London, which is very much your immediate experience, and yet there's something very reminiscent in all your later work of the early plays. Is that the way the plays are building, complicating themselves as they go on, and maybe becoming more interesting the more complicated they get?

Well, I don't know if they're more complicated, they're *different*, because, yes, you accumulate the experience of having written all those other plays, so they're all in you somewhere. But sometimes it gets in the way—you sit down and you find yourself writing the same play, which is a drag. Terrible feeling when you suddenly find yourself doing the same thing over and over again. . . .

How conscious are you of length when you write—do you write a short play consciously, or a long play, or does it just make its own length?

Oh yeah, it makes its own length. The term full-length to me doesn't make any sense, because people call a two-act or a three-act play, or a play with a certain number of pages, a full-length play, but I think it's ridiculous, because . . . well, Beckett wrote *Come and Go* and it's five pages long but it's full-length, whereas some of O'Neill's . . . No, people are always making distinctions about full-length plays, and I think it's really a shame that it's gotten into that kind of groove.

Well, I was going to ask, and perhaps I'll ask it anyway—it seems to me that quite apart from one being an early play and one being a later play, a great deal more conscious craftsmanship, or shaping, would have to go into writing say Tooth of Crime *than say* Chicago.

No, I don't think so. Your craftsmanship always comes from some interior thing, it's not something you can stick onto the play to make it have a style or a form—it has to come out of what's making the play, what's motivating the play. It's not the size of it, it's the quality of it. I guess it's just a matter of terms really, but to me *Tooth of Crime* performs a different quality than *Chicago* does. Put another way, it's playing for different stakes. You can play for the high stakes or the low stakes, or you can play for compromise in between: maybe *Geography* was playing for more modest stakes than *Tooth of Crime.* But what makes a play is how true it is to the stakes that you defined at the beginning.

But how do you define them—how did you know, say, that Tooth of Crime *was going to play for high stakes?*

It's an interesting thing that happened with that play, because I wrote it in London—it's been called an American play, right, but it was written in the middle of Shepherds Bush, and for about a month before that I was struggling to write this other play called *The Tooth of Crime,* which was a three-act epic number in a jail . . . and at the end it was a complete piece of shit, so I put it in the sink and burnt it, and then an hour later I started to write this one that's been performed. So, no, it's not so easy to say what it is when you sit down and write a play. You can sit down and say, now I know all the ingredients that are going to go into this and I'm shooting for something very big, and then you begin to write, and it may work out or it may not. The next time you may sit down, and say, I don't have an idea in my head, and yet something incredible may come out, you know. It has to do with the conditions at the time you sit down and write.

Fair enough. So say Chicago *starts with the idea, the image, of a bloke in a bathtub—what does something like* Tooth of Crime *start with—what did it start with?*

It started with language—it started with hearing a certain sound which is coming from the voice of this character, Hoss. And also this sort of black figure appearing on stage with this throne, and the whole kind of world that he was involved in, came from this voice—I don't mean it was any weird psychological voice in the air thing, but that it was a very real kind of sound that I heard, and I started to write the play from there. It just accumulated force as I wrote it.

We've rather jumped to this very American play written in Shepherds Bush: can you say something about your reasons for coming to London from New York?

Well, when I first got to New York it was wide open, you were like a kid in a fun park, but then as it developed, as more and more elements came into it, things got more and more insane—you know, the difference between living in New York and working in New York became wider and wider, so that you were doing this thing called *theatre* in these little places and you were bringing your so-called experience to it, and then going back and living in this kind of tight, insular, protective way, where you were defending yourself. And also I was into a lot of drugs then—it became very difficult you know, everything seemed to be sort of shattering. I didn't feel like going back to California, so I thought I'd come here—really to get into music, you know. I was in a band in New York, and I'd heard that this was the rock 'n' roll center of the world—so I came here with that kind of idea. London was notorious for its rock 'n' roll bands, and my favorite bands are The Who, groups like that, so I had this fantasy that I'd come over here and somehow fall into a rock 'n' roll band. It didn't work. . . .

In spite of the fact that people were already saying that you were the darling of off-off-Broadway, you wanted to get into something else?

I really wanted to find another kind of thing over here. I much prefer playing music to theatre, but it's hard to find the right situation.

Yet music doesn't seem to have played a large part in many of your plays, has it? People talk about there being a musical structure to your plays, which I'm sure is intuitive, and there have been a couple of plays which have had music connected with them—the one where it's most integral is Mad Dog Blues. But certainly in The Tooth of Crime, though it may have been the production I saw rather than anything else, the music seemed rather superficially connected. . . .

It depends what you mean by music. I think music's really important, especially in plays and theatre—it adds a whole different kind of perspective, it immediately brings the audience to terms with an emotional reality. Because nothing communicates emotions better than music, not even the greatest play in the world. But it's not a question of just putting music in plays. First of all there may be some plays that don't require music, like *Geography of a Horse Dreamer*—I've used music from records, but there wasn't any opportunity really for songs or anything like that.

But there was lots of room for it in Tooth of Crime, and yet it wasn't really used integrally?

Yeah, I know what you're saying. I wanted the music in *Tooth of Crime* so that you could step out of the play for a minute, every time a song comes, and be brought to an emotional comment on what's taking place in the play. When you go back to the play you go back to the spoken word, then when a song comes again, it takes you out of it just a little bit. I wanted the music to be used as a kind of sounding-board for the play, you know. At The Open Space, I worked with the band that did the music, Blunderpuss, and it was never right—they're a really good band, but *because* they're a band, that already has an identity of its own, you're starting with the type of music that they can perform, that they've been used to performing, and the most you can get is a good compromise. The only way to do it really is to gather musicians together independently who can get along with each other and know how to play and create the music from scratch. That's what we'll do in the Royal Court production, so hopefully the music will be a little truer to the way it was written.

You say you think music can potentially affect an audience much more strongly than even the best playwright's words. . . ?

Oh, yeah.

How do you feel about the vogue for so-called rock operas?

I haven't ever seen a good rock opera. But I don't think that the music in theatre necessarily has to take on a rock 'n' roll idiom—it could be any kind of music. What I think is that music, no matter what its structure, has a very powerful emotional influence, it can't help but have that—it's in the nature of music, it's when you can play a note and there's a response immediately—you don't have to build up to it through seven scenes.

Can you think of a play or a production which achieved the impact you're talking about?

With music? Brecht's plays. Plays like *Mahagonny*. He's my favorite playwright, Brecht. If you look at *Jungle of the Cities*, it's a play—a bout, between these two characters, taken in a completely open-ended way, the bout is never defined as being anything but metaphysical.

Do you think the music works in Brecht in the way he wanted it to work, as a means of distancing?

I never saw a production that he did, and I've seen very few good Brecht productions. It's very hard to do.

What effect would you like a play of yours—one that you really felt totally happy with, play and production—to have on an audience?

Well, it depends on the play, but hopefully it would be something that would transform the emotions of the people watching. People come into the theatre in very different circumstances, expecting something to happen, and then hopefully when they walk out of the theatre the chemistry's changed. What specifically that is depends on the material of the play, because every play's different.

I find it rather surprising when you say things like that, that you haven't written a play that has required an environmental situation—some sort of a situation in which the audience comes in to the play, or comes into a space that the play has taken over. . . .

There's a whole myth about environmental theatre as it's being practiced now in New York. The myth is that in order for the audience to be actively participating in the event that they're watching they have to be physically sloshed into something, which isn't true at all. An audience can sit in chairs and be watching something in front of them, and can be actively participating in the thing that's confronting them, you know. And it doesn't necessarily mean that if an audience walks into the building and people are swinging from the rafters and spaghetti's thrown all over them, or whatever the environment might be, that their participation in the play is going to be any closer. In fact it might very well be less so, because of the defenses that are put up as soon as that happens.

Can one relate that to Dick Schechner's production of Tooth of Crime?

Well, I think he's lost. I think he's lost in a certain area of experimentation which is valid for him. He feels that he wants to experiment with the environment of theatre, which is okay, I've nothing against it. Except when you write a play it sets up certain assumptions about the context in which it's to be performed, and in that play they had nothing to do with what Schechner set up in the theatre. You can take that or leave it. It can be okay—the playwright isn't a holy man, you know. Except I'd rather that the experimentation took place with something that left itself open to that—a play that from the start defines its context as undefinable, so that you can fuck around with it if you want to.

Do you visualize a particular type of performance space when you're writing—proscenium arch, open stage conditions, or whatever?

Yes, sometimes I see a play in a particular theatre, in a particular place—like I used to for Theatre Genesis, because I was so familiar with that environment. . . .

Has it proved important that those plays should go on being done in that sort of theatre?

It's important in terms of the size of the play—in other words the number of characters. For one thing you feel that if you have too many people involved in a production it can only be done in very special financial circumstances—you can only have it done in Lincoln Center, for instance, which turns out to be a disaster, and from there on it can't really be performed in colleges or anything like that because it's too expensive. It's important to take into consideration the general environment the play's going to hit. It's more important to have a five-character play or less that can be done in a close, non-financial situation than it is to have a circus.

Have you seen many amateur and student productions of your plays? Do you think they work with amateurs and students?

Yeah, sure. Again, it depends on the play, some plays work very well with amateurs.

I was thinking, almost by analogy with Brecht, that maybe amateurs and students, not approaching your work with actorish preconceptions, might find a better style on occasions.

Well there's a certain excitement goes on with that kind of thing, because you know it's not being performed in this kind of blown-up way, it's not being performed for an anonymous audience—it's being done very specifically for people everybody knows.

How specifically do you conceive a play being staged when you're actually writing it?

This experience with *Horse Dreamer* opened my eyes to all possibilities of productions, because I've been very opinionated about productions before.

You've not found yourself getting on with your directors?

Very rarely have I got on with them, except for a few instances.

You take an active part in rehearsals none the less? Where you can?

Sometimes—it depends on the situation, it depends who you're working with. I like to take part in rehearsals, it's just very delicate, you have to watch out, it's easy to say the wrong things to the actors.

Was Horse Dreamer *the first play of your own you've directed?*

Yeah, first time I ever did it. I much prefer working in England, though, because the actors I've found are much better equipped to do things. . . .

Technically?

No, not only technically, but in other ways, like these guys I've gotten in *Horse Dreamer*, who are fantastic—the best actors I've ever worked with, they're really great. In New York you're lucky if you find anybody. Everybody's acting, and doing some lifestyle sort of thing at the same time, sort of mixing their lifestyles with their acting, so it's very hard to get the same dedication.

In terms of your future relationship with directors have you learned anything from directing Horse Dreamer?

Well, I've learned that it's very important to have patience, and that things can't be rushed. I've learned that the rehearsal process is actually a process.

The reason it takes three or four or five or six weeks is because it actually needs that amount of time to evolve. Whereas I used to think that a production was a miracle act, that actors very suddenly came to the play and it was realized in a matter of days. But that's not true, it takes a great deal of time, and in the production at the Court now, they're still finding things, still working on things and bringing new things to it.

Do you think you've found that a particular kind of rehearsal process suits your plays—from reading to blocking to working, or whatever?

When I first went into this thing, because I didn't have any experience I called up several different directors that I knew and said, could you fill me in on the details? And some of them told me some very interesting things about the way they worked, the sort of process, but I found none of it held true for this particular experience. It's very like writing—you can't have any set kind of preconceptions about what it's going to be. You can *say* first week we're going to read it, second week we're going to block it, third week we're going to churn it out, but it doesn't make any difference, because when you get to the actual thing it makes its own rules.

So how did the rules work out?

The rules came from the actors. Because they were so good and they've had so much experience, it wasn't me making absolute decisions, though I saw things that they were doing and pointed them out, and then tried to mold a little bit from what they were doing.

There is a problem it seems to me, insofar as there are styles of playing on the one hand, and there are very clear literary things happening in the writing on the other, and sometimes the two don't quite go together. Did you find that at all with Geography of a Horse Dreamer?

That play is different because it's more structured, it's more straightforward in its plot and that kind of thing. I think what you're talking about does come into a play like *Icarus's Mother*, though, which is really a bitch to produce. It's very difficult for actors to do—being physically there on stage and having monologues that run for a page and a half—to bridge that gap between the language and the physical acting of the play. Is that what you're talking about?

Yes—do you think you're getting closer to bridging that gap now?

Yeah. One of the things I've found is that it's too much to expect an actor to do a vocal aria, standing there in the middle of the stage and have the thing work in space, without actually having him physically involved in what he's talking about. The speeches have been shaved quite considerably since the early plays, I don't go in for long speeches any more.

Although there are some quite beautiful and very long speeches in The Unseen Hand.

Yeah, right. But even so, even that is difficult, like I said.

But the first speech, for example, where Blue is on stage by himself. . . .

He's got something to do, he's working with the car, and he's on the highway . . . The imagery comes out of the situation. It also does in the earlier plays, except that there the characters are physically marooned by their speaking, which makes it hard.

What do you think about the criticism that's been made of Geography of a Horse Dreamer, *that it doesn't contain the intensity of language of* Tooth of Crime *or* The Unseen Hand?

Well, I can see how people would be disappointed if they found that the language filled them out more, gave them more of a thing to spring from, but it's just not right for this play. It's not a play that's investigating a whole complicated language scheme. I was using language from Raymond Chandler, from Dashiell Hammett—from the thirties, which to me is a beautiful kind of language, and very idiomatic of a period in America which was really strong.

Is this something you can turn on without thinking—a particular idiom, whether it's of rock music or Dashiell Hammett—or do you have to think yourself into it?

You have to make an adjustment, you have to sort of click into something: a trigger is set off, and then you're able to do it. . . .

Why the combination of the dog-racing theme and the Raymond Chandler style? They're pretty disparate elements, aren't they?

Not really, no, they both have to do with crime and the underworld. Raymond Chandler actually visited London a lot—he dug London. He never got involved in dog-racing, but I think the kind of working-class people here who go to dog-racing talk in the English version of what that American idiom is.

How did you get involved in the dog-racing scene—what was the fascination?

Well, I loved horse-racing before, I really used to like the horse-track, we lived right near one. But it's very expensive, as far as actually getting involved in it. Then when I came here I found dog-racing is the second biggest spectator sport in England, you've got twelve tracks or something, and suddenly it was like all your romantic childhood dreams come true—only with dogs. So I thought, shit, this is great, and I got involved in it. It's really a sort of romantic impulse, you know. Being around the track, punters and all that kind of stuff—I like that world.

Do you consider yourself a romantic?

What does that mean?

Well, you've been talking about things being romantic, in that they obviously have a primarily emotional pull. . . .

Like for instance Wyoming . . . Yes, just in that a thing pulls me in a certain way. In that sense I'm a romantic.

And in the sense that you don't pre-structure your plays?

Yeah, but I wouldn't say that that was necessarily romantic. I like poetry a lot, I like the impulse that makes poetry happen, the feeling that language can occur out of an emotional context. I mean, it's not any specific poetry, it's just that I think that theatre especially has a lot of room for that.

Is there maybe something romantic about your preoccupation with death, too?

Death? The idea of dying and being reborn is really an interesting one, you know. It's always there at the back of my head.

In a religious, or metaphysical, or philosophical way, or what?

In real terms, what it means to die and be born again. I mean, you can call it religious if you want. It's something I've wanted somehow to get into, but I've never really found how to make it work in the plays.

Were you raised in a religion?

Yes, I was, but that's not necessarily where it's coming from—I was raised as an Episcopalian . . . But that was another kind of prison to get out of, you know. There's nothing worse than listening to a lot of people mumbling, and outside the sun is shining . . . But you have this personality, and somehow feel locked into it, jailed by all of your cultural influences and your psychological ones from your family, and all that. And somehow I feel that that isn't the whole of it, you know, that there's another possibility.

You still feel yourself escaping from those influences?

You can't escape, that's the whole thing, you can't. You finally find yourself in a situation where, like, that's the way it is—you can't get out of it. But there is always that impulse towards another kind of world, something that doesn't necessarily confine you in that way. Like I've got a name, I speak English, I have gestures, wear a certain kind of clothes . . . but once upon a time I didn't have all that shit.

Do you have any ideas about the way you're going as a dramatist?

I wish I did. I don't know. I'd like to try a whole different way of writing now, which is very stark and not so flashy and not full of a lot of mythic figures and everything, and try to scrape it down to the bone as much as possible.

But not realism?

Well, it could be called realism, but not the kind of realism where husbands and wives squabble and that kind of stuff.

Are you keen to direct your plays again, or to consider directing somebody else's?

Yeah, without having a great deal of time to think about it first, though I wouldn't want to plunge right into another one. But that's a whole area of possibilities—where you begin to find out what it really means to write a play. That it isn't a piece of paper, it's something that's really happening in real life. And the more you find out about it the more you can grow as a writer. I'm very interested in the kind of chemistry that goes on with directing, finding the right language to use with the actors, finding the way an actor works. Every single actor in *Horse Dreamer* worked in a completely different way, and it took a couple of weeks to find that out. I was saying the same things to everybody, and then I began to find that you have to talk differently to each actor—something you say to one guy doesn't mean a thing to the next guy.

Is it important what people, professional critics or others, say about your plays?

Well, it would be silly to say that I'm immune to it, because it affects you in one way or another. But with this particular play I'm not particularly concerned about the press criticism, because it's been such a strong experience. For three weeks you've been working with people, going through this very intricate process, and you arrive at this thing, and then it's judged by people who've never seen anything until that moment. So whatever they say about it, whether they like it or don't like it, whether it's constructive criticism or not, it doesn't have anything to do with that process that went on. I mean, that's what's important to me, and that's really the life of the play.

Anything else in England that has really turned you on, like dog-racing?

I like pubs and football a lot. There's nothing like pubs in America. And Guiness, I like Guiness.

Any of those going to be dramatically productive?

Football . . . yeah, football very well might.

TIME

In the realm of experimental writing for the theatre, a young writer is gradually persuaded that the "one act" form is a stepping stone toward the creation of "full-length" plays and that, finally, when he begins to grind out these monsters they alone can serve as proof of his literary value to the public. The term "full-length" has for a long time been synonymous with a play of two acts or more and has relegated shorter works to the status of "experimentation." The cultural machine that encourages young writers to experiment, in the same breath encourages them to quickly grow out of it and start producing "major works."

Somewhere in this is the old idea that the public deserves to get its money's worth and that this value lies in length rather than quality, or that only in length can there be any quality. I'm not sure which. This isn't to say that because a theatrical event takes a long time to unwind that there can't also be experimentation involved. Robert Wilson and Richard Foreman have opened up areas in that direction. My concern is mainly with the playwright and his personal sense of time in relationship to his work. How that sense of time is correlated between his work on paper and its appearance in three dimension. And finally how that sense of time becomes squeezed and pulled into conventional lengths for the viewing public. Writers are still under the influence of producers, critics, agents, etc., who demand that the real value of a piece of work has to be gleaned from its content only and that the total experience of the piece (including its length) is something set apart and even something that can be "doctored up" to suit the needs of the individual theatre and its audience.

Another part of this syndrome is the difficulty a playwright has in returning to attempts at shorter works after having "accomplished" one or two longer plays. The demand from the outside is always for the next "full-length, major opus" and anything shorter can only be taken as either some regression or an intermediary to something bigger. Rarely is it seen for what it is—a part of the gradually unfolding process of a playwright's total work.

I'm not trying to make a case for the playwright as victim to the forces of outside evil because in the end it has to come down to his own personal relationship to his work. I'm just pointing out that these influences are very strong in the direction of confusing a writer's true aims and that these aims have to be continually re-evaluated. If this re-evaluation is sincere he has to come back to the point where he feels he knows nothing at all about the heart of what he's after. He knows a great deal about things like: timing, rhythm, shape, flow, character (?), form, structure, etc., but still nothing about the real meat and potatoes. So he begins again. He strips everything down to the bones and starts over. And in this is where he makes his true discoveries.

AMERICAN EXPERIMENTAL THEATRE
Then and Now

It feels awkward to make definitive statements concerning a subject like experimental theatre. If experimentation truly has to do with taking steps into the unknown with the hope of knowing, then it seems that each time those steps are taken they are brand new from the last time. There are certain things that you always drag with you but when the time comes to step off the edge you leave those things behind. If you hang onto them you find yourself in the same place you started. So you start over again.

To me the influence of the sixties and the off-off-Broadway theatre and the Lower East Side was a combination of hallucinogenic drugs, the effect of those drugs on the perceptions of those I came in contact with, the effects of those drugs on my own perceptions, the Viet Nam war, and all the rest of it which is now all gone. The only thing which still remains and still persists as the single most important idea is the idea of consciousness. How does this idea become applicable to the theatre? For some time now it's become generally accepted that the other art forms are dealing with this idea to one degree or another. That the subject of painting is seeing. That the subject of music is hearing. That the subject of sculpture is space. But what is the subject of theatre which includes all of these and more? It may be that the territory available to a theatrical event is so vast that it has to be narrowed down to ingredients like plot, character, set, costume, lights, etc., in order to fit it into our idea of what we know. Consequently, anything outside these domains is called "experimental."

I don't really feel that the American theatre underwent any enormous changes as a result of what went down in the sixties. It was only added on-to. Generally speaking, the attitudes of the press are still the same as they always were toward new work. Bemused condescension or outright in-dignance. The main theme of the press in reaction to my own work has been "It's fine if you like that kind of thing and he certainly has a way with words but when is he going to stop playing around and give us a really MAJOR NEW AMERICAN PLAY."

By now, it's obvious that there is an audience for new theatre. For a theatre that takes chances and risks going into dimensions other than the ones we've already seen and heard of. That audience creates the need for theatre as an art form and that need can't be measured by widespread popularity or even failure. It's the same need that causes someone to write.

LANGUAGE, VISUALIZATION AND
THE INNER LIBRARY

I feel a lot of reluctance in attempting to describe any part of a process which, by its truest nature, holds an unending mystery. At the same time I'm hoping that by trying to formulate some of this territory I can make things clearer to myself.

I've always felt that the term "experimental" in regard to theatre forms has been twisted by the intellectual community surrounding the artist to the extent that now even the artist has lost track of its original essence. In other words, a search for "new forms" doesn't seem to be exactly where it's at.

There comes a point where the exterior gyrations are no longer the most interesting aspects of what you're practicing, and brand-new exploration starts to take root. For example: In the writing of a particular character where does the character take shape? In my experience the character is visualized, he appears out of nowhere in three dimensions and speaks. He doesn't speak to me because I'm not in the play. I'm watching it. He speaks to something or someone else, or even to himself, or even to no one.

I'm talking now about an open-ended structure where anything could happen as opposed to a carefully planned and regurgitated event which, for me, has always been as painful as pissing nickels. There are writers who work this way successfully, and I admire them and all that, but I don't see the point exactly. The reason I began writing plays was the hope of extending the sensation of *play* (as in "kid") on into adult life. If "play" becomes "labor," why play?

Anyway, to veer back to visualization—right here is where the experiment starts. With the very first impulse to see something happen on a stage. Any stage. This impulse is mistakenly called an idea by those who have never experienced it. I can't even count how many times I've heard the line, "Where did the idea for this play come from?" I never can answer it because it seems totally back-assward. Ideas emerge from plays—not the other way around.

I don't mean to make this sound like a magic act or a mystical experience. It has nothing to do with hallucination or drugs or meditation. These things may all have an influence on the general picture, but they aren't the picture itself. The picture is moving in the mind and being allowed to move more and more freely as you follow it. The following of it is the writing part. In other words, I'm taking notes in as much detail as possible on an event that's happening somewhere inside me. The extent to which I can actually follow the picture and not intervene with my own two-cents worth is where inspiration and craftsmanship hold their real meaning. If I find myself pushing the character in a certain direction, it's almost always a sure sign that I've fallen back on technique and lost the real thread of the thing.

This isn't to say that it's possible to write on nothing but a wave of inspired vision. There has to be some kind of common ground between the accumulated knowledge of what you know how to do (because you've done it before) and the completely foreign country that always demands a new expression. I've never written a play that didn't require both ends of the stick.

Another part of this that interests me is: How is this inner visualization different from ordinary daydreaming or ordinary nightdreaming? The difference seems to lie in the idea of a "watcher" being engaged while writing, whereas ordinarily this watcher is absent. I'm driving a truck and daydreaming about myself in Mexico, but, in this case, I'm not really seeing the dream that's taking place. If I start to see it, then it might become a play.

Now, another thing comes into focus. It must be true that we're continuously taking in images of experience from the outside world through our senses, even when we're not aware of it. How else could whole scenes from our past which we thought we'd long forgotten suddenly spring up in living technicolor? These tastes from our life must then be stored away somewhere in some kind of inner library. So this must mean that if I could be truly resourceful, I could draw on this library at any given moment for the exact information needed. Not only that, but the information is then given back to me as a living sensation. From this point of view, I'm diving back into the actual experience of having been there and writing from it as though it's happening now.

This is very similar to the method-acting technique called "recall." It's a good description—I'm recalling the thing itself. The similarity between the actor's art and the playwright's is a lot closer than most people suspect. In fact the playwright is the only actor who gets to play all the parts. The danger of this method from the actor's point of view is that he becomes lost in the dream and forgets about the audience. The same holds true for the writer, but the writer doesn't really realize where he became lost until he sees an audience nodding out through what he'd thought were his most blazing passages.

This brings me down to words. Words as tools of imagery in motion. I have a feeling that the cultural environment one is raised in predetermines a rhythmical relationship to the use of words. In this sense, I can't be anything other than an American writer.

I noticed though, after living in England for three straight years, that certain subtle changes occurred in this rhythmic construction. In order to accommodate these new configurations in the way a sentence would overblow itself (as is the English tendency), I found myself adding English characters to my plays. *Geography of a Horse Dreamer* was written in London, and there's only one truly American character in the play.

Still, the power of words for me isn't so much in the delineation of a character's social circumstances as it is in the capacity to evoke visions in the eye of the audience. American Indian poetry (in its simplest translation) is a prime example. The roots of this poetry stem from a religious belief in the word itself. Like "crow." Like "hawk." Words as living incantations and not as symbols. Taken in this way, the organization of living, breathing words as they hit the air between the actor and the audience actually possesses the power to change our chemistry. Still, the critical assessment of this kind of event is almost always relegated to the categories of symbolism or "surrealism" or some other accepted niche. In other words, it's removed from the living and dedicated to the dead.

I seem to have come around now to the ear as opposed to the eye, but actually they work in conjunction with each other. They seem to be joined in moments of heightened perception. I hear the phrase a lot that this or that writer has a "great ear for language." What this usually means is that the writer has an openness to people's use of language in the outside world and then this is recorded and reproduced exactly as it's heard. This is no doubt a great gift, but it seems to fall way short of our overall capacity to listen. If I only hear the sounds that people make, how much sound am I leaving out? Words, at best, can only give a partial glimpse into the total world of sensate experience, but how much of that total world am I letting myself in for when I approach writing?

The structure of any art form immediately implies limitation. I'm narrowing down my field of vision. I'm agreeing to work within certain boundaries. So I have to be very careful how those boundaries are defined at the outset. Language, then, seems to be the only ingredient in this plan that retains the potential of making leaps into the unknown. There's only so much I can do with appearances. Change the costume, add a new character, change the light, bring in objects, shift the set, but language is always hovering right there, ready to move faster and more effectively than all the rest of it put together. It's like pulling out a .38 when someone faces you with a knife.

Language can explode from the tiniest impulse. If I'm right inside the character in the moment, I can catch what he smells, sees, feels and touches. In a sudden flash, he opens his eyes, and the words follow. In these lightning-like eruptions words are not thought, they're felt. They cut through space and make perfect sense without having to hesitate for the "meaning."

From time to time I've practiced Jack Kerouac's discovery of jazz-sketching with words. Following the exact same principles as a musician does when he's jamming. After periods of this kind of practice, I begin to get the haunting sense that something in me writes but it's not necessarily me. At least it's not the "me" that takes credit for it. This identical experience happened to me once when I was playing drums with The Holy Modal Rounders, and it scared the shit out of me. Peter Stampfel, the fiddle player, explained it as being visited by the Holy Ghost, which sounded reasonable enough at the time.

What I'm trying to get at here is that the real quest of a writer is to penetrate into another world. A world behind the form. The contradiction is that as soon as that world opens up, I tend to run the other way. It's scary because I can't answer to it from what I know.

Now, here's the big rub—it's generally accepted in the scholarly world that a playwright deals with *"ideas."* That idea in itself has been inherited by us as though it were originally written in granite from above and nobody, but nobody, better mess with it. The problem for me with this concept is that its adherents are almost always referring to ideas which speak only to the mind and leave out completely the body, the emotions and all the rest of it.

Myth speaks to everything at once, especially the emotions. By myth I mean a sense of mystery and not necessarily a traditional formula. A character for me is a composite of different mysteries. He's an unknown quantity. If he wasn't, it would be like coloring in the numbered spaces. I see an old man by a broken car in the middle of nowhere and those simple elements right away set up associations and yearnings to pursue what he's doing there.

The character of Crow in *Tooth of Crime* came from a yearning toward violence. A totally lethal human with no way or reason for tracing how he got that way. He just appeared. He spit words that became his weapons. He doesn't "mean" anything. He's simply following his most savage instincts. He speaks in an unheard-of tongue. He needed a victim, so I gave him one. He devoured him just like he was supposed to. When you're writing inside of a character like this, you aren't pausing every ten seconds to figure out what it all means. If you do, you lose the whole shot, because the character isn't going to hang around waiting for you. He's moving.

I write fast because that's the way it happens with me. Sometimes long stretches happen in between where I don't write for weeks. But when I start, I don't stop. Writing is born from a need. A deep burn. If there's no need, there's no writing.

I don't mean to give the impression from all this that a playwright isn't responsible toward the audience. He is. But which audience? An imagined one or a real one? The only real audience he has at the moment of writing is himself. Only later does the other audience come into it. At that point he begins to see the correspondence or lack of it between his own "watching" and the watching of others.

I used to be dead set against rewriting on any level. My attitude was that if the play had faults, those faults were part and parcel of the original process, and that any attempt to correct them was cheating. Like a sculptor sneaking out in the night with his chisel and chipping little pieces off his work or gluing them back on.

After a while this rigid "holy-art" concept began to crumble. It was no longer a case of "correction," as though what I was involved with was some kind of definitive term paper. I began to see that the living outcome (the production) always demanded a different kind of attention than the written form that it sprang from. The spoken word, no matter how you cut it, is different than the written word. It happens in a different space, under different circumstances and demands a different set of laws.

Action is the only play I've written where I spoke each line out loud to myself before I put it down on paper. To me that play still comes the closest to sounding on stage exactly like it was written. This method doesn't work for every play, though, since it necessarily sets up a slower tempo. It just happened to be the right approach for that particular piece.

La Turista was the first play I ever rewrote, under the urging of Jacques Levy, who directed it. We were in the second week of rehearsals at the American Place Theatre when I walked in with a brand-new second act. It's a tribute to Wynn Handman that he allowed this kind of procedure to take place. That was the first taste I got of regarding theatre as an ongoing process. I could feel the whole evolution of that play from a tiny sweltering hotel in the Yucatan, half wasted with the trots, to a full-blown production in New York City. Most of the writing in that piece was hatched from a semidelirious state of severe dysentery. What the Mexicans call "La Turista" or "Montezuma's Revenge." In that state any writing I could manage seemed valid, no matter how incoherent it might seem to an outside eye. Once it hit the stage in rehearsals and I was back to a fairly healthy physical condition, the whole thing seemed filled with an overriding self-pity. The new second act came more from desperation than anything else.

I think immediate environments tend to play a much heavier role on my writing than I'm aware of most of the time. That is, the physical place I'm in at the time of sitting down to the machine. In New York I could write any time in any place. It didn't matter what was happening in the streets below or the apartment above. I just wrote. The funny thing is that I can remember the exact place and time of every play. Even the people I was with. It's almost as though the plays were a kind of chronicle I was keeping on myself.

It seems that the more you write, the harder it gets, because you're not so easily fooled by yourself anymore. I can still sit down and whip off a play like I used to, but it doesn't have the same meaning now as it did when I was nineteen. Even so, writing becomes more and more interesting as you go along, and it starts to open up some of its secrets. One thing I'm sure of, though. That I'll never get to the bottom of it.

CONTRIBUTORS

JOYCE AARON is an actress, director and playwright who appeared in the original productions of Sam Shepard's *Up to Thursday, Red Cross* and *La Turista*. An original member of The Open Theater, she has performed in many off-Broadway theatres since the sixties.

MICHAEL BLOOM is a director and critic, and Theatre Associate for the Great Lakes Colleges Association.

EILEEN BLUMENTHAL reviews theatre for the *Village Voice*, and also teaches in the Department of Theatre Arts at Douglass College, New Jersey.

ROBERT COE is a Contributing Editor of *Performing Arts Journal*, and has also written for the New York *Times* and *Village Voice*.

KENNETH CHUBB and the Editors of *Theatre Quarterly*. Mr. Chubb is one of the founders of Britain's Wakefield Tricycle Company. *Theatre Quarterly* is a British theatre journal.

GAUTAM DASGUPTA is co-Publisher/Editor of *Performing Arts Journal* and PAJ Publications, and (with Bonnie Marranca) co-Editor of *Theatre of the Ridiculous* and *Animations: A Trilogy for Mabou Mines.*

MICHAEL EARLEY, Associate Editor of *Performing Arts Journal*, is Director of the Playwrights Program at the Theatre Center of The Juilliard School.

FLORENCE FALK is a director and critic whose work has appeared in *Performing Arts Journal, The Drama Review* and *Theater Journal*. She recently staged Charlotte Perkins Gilman's *The Yellow Wallpaper*.

REN FRUTKIN, now a lawyer practicing in Indiana, was the founding Editor and Chairman of the *yale/theatre* editorial board.

JACK GELBER is a playwright and director. His plays include *The Connection, The Apple, Sleep* and *Jack Gelber's New Play: Rehearsal*.

SPALDING GRAY is a performer who worked for several years with The Performance Group, and is now with The Wooster Group for whom he co-conceived *Three Places in Rhode Island*, a trilogy. His most recent work is in solo performance.

ELIZABETH HARDWICK is a critic and novelist whose most recent book is *Sleepless Nights*.

STANLEY KAUFFMANN writes on theatre for *Saturday Review* and film for *New Republic*. His autobiographical *Albums of an Early Life* was recently published.

WILLIAM KLEB is a Contributing Editor of *Theater* and teaches in the Department of Dramatic Art at the University of California-Davis.

JOHN LAHR is a theatre critic and novelist who recently published a biography of Joe Orton entitled *Prick Up Your Ears*.

BONNIE MARRANCA is co-Publisher/Editor of *Performing Arts Journal* and PAJ Publications, and Editor of *The Theatre of Images*. She co-authored (with Gautam Dasgupta) *American Contemporary Playwrights: A Critical Survey*.

RICHARD SCHECHNER, who teaches in the Department of Performance Studies at New York University, is the author of several books of essays on performance. He was founder-director of The Performance Group, 1967-1980.

MICHAEL SMITH, an early theatre critic for the *Village Voice*, is a playwright and director and resides in Connecticut.

GEORGE STAMBOLIAN teaches in the French Department at Wellesley College, Massachusetts.

GERALD WEALES teaches in the English Department of the University of Pennsylvania. He has written widely on American drama.

ROSS WETZSTEON is a Senior Editor of the *Village Voice*, and writes frequently on theatre.

ROBERT WOODRUFF is a founder of the Bay Area Playwright's Festival and has directed plays at the Magic Theatre, Manhattan Theatre Club, Phoenix Theatre, and Public Theatre. He directed Sam Shepard's Pulitzer Prize-winning *Buried Child* and *Curse of the Starving Class*.